ONE MORE NIGHT

Bob Dylan's Never Ending Tour

Andrew Muir

ISBN: 1482632365
ISBN 13: 9781482632361

DEDICATION

With love and gratitude to my big sister, Olive, who could never even begin to contemplate treating me 'like a stranger'.

Thanks for always being there for me and in teenage years letting your young brother hang out with your friends, the cool gang, from whom I first heard the names 'Bob' and 'Dylan' combined into the three-syllable rhapsody that has never stopped playing.

Contents

Foreword

This book concerns itself with what Bob Dylan fans have come to call the Never Ending Tour (NET), which began on 7th June 1988 at the Concord Pavilion, Concord, California. It is still going strong as I type this in the year 2012, approaching two and a half thousand shows and 25 years later.

Dylan dislikes the name 'the never-ending tour'. He sees the tours since 1988 as disparate in nature and claims in the liner notes to *World Gone Wrong* that the first of these tours ended when guitarist G.E. Smith left the band. Dylan has gone on to make the reasonable points that nothing lasts forever, and that touring is his trade and no one talks of never-ending bricklayers or suchlike.

Notwithstanding Dylan's valid points, the series of tours since July 1988 stands in stark contrast with all Dylan's tours prior to that date, as I shall detail below, and a term is needed to allude to this. Never Ending Tour is the commonly used term and, it has to be acknowledged, it is tremendously more wieldy as a term of reference than 'a series of disparate tours, only the first one of which (from 1988-1990) can be referred to as the Never Ending Tour, but which nonetheless share a distinct difference from all of Dylan's tours pre-1988 and have been continuing every year since then.'

The term was first defined, if not actually coined, by Dylan himself: "*It's all the same tour –The Never Ending Tour – it works out better for me that way. You can pick and choose better when you are just out there all the time and your show is already set up. You know, you just don't have to start it up and end it; it's better to keep it out there with breaks – extended breaks."*[1]

We even have Presidential backing for continuing to use the term. In February 2010 Dylan took part in 'Performance at the White House: A Celebration of Music From the Civil Rights Movement'. President Obama introduced Dylan as "The man who was good enough to take time off from his never-ending tour, Mr Bob Dylan."

The NET tours are different to those that preceded them in style, format, presentation and frequency. The Dylan of the NET plays around or over 100 shows per year. The only time Dylan had ever exceeded 100 shows in a year prior to 1988 was during 1978's world tour. His (in)famous 1966 tour numbered just 41 gigs. Nineteen seventy five's legendary "Rolling Thunder Revue" was ten fewer than that and the year immediately preceding the NET, 1987, was exactly midway between those two at 36 shows.

As we shall see, the NET that began in 1988 was a startling contrast to the Dylan tours of 1986 and. It was, and remains, a travelling show that allows him to focus on the here and now, presenting the songs and himself as present and changeable, rather than ossified in some former incarnation.

My aim is to put the vast and unwieldy NET into some kind of perspective: to examine its importance in the context of Dylan's overall career; and to chronicle the comparisons and contrasts between individual legs of the tour. However, this book is not just about the NET as a lengthy episode in the life of Bob Dylan. The Never Ending Tour has also become a phenomenon in my own life, so it is also the tale of a fan who has travelled to a substantial number of these shows over the years and who has listened to tapes, and watched video footage, of many of the others. These unofficial recordings have been obtained over the years via fan networks, initially on C-90 tape, then CD-Rs and now as computer files. At the beginning it took time and dedication to acquire every tape; nowadays any live debut of a song is instantly available around the globe.

---

1 *Adrian Deevoy interview:* Q Magazine issue 39, December *1989*. This printed interview was inaccurate, it was actually Deevoy who interrupted with the phrase 'Never Ending Tour' and Dylan continued the conversation, albeit in agreement ("yeah...yeah").

I want to tell you about this fan's experience of the NET. That experience has been both a cherished and an exhilarating one, though admittedly not without a degree of obsession that borders on the unbalanced. At the same time, this is not simply a fan's memoir; I do intend to bring some critical analysis, objectivity and balance to my account, though these are not always qualities I can guarantee to take to the shows themselves.

The sheer scale of the NET is overwhelming. For those who have been there since it started, the NET forms a large portion, probably over half, of our adult lives. It is amusing to imagine what a fan would have felt in 1988 had s/he been told that Dylan would tour continually for at least the next quarter of a century, and then that he would be playing mainly with a small back-up band in relatively intimate settings as well as the occasional arena and stadium tour. No fan would have believed it, far less that Dylan would play countless, wonderful, unexpected songs, and undertake residencies at favoured venues where the set-lists would change so dramatically from one night to the next that sometimes not even one song would be repeated at consecutive shows.

Yet that is exactly what did happen, and here is one fan's story of how it unfolded for him.

CHAPTER ONE

Before the Never Ending Tour

From Greenwich Village to Vineyard Fellowship

Any study of Dylan's career prior to the NET would demand a huge book in itself, and I do not plan to repeat that well-documented story in detail. However, as the NET began at what was widely regarded as a commercially and artistically low point in his career, it may be worth pointing out, albeit using the broadest of brush-strokes, just what Dylan had already given to the world before I pick up his story in the late 1980s.

Dylan's early years could be characterised as a journey from Woody Guthrie clone to Prince of Protest. Emerging from the early 60s Greenwich Village music scene, he quickly became the acknowledged master of the protest song, wielding an enormous influence on the Civil Rights movement with songs that denounced racism, warmongering, poverty and injustice. Acoustic anthems and legendary ballads such as "Blowin' In The Wind", "Masters Of War", "Oxford Town", The Times They Are A-Changin'" and "The Lonesome Death Of Hattie Carroll", to name but a very few, not only profoundly affected millions of listeners but also arguably became part of the history of the times.

At the same time, Dylan was producing some of his most affecting love songs, including "Girl From The North Country", "Don't Think Twice, It's All Right", "One Too Many Mornings", "Boots Of Spanish Leather" and "Tomorrow Is A Long Time".

These early years alone would have been enough to make Dylan a legend. However, in 1964 he upped the ante, moving from Folk Idol to Rock DemiGod by producing, over the course of little more than two years, a string of visionary social critiques, intense profiles of the psychological minefields of relationships and truly rapturous love songs. In so doing, he changed the world of popular song forever.

At this time, Dylan seemed to be a veritable fountain of poetic insight. The many highlights from this period of inspiration form a breathtaking oeuvre that includes "Chimes Of Freedom", "It Ain't Me, Babe", "Maggie's Farm", "Love Minus Zero/No Limit", "Mr. Tambourine Man", "Gates Of Eden", "It's Alright, Ma (I'm Only Bleeding)", "It's All Over Now, Baby Blue", "Like A Rolling Stone", "Ballad Of A Thin Man", "Queen Jane Approximately", "Desolation Row", "Visions Of Johanna", "I Want You", "Stuck Inside Of Mobile With The Memphis Blues Again", "Just Like A Woman" and "Sad-Eyed Lady Of The Lowlands".

Dylan's plunge into the maelstrom of his 'electric' tour of 1966 was followed by media reports of a motorcycle crash and a subsequent retreat from the madness his life had become into rural tranquillity, though it was the opposite of a retreat from musical and lyrical exploration. The first fruits of this 'post-accident' artist, *The Basement Tapes* and *John Wesley Harding*, can stand proudly alongside anything in his canon. The focus may have changed but, at first, anyway, the fecundity and profundity were unchecked. Key songs from 1967 include "Tears Of Rage", "I Shall Be Released", "You Ain't Going Nowhere", "This Wheel's On Fire", "Quinn, The Eskimo (The Mighty Quinn)", "I Dreamed I Saw St. Augustine", "All Along The Watchtower", "I Pity The Poor Immigrant" and "I'll Be Your Baby Tonight". The last-named signified Dylan moving on into a period of creativity-diminishing contentment.

Although the next album, *Nashville Skyline*, had its moments ("I Threw It All Away", "Lay, Lady, Lay", "Tell Me That It Isn't True", "Tonight I'll Be Staying Here With You"), it was essentially a slight offering compared to its predecessors. Nevertheless, for the counter-culture's undisputed leader to emerge with an album of 'redneck' country music was extremely brave, not to say provocative. Dylan's courage was rewarded when the hit single "Lay, Lady, Lay" helped make *Nashville Skyline* Dylan's best selling, if least compelling, album to date.

Still, with much of the rock world following Dylan 'back to the garden' (to borrow Joni Mitchell's phrase), like the eponymous 'hero' of "John Wesley Harding" he could reasonably be said during the 60s to have been "never known to make a foolish move". Decades later, 1962-1968 are still the years for which Dylan is lauded: honoured at award ceremonies and fêted by fellow artists, national leaders, distinguished academics and cultural gurus as one of the great artistic geniuses of the 20th Century.

The huge influence – on musicians, on society, on history – of Dylan's songs from this period is something that he has had to live with ever since, and it would be fair to say that he has not found doing so an easy task. The man had opened millions of eyes to the inequalities of the day: he not only told them what to see but also, in the words of David Bowie's "Song For Bob Dylan", "sat behind a million eyes and told them how they saw".[1] Indeed, he had assumed a central place in the lives of an entire generation. Such a level of responsibility was an intolerable burden, and one Dylan has tried to shake off ever since his mystery-shrouded 1966 motorcycle accident.

As the album market continued to expand at the turn of the decade, Dylan's reputation and mystique did likewise, making 1970's *Self Portrait* another big seller. It was also a huge disappointment, being a portrait of a self that nobody wanted to know, far less acknowledge as Bob Dylan. The "I am not the person you think I am" battle was set to run and run. Indeed, more than forty years later Dylan's first shows in China showed that it still has legs in it to this very day.

Patchy success followed with 1970's *New Morning* and the subsequent, and rather lovely, *Pat Garrett and Billy The Kid* soundtrack album, which yielded one of Dylan's biggest and most enduring hits, "Knockin' On Heaven's Door". Nonetheless, the period 1968-1973 was pale in comparison to the brilliant light of 1962-1967.

Fortunately, the mid-70s brought about a reawakening. Nineteen seventy four's *Planet Waves* album, a hastily-produced mix of the banal and the brilliant, reunited Dylan with his old sparring partners from 1966-67, The Band, and their

---

1 From the *Hunky Dory* album, the lyrics that come with the (otherwise superb) remastered CD manage to get this, as well as most other lines, incorrect. Apt, I suppose, given Dylan's own published error-strewn lyrics.

resulting 'comeback tour' of stadiums, capitalising on the return of the supposed '60's idol[2], was a huge commercial, though qualified artistic, success.

The genuine 'return' of Dylan's mercurial genius came in 1975 with the release of *Blood On The Tracks*, a record that not only lived up to his previous achievements but proudly stood as the single greatest album he had produced. On the road, too, his creativity again attained a peak of splendour, with 1975 and 1976 witnessing Dylan deliver two of his finest ever tours. Nineteen seventy-six also saw the release of his chart-topping *Desire* album, a musically adventurous and fine work, though it did not match the overall brilliance of its predecessor.

For all the success of *Blood On The Tracks* and *Desire*, Dylan's popularity in the States was beginning to diminish from 1976 onwards, the second Rolling Thunder Revue tour being very different to, and differently received from, its predecessor. Then his four-hour epic art-house movie *Renaldo and Clara* was ripped to shreds by the press. Worse was to follow. Dylan's next studio album, *Street-Legal*, was by far his least successful release of the decade in the US.

On the other hand, it was a completely different story beyond American shores. Dylan's 1978 world tour, his first for twelve years, garnered enormous media attention. Magnificent shows and legions of delirious fans kept Dylan very much in the international spotlight, and *Street-Legal* topped the charts in many countries. In the UK, the album's first single, "Baby Stop Crying", even made the Top 20 and was played on *Top Of The Pops*. *Renaldo and Clara* also received a somewhat more sympathetic press in Europe (especially France), though it was still a financial flop and more often than not heavily panned. Meanwhile, a messy divorce from Dylan's first wife, Sara, was turning his life upside down.

And in perhaps the biggest shock of a shock-filled career, after Dylan lost Sara, he found Jesus....

From finding Jesus to getting lost in Philadelphia

Street-Legal's poor US sales notwithstanding, Dylan was still very much regarded as rock's main man in 1978. He had, after all, largely survived punk along with perhaps only Neil Young and David Bowie from the old guard. The UK's hugely

2 A term Dylan was still dismissing vehemently – idols, he remarked, were little wooden carved things.

influential *New Musical Express* may have switched to a predominately punk-based content, but it still lauded Dylan's shows and excitedly revealed the mutual admiration that he and the Clash felt for each other's work.

In this context, Dylan's highly-publicised conversion to evangelical Christianity in 1979 dealt a hammer blow to his worldwide following. Dylan had taught his fans to think for themselves and reject false leaders. Dylan espousing any kind of authoritarian belief system would have been difficult for them to cope with, and his chosen religious path was downright unthinkable for many fans. It wasn't just that Dylan had become a born-again Christian[3], but that his conversion seemed to have taken him in a disturbing direction, where authoritarianism – "*Well, it may be the devil or it may be the Lord/ But you're gonna have to serve somebody*" ("Gotta Serve Somebody") was to be found alongside racism: "*Sheikhs walking around like kings, wearing fancy jewels and nose rings/ Deciding America's future from Amsterdam and Paris*" ("Slow Train").

Even more disturbing statements could be heard in Dylan's 'preaching' at concerts, where homophobia[4] was accompanied by paranoid 'political' ranting[5] and pure out-to-lunch wackiness:

> *"....god of this world, prince of the power of the air. That's the devil and he's infiltrated into e-v-e-r-y thing. Medicine, science, you name it, he's there. You know we read in the newspapers every day how bad the world is getting. The situation in Iran, the students*

3 This is not a term Dylan himself accepts, despite the specific references to being 'born again' in many lyrics.

4 *"Joshua, ... he went into, .. Canaan land, and God told him that in certain times He would destroy all the people, every man, woman, children there. .... And there was some cities. God said, 'Don't go in there yet', so Joshua wondered why, and God said 'Because the iniquity is not yet full'. So now, you look around today, when we started out this tour we started out in San Francisco. It's a kind of unique town and these days, I think it's either one-third of two-thirds of the population that are homosexuals in San Francisco. I heard it said. Now, I guess they are working up to a hundred percent. I don't know. But anyway, it's a growing place for homosexuals, and I read they have homosexual politics, and its political party. I don't mean it's going on in somebody's closet, I mean it's political! Alright, you know what I'm talking about? Anyway, I would just think, well, I guess the iniquity is not yet full. And I don't wanna be around when it is!"* Hartford CT, 8th May, 1980.

5 *"Russia will come down and attack in the Middle East. China's got an Army of two million people. They're gonna come down in the Middle East. There's gonna be a war called the Battle of Armageddon which is like something you never even dreamed about. And Christ will set up His Kingdom and He'll rule it from Jerusalem. I know, far out as that may seem this is what the Bible says..."*

> *rebelling, you know, even over here they're rebelling. They don't let the Iranians sneak into the whorehouses. But that don't matter much because we know this world will be destroyed.*
>
> *"Well, let ...me tell you now: the devil owns this world: he's called the god of this world.*
>
> *"Every time God comes against a nation, first of all he comes against their economy. If that doesn't work, He comes against their ecology ... He did it with Egypt. He did it with Persia. He did it with Babylon. He did it with the whole Middle East. It's desert now. It used to be flourishing gardens. Alright. If that doesn't work He just brings up another nation against them. So one of these three things has got to work. Now Jesus Christ is that solid rock. He's supposed to come two times. He came once already – He's coming back again. You gotta be prepared for this. No matter what you read in the newspapers, that's all deceit. The real truth is that He's coming back already. You just watch your newspapers, you're gonna see – maybe two years, maybe three years, five years from now, you just wait and see."* ***(Thus saith Dylan on April 20th, 1980 at Toronto.)***

John Lennon is perhaps the only other rock writer-performer to have enjoyed as iconic, and iconoclastic, a status as Dylan. While discussing Bob's Christian song "Gotta Serve Somebody", Dylan's first 'Christian' single and winner of that year's Grammy for Best Male Vocal, the former Beatle publicly avowed that Dylan should be allowed to do and say what he wanted. "Whatever reason he's doing it ... it's a personal reason for him and he needs to do it," Lennon maintained, in a 1980 radio interview: "I'm not distressed by the fact that Dylan is doing what Dylan wants to do ... If that's what he wants to do, he has to do that now, you know, let him do it ... "

Tellingly, Lennon added: "But I must say I was surprised ... when old Bobby Boy did go that way. You know, very surprised. I'm sure I wasn't the only one ... because all I ever hear whenever I hear him ... is: 'Don't follow leaders/Watch your parking meters' [sic]." Lennon's off-the-cuff remark echoed the widespread shock engendered when Dylan seemed oblivious to the irony that he, of all people, was denying others the freedom to think for themselves. Even as he was preaching: *"I told you that 'the times they are a changin'' 20 years ago, and I don't believe I've ever lied to you.... Never told you to vote for nobody; never told you to follow nobody"* he was singing: "*You're gonna have to serve somebody.*"

Perhaps unsurprisingly, given Dylan's fervent commitment to his new faith, the 'Christian tours' found him performing at an astonishing level, vocally and musically. Only the very best of his mid-sixties and mid-seventies shows can match the passion, subtlety and mesmeric vocal power of those performances. The message may have been unpalatable, but few who have heard the shows with open ears have been anything less than enthralled by its delivery.

By the time of his 1981 tours of Europe and America, Dylan was mixing old and new songs rather than sticking to the 'Christian ones'. It was a year of many wonderful vocal performances, as Dylan toured with a magnificently talented band. I saw the shows in London at Earls Court and was appalled that swathes of seats were empty till the moment Bob was due to take the stage. This casual attitude was a graphic illustration of the shocking drop in audience reverence towards Dylan when contrasted to his previous, pre-conversion, visits to Earls Court; then, the hall had been packed long before Dylan appeared.

The shows themselves were fine. In particular, the newer songs shone. "In the Summertime" was gorgeous while "I Believe In You" was literally spine-tingling; but there were also notable performances of older material like "Simple Twist of Fate" and "Girl From The North Country".

"In the Summertime" hailed from *Shot Of Love*, an album released to poor reviews and even poorer sales. Its follow-up, *Infidels*, and associated videos and TV appearances improved matters somewhat. (Though goodness knows how much more of a positive impact *Infidels* would have made had the released album included the best tracks from the sessions. Then again, the same could be said of *Shot Of Love*.) Although *Infidels* was initially panned by *Rolling Stone*, the magazine, like other commentators, subsequently deemed it a 'return to form'. The cliché-driven headline business proclaimed that 'Dylan was back', 'the radical 60s man was singing protest songs for the 80s' and all that kind of nonsense.

Dylan built on this resurgence of critical acclaim by giving a great performance on the *Late Night With David Letterman* TV show in March 1984. He then played a tour of European stadiums, co-headlining with Santana. The shows had a somewhat mixed reception amongst fans, but certainly sold well and garnered a fair share of media attention. Still, these were small victories. Undeniably, as the decade reached its mid-point, Dylan's career badly needed a shot in the arm. Instead, Dylan nearly shot it dead.

From Philadelphia to Concord

Nineteen eighty-five's massive Live Aid charity rock concert, in aid of African famine relief, drew a worldwide audience estimated at anywhere up to two billion. When guitar icon Eric Clapton was asked who he thought should close the event, he opined that Dylan was the only possible choice. In fact he seemed astonished the question should even be asked. Certainly Dylan's career achievements dwarfed those of any rock act still performing, but it was equally clear that his lofty reputation had little to do with his work in the 1980s. Still, here was a chance for Dylan to reassert both his primacy and contemporary relevance.

It is arguably admirable that, as we will see, he chose not to exploit this fund-raising event as a way of rejuvenating his career. The album charts, on both sides of the Atlantic, would soon be full of records by people who had impressed at Live Aid, with the Greatest Hits of apartheid-era Sun City patrons Queen the most conspicuous. Dylan albums would not be joining them, for Bob ended the immensely successful day-long spectacular on a sour, deflating note.

I watched the event on television, along with hundreds of millions around the planet. There were one or two performers on the bill that I still admired, Elvis Costello for example, and a few other senior acts I was curious to see. However, I watched the Global Jukebox, as it became known, as a Bob fan. As well as, obviously, hoping it would raise the necessary money to bring aid for those in such dire need of help, for me, Live Aid was also another concert that Dylan would be headlining and I spent the entire day geared up in anticipation of his appearance.

Reservations about the make-up of the bill and worries about how the aid would get to where it needed to notwithstanding, I was unquestionably aware that the fund-raiser was palpably a good and extraordinary thing. Yet I was so excited by the promise of Dylan's performance that, throughout the event, I kept my ears pinned back for any mention or cover of his Bobness. A completely over-the-top, soul version of "Forever Young" by Patti LaBelle further whetted my appetite for the man himself.

Finally, at 3:39am UK time, Dylan was given a magnificent introduction by Jack Nicholson. This turned out to be the best part of Dylan's 'set'. "Some artists' work speaks for itself," Nicholson began. "Some artists' work speaks for its generation. It is my deep, personal pleasure to present to you one of America's great voices of freedom. It can only be one man – the transcendent BOB DYLAN...."

A rather puffy, soon to be sweaty, Dylan emerged onto the stage, looked around and then addressed the audience: "Let me introduce some people who just came along tonight, Keith Richards and Ron Wood ... I don't know where they are."

When Wood and Richards appeared a few moments later, they too seemed not to know where they were. Both were looking and acting as though they had just been interrupted in the middle of a backstage party. It all looked very spontaneous but, in fact, Dylan had invited them to join him well before the day of the show. As the whole planet watched, it soon became apparent that our boys did not seem to be on it. 'Keef and Ronnie' were certainly appropriate guests, especially given Mick Jagger's preceding piece of dire showmanship with Tina Turner, but they were on acoustic guitars and, especially in Keith's case, didn't seem to realise this. Nor did they seem to have any idea which songs they were playing. Wood was concentrating so hard on smoking his cigarette that he completely ignored his guitar until well into the first song. While Richards did not shun his instrument quite so blatantly, it was not entirely clear what he was doing with it.

Still, initially things looked fairly hopeful. When Dylan began singing "Ballad of Hollis Brown" his voice was clear and strong and the line "Is there anyone who knows, is there anyone who cares?" got a cheer from some attentive folk in the audience. Unfortunately, some terrible feedback immediately unsettled Dylan. He just about managed to hold it together, but the song fizzled out pretty weakly.

Dylan followed this inauspicious version of a well-chosen song with a startlingly inappropriate little speech. He initially explained that he "thought that was a fitting song for this important occasion." However, it soon became clear that he had something more on his mind, something the song was specifically 'fitting' for. "I'd just like to say," he continued, " I hope that some of the money that's raised for the people in Africa, maybe they could take just a little bit of it, maybe one or two million maybe, and use it say to pay the, uh, the mortgages on some of the farms, mmmmm, that the farmers here owe to the banks."

Given the situation, I found, and still find, the comments indefensible. Many others have been determined to find a defence for them, though. There are two main points people make when they attempt to justify Dylan's bizarre speech. The first is that Dylan was bucking the trend by speaking out about something important on a day of self-satisfied superstar smugness and cynical careerism, and the second that he was only bravely standing up for the truth in the old saying 'charity begins at home'.

On the first point, far be it from me to be against Dylan bucking a trend. There were undeniably cynical elements to the day. Seeing Status Quo and Queen, who had broken the boycott by Western artists in protest over the cancer of apartheid by playing Sun City, now boosting their career while getting credit for helping starving Africans, made one even keener than usual to discover what a true individual like Bob Dylan would make of the whole event. However, the cynicism of some performers should not be allowed to colour one's judgement of the entire event. "The purpose of Live Aid was to raise money," event organiser Bob Geldof maintained. "If a band sold a million records, it meant more people would watch than if they sold a thousand. If more people contributed, more people lived. If I have a choice between Steel Pulse or Wham! on this show, I'll take Wham!"

To fully appreciate the appalling impact of Dylan's speech, it is essential to see it in the exact context of the night. Just before 3.30am, a shattered, ill-looking Geldof appeared on UK television to thank those who had pledged donations and to implore the viewers to donate further. He also made a final plea against the insanity and inhumanity of mass starvation in the Third World during an era of Western prosperity, railing against the ignorance and indifference of Western political leaders.

"Again I pose the question that I've yet to receive an answer to," he raged, "Why, if we sit on food surplus stocks, why are there people dying? Why don't they simply open the gates to these silos and send it to those people?"

Asked how he pulled the event off, Geldof retorted "You have to find a cause that is above moral or political argument – everybody agrees 130 million people dying is wrong...." With eyes nearly closing with fatigue, Geldof made one last plea to the audience to open their wallets. The camera then switched to the studio presenter. "You are looking absolutely shattered," he told Geldof. "Quite obviously it has been a very long day for you .... Well, sit back and enjoy this, because at JFK Stadium in Philadelphia we can now go to Bob Dylan and the finale."

Minutes later, the bleary-eyed Europeans who had stayed up for the great finale heard Dylan ask for money to be taken away from the starving African children, whose desperate plight Geldof had just so passionately expounded upon, to be used to pay mortgage loans to rich American banks. Regardless of Dylan's motives, this was a slap in the face to all that was good about the day. Also, it is hard to determine how daring Dylan actually was: his words were greeted by a large cheer from the American crowd. It is impossible to tell, though, if this was because the well-heeled, mostly white Philadelphia crowd agreed with him, or because they were simply ready to cheer anything Dylan said.

Sadly, Dylan just came across as petty and mean; there was certainly no offer of any of his own millions to help kick the 'one or two million' off.

Even if one agrees with the second point, that 'charity begins at home' this was hardly the time or the place to launch a campaign for it. Why not wait a week and hold a press conference acknowledging Live Aid's success and suggesting a similar fund-raiser for American farmers? Even the next day would not have seemed so crass, but to make this point at the climax to the whole Live Aid day was nothing less than shameful. To directly equate the plight of struggling US farmers, for all they too were deserving of help, to that of the dying babies with their starvation-distended stomachs, disease-ridden bodies, and faces covered in flies they were too weak to brush off; desperate for any water or food at all, far less medical aid was ... well, the last words on this issue should go to Geldof himself. Geldof accused Bob of "a complete lack of understanding of the issues raised by Live Aid". Clearly riled, Geldof continued: "Live Aid was about people losing their lives. There is a radical difference between losing your livelihood and losing your life. It did instigate Farm Aid, which was a good thing in itself, but it was a crass, stupid, and nationalistic thing to say."

Having made his little speech, Dylan went into his second song, "When The Ship Comes In". It sounded passable at the beginning, if a little thin. However, by now the level of intrusive background noise was so loud that it must have seemed like retribution for his insensitive outburst. Dylan, who later used the word 'sabotaged' when talking about it, occasionally glanced at Keith Richards, who remained obliviously happy, as he preened himself in smiling rock guitarist mode.

Dylan began to sweat more heavily; the strain was beginning to tell. The song became increasingly tuneless and Dylan's attempt at a harmonica break had to be curtailed. Presumably by now almost unable to hear himself, he screeched towards the song's conclusion; shouting the lyrics and vainly trying to put emphasis in the right places. A wry grimace and self-deprecating smile after "conquered" let us know he probably had a good idea how this sounded. Ron and Keith tried to buddy-buddy him on stage and lift his spirits, but things were going very badly. The song ended to muted cheering. Dylan asked the crowd if the sound was OK, and then asked how much time he had left. To be honest, you felt he was hoping the answer would be "not much".

Then it was into "Blowin' In the Wind", again pretty apt considering another hugely obvious answer was blowin' around the whole world, Dylan's voice cracking in the second line. He recovered sufficiently to give it a fair reading. Dylan then introduced a Keith Richards' solo. The camera caught Dylan turning his face to Ron and looking to the sky. It was a clear gesture that Dylan had no idea what Keith would do, and Ron seemed to feel the same. To be fair to Keith, the solo was probably completely unplanned and a cover for Dylan to do something to his own guitar, which had by now broken down completely. Dylan ended up taking Ron Wood's guitar. Keith ended his solo before the instrument swap was completed and Dylan did really well to keep singing as he tried to strap on his replacement guitar. Ron got another guitar from a roadie a verse later but it seemed, to put it mildly, to be a stranger to him. I am not sure it had a single string properly tuned.

The whole thing ended with a "thank you". Lionel Richie came on and cuddled them all and the curtains opened to reveal nearly all of the day's participants gathered for a massed finale. Bob initially remained near the front of the stage, playing a few guitar licks, then, somewhat comically, he ran off to the side like a small schoolboy rushing away to meet his pals. He nudged Richie in the back on his way past, presumably to let him know he would not be singing his line in "We Are the World".

There are many excuses for Dylan's performance; not least, the situation on stage was chaotic at best. Perhaps, though, proper preparation would have helped. The circulating tapes of rehearsals (discovering the Loch Ness Monster would have been slightly less of a surprise than finding evidence that this shambles had been rehearsed), shows that the boys had been enjoying themselves. The quality of the rehearsal performances was so bad that Ron Wood speculated on how terrible it would be if Dylan were to mess things up on the night in front of so many people. Completely mistakenly, he and Richards reassured themselves that this could never happen.

Perhaps, also, less partying before the event would have helped; but to be fair to Dylan, lack of preparation and excessive indulgence in pre-concert 'refreshments' have, both before and since, led to some sparkling performances. Certainly, at the start Dylan's voice sounded unaffected by any backstage revels. In addition, a further batch of rehearsal tapes that made their way into collectors' hands show that, on another day, the musicians were treating the event more respectfully. This recording also contained the surprising news that Dylan had been planning to play "Dark Eyes". The set-up at the event would have made this impossible but it is more than a little intriguing to imagine how that could have sounded and what a triumph it might have been. We were faced with disaster rather than triumph, as it transpired.

When questioned about the catastrophe, another Sun City boycott-buster, Rod Stewart, commented that they should have let Bob Dylan go on stage alone: "He's the best in the world at that". Unfortunately, it was Dylan's decision to have two Stones with him. And, to some degree at least, it was Dylan's fault that they had no idea what they were supposed to be doing on the stage. To make things worse, Dylan looked in a dreadful condition. His bloated and sweaty frame was such a depressing contrast to the wiry, ultra-cool Dylan of previous years. He seemed a sad, bitter and marginalised figure at an event that he should have totally dominated. His appearance, performance and embarrassing words brought him to an all-time low. Quite an achievement to time this for an appearance that handed him a potentially adoring audience of somewhere between one and two billion on a plate.

So, by the summer of 1985 Dylan had managed to lose any ground he had regained with *Infidels*, and his career had reached its nadir. He had to start turning things around. Dylan followed Live Aid's global showcase with a low-key performance at a poetry festival in Moscow. His next gig was at the at the first

Farm Aid show at the Memorial Stadium, Champaign, Illinois. This was inspired by his ill-judged remarks at Live Aid, organiser Debra Winger heard Dylan's comments and thought, "Yes, I agree with that". So, in a way, Dylan had given himself the chance of redemption in front of another vast audience.

Farm Aid united another all-star cast and, enjoyed, if not a global audience to begin with, a huge American one. This time, though, the Dylan fan did not need to worry; the contrast with Live Aid could not have been more marked. Dylan was alert and clearly enjoying the experience. He was backed by the accomplished and professional Tom Petty and the Heartbreakers, and four black female back-up singers (known as the Queens of Rhythm).

In the US at least, Dylan's Live Aid débâcle had not alienated too much of the audience. There was an enormous ovation when his name was announced. He was still a huge name, if no longer the automatic headliner, and was introduced as a 'superstar' by American TV. Gone was the puffy-looking Dylan: in fact, earring aside, he looked great, with his trademark hair and profile, leather jacket, and jeans tucked into motorbike boots.

He opened with "Clean Cut Kid", a song I have no enthusiasm for, its irony being about as subtle as that of "John Brown", but it was a good number for Bob and the Heartbreakers to rip into with gusto. The televised segment then began as Dylan launched into "Shake", one of a number of fun old rock 'n' rollers the band had rehearsed. Complete with suitable guitar hero poses and Dylan trading licks with Petty, it was very well received.

Next was the potentially mawkish "I'll Remember You", but it sounded wonderful; as, indeed, it has at various times on the NET. Dylan managed to bring out the song's intimacy, which was no small feat in such a setting, and also appeared to be brimming with confidence, another contrast with his Live Aid persona. There was more intimacy, too, in his glances at his co-singer, Madelyn Quebec. When Dylan sings this song well, he transcends its saccharine platitudes and turns it into something deeply moving.

By the time Dylan got to "Trust Yourself" he had been joined by a crowd of musicians, including Willie Nelson, and was clearly having fun. This was a new song, a live debut indeed (as was "I'll Remember You"), and he usually performs his newest songs with special, extra presence

Towards the song's conclusion, Dylan approached the front of the stage and stared out at the crowd while rocking out on his guitar. It was as if he were looking to see if they were still his audience. He appeared confident that they were. "That Lucky Old Sun" was fabulous, worth all the rest of the set put together, a tremendous treat for the crowd though not, alas, for the TV audience as, like "Clean Cut Kid", it was omitted from the broadcast. The song's contrast of earthly toil and heavenly ease was also poignant for an event in aid of those who were being denied the chance to toil on their farms.

Dylan ended his set with a solid, rocking ensemble performance of a song that demanded to be played at Farm Aid: "Maggie's Farm". Dylan's set at Farm Aid was pretty damn good. If "That Lucky Old Sun" plus any two of the other tracks could have been transplanted to Live Aid, Dylan's set there would have been a triumph rather than an abject failure, so long as he had stuck to performing and dropped his between-song patter.

Another glaring contrast between Farm Aid and Live Aid is the evidence we have of the rehearsals for the two events. There is a circulating video of the Farm Aid rehearsal sessions which gives a magnificent glimpse into Dylan at work. In these rehearsals Dylan looks well and sounds sublime and is extremely focused on what he is doing. As far as the event itself was concerned, Dylan's set helped re-establish some credibility, even in its truncated televised form.

The collaboration with Tom Petty and the Heartbreakers continued for two very different tours, in 1986 and 1987. The 1986 double-headers encompassed New Zealand, Australia, Japan and then Dylan's first US tour since 1981.

This US leg of the tour was described by Rolling Stone as "the hottest ticket of the summer". The tour as a whole was immortalised in the video *Hard To Handle*, filmed at Sydney on 24th and 25th March. However, this tour is not rated highly by most Dylan fans. The tapes of the US shows capture some good, hard-hitting rock 'n' roll, fun for the audience on the night, but, as with the 1974 tour, these are not tapes one returns to often. Unless Dylan is on his most transcendent live form, say 1966, 1975 or 1979, Dylan fans demand radical changes in set-lists from night to night. It is all relative, of course; this tour would probably seem full of quality, variation and surprise compared to many touring performers who actually do play the same songs in the same way and the same order night after night. Despite the overall similarity of the set-lists, Dylan certainly did not do that. There were variations and introductions of fresh songs throughout the tour; especially, and significantly for the NET, in the cover versions.

"Shake" prefigured a succession of delightful, and often obscure, covers from the back pages of R&B, rock 'n' roll and other vintage sources that would light up the following decades. "That Lucky Old Sun" was also reprised to fabulous effect, and special mention has to be made of two other magnificent covers: "Lonesome Town" (by Baker Knight, but made famous by Ricky Nelson) and Ry Cooder, John Hiatt and Jim Dickinson's "Across The Borderline". The latter, as performed by Dylan, takes on the whole range and power of frontier American literature. He inhabits and then projects the song so fully that it is extremely difficult to remember that it is not a Dylan original.

Delightful covers aside, the sets were a high-energy romp spanning songs from throughout his career. Although leaning heavily on the 'greatest hits', Dylan also showcased his recent album, *Empire Burlesque*. One should also not overlook Dylan's pointed performance of "In The Garden" from *Saved* as a centrepiece of the sets, prefaced with remarks about how Jesus was still his 'hero'.

The change in Dylan's appearance from the previous year was startling. "Dylan on stage in 1986 looked muscular and healthy," Paul Williams[6] comments, "a relaxed, confident performer who had prepared carefully for this tour, this set of shows. It is as if a year earlier he watched footage of himself at Live Aid and resolved to do whatever he had to, to regain his power and dignity." Dylan's new look appeared to have been deliberately chosen to banish the memory of that Live Aid footage, but it involved curiously non-Dylan-like attire. Apart from his predilection for an absurd earring, the wearing of leather vests and the macho bare-arm posturing seemed much more of a sub-Springsteen stereotypical rawk'n'roll-look than a Dylan one.

The 1986 trek was a very high-profile tour; backing band Tom Petty and the Heartbreakers were huge album sellers in their own right and on something of a commercial roll. In fact, one interviewer quizzed Petty about opening for someone who sold so few records in comparison with himself. Petty wondered aloud how it could be any other way, finding the idea of Dylan opening for someone else ludicrous. One wonders how Petty has viewed Dylan at various

6 Paul Williams passed away after a long, tragic illness on March 27th 2013

times opening for the Rolling Stones, Van Morrison, Joni Mitchell, Santana and the Grateful Dead amongst others, including the Dead's ex-bass player, in the years since.

So how would Dylan follow this big 'event of the year' tour that introduced him to the huge fan base of a multi-platinum selling group? Well, why not go for the biggest fan base of any touring band? Which is what he did by teaming up with the Grateful Dead, the legendary '60s survivors who continued, year in and year out, to draw the biggest concert audiences in the USA.

In fact, Dylan's live adventure with the Grateful Dead would have very unfortunate results. He played in front of huge audiences, but the vast majority of them were there to see the Dead. The opening show, on July 4th 1987, found Dylan looking much older and frailer than in the previous year, wearing a too-obviously-casual-to-be-accidentally-thrown-together outfit as if to please the Deadheads. He hunched over the microphone as though in pain, and the light, it was an outdoor show, seemed to bother him greatly. The group and Dylan played as though they had never met, far less spent time rehearsing. It later transpired, however, that they most certainly had, collectors now have recordings of these rehearsals.

Dylan's voice was reduced to a thin rasp as he proceeded to slaughter most of his set. He sounded for all the world like an under-rehearsed Dylan impersonator. Unfortunately, this poor display was not greatly improved upon during this curious little mini-tour of stadiums. But if the performances were, at best, erratic, the selection of songs was simply stunning.

Songs that Dylan fans would never have predicted came tumbling out– songs never before played live, or in the case of "Chimes of Freedom" not for almost a quarter of a century. (I mention "Chimes of Freedom" particularly, because if there was one redeeming feature of these shows, it was to be found in the sublime versions of this brilliant song.) To hear Bob perform "Queen Jane Approximately", "The Ballad Of Frankie Lee And Judas Priest", "John Brown", "Joey", and "The Wicked Messenger" was simply extraordinary. I have to give Jerry Garcia and his cohorts great credit for galvanising Dylan to rediscover old gems from his back pages, especially those songs that they themselves were wont to cover.[7]

Dylan himself was later to specifically credit The Dead with giving him back the idea of what touring was all about. "*Ten years ago*", Dylan told *Newsweek*'s David Gates in 1997[8]:

> *"I'd kind of reached the end of the line. Whatever I'd started out to do, it wasn't that. I was going to pack it in."*

(DG) Onstage, he couldn't do his old songs.

> *"You know, like how do I sing this? It just sounds funny."*

(DG) He goes into an all-too-convincing imitation of panic: *"I - I can't remember what it means, does it mean - is it just a bunch of words? Maybe it's like what all these people say, just a bunch of surrealistic nonsense."*

(DG) When the Grateful Dead took him on tour in 1987, Jerry Garcia urged him to try again.

> *"He'd say, 'Come on, man, you know, this is the way it goes, let's play it, it goes like this.' And I'd say, 'Man, he's right, you know? How's he gettin' there and I can't get there?' And I had to go through a lot of red tape in my mind to get back there."*

Then, in October 1987, playing Locarno, Switzerland with Tom Petty's band and the female singers he now says he used to hide behind, Dylan had his breakthrough. Soon, we will see exactly how he was going to "get back there", but first things had to get worse before they could get better.

What a contrast the 1987 tour was to the Dylan/Heartbreakers shows of 1986. The greatest hits were still present but were often mangled and contemptuously

---

7 I still do credit them with this though I am no longer clear to what degree the Dead influenced Dylan's song selection and how much came from Dylan himself. Via Susan Ross's testimony and the songs rehearsed it appears now that Dylan himself was originally in an even more experimental mood than the shows evinced.

8 "Dylan Revisited", David Gates, *Newsweek Magazine* Oct 5th, 1997

tossed aside in wildly unpredictable set-lists. This certainly made it exciting for those who went to more than one show, and substituting a more 'obscure' title in place of another big crowd-pleasing finale of "Like A Rolling Stone" is fine by me. Nor am I against the fact, which seemed to upset so many reviewers and attendees, that Dylan never spoke to the audience.

However, Dylan did seem wilfully sullen on this tour. He dressed bizarrely badly and looked dreadful, or at least insofar as one could see him on the barely-lit stages. It was hard to comprehend the disparity between his current sorry appearance and the re-energised rocker of the US Heartbreakers tour. "He came on stage ... contorted in a Keef Richards slouch," Gavin Martin wrote of 1987's Wembley Arena Dylan, "with semi-biker gear and what looked like a dead rodent on his head. His strained, strangled wretch of a voice seemed to fit his appearance."

Dylan did look utterly wasted. Seeing him this way I felt he was pushing himself to an early grave. Without wanting to invade Dylan's privacy, such incontrovertible evidence of drug use is impossible to ignore – especially in relation to its effect on his stage performance. In fact, as with the whole of rock's history, Dylan's career was heavily influenced by drug usage. And around this time he was not hiding it. In the fascinating BBC *Omnibus* interview, recorded on 18th October 1986, Dylan sniffs with what is clearly not a cold and even makes a point of going out to 're-energise' himself. A security guard at Birmingham's NEC reported that he saw Dylan alone in a room, just prior to the show, snorting from a "mountain of cocaine" that was larger than the guard had ever seen before, including, even, the entire stash of a notoriously indulgent heavy metal group. While that story is, naturally, hearsay, it certainly appeared to be corroborated by Dylan's appearance that night.

On Dylan's legendary 1966 tour the use of drugs seemed overwhelmingly present on every song, yet his control was total and exquisite, from the dopey haze of the gorgeous acoustic sets to the speed-fuelled rush of the second half – night after night, country after country. When it works for Dylan it works unimaginably well, but, whatever uppers and downers one indulges in, the outcome can be hard to predict. What can be said with a greater degree of certainty is that the older one gets the harder it becomes for the body to recover, especially during gruelling tours. In the Band's farewell concert film *The Last Waltz,* Robbie Robertson said of touring "It's a goddamn impossible way of life". Dylan seemed a physical embodiment of that statement during his 1987 and 1991 European tours, although he has gone on to confound the claim in the most emphatic of terms.

There is, though, something to be said for this 'scorched earth' policy toward touring. (Well, not in early 1991, but more of that later.) The 'Temples In Flames' tour also produced performances of beauty, often of songs that one had had no expectation of ever hearing in concert, let alone in such intensely felt, close-to-the-edge performances. The varied set-lists, the spontaneous recreations of songs, the surprising selections all prefigured the NET. And Tom Petty and his band certainly found it startlingly innovative and a steep and highly beneficial learning curve:

"I learned so much from Bob Dylan," says Tom Petty. The Heartbreakers toured as Dylan's backing band from 1986 to 87. "He gave us a kind of courage that we never had, to learn something quickly and go out on stage and play it. You had to be pretty versatile because arrangements could change, keys might change, there's just no way of knowing exactly what he wants to do each night. You really learnt the value of spontaneity, of how a moment that is real in a concert is worth so much more than one you plan out."[9]

Nonetheless, at the time the general impression amongst (many) Dylan fans and (most) reviewers was that Dylan was losing the plot altogether. Looking ill and sporting bizarre, ill-chosen headgear he skulked in the shadows throughout incredibly short sets, wherein he distorted his best melodies in a strangulated vocal parody of himself more hurtful than any malicious satirist has ever managed. Later, once they started listening to the tapes, Dylan fans would discover that rare jewels and fabulous performances lay within. Mostly, though, only negativity remained amongst onlookers as Dylan's last pre-NET tour wound its way to a close.

It was amidst this backdrop, and on an uninspiring, windy and foggy, evening at an outdoor show at Locarno, Switzerland, that Dylan had an epiphany as he stepped up to the microphone.

"It's almost like I heard it as a voice," Dylan recalled to Newsweek's David Gates. *"It wasn't like it was even me thinking it. I'm determined to stand, whether*

---

9 "Telegraph reporter"; *Tom Petty's debt to Bob Dylan* June 18th 2012

God will deliver me or not. And all of a sudden everything just exploded. It exploded every which way. And I noticed that all the people out there – I was used to them looking at the girl singers, they were good-looking girls, you know? And like I say, I had them up there so I wouldn't feel so bad. But when that happened, nobody was looking at the girls any more. They were looking at the main mike. After that is when I sort of knew: I've got to go out and play these songs. That's just what I must do. "[10]

He's been at it ever since.

As 1988's tour kicked off, all Dylan's 1980s touring paraphernalia – huge stadiums, big-name groups, backing singers etc. – were to be swept away. The new shows would mark a whole new approach, or, rather, a return to an earlier format. Dylan was ready for the Never Ending Tour. His fans had no idea what was about to hit them.

The Fan's Never Ending Tour

Despite what historians might argue, I need to stress that, from the fan's perspective, the NET itself is not a single, monolithic entity. No two people witness a show with the same dispassionate objectivity. Even more pertinently, no one aside from Dylan has attended every show on the NET. As a result, dedicated fans each carry our own version of the Never Ending Tour around with us, based not only on memories of the shows we attended, but also, indeed mainly, on our after-the-fact exposure to recordings on cassettes, DATs, minidiscs, CDs, MP3s, WAVS and from audience and professional video footage. This leaves us at the mercy of our distorted memories, the quality of our recordings and our particular moods and circumstances when listening to them.

One of the Dylan 'voices of authority' that I most respect, a really careful listener, received two tapes from me in February 1994. I thought I had sent him the 7th and 9th of February. In those days I was getting tapes directly from the Japan shows and copying and forwarding them to as many friends and as quickly as possible. It was the routine of 'listen as you copy, label, package, post'

10 "Dylan Revisited", David Gates, *Newsweek Magazine* Oct 5th, 1997

that obsessive fans performed so often. So, my error in sending the tape of the 7th twice to the same person, one labelled correctly, one as the 9th, is perhaps understandable.

What is also understandable, though it initially seems surprising, is that the recipient of these tapes did not like the show labelled as the 7th at all, but thought the '9th ' was a big improvement. On the next listen he realised that it was the same show and compared the two tapes to see if there was a difference in recording quality; there was not. The difference had been in his personal circumstances. When first listening, he was pressed for time, and tried to make the most of his one listen by studiously concentrating on every moment of the tape. The tape did not repay this level of concentration.

Also, crucially, it was the first tape he had heard from this leg of the tour (the first of the year at that) and he had expectations that were not met. By the time he got the next tape, a couple of days later, his expectations were considerably lower and he had less time pressure. He was listening further away from the sound source (this can be remarkably beneficial in non-professionally made concert tapes, unless one has the very best sources) and so forth. And he liked it, the same tape he had not enjoyed only two days earlier. When you remember the highly subjective way in which we listen to music in private, this is perfectly understandable, and it is a major reason why the NET is so much easier to talk about in general terms (various legs of the tour, for example) than via particular shows.

Other personal circumstances also come into play. I have tapes that resonate with what I was doing when I first heard them, and I have 'favourite shows', because they were the only ones that I had in good enough quality to play on my Walkman as I travelled to and from work. Other people I know have favourite 'car tapes'. And these are people who have a vast number of shows on tape, who dedicate time to listening to these tapes; a more casual listener may have only a few tapes from a given year, with the result that their feel for that whole year will be based on those gigs. Given Dylan's variable performances from night to night on the NET, the possibilities for misinterpreting the artistic worth of a given year are immense. Someone listening to three shows from Europe 1991 and three shows from the fall tour of the USA that same year might almost believe they are listening to two different people, or at the very least the same person from two shows many years apart in his career.

The same difficulties in discussing individual shows are exacerbated by one's personal attendance. What mood were you in? How was your personal life going at the time? Were you clear-headed, or in party mood? Was it the first show you had seen in years, or that particular year, or that month or week, or was it one of eight shows you were seeing in a row? Did you have a good seat/standing position? Could you see Dylan's face clearly? Did you have an annoying person near you, in front of you, or did you have a nice enough person in front of you, but alas s/he was a foot taller than you? On and on this litany could go, and the likelihood of some kind of personal, travel or emotional problem is exacerbated by the very intensity that diehard fans bring to the shows. In their excited state, functioning properly can be a task too far. Oh, and we have not even mentioned Dylan's 'mood' yet.

The first NET concert I attended was Glasgow 1989. While writing *Razor's Edge* twelve years ago, the Glasgow '89 show I listened to on a cassette was not the same event at all. For a start, I was eleven years older: my life and my perceptions had changed. To put that in perspective, eleven years before Glasgow I saw Dylan live for the first time at Earls Court, London. I wonder what my 19-year-old self would have made of the Glasgow '89 show, or of some of the later shows that I was to hurry to listen to in the years that followed; I doubt he would have shared my excitement.

This is not to decry the NET as an inevitable decline, it is far from that. But even the most fanatical of Dylan fans must admit that he is only human, and age brings an inevitable waning of powers: vocal cords, stamina, concentration levels all deteriorate. In the sixties Dylan was in his 20s, in the seventies his 30s. He was also, in the middle of both those decades, at performing heights that the word Olympian fails to do justice to. His backing musicians were of the highest calibre, too, constantly pushing him to further heights. Dylan was 71 when he concluded 2012's year of touring, so comparisons are unfair to the point of being preposterous. And yet, and yet ... the fan who goes to shows on the NT is also the fan who still collects recordings and videos of those earlier years. Dylan's record company are forever releasing gems from his jewel-encrusted past. While for Dylan it seems that he must ignore this legendary past in order to keep working; for the fan Dylan's past is always present.

One also has to embrace the consequences of Dylan continuing to play over 100 shows per year. A variation in quality is an inevitable side effect of the NET's annual slog, night after night, city after city. Thinking otherwise will spark vain comparisons to times when a younger Dylan, virtually always playing far fewer times per tour, consistently performed with that intensity, menace, concentration and presence that set his concerts apart from anything else you could experience. This is not to say that the NET has not at times afforded us opportunities to witness Dylan in all his raging glory. It has, but it does not, indeed, could not, do so at each of 100 or so shows every single year.

That is why, despite all its limitations and distortions, the recorded medium offers a better chance of a balanced judgement of the NET phenomenon than attendance at a few, or even many, of the shows. If I picked my favourite fifty Dylan shows of all time, I would have attended none of them; if I picked my favourite ten NET dates, I would have attended none of those either. If I were only to write about the shows I have attended, this would give neither a feel for their place in the unfolding story of the NET, nor how they came to be heard by me and the effect they had on me. The shows I have attended are just one facet amongst many in my experience of these extraordinary events; I was also listening to tapes, watching videos, sharing stories with friends, avidly following set-list changes in far-off countries I could not visit and so on. The entirety of this NET experience is the subject of this book.

Nonetheless, for the fan there will always be a particular thrill about a live show. The special connection that you feel when you are in the same hall as the singer; that bond is at the centre of what the NET is all about. So the shows I attended, as well as the tapes I hold in high esteem, form the basis of my Never Ending Tour.

What follows is one fan's experience of this utterly unpredictable, constantly changing and regularly inspiring period in the career of an artist who has been attracting exactly those adjectives from the press and public for over fifty years.

CHAPTER TWO

1988: "The people themselves will tell you when to stop touring"

"I really don't have any place to put my feet up. We want to play because we want to play. Why tour? It's just that you get accustomed to it over the years. The people themselves will tell you when to stop touring."

BOB DYLAN, AUGUST 5TH 1988[1]

I cannot recall exactly who told me, but early in the summer of 1988 I became aware that Dylan had started a new tour with a small band, was playing some hard-hitting, rock-driven shows and was looking far healthier than in 1987. I also knew that Neil Young had guested on guitar for a number of shows and that Dylan was tending to play theatres rather than arenas. It all sounded very exciting. As I had been living abroad and was not part of the world of Dylan fandom at the time, I had to settle for what few scraps of information were given out by the regular music press and what I garnered from my cousin Andy. This only heightened my anticipation, so it was with great expectation that I

1 Interview by Kathryn Baker, Associated Press.

awaited the tapes Andy would forward to me. Unsurprisingly, the first ones I received were from the opening shows. So let us go back in time to Concord, to where it all began.

FIRST NET SHOW: June 7th 1988 Concord Pavilion, Concord CA

1 Subterranean Homesick Blues
2 Absolutely Sweet Marie
3 Masters Of War
4 You're A Big Girl Now
5 Gotta Serve Somebody
6 In The Garden
7 Man Of Constant Sorrow (Traditional, Acoustic)
8 The Lakes Of Pontchartrain (Traditional, Acoustic)
9 Boots Of Spanish Leather (Acoustic)
10 Driftin' Too Far From Shore
11 Gates Of Eden
12 Like A Rolling Stone
13 Maggie's Farm

After the years of big bands, string sections, horns and female backing singers, it must have been quite a shock to see Dylan take the stage flanked only by a three-piece band: Chris Parker on drums, G.E. Smith on lead guitar and Kenny Aaronson on bass. They looked and sounded like a band of rock and roll gangsters from the wrong side of the tracks. Neil Young was there too, though his presence was barely audible.

The opening show started with a shock as a fairly throaty Dylan sped through his first ever live performance of "Subterranean Homesick Blues". This proved so successful an opener that it remained in the starting slot throughout 1988. It was followed by an even greater live debut in "Absolutely Sweet Marie", a point often overlooked by commentators in their excitement over "Subterranean". This classic *Blonde On Blonde* song was treated to an aggressive rendition, with

Dylan's voice exploding into action as though he had been longing to get back to stripped-down rockers.

Guitars riffing like machine guns propelled Dylan next into an ominous "Masters Of War". After this opening hard-hitting three-song salvo, Dylan's voice had shed all vestiges of rustiness and the subsequent "You're a Big Girl Now" had strong, clear vocals. Dylan now allowed himself a bit of space to squeeze tremendous emotion from phrases such as "back in the rain". There were many more fine versions of this song to come in 1988, Dylan even rewriting a verse as the shows progressed. This was hardly remarked upon at the time, as rewriting a song from *Blood On The Tracks* for live performance was not unusual in those days; it certainly would cause more than a ripple in fan circles in later years.

Dylan's first address to an NET audience followed: "All right, thank you; we got Neil Young here playing tonight." Then he swung into "Gotta Serve Somebody", a song that allows him the pleasure of playing around with rhyming couplets without changing the import of the chorus. Despite being given a kick-ass treatment it displayed a refreshing jauntiness, with Dylan enjoying changing the emphasis and playing with the song's title line.

A dramatic, declamatory "In The Garden" was next, just in case anyone had missed the previous song's Christian message amidst the exuberant, playful delivery. As a song, "In The Garden" just shades the early finger-pointing of "Who Killed Davey Moore?" in subtlety; the browbeating, rhetorical questioning has the same bludgeoning effect. When Dylan is into the song, though, as he was here, it drives along with power and sweeps you up in the moment. He performed it in a challenging, ranting style to close the first electric set; setting a trend for this spot in NET sets to be occupied by a theatrically key song. A trend which was, with only a few exceptions, to last for a long time.

The shocks did not stop. The acoustic set opened with "Man Of Constant Sorrow", a traditional song that Dylan had covered on his debut album so many years before. This alternate version was beautiful, a splendid arrangement with expressive vocals. It was a worthy beginning to the extraordinary procession of traditional songs that Dylan would cover over the years of the NET. Night after night, year after year, they have supplied many of the high points. So fully does Dylan inhabit these numbers that they often sound more like Dylan songs than some he has penned himself. This was especially obvious in some later years, when, unlike 1988, he would sometimes toss off his own most familiar material with no feeling of being engaged in his own songs at all, and then suddenly come to life when interpreting a folk standard.

Back at Concord '88, he was about to play another: "The Lakes Of Pontchartrain", a magnificent, timeless song of unfulfilled love ("I asked her if she would marry me, she said that never could be/For she had got a lover, and he was far off at sea"). In Dylan's hands, both here and many times since, you live the story with and through him. The same theme of unfulfilled love shot through Dylan's contemporary album *Down In The Groove* in songs such as "Ninety Miles An Hour (Down A Dead End Street)": "You're not free to come along with me/ And you know I could never be your own".

So, the new record seemed, at this moment, to be present in spirit, though I doubt that this was much comfort to the record company executives who would surely have preferred to hear Dylan sing actual tracks from *Down In The Groove*. Then again fans who bought that release, which was so short on quality and in length, would have preferred the inclusion on the record of a few more traditional songs like "The Lakes Of Pontchartrain".

Dylan brought this riveting acoustic set to an end with one of his own 'traditional' sounding songs, giving us an appealing version of "Boots Of Spanish Leather".

Somewhere along the way the audience may have noticed they had no opportunity to give the customary rousing acclaim to Dylan's harmonica-playing. In yet another surprise, Bob never played harmonica on the 1988 tour.

The second electric set opened with another debut, "Driftin' Too Far From Shore". It was too much to expect this feeble work to follow comfortably in the footsteps of the marvellous songs just played. Nonetheless, the first live outing of a newish Dylan song was exciting in itself, even if it was played as though it was the "Julius And Ethel" out-take from *Infidels*. The song itself is such a minor one that it was held over from the impoverished *Empire Burlesque* album and released on its near-catastrophic successor, *Knocked Out Loaded*. It shows. "Driftin' Too Far From Shore" also formed the B-side of Dylan's current single. The A-side, "Silvio", was soon to be unveiled in concert and would feature prominently for years to come.

Another surprise followed in an electric version of the usually acoustic "Gates Of Eden"; it was slow, but punchy and dramatic with a biting delivery. The guitar parts had obviously been worked on, and formed a compelling backdrop against which Dylan revealed his vision.

"Like A Rolling Stone" was the crowd-pleasing closer; Dylan was clearly enjoying himself too, giving an open throated laugh as he sang "secrets to conceal". The audience's rapture was further increased by a foot-stomping encore of "Maggie's Farm", preceded by Dylan thanking, with marvellous intonation, "You people for being so nice".

And that was that: 13 songs, approximately 70 minutes of prime Dylan, classic rock 'n' roll with an acoustic set from folk heaven, a hugely enthusiastic crowd and a patently in-high-spirits performer. What more could you want? Well, quite a lot more if you were writing for the San Francisco newspapers. With a history of antipathy towards Dylan, they launched yet another offensive.

The Examiner's Philip Elwood, in an article entitled "Dylan Show Sinks Like A Lolling Stone", gleefully crowed that the Concord Pavilion was "barely half full", that Dylan "mumbled" and that nearly all the songs were "both unrecognisable and unintelligibly sung", while "Dylan's vocals were so poorly defined and so lacking in melody that most were at a loss to catch any lyric thread or phrase."

Now this book is not going to claim that all of Dylan's thousands of shows have been magical and I freely, admit to having been to shows where Mr Elwood's comments would have been very hard to refute. However, even though my original tape was rather lo-fi, I could always tell that he was misreporting here. Most songs were played at a fast pace, but the vocals were clearly intelligible. In more recent years a soundboard[2] recording has emerged which further underlines the point that this review is a wilful misrepresentation of Dylan's singing that night. Mr Elwood may have been right that Neil Young's guitar was "kept

2 A soundboard recording comes directly from the mixing board at a concert. The sound quality is obviously much superior to that of a concert recording as the sound is captured close to the artist's mouth. In many cases these give a more faithful impression of the show than even officially released live albums which are often edited, spliced from various shows and 'enhanced' in the studio. The downside is that although the lack of audience noise is usually a boon, the lack of it also changes the atmosphere. Audiences are not necessarily totally unheard on soundboard tapes but they are so muted that you often can lose the feel of 'being at' a show. Another drawback is that the mixing board sound is not intended for audiences' ears and can be rather flat sounding. Overall, however, their near studio quality makes them highly prized and they give the best chance to relive the event.

so low his playing was seldom clearly defined"; however, Neil was just a guest dropping in, his prominence or lack thereof was no great matter.

Joel Selvin of *The Chronicle* also accused Dylan of "mumbling" and even went to the unforgivable length of unfavourably comparing Dylan's rendition of "Like A Rolling Stone" to a live version by John Cougar Mellencamp. He also wrote, in comments that make one doubt he actually heard, say, "You're A Big Girl Now":

"(Dylan) failed utterly to appear as if he cared in the slightest about what he was doing.... Dylan managed to perform the set in relative darkness.... There were ragged endings, a sloppy mix and a tentative, uncertain ensemble sound.... There were no particular highlights or dramatic moments, just a flat, uninspired, almost rote recitation of inconsequential selections."

Selvin further complained that Dylan stuck to "an undistinguished lot of songs drawn from throughout his career". This is 'criticism' that should surely be praise; needless to say, Dylan often gets castigated for doing the opposite. For many years after this, Dylan's set-lists relied heavily on songs from a handful of famous albums. When asked in an interview why he played all the old 'hits', Dylan replied that when he tried to play new songs people didn't like it.

With comments such as "He boasts one of the deepest repertoires of great songs anybody could claim but roundly ignored the cornerstones, other than the obligatory 'Like A Rolling Stone'", this journalist might be one of those responsible for Dylan's frequent reliance on old material. It was such a ridiculous complaint and meant that the audiences, who wanted something new, were denied it due to Dylan's stated perception that when he tried to play new songs "people didn't like it". People did like it; the more influential San Francisco journalists, alas, did not.

Dylan was also criticised for the brevity of his Concord set, an extremely odd reaction when you consider the superlative quality of those 70 minutes. It makes one wonder if the reviewers would prefer two hours of someone in third gear followed by a high energy encore to over an hour of someone in top gear throughout.

Dylan's next stop was at Sacramento. After an opening show that was wonderful for the fans, but rocky in terms of attendance and press reaction, the tour was about to nearly run aground. If Concord was not a long set, the Sacramento show, twelve songs and no encore, clocking in at under one hour, was to be by far the shortest of the tour.

The story goes that Dylan was in a foul mood and stormed off without encores as he was disappointed by the size of the crowd, which was less than half the 12,000 capacity. It is also possible that he had seen the *SF Examiner* and *Chronicle* reviews. Dylan may say that he ignores reviews but there's been many a bitter retort from him to negative press comments over the years, and he was to answer one of the newspapers' jibes just a couple of shows later. Certainly the show was so much shorter than any other gig on the tour that you feel Dylan must have been disturbed by something, but writing the whole show off as a disaster simply cannot be supported by the recorded evidence. By the end of the set Dylan may well have been upset, but there seems no indication that he was at the beginning when one listens to the audio.

SECOND NET SHOW: June 9th 1988 Cal Expo Amphitheatre, Sacramento CA

1 Subterranean Homesick Blues
2 It's All Over Now, Baby Blue
3 The Man In Me
4 Stuck Inside Of Mobile With The Memphis Blues Again
5 I Shall Be Released
6 Ballad Of A Thin Man
7 Baby, Let Me Follow You Down (Eric Von Schmidt, Acoustic)
8 Two Soldiers (Traditional. Acoustic)
9 Girl From The North Country (Acoustic)
10 Had A Dream About You, Baby
11 Just Like A Woman
12 Maggie's Farm

The first thing to mention about the Sacramento show is that only two songs – the opener and closer – were repeated from the first night, repaying fans who went to consecutive shows as well as highlighting that the tour was in its formative days.

A typically rambunctious 1988 performance of "Subterranean Homesick Blues" was followed by an unexpected electric set slot for "It's All Over Now, Baby Blue". A brave choice this, especially before his voice had warmed up, but it was a fine performance, although there are elements of what Mick Ronson once termed Dylan's 'Yogi Bear' voice[3]. "The Man In Me" was another bolt from the blue and another excellent delivery. With the story surrounding this show, I was prepared for a Verona 1984-type shambles, where Dylan treated the opening gigs of the tour as rehearsals; however, this is not at all what you hear when listening to the opening of the show. A scorching "Stuck Inside of Mobile With The Memphis Blues Again" got the biggest cheer of the night so far, and was followed by "I Shall Be Released" and "Ballad Of A Thin Man" with both featuring strong vocals.

Even though the songs changed so much between the opening nights you can see that Dylan had a fixed set structure in his mind. As at Concord, the acoustic set opened with a song covered by Dylan at the beginning of his career, then there was a traditional folk song and finally an old favourite from the early days. Then, again as at Concord, Dylan opened the second electric set with a new song, or 'obscure song', as the press would call them. In another indication that he does indeed read the press coverage, this led to Dylan's remarking, after playing "I'll Remember You" at the fourth show of the tour, at Mountain View, California: "I don't think that's an obscure song. Do you think that's an obscure song? I don't think so!"

Concord	Sacramento
7. Man Of Constant Sorrow (Traditional)	7. Baby, Let Me Follow You Down (Eric Von Schmidt)
8. The Lakes Of Pontchartrain (Traditional)	8. Two Soldiers (Traditional)
9. Boots Of Spanish Leather	9. Girl From The North Country
10. Driftin' Too Far From Shore	10. Had A Dream About You, Baby

3 Considering Mr Ronson was referring to the Rolling Thunder Tour he could not have been more wrong at the time, though there have certainly been times in the NET when the remark has been ruefully recalled.

"Baby, Let Me Follow You Down", a song that saw sterling service in 1966 and at the Band's farewell concert, 'The Last Waltz', appeared in the same slot as "Man Of Constant Sorrow", another cover song that appeared on Dylan's first LP. It was great to hear it again and the audience responded enthusiastically. "The Lakes of Pontchartrain" was replaced by a cover of another traditional folk song, "Two Soldiers". Dylan was straining his voice, a little uneasy at having to hit some difficult notes, and yet this was far from a poor performance. On first receiving the tape I already knew of the furore surrounding the gig but re-listening to it later, searching, as I did back then, for things that sound wrong, I cannot hear them. If you start to look for something, you can wrongly convince yourself you have found it and I think that may have affected some commentators looking back at this controversial night. Unsurprisingly, given the quality of the performance, there was loud applause at the song's end. So, there has been no sign yet that Dylan was in the reported 'sulk', 'foul mood' or 'rage'.

Certainly, the noise the crowds made throughout Dylan's beautifully crafted and executed acoustic set would give him just cause for being angry. However, this happens every night and either he doesn't hear it or he rises above it. There is no reason to suppose Sacramento should be regarded differently to every other night in this regard. "Girl From The North Country" followed "Two Soldiers", it was not outstanding but it was more than passable. You can hear somebody shouting: "Everybody back! Everybody back!" followed by an excited melee and much cheering. Perhaps there was a stage rush, but this usually delights rather than irritates Dylan. Nonetheless, it was from this point onwards that the show began to deteriorate.

The electric set opened with yet another debut, and for a new Dylan song at that, from *Down In The Groove*. Unfortunately, it was the sub-standard "Had A Dream About You, Baby", but at least live Dylan and the audience could have some fun with it. Not surprisingly, given that the song dates from the ill-advised and ill-fated 1986 *Hearts Of Fire* movie, Dylan sounded more like he did in 1986 than 1988. It is not possible to tell if there is a real problem with Dylan singing this song or not as it is just a thrash. However it is undeniable that the feeling of the more 'distant' Dylan of 1986 rather than the, up to now, vibrant 1988 version persisted in the old favourite that followed, "Just Like A Woman".

Some of the early part of the show's freshness and vitality had been lost; nonetheless, Dylan does not sound like he was merely going through the motions and it is significant that the crowd certainly were loving it. When the predictable choice of "Maggie's Farm" closed the second electric set, there was still no sign that Dylan was annoyed. Granted, he was galloping through the set, but then he did so throughout the 1988 tour. Granted also, he sounded nowhere near as strong at the end of the show as he did at the beginning; but, again, this is hardly shocking. We were only on the second night of a new tour, and his voice and energy levels might just have been flagging before he got back into the touring routine.

Whatever the problem was, Dylan left after twelve songs and did not return. The set was only one song shorter than at Concord, but the unannounced, abrupt ending and the psychological effect of the show being under an hour made it seem far shorter. Encores were expected, at the very least. Some in the audience no doubt hoped that Dylan's departure signalled only a mid-show break, with the second half still to come. Their disappointment soon turned to anger and the night ended in acrimony that further inflamed the long-standing bad feeling toward Dylan in the local press. A vicious circle was in danger of dragging down the tour that had started so well at Concord.

After the dust had settled on Sacramento, renowned concert promoter Bill Graham is alleged to have informed Dylan that this would not do; that Bob would have to make a greater effort to please his audience or he would lose it altogether. The result? Dylan pulled up his socks and delivered a brilliant 17 song, 90-minute+ set at Berkeley and went on to complete a glorious tour. This is the received wisdom, yet it just does not sound at all like Dylan. It seems absurd, given his career, to view him as a naughty schoolboy, who, when rebuked, turns into a star pupil. In addition, Berkeley is often blessed with special shows, and opening concerts are often greatly at variance with what follows on Dylan tours. As a strong example of that, the first four shows in 1988 contained about half of the songs played in the whole year.

Whether the alleged warning from Bill Graham changed Bob Dylan's plans for the tour, or whether Dylan just had an 'off' ending to the night after the acoustic set at Sacramento for some reason or another, we will probably never know for sure.

Still, after Berkeley's 17-song feast (including many songs that were not played in the first two shows, "Rank Strangers To Me" among them), the set lists/structure settled down to a fairly consistent pattern of 15 or 16 songs per night (though there were a large number of 14s and 17s too), rising on special occasions and peaking with a 21-song set at Upper Darby, Pennsylvania on October 13th, as Dylan warmed up for the concluding dates that had been added at New York's Radio City Music Hall in response to the rave notices posted as the tour progressed.

Generally speaking there were six or seven electric songs, followed by three or four acoustic numbers (on which G.E. Smith accompanied Dylan). Dylan would then return for another three or four electric numbers and round it all off with a one- or two-song encore. Surprises continued throughout the 71-date tour, with some 87 different songs being played.

Contrary to the poor turnouts early in the tour, the Radio City residency was a complete sell-out; and, in the middle of those shows, The Travelling Wilburys (a 'supergroup' consisting of Bob Dylan Roy Orbison, George Harrison, Tom Petty and Jeff Lynne) released their first album, to huge acclaim and impressive sales.

Throughout 1988 I continued to receive tapes of the tour, and it soon became evident that a key facet of the shows was the way in which Dylan was, yet again, defying attempts to pigeon-hole him. Though set-lists were dominated by the greatest hits from his folk and rock phases from the 1960s, the mixture of songs played included country, rockabilly, gospel, Tin Pan Alley and traditional folk. I remember various shows that I carried around on my Walkman; the one from George WA on August 20th, for example, where there was the following comment from the audience after "Highway 61 Revisited": "It's much better than I thought it would be". This simple statement could stand as a verdict on the whole tour.

I remember from that show, too, the pile-driving rhythm and the glorious extended "eee" endings in "Absolutely Sweet Marie", and I recall listening intently to the way he enthusiastically pronounced the words to fit a new stop-start rhythm in "You're A Big Girl Now". There were so many other gems from other shows that people started making and trading compilation tapes. These tapes included celebrated performances such as that of the rarely played, exquisite "I Dreamed I Saw St. Augustine" from *John Wesley Harding*. It was almost as if Dylan had deliberately plucked out a song from his own back catalogue which, although seldom played live, would surely survive for as many hundreds of years as the treasures from the trove of traditional songs that he was performing nightly with such care and intensity.

There was even a splendid "Joey", a modern tale told as a fable with truth so far removed in its words that it seems at home amongst the myths from yesteryear. This song would often be attempted live in the years that followed (albeit seldom with its lyrics correctly remembered), but never more successfully than in 1988. Then there was "My Back Pages", which was totally recast with, aptly enough, Byrds-like celebratory guitars chiming while Dylan's voice veered from anxious to a laughing, dismissive tone on "rip down all hate". As the performance progressed, the song regained its original, confident declamation due to the driving beat of the tight band.

There were tremendous single outings, too, for "License To Kill", "One More Cup Of Coffee", and "Tomorrow Is A Long Time". Dylan also gave us, though you'd be forgiven for thinking this was not the musical setting for it, a one-off performance of "Visions Of Johanna". When he played "Ballad Of Hollis Brown" at Alpine Valley WI on June 18th (another "Walkman" favourite show, incidentally) it was interpreted as an oblique sign of support for local farmers then enduring a drought. Since it was the sole performance in the year, this seemed a reasonable assumption; and even though its next appearances would be at Helsinki, Dublin and London (in 1989) and would be harder to fit into this theory, the 1989 performances were electric, while the 1988 one was both unique to that year and acoustic. "Song To Woody" made it four songs from Dylan's debut album, and there were a few outings for "The Ballad Of Frankie Lee And Judas Priest", for which, presumably, we have to credit the Grateful Dead. Even "Bob Dylan's 115th Dream" was unexpectedly debuted in one of the Upper Darby 'warm-up' gigs for the Radio City Music Hall residency. It was a year of surprises and of magnificent shows.

Most of all, though, I remember marvelling at the wonderful cover versions. They sprang up all over the place, in show after show, compilation tape after compilation tape. Some were played but once, some a few times and others became commonplace. But it was the breadth of sources that was most impressive: from "Across The Borderline" to "Give My Love To Rose"; "Eileen Aroon" to "Pretty Peggy-O"; "Wagoner's Lad" to "Wild Mountain Thyme" and "I'm In The Mood For Love" to "Trail Of The Buffalo".

Of these, the first to strike home were the traditional songs. As far back as 1966, in the *Playboy* interview with Nat Hentoff, Dylan had hinted at how important these songs were to him:

"Traditional music is based on hexagrams. It comes about from legends, bibles, plagues, and it revolves around vegetables and death... All these songs about roses growing out of people's brains and lovers who are really geese and swans that turn into angels...I mean you'd think that the traditional-music people could gather from their songs that mystery is a fact, a traditional fact. I could give you a descriptive detail of what they do to me, but some people would probably think my imagination had gone mad."

The NET has been honoured, year after year, by Dylan singing traditional songs and giving us every 'descriptive detail' his immense interpretative powers can imbue them with.

"Barbara Allen", played in a variety of ways, was a regular standout. I swear that on some nights the way he sang the words: "Oh yes oh yes, I'm very sick, and I will not be better" was worth the admission price alone. The same could be said for any version of "Lakes Of Pontchartrain" or "Eileen Aroon" both of which consistently provided yet further evidence of how incomparable a communicator Dylan is. Here, in later life, if he could not manage the vocal brilliance of his staggering early '60s rendition of the traditional "Moonshiner Blues", as his vocal range was already diminished (relative to those heady days), he could still manage a breathtaking delivery.

The brilliance of the song, with a melody, lyric and conceit that seem as old as expression itself, was given full and deserved embodiment in Dylan's delivery. The following lines, when sung by Dylan in 1988, surpassed even Robert Browning's masterly poetic encapsulation of the identical sentiment in "Love Among The Ruins".

Youth will in time decay,
Eileen Aroon
Beauty must fade away
Eileen Aroon
Castles are sacked in war
Chieftains are scattered far
Truth is a fixéd star
Eileen Aroon

The deliberate emphasis on the ending of fixéd was only one of many 'goose-bump' moments.

And all this from a man they say can't sing. You want to ask such detractors to define 'singing', for whatever they mean by the word can only be a limited sub-branch of what we hear when Dylan performs like this. We are not just listening to a singer, accomplished or otherwise, retelling a tale and pushing the buttons of our emotional responses. Instead we are involved in the story, in myth. We are dragged, perhaps even reluctantly, towards what Dylan described in that famous 1966 *Playboy* interview as "the one true, valid death you can feel today off a record player".

Dylan could also cover modern songs to similar dramatic effect. The pick of these was Leonard Cohen's "Hallelujah", unveiled in Montreal on July 8th, presumably as a tribute to the Canadian poet and songwriter. The way Dylan performed it made it sound like a brand new masterpiece of his own. I first heard the song when Cohen closed a fine show in Helsinki with it three years earlier; but listening to Dylan perform this notable song, which was later to become a hit in more than one cover version, was like hearing it for the first time. Cohen was reportedly delighted when hearing the news of the tribute, but he would have been ecstatic if he had heard what a majestic version it was. (Dylan played it one more time, and in a very different but equally effective style, on August 4th, the last of three splendid nights at the Greek Theatre, Hollywood.)

The tour 'ended' on September 24th in New Orleans, but this was not quite the finish. As previously mentioned, popular demand had led to four further nights being added at Radio City Music Hall in New York. These shows quickly became a focus for the press and fans alike. The former, previously misguided critics of the tour, now praised Dylan to the skies; the latter, trying to read the runes of relatively unchanging set-lists, talked of a live album being released from the shows. All this is rather ironic as the shows themselves, although fine, were far from being the best, or even up to the average standard, of the year.

Certainly, press coverage of Dylan has always been extremely erratic, but to be fair to the journalists Dylan's NET shows are bound to be challenging for music critics uninitiated in his current art of performing. If a writer prepared for a Dylan show by playing Bob's "Greatest Hits" or his latest album, the scribe would be lucky to recognise any of the former until the song was well underway, and in the case of the latter he might be lucky to hear any tracks from it at all at this point in Dylan's touring. At times on the NET, inspired reinvention can seem much the same to the layman as massacring a classic song. In later decades it was to become a matter of confusion amongst fans too, come to that.

Dylan's performing art during the NET is not beyond reproach, but much of the ill-founded criticism he has garnered can get wearing[4], and it is clear that under pressure to produce copy some journalists will simply echo the bad reviews of the shows preceding the one in their town. Still, it works the other way too: when somebody is 'hot', good reviews beget more good reviews – merited or otherwise. As the Radio City Music Hall shows became hot news, so the good reviews multiplied.

As for the fans, they were pleased with the attention and praise Dylan was receiving, but also rather miffed that the shows which attracted all this press euphoria were attended by those drawn solely to this month's 'hot ticket'. This was in stark contrast to the previous months' shows, when diehard fans had witnessed Dylan in top vocal form with a rapidly changing set-list. Also, by the time he got to Radio City Music Hall, Dylan's voice was under pressure both from the year's touring and a cold which coincided with the residency. This is not to say that the Radio City shows were poor, but they became, due to the wide circulation of soundboard tapes of the closing show allied to the media buzz, falsely representative of the whole year.[5]

LAST NET SHOW of 1988: 19th October 1988 Radio City Music Hall, New York NY

1 Subterranean Homesick Blues

2 I'll Remember You

---

4 *The Guardian* newspaper fulminated against Dylan's delivery of "Blowin' In The Wind" at a festival one year. It was not played at all. This has happened in other reviews too and it makes you wonder when some reviewers actually write their reviews in advance at times, or if they actually attend the shows.

5 Still, at least they were more typical than the February 1989 release of the shambolic Dylan and the Dead live album (from the 1987 shows), which might as well have been subtitled "the very worst songs from a very poor tour".

3 John Brown

4 Stuck Inside Of Mobile With The Memphis Blues Again

5 Simple Twist Of Fate

6 Bob Dylan's 115th Dream

7 Highway 61 Revisited

8 Gates Of Eden (Acoustic)

9 With God On Our Side (Acoustic)

10 One Too Many Mornings (Acoustic)

11 Barbara Allen (Traditional, Acoustic)

12 Silvio

13 In The Garden

14 Like A Rolling Stone

*

15 Wagoner's Lad (Traditional, Acoustic)

16 The Lonesome Death Of Hattie Carroll (Acoustic)

17 Knockin' On Heaven's Door (Acoustic/Electric)

18 All Along The Watchtower

19 Maggie's Farm

As mentioned above, by now Dylan's voice was showing some wear and tear, but he started this last show in strong form by ripping through "Subterranean Homesick Blues", before calming things down with "I'll Remember You", a slight song redeemed by a few well-chosen couplets and Dylan's powers of delivery. The subsequent "John Brown", while laudable for its sentiments, remains one of my least favourite songs in Dylan's entire catalogue; but he performed it splendidly. In fact, this was about as good as you could ever expect to hear it.

A splendid "Simple Twist of Fate" was the next treat, but Dylan's voice was starting to go in places and the song came to a hesitant, oddly stumbling end. One of the revelations of the tour had been saved for the October shows, with the first ever live version of "Bob Dylan's 115th Dream" at Upper Darby on 13th October. I don't think there was any fan who could have envisaged this long, comic monologue being pulled from his back pages; but Dylan clearly enjoyed tackling it. You could hear the relish in his voice, particularly when he sang the words "my way" near the song's conclusion.

"Gates of Eden" was back in the acoustic set, while Dylan's old protest classic "With God On Our Side" now included a verse on Vietnam, which had been added by the Neville Brothers in their version. It was strange in 1988 to hear Dylan, the definitive '60s protest-singer, for the first time ever sing lyrics explicitly about the Vietnam war. Stranger still that he was singing someone else's words in one of his own songs; the new verse brought a huge cheer from the audience.

If you wanted two songs to round off an acoustic set and were allowed to pick one Dylan original and one traditional, you would be hard pressed to beat the 19th October pairing of "One Too Many Mornings" and "Barbara Allen".

"Silvio" opened the second electric set, Dylan having decided to 'promote' his current single and album by playing this regularly from 21st June onwards. The 1988 version was certainly better than the bloated, falsely theatrical renditions he was to inflict on us in future years, though even here it still sounded somewhat like a Dylan parody.

"In the Garden" was preceded by a little speech, the impish Dylan of yore well evident as he managed to be charming while giving a pointed barb to those who are not as keen on this song as its author is.

> *"Thank you, I was really honoured last year when the Amnesty tour chose a Bob Dylan song as a theme song. A song called 'Chimes Of Freedom'. This year, to my great surprise, they chose another Bob Dylan song. Actually that one was this year. 'I Shall Be Released' was the song they chose last year. Anyway I guess they're gonna have another Amnesty tour next year. I think the theme song they're gonna use is another Bob Dylan song called 'Jokerman'. But I'm trying to get them to change their minds. Trying to get 'em to use this one."*

With that he swung into a strong, clear rendition; a bit less actively aggressive than the one at Sacramento, but in the same basic style.

Having made his point Dylan gave the crowd the rousing "Like A Rolling Stone". However, by the time he got to "secrets to conceal" his voice had been reduced to a growl, and sounded shot. He left the stage when the song finished.

Somehow Dylan's vocal powers recovered sufficiently for him to pull out a half-acoustic/half-electric five-song encore. He accomplished this feat by making the third song of the five, "Knocking on Heaven's Door", start acoustic but switch to electric midway through.

The encores opened with that wondrous traditional lament to woman's lot, "The Waggoner's Lad", sung with such empathy it is hard to believe he is the same man who in life, interview and song has often seemed far from understanding the female perspective. All that is forgotten whenever you play a recording and hear Dylan sing the opening lines:

"Hard is the fortune of all womankind
It's always controlled, it's always confined
Controlled by her parents until she's a wife
Then a slave to her husband for the rest of her life."

Following the yearning pleas of this heartbreaking traditional song, Dylan's voice becomes stronger and deeper for one of his own masterly songs about injustice and the hard lot of womankind, the remarkable and humbling "The Lonesome Death of Hattie Carroll".

That remarkable pairing was succeeded, without pause, by the half acoustic/half electric "Knockin' On Heaven's Door". The evening, the residency and the 1988 tour then closed with the double-barrelled electric blast of "All Along The Watchtower" and "Maggie's Farm".[6]

After the disappointment of the *Down In The Groove* album, Dylan fans had been boosted by Bob's blistering June-onwards live performances. What would make 1989 perfect would be for the tour to continue and Dylan to release an album of impressive original songs.

---

6 A footnote to the year's touring was Dylan and GE Smith performing an acoustic set at Neil Young's annual Bridge School Benefit; where along with four of his own songs Dylan sang "San Francisco Bay Blues" and "Pretty Boy Floyd".

CHAPTER THREE

1989:
"The songs themselves do the talking"

"It's not stand-up comedy or a stage play – it breaks up my concentration to have to think of things to say or to respond to the crowd. The songs themselves do the talking."

BOB DYLAN, 1989[1]

The 1989 tour, just like the 1988 one, started amidst controversy and recriminations, but I was still not part of the Dylan fan world and did not know much about that until later in the year. My Dylan year really began with my first NET show, at Glasgow on the 6th of June, Dylan's sixth show of a year that was to encompass 93 more.

In 1989 I had very little cash available for Bob-trekking. I certainly couldn't afford to take leave to see Bob, particularly as at the very time he was touring the UK I was working in Eastbourne on the southern coast of England, just about as far from Glasgow as one could get without leaving the UK.

1 Talking to Edna Gundersen, *USA Today*

My boss kindly covered my evening duties, so I did a morning shift and then headed for the train to Gatwick Airport to catch a flight to Glasgow and meet my parents, who were going to the show with me.

My parents, like most parents of obsessive Dylan fans, I guess, were long-suffering; though I am certain they were more open to Mr. Dylan's charms than most who had endured his voice permeating every corner of their homes for years on end. Their healthy approach to parenting, which seemed almost revolutionary at the time, was to take an interest in what their teenage offspring were 'into'. And, as we all know, if Dylan is approached with an open mind he will captivate it, if it is at all worth captivating. So, long before this concert, both my parents had become 'fans' to an extent themselves; what with my father using "John Wesley Harding" in a lecture he was giving on poetry and both having a number of songs that they particularly related to.

Still, it had never occurred to my parents to go and see Dylan themselves, although this may have been partly because he had not played in Scotland since 1966. Anyway, they expressed a convincing display of delight when I suggested they go. Also going with us would be my aforementioned cousin, Andy, who was once described as my 'Frankenstein creation' because of the convenient way he got into Dylan and started collecting tapes with fanatical completism just as I left the UK for mainland Europe and, perforce, stopped collecting them myself.

So you can see why this concert, Dylan's first in my homeland for 23 years, was so very special despite there being more UK dates to follow for me. Besides, I had not seen a Dylan show since October '87.

So, June 6th 1989 found me in Eastbourne in a state of some excitement. I was on my way to see Bob....

... Or was I? Because the kind of panic-inducing crisis that seems to occur so often to fans on their way to see Dylan was waiting for me at Eastbourne station. Oblivious to the fact that the station was almost deserted, already in the holiday spirit, I happily strode straight up to the designated platform only to be confronted by a big metal barrier with a sign that said "Train to London cancelled".

While I was on a comfortable enough schedule given the proviso that I had made this (now cancelled) train, the next one would not guarantee that I caught the plane. This was presuming the next one would run. I had already decided, with the inherent fatalism of a panicking fan, that it would probably be cancelled too. In fact, I was in the icy cold grip of a creeping realisation that I might not make it at all.

I was quickly reduced to a gibbering wreck and reeled about the station moaning, unable to deal with the reality of my situation. And then I spotted a woman reacting to the sign on the platform with horror. Given that there was no mirror for me to see myself in, I could declare that I had never seen anyone so distressed at missing a train. "Taxi", we both intoned simultaneously, "we could share a taxi." And so we did. The cost nullified the whole point of me working in Eastbourne but this seemed totally irrelevant as long as we still had a chance of making our plane(s). I did make mine and got to Glasgow in time to meet my family before the concert, seeing old friends from years before as we went in. I have every reason to believe that my fellow taxi traveller caught her flight too. I hope so.

The Glasgow show took place in the Scottish Exhibition Centre, a hangar-like place built for exhibitions of ideal homes and yachts, copper kettles for fake mahogany kitchen ranges or whatever – the kind of absurd events thronged by people who think that following Dylan around is a sign that one 'needs to get a life'. It is a cavernous venue with appalling acoustics; I would only ever consider visiting it in order to see Bob. Nineteen eighty-nine would be the first but far from the last time I would do so.

There is only a small area in the hall where the acoustics are not completely ruined and none of the experienced tapers with expensive equipment happened to be seated there, so the best tapes of this event actually came from less costly recorders that just happened to be in the right place. As, by pure luck, were we, although I only realised this later when talking to others who had not been so fortunate.

"Subterranean Homesick Blues" was the first song. Though predictable, it was a great opener for this band and, as has become increasingly important as the years have passed, allowed Dylan's vocals to warm up. Not having to listen too carefully to a surprise song choice also permitted me to soak in every image of Bob that my Dylan-starved-for-nearly-two-years retinas could absorb. Unlike many, we could hear every word as Dylan attacked the song with gusto, throwing in the odd bit of inspired intonation.

The second song, "Congratulations", was as unexpected as the opener was predictable, but it was equally enthusiastically received. Well, this was Glasgow, after all: if the audience there love you, they really love you; if they don't, well, it's safest to go to Edinburgh. Dylan sang in a deep growl of disenchantment, and played some neat harp, too.

A magnificent rendition of "Stuck Inside Of Mobile With The Memphis Blues Again" followed and then came a driving "Ballad Of A Thin Man" which emphasised how much stronger Dylan's voice was compared to 1987's frequent bouts of frailty. Most live versions of this song are much more declamatory than the original, sometimes even just shouted. However, there was still a clarity and force in this take. His vocals had fully warmed up and this was well sung, with the spirit of the original still intact. I loved the way his voice descended into the "You've been with the professors" line.

Yet another of Bob's mid-sixties classics, "Just Like A Woman", followed. There was no way the 1989 Glasgow performance of it could have the warmth, depth, control and wit of the 1966 incarnations (or, for that matter, the beautiful 1981 versions) but nonetheless it was utterly splendid. Dylan was clearly alive to the song, still exploring its (endless?) possibilities, and producing all kinds of interesting stresses.

The first electric set closed with a hard-rocking, guitar-driven "All Along The Watchtower" pushing the crowd to further heights of passion.

The acoustic set opened with the traditional Scottish ballad, "Barbara Allen". It had featured in nearly half the 1988 shows, so there was good reason to hope for it; yet, with a paranoid fan's dread, I had feared it would be dropped. Now it was magical to be back home with my family, who were hearing Dylan sing a ballad they had known long before they had heard of the Minnesota Minstrel who brought us together that night.

The Glasgow Herald not only reviewed the show, but even included a wonderful editorial extolling Dylan's unique ability to "transcend the transitory". At the same time they claimed that despite Dylan not saying a word to the audience he acknowledged them by playing this song. Given the song's presence in almost half of the 1988 shows and its occurrence in Dublin two nights earlier, *The Herald*'s comment is factually inaccurate; nonetheless it conveyed the feeling within the hall that Dylan was singing this song specifically for us, a Scottish ballad for a Scottish audience.

The opening chords of "Mr. Tambourine Man" brought huge applause, practically drowning out the first words until Dylan's strong, confident vocals came sailing through the quickly quietening hubbub. Dylan was now in complete control of everything: the crowd, the night, his vocals, the band and the entire venue. We were indeed "ready to go anywhere", following this musician as he followed that famous Tambourine Man.

The audience tried to show its appreciation with a determined effort to sing along on "It Ain't Me, Babe", though this was easier said than done. There was a huge guitar build-up as the groundswell of crowd approval rose; then Dylan pulled back and 'tricked' the crowd before singing "melt back into the night".

One of the inevitable effects of Dylan's relentless touring over the last quarter of a century, for those that follow his every step,. is that over-exposure to certain songs affects one's judgement and memory. When I first wrote of this show, in *Razor's Edge*, my feelings about the third song were totally dominated by an overwhelming sense of joy that it was not "All Along the Watchtower". This was because, at the time of my writing it, show after show had featured "All Along The Watchtower" as the set's third song for year after year after year. This had driven myself and many other Dylan followers into a peculiarly intense state regarding the possibility of the third song being something else every time we went to a show, and had become so pervasive I even felt it when listening to recordings of shows.

Similarly, my memories of "It Ain't Me, Babe", like all Dylan's classics that I have by now heard live so very often, suffer from this over-exposure. Notwithstanding this, it was just so well performed in Glasgow that it still sounds irresistible; take the "die for you and more" line, for example; I cannot remember when I last heard it sung like this. "Silvio" kicked off the second electric set, a song that, following the pattern above, Dylan touring fans lost all patience with after a decade's worth of repeated, near ever-present outings. In addition it was very far from being a Dylan classic and so tolerance was much more quickly eviscerated amongst the demanding diehards. Back in 1989 however that was all ahead of us, and it provided a release of rock energy after the acoustic set.

"I Shall Be Released" was next, another 'greatest hit'; though 'hit' is meant in a very Dylanesque way. It was famous, yet had never been a hit single nor even properly released. To my mind there are only two versions which really get to the heart of this song: the original Big Pink sessions take, criminally omitted from *The Basement Tapes*, and the extraordinary, one-off adaptation Bob unveiled for the Martin Luther King Birthday celebration show in 1986. This version in Glasgow 1989 was passable, though the lovely finale surpassed that description.

Then, in time-honoured fashion, the opening chords of "Like A Rolling Stone" were the crowd's cue to 'go nuts'. I still had the 'this is the special song that going to Dylan's shows is all about' attitude back then. The whole 'Royal Albert Hall' legend, the intrinsic value of the song itself and its pivotal role in Dylan's career make it so very special. So even Bob Dylan was not going to be able to stop the Glasgow crowd singing along to this one, especially as by now a large portion of the crowd had surged to the front of the stage to party in front of him.

Suddenly we were into the encores; the night had simply flown by. "The Times They Are A-Changin'" quietened things down to an extent, with Dylan somehow playing it simultaneously as a crowd-rousing anthem and an attempt to discourage a sing-along. Eventually, he managed to wrestle it back from the audience, rediscovering the song beneath the anthem. From there he launched into "Knocking On Heaven's Door", a superb choice of song at this stage; elastic enough to encompass everything from meaningful communication to catchy pop, and, in this arrangement, to serve as both an acoustic and electric rock treat. Dylan sounded, unsurprisingly, a bit strained in the opening verses. However, just when I thought he'd given us all he could, he got a second (third? fourth?) wind and pulled off a strong verse and a fine second harmonica solo before launching into a blistering rendition of the show's closer, "Maggie's Farm", of which a long term Dylan disdainer wrote, in a grudgingly enthusiastic review in *The Glasgow Herald*: "During Maggie's Farm I swear I heard a government topple."

The reporter's name was David Belcher, a fine man really though he does enjoy winding up Dylan fans, and he was taken aback by the sheer power of the show and the experience, summing up the whole evening as: "an experience much more intense than I had bargained for and one I'll always be glad I felt". Ian Woodward, in his splendid diary of all things Dylan, *The Wicked Messenger*, was equally enthusiastic: "There was an energy and urgency in these shows we haven't seen for a long time."

"Energy and urgency" were indeed much in evidence and I don't know if it the whole experience had been draining for Dylan, but I was exhausted. Thankfully the adrenaline boost of seeing Dylan kept me going. I had little time for sleep as I had to reach Eastbourne and start work by 9 a.m. I made it with a comfortable two minutes to spare.

By all accounts that evening's Birmingham show was one that I should not have missed. *The Guardian*'s Bob Flynn was gushingly enthusiastic: "What we got was the happy shock of Dylan not only playing the best of his extraordinary song book but playing it with the glorious intensity of that star-burning ruthless youth ... We were expecting an old man to be wheeled into the arc lights, we were faced with this extraordinary vision of a withered priest somehow plugging himself back into his unique, mystic jukebox of hits." I couldn't really enjoy reading Mr Flynn's fine writing as I really should have been in Birmingham that night when "Congratulations" was played again, this time in the encores.

Never mind, two nights after Glasgow I was as bowled over by Wembley as Mr Flynn had been by Birmingham. With the first rush of seeing Dylan over, I was able to concentrate harder on the actual performances. Remembering back now, the clearest song in my mind was a spectacular, edge-of-despair rendition of "Ballad of Hollis Brown". Then, fittingly enough, another from the same album, "The Lonesome Death of Hattie Carroll". There was no "Congratulations" here, in the encores or anywhere else; the 'surprise' number two slot was taken by "When Did You Leave Heaven?" (in Birmingham it had been the gorgeous "Lonesome Town").

The heavyweight music press was full of praise for the Wembley show. "Oh yes: this was a rejuvenated Dylan," *Melody Maker*'s Allan Jones concluded, "the master in all his raging glory. Unforgettable, unsurpassable." *NME*'s Gavin Martin enthused: "Tonight all the images of Dylan fused into the crucible of his raw genius.... Poet, seer, mystic, iconic rocker, ravaged salvationist, virulent misanthrope – such descriptions are paltry. The meaning of the songs weren't simply buried in nostalgia or in the lyrics, it was in the way he played with inflections and the sounds of the words, the way he changes the timbre of his voice to exact the most from the frazzling guitar cauldron or the weird, disfigured acoustic interludes ... tonight he proved that on form he was still unimpeachable, miles ahead of pretenders both young and old."

There was a coda to the Wembley show, something that became of relevance to my NET over the next few years.

The Monday morning after the Wembley show finds me back on my way to Eastbourne, tired and laden down with luggage. I collapse on to the London tube, put down my bags and cases, and switch on my Walkman to listen to the Glasgow show. Out of the corner of my eye, I spot someone in the next carriage, also wearing a Walkman. This guy has long hair, an eccentric hat, a wolf-like grin and an alarmingly intense stare. He looks like a 'nutter' and the music in his Walkman appears to be driving him mad. Impossible as this sounds, his arm seems to be beating the empty air and to be angry with the air for being empty, while his right leg simultaneously pounds the floor. I assume he is listening to heavy metal.

In these situations, you simultaneously wish to distance yourself from attracting the nutter's attention and are so drawn by their eccentric behaviour and appearance that you cannot look away. My 'excuse' for staring was that I needed to confirm my earlier thoughts regarding his choice of listening. I glanced across to sneak a look at his T-shirt... and, yes, you've guessed it, it was a Dylan T-shirt ('Temples In Flames', if I recall correctly).

The inevitable result of not resisting the temptation to look at a nutter is that said nutter immediately homes in on you. He caught my eye as it left his T-shirt and he appeared to notice that the Walkman-listening eccentric in the next carriage to him, i.e. me, was wearing a Dylan T-shirt too. He immediately came over to talk. Within about 33 seconds he had announced that the tape in his Walkman was not only more recent than mine from Glasgow (true – by all of a day!) but also, without hearing mine, he absolutely guaranteed that his was better quality. We swapped tapes for a moment to test his theory, which was quickly proved.

We gibbered Bob at high speed for the next couple of stops; he informed me that he had been on his way to give this Birmingham tape to *Melody Maker*'s Allan Jones, but would now leave it with me, as he clearly thought someone with such a dated tape in his Walkman was in need of charity. With a scribble of his phone number he was off, taking the tube in the opposite direction to return home and dub another copy for Mr. Jones.

This was my first encounter with the man they called Lambchop.[2]

And that was my NET year as far as attending live shows went; for Dylan these concerts came after the European tour had got off to a shaky start, and there were months of touring to follow afterwards.

At Glasgow and Wembley I had heard plenty of stories about the start of the 1989 leg of the tour: like the previous year, controversy had dogged the opening concerts. The tour kicked off on the 27th May with a ragged show at Christinehof Slott, Andrarum, in Sweden, that nonetheless had its moments, like a splendid "Gates of Eden". Dylan seemed very unhappy and his peculiar get-up of windcheater, cap, and hood pulled up over the cap meant that not only did the Swedes get a surly, non-communicative Dylan but a mostly hidden one to boot. Covered up though Dylan was, he still clove to the darkness on stage, revealing as little of himself as possible. A similarly bizarre appearance and erratic performance the next night at Stockholm was at least partly redeemed by an adventurous set list that included "My True La-La", "Eileen Aroon" and "When Did You Leave Heaven?".

The Swedish press were taken aback. "Bob Dylan doesn't smile...the mouth grimaces in a grotesque manner at times but his eyes never smile. Somehow, he might as well be in pain," said one. The tabloid *Kvällsposten* had a photo of the strangely garbed Dylan on its front page under the banner headline: "SKANDAL" (no translation necessary!) and deemed the show "pure catastrophe"! "Dylan appeared stand-offish both on and off the stage," the article continued. "He ignored the audience as well as the many journalists who attended. *Kvällsposten* can reveal that Dylan earned nearly 1.5 million Swedish kronor for the scandalous performance."

2 As you can guess from my comments here, there is more to come about Lambchop later in this book. Sadly, I have to report, as is perhaps inevitable given the timescales involved, that some fans who feature in these pages are no longer with us. Lambchop is amongst those whom death has claimed.

Other reports were fairer; one even stressed that "Differently from so many other performers Bob Dylan doesn't go on auto-pilot when he performs. His mood, how he feels, always becomes apparent – whether good or bad." Nonetheless, all the Swedish journalists were baffled or outraged, or both, by the short sets and by Dylan's appearance – hidden in hood, cap and darkness.

This did not sound like the man I had seen at Glasgow, and it was the next show in Helsinki, Finland, that proved the turning point on his road to the stunning performances later in the year. That night was also when a contrast between the European tours of 1989 and 1987 began to emerge – a theme that would run throughout that summer so it is worth exploring briefly here.

My own feelings on 1987 are very mixed: there were plenty of high points, but I find it an incredibly erratic tour. While the peaks are mountainously high, so the low points are buried way below what you expect from someone of Dylan's stature.

I had lived in Helsinki in 1985-1986 so, typically, Dylan popped up there for his first ever visit the very next year, on 23rd September 1987! The anticipation amongst my Finnish friends for Dylan's first show in their country was acute. Their expectations were dashed, and they came out bitterly complaining that Dylan looked and sounded appalling, and didn't seem to care. Dylan had played for approximately one hour and appeared and acted as though he had the worst hangover of his life. Looking 25 years older than he had in 1986, he contemptuously mangled the melodies and spat out the lyrics to his audience's favourite songs.

And yet, and yet ... one man's 'mangled melody' is another man 's 'artistic bravery'. 'Spat out lyrics', for some, mark a "stunning re-creation, evoking new emotions from tired old words". I defy anyone to say that Helsinki will ever again hear anything of the quality of 1987's sublime "Simple Twist Of Fate", the brooding yet hopeful "Señor", and the moving "It's All Over Now, Baby Blue" – to say nothing of a magnificent, first encore, "Desolation Row", and a set-list that mixed the familiar 60s songs with less well-known material like "Dead Man, Dead Man" and "Gotta Serve Somebody".

At that first Helsinki show in 1987, as with most performances from that year's inconsistent but often mesmeric European tour, there was golden wheat to be found among the chaff. However, the 'presentation' of the show, not least

Dylan's overall demeanour and startling appearance, made this hard to appreciate at the time. Not just for live Dylan 'newbies' like my Finnish friends, but also for even the most experienced Bob-cats such as *The Wicked Messenger*'s Ian Woodward, who was particularly disappointed by Dylan's own indifference to his performance during "the glum 1987 shows".

Initially, to be frank, I also preferred 1989. However, having listened to numerous shows many times since then, 1987 seems to grow better and better in retrospect. Which is not to say that the 1989 Helsinki gig I am about to focus on was a poor show, very far from it; it is just that to praise it to the rafters while pouring scorn on the 1987 show seems unjustified, and I want to make it clear that I am not following that oft-quoted but to these ears patently inaccurate, comparison

Putting all that to one side, as far as 1989 is concerned, it is fair to say that Helsinki saw the first satisfactory show of what was to be a very gratifying year.

May 30th 1989 Jäähalli Ishallen, Helsinki, Finland

1 Subterranean Homesick Blues
2 Confidential (Dolinda Morgan)
3 Ballad Of Hollis Brown
4 Just Like A Woman
5 Stuck Inside Of Mobile With The Memphis Blues Again
6 All Along The Watchtower
7 To Ramona (Acoustic)
8 Mr. Tambourine Man (Acoustic)
9 Eileen Aroon (Traditional, Acoustic)
10 Knockin' On Heaven's Door(Acoustic/Electric)
11 Silvio
12 In The Garden
13 Like A Rolling Stone
*

14 The Times They Are A-Changin' (Acoustic)

15 Maggie's Farm

After the standard opener, "Confidential" was a real treat. Dylan's vocals, awakened by the blistering opening song, caressed the words, extracting the most out of line endings like "To my hee-e-e-aa-art". He also embellished the song with a sympathetic little harp flourish.

His early 'protest' classic "Ballad Of Hollis Brown" was moody and magnificent; after the words "ocean's pounding roar", there was the added effect of a thrashy electric guitar approximation of that sound. Then it was straight into a marvellous, inventive rendition of perennial classic "Just Like A Woman". And so it went on: an enthusiastic crowd served with "Stuck Inside Of Mobile With The Memphis Blues Again" and "All Along The Watchtower", the latter having a striking guitar opening, piercing the night air even more sharply than the harmonica that punctuated the song.

Although "To Ramona" was far from convincing, it was well received and formed part of an acoustic set that included a powerful "Mr Tambourine Man" and "Eileen Aroon", which was received in the silence it deserved, in contrast to the cacophony of audience chatter that had spoiled it a year before in the States. The audience's fervent applause for this classic old folk song had not subsided when Dylan and the band ripped straight into "Knockin' On Heaven's Door". This was introduced with a strange and effective start-stop-(mournful harp)-start tempo that brought the crowd's euphoria back up to the 'greatest electric hits level' of the pre-acoustic slot. Dylan was experimenting with the lyrics and tempo on stage, though not for a moment leaving the audience behind.

It was a pretty impressive show thus far and while "Silvio" and "In The Garden" simply did not belong in this company, you could not have faulted Dylan's commitment to performing them. "In The Garden" segued into a barnstorming "Like A Rolling Stone" and when Dylan sang "kicks for you" it sounded as if he really remembered what it meant.

After Helsinki and just before the Glasgow show described above, Dylan played two nights in Dublin, still swathed in darkness and sporting the same ridiculous outfit as in Sweden. The shows were improving, though. The first Dublin concert's splendid set-list boasted "You're A Big Girl Now", "Every Grain Of Sand",

"Gates Of Eden", "The Lonesome Death Of Hattie Carroll", "The Water Is Wide" and "Eileen Aroon", the last two traditional songs being particularly outstanding. The electric take on "The Water Is Wide" was, in fact, one of the highlights of the year and would be a contender in a list of 'best ever NET performances'. As Dylan's vocals took off, the band cut loose and proved their worth in a classic performance. The next day was also a good show, although it had two fewer songs, a less adventurous set-list and the horror of that walking ego, U2's Bono, joining Bob on stage.

After the three already-discussed UK shows which followed Dublin, bass player Kenny Aaronson left the band to return to the States for an operation. His place was taken by Tony Garnier, who has remained in every NET line-up since. The band now consisted of G.E. Smith on lead guitar and occasional backing vocals, Christopher Parker on drums and Tony Garnier on bass.

After London, Dylan went a-rocking other parts of Europe, in outfits that varied from leather waistcoat to the kind of horrible jackets that he seems to specialise in. The concerts were looser than his '88 US shows, though they followed the same basic structure: a mixture of the ragged and the swagger. These were enjoyable shows, with sterling rock 'n' roll performances punctuated with some more sensitive readings. The crowds were enthusiastic and the reviews generally good. One big difference to the US shows was Dylan's use of harmonica, though this was not always successful.

By now we were used to 'odd songs' popping up in Dylan's live shows, and this leg of the tour did not disappoint in this respect. Immediately after London, the Hague got that fine traditional song "Trail Of The Buffalo". There were two outings for the rarely played "Song To Woody" in July, "Tangled Up in Blue" appeared in the opening slot one night in Spain, and one of my all time favourite non-Dylan songs, Townes Van Zandt's remarkable "Pancho And Lefty", appeared on 21st June. The 13th of June concert at Frejus in France included outings for "Hey La La (My True La La)", "The Lakes Of Pontchartrain" and, most startling of all, a spellbinding rendition of Thomas Dorsey's "Peace In The Valley".[3]

Italy saw some hard-rocking shows, with enthusiastic crowds feeding back the energy. A compilation double bootleg CD, *All The Way Down To Italy,* carried the Italian electric charge around the Dylan world. Next, Dylan marked the NET's first foray into Turkey with an extended 21-song set, including four acoustic songs in the encore.

Greece, appropriately enough, staged some classic Dylanesque drama. Patras, on 26th June, found Dylan in a foul mood; the fact that his nose sounded completely blocked didn't help. His temper completely snapped part-way through "Silvio", when he stopped playing and shouted to the light engineers: "Shut that light off please!" Given the minimal lighting normal for Dylan shows in those days it meant that for the rest of the show the stage was in near complete darkness. Meanwhile the star act was apparently more concerned with the effort of drawing breath than with projecting his voice around the darkened arena. This low point of Dylan's performing year drew predictable boos at the end.

The shouted instruction and the darkness of so many stage sets had fans worried that Dylan had a serious eye problem. A long-standing back complaint was also presumed to be playing up at the time, given his relative immobility on stage. In addition, he had been pushing his voice to the limit with his barnstorming electric sets, so perhaps it all came to a head that night. At least the Patras audience got the first-ever live performance of "Tears of Rage" as some consolation. Technically, as neither "Quinn The Eskimo" nor "I Shall Be Released" feature on the official release of *The Basement Tapes*, this was the first performance at a Dylan show of any song from that album, 22 years after it was recorded and 14 years after it was released. (Though "Down In The Flood" and "Don't Ya Tell Henry" were performed when Dylan guested at a Band show in 1972).

---

3 Years later the rehearsals for this tour were to emerge and "Peace In The Valley" was there, as were Buddy Holly and Gram Parson songs and Robert Johnson's "Queen Of Spades". Not on this circulating tape, but also run through, were a huge number of covers including the Who's "I Can See For Miles" and the Beach Boys' "God Only Knows" among the more mind-boggling. (Christopher Parker, interview, *The Telegraph* #36)

This European jaunt came to an end at Athens on June 28th. Dylan gave an extended 19-song set and "Highway 61 Revisited" was filmed for a Greek TV special. In addition, Van Morrison joined Dylan for two of the Ulsterman's songs in the encores. These were filmed for, but not shown in, a BBC TV Arena special on Van. The programme did, however, show us the pair at large in Greece.

The Greek segment of the show opened with a shot of Dylan on the Hill of Muses. It was a wonderful treat for fans, used to Dylan's murky appearance on a darkened stage, to see him so clearly in brilliant sunlight; though it didn't appear to be a pleasure for Dylan, who squinted uncomfortably in the glare. As the camera panned out, it revealed the marvellous, classical Greek scenery in the background and Bob and Van in the foreground, performing the latter's "Crazy Love". Well, Van performed it, while Dylan hesitantly joined in late as he studied Van intently to glean the words as they went along.

Interestingly, during the Dylan section of this Van Morrison TV special the camera concentrated on Bob as though he were the subject of the programme; it rarely left his face during a duet on "One Irish Rover", which once again found him trying to figure out the words as Van sang them, and then eventually giving up singing altogether. Still, the film clip acts as a nice footnote to this leg of the NET. It provides some of the best Dylan visuals you could wish for; and, having learnt the words subsequently, Dylan would feature "One Irish Rover" some 14 times in the US legs of 1989's tour. It would also be far from the last time in the NET that Bob and Van would prove that they couldn't duet.

After the exertions of his European tour, you would have been forgiven for thinking that Dylan was ready for a rest. He had other thoughts: the European leg ended on June 28th, and by July 1st Dylan was on stage in Peoria, Illinois to kick off a 47-date tour, the first of two separate US legs.

Not only that, but he opened the Peoria concert with a triple surprise blast of "Pancho And Lefty", "One Irish Rover" and "I Believe In You", The first was making only its second-ever appearance on a Dylan set-list, the second was a debut performance, and the third was having its first outing since November 1981.

Clearly in the mood to experiment, Dylan opened the next night's show with the rarely-played Glen Trout song "Everybody's Movin'", following it with "Absolutely Sweet Marie", "Ballad Of Hollis Brown", "Tears Of Rage", "Seeing The Real You At Last", and "Gotta Serve Somebody". Usually only one or two of those songs featured in any given show. The next day, Gordon Lightfoot's "Early Morning Rain" (like "Pancho and Lefty", a song tailor-made for Dylan) was followed by the sole 1989 outing for both "Driftin' Too Far From Shore", and (a few songs later) "I Dreamed I Saw St. Augustine". Even more startlingly, two songs after that, Leadbelly 's "In The Pines" made its first appearance since the 1960s. Things generally settled down after this, though surprises continued: from Van Morrison's "And it Stoned Me" on July 6th right through to "Rank Strangers To Me" in September. Not for the first or last time on an NET leg, most of the highlights were to be found in these covers.

Despite all this, some fans were disappointed not to have heard songs from Dylan's completed, but yet to be released, *Oh Mercy* album. It was said that Dylan was not playing this material for fear of bootleggers distributing the songs before the album appeared.

Notably for later NET developments, Steve Earle was the support act during this part of the tour and Bucky Baxter, Earle's steel guitarist, sat in on some sets.

The reviews of these shows were mainly positive – though there were some familiar criticisms, especially: "It doesn't sound like the records"; "He can't sing"; and "He doesn't speak".

A few months later Dylan gave journalist Edna Gundersun a fairly straightforward explanation as to why he doesn't talk to audiences. "It just doesn't seem relevant anymore," he told her. "It's not stand-up comedy or a stage play. Also it breaks up my concentration to have to think of things to say or to respond to the crowd. The songs themselves do the talking." Later in the NET, Bob would give completely different answers to the same question.

In the meantime, *The Cleveland Plain Dealer*'s Michael Heaton was particularly enthusiastic about Bob's performance: "When Dylan's revved up as he was all night at Blossom Sunday, it's a privilege to watch him play ... It was the best show of the summer so far. He's the last real deal. The genuine article. A true star." At the same time, like many other reviewers, Mr Heaton could not help pointing out that the audience was about half the size of the previous year's 9,000.

The Boston Herald's Greg Reibman opened a rave notice with an interesting comparison that was echoed by a number of other critics. "The summer of 1989 will be remembered as a time when tours by the Who, the Rolling Stones, Ringo Starr and other veteran rockers dominated the concert stages and rock headlines," Reibman noted. "In contrast, without the now customary hype, tour sponsorships and press conferences, Bob Dylan practically snuck into Great Woods Thursday night. It turned out to be an inspired concert that his fellow '60s superstars would be hard pressed to match ... The 90-minute career-spanning concert was a Bob Dylan fan's dream come true. To 15 of his best songs, he brought fresh arrangements and vitality ... The show didn't come across as a night of nostalgia, nor as an attempt to capitalise on past glories."

"He slammed through his 90-minute set like a small gale passing through the beach," *Newsday*'s Stephen Williams enthused of the Jones Beach show. "[Dylan's] no-nonsense posture – he'd lean forward sometimes, his guitar neck pointed at the wings like a machine gun – supplemented [his] aura of aggression." It was a posture he adopted for most of 1989.

However, not all the media coverage was positive. In the first of many NET "Bob's sold out, the Sixties are dead" stories, Dylan's decision to play at an Atlantic City casino on July 20th caused something of a press furore. This served as a stark reminder of just how big an icon Dylan still was, regardless of his current record sales. The reaction of *The Montreal Gazette*'s Michael Farber was fairly typical. "The revolution is over," Farber fulminated. "We lost ... On the 20th anniversary of Woodstock the man who wrote 'money doesn't talk it swears' and meant it, sang for the first time in capitalism's playground."

Intriguingly, *The New York Daily News*'s David Hinckley saw Dylan as following in the footsteps of rock' n' roll's first icon. "It's Elvis and Dylan," he explained, "and their common ground, which begins with youths of talent, fire and charisma, when they were so good that even people who didn't understand or like them often sensed, correctly, that there was reason to be afraid of them." Dylan came out of the comparison on top, as Hinckley contrasted Elvis's unchallenging casino days with Dylan "ripping into songs" at Atlantic City. The reviewer placed particular emphasis on the way Dylan used "It Ain't Me, Babe" as a personal anthem, "because it's both close to and far from the hollow 'My Way' with which Elvis tried to convince himself, and maybe the world, that he controlled his life. Dylan, more modestly and accurately, says only that he won't be what he ain't."

In the meantime, the NET resumed with one of its most exciting and rewarding legs. Much of the excitement was due to the release during the break of the *Oh Mercy* album. One of the great joys of following Dylan on tour is to observe the evolution of new Dylan originals, especially when the material is as strong as the tracks from *Oh Mercy*, though not all of them were played live in 1989.

"Everything Is Broken" was performed at all but one of the shows (26 times), which in a way was a pity, as it is probably the weakest song from the record. However the next most played was "Most Of The Time" (23 times, at the beginning of the first encore); a majestic, searing song that grew in the playing and has a fair claim to be the best track on an album bejewelled with standout songs. "What Good Am I?" featured 18 times, while "Man In The Long Black Coat" was performed on 15 occasions and "Disease Of Conceit", with Dylan on piano, 11 times. Dylan also made one under-rehearsed stab at a solo piano take of "Ring Them Bells" at the request of his manager. This left "Political World", "Where Teardrops Fall", "What Was It You Wanted" and "Shooting Star" from *Oh Mercy* still to be played live.

The introduction of these new songs necessitated a change in the way Dylan and the band played. The garage band sound that had the *NME* claiming earlier in the year, "This is the way the Clash should have sounded", would not do for brooding and introspective material like "What Good Am I?", "Man In A Long Black Coat" and "Most of the Time". As "What Good Am I?" was most commonly to be found as the second song, this change was noticeably almost immediately and it affected the tempo of many of the songs. There was still room for some all-out rockers, but the overall mood and pace of the shows had changed.

The first *Oh Mercy* songs were debuted in October 1989 during an enthralling residency at New York's Beacon Theatre. This was one of Dylan's most memorable series of shows. Listening to a tape of the first night, 10th October, in particular, an almost demonic rage seems to spill through the speakers.

"[On the first night, Dylan] took the stage like a wild man," audience member Peter Vincent recalls, "stalking back and forth and tearing into the first song at a furious pace. He slowed slightly for the second song, the debut of 'What Good Am I?', the first *Oh Mercy* song ever to be played live, but there were no niceties like pauses for applause; one song segued into another while the musicians flogged themselves to keep up. Without good peripheral vision this would have looked like a solo electric appearance, as the band was hovering at the edge of the stage, eager to keep as far away from Dylan as the leads on their instruments would allow." No fewer than three *Oh Mercy* songs were debuted that night: "What Good Am I?"; "Everything Is Broken" and "Most Of The Time".

On tape the show sounds quite erratic in places, but when it is good it is great, and it is never less than gripping. Dylan's foul mood caused sparks to fly, not just from the rejected harmonicas he threw across the stage when he couldn't find one in the right key, but from his intuitive sense of theatre. This stands in complete contrast to Patras, where his anger merely resulted in a sullen and lacklustre show.

Things at the Beacon calmed down on the 11th and 12th, though the first of these dates still featured a stand-out "The Lakes of Pontchartrain" – Dylan's phrasing here has to be heard to be believed – and a never-bettered "It Takes A Lot To Laugh, It Takes A Train To Cry". Most especially, there was a breathtaking performance of "Queen Jane Approximately" on the 12th – the song's 9th NET outing (starting on August 16th 1989). Dylan had already performed other fine renditions of the song, and would continue to do so, but it seemed to peak here. Dylan writer Robert Forryan praised it for "an opening that is all low-down, brooding guitar complemented by Dylan's slow, achingly sweet harmonica, and a stately, marching drum-beat." Forryan saw the song's high point as when Bob sings "'You want someone ... aaarrr ... you don't have to speak to' ... that 'aaarrr' is stomach-churningly gorgeous; divinely sensual; just plain sexy!"[4]

"Everywhere they went with the music seemed totally and absolutely right," Peter Vincent recalls, "a combination of power and spontaneity the like of which I have practically never encountered. It may have been the single greatest performance by Dylan I have ever had the good fortune to attend, and no-one in the band was willing to let it go ... It seemed like they were going to keep playing 'Queen Jane' all night, endlessly finding fresh variations on the song's themes."

Bob biographer Clinton Heylin, not given to hyperbolic praise, was almost as enthusiastic, considering "Queen Jane" not just the highlight of the night, but

4 Robert Forryan: "Queen Jane – An Incomplete History". *Dignity* issue 8 : Jan/Feb 1997

"One of the two or three greatest performances of the Never Ending Tour". It is certainly among the contenders. The original *Highway 61 Revisited* version was stately, but in this truncated performance (Dylan drops verses 2 and 4; but it is truncated in terms of words only, not at all compromised in feeling) there was a lived-in humanity mixed with a different yearning. It is this kind of performing art that makes following the NET so rewarding.

It would have been hard for Dylan to top the drama of the opening three Beacon gigs, but he managed to pull out more surprises on the final night. "Precious Memories" and "Man In The Long Black Coat" were played for the first time, which may have surprised the audience, though perhaps not as much as the sight of Dylan clad in a gold lamé suit. Mr Hinckley could have extended his 'Dylan following in Elvis's footsteps' theory further had he been writing later in the year. An even bigger shock was kept until the end, though, after "Man In the Long Black Coat" led onto a hand-held-microphone version of "Leopard-Skin Pill-Box Hat". During a harmonica solo, Dylan shook hands with members of the audience, leapt off the stage and walked out through a fire exit. The band was as bemused as the audience were, and G.E. Smith only brought the song to an end when it finally became clear that Dylan was not going to return.

Without the same dramatics, the 1989 shows that followed the Beacon featured many fascinating highlights; especially, once again, in the covers (including the surprising "When First Unto This Country" and "Everybody's Movin'") as well as the *Oh Mercy* songs discussed above. In addition, a number of debuts and unusual choices were unveiled, such as "Man of Peace" from *Infidels*. "Lay, Lady, Lay" also made its NET debut and "To Be Alone With You" made its first appearance in any Dylan live show. A number of old friends appeared in different guise: "Don't Think Twice, It's All Right" found itself, for the first time on the NET, in the electric set, while "Tangled Up In Blue" popped up in an acoustic slot for the first time in five years.

In the insatiably greedy way that a fan forever demands more, my main complaint about this 1989 NET leg is that I would have liked Dylan to have spent more time at the piano. After the disappointing debut of "Ring Them Bells", Dylan used "Disease of Conceit", when it was on the set-list, as his one piano piece, other than a one-off version of "Gotta Serve Somebody". Still, as I said, I am being too greedy. Not only were the shows high-quality and adventurous, they also introduced a new style of NET performance and more than whetted the appetite for what was to be an extraordinary end to the decade.

CHAPTER FOUR

1990:
"Better than quittin' anyway"

"Don't be bewildered by the Never Ending Tour chatter, there was a Never Ending Tour but it ended... with the departure of guitarist G.E. Smith."

BOB DYLAN, LINER NOTES TO 1993'S *WORLD GONE WRONG*

Though Glasgow 1989 was the first NET show I attended, in many ways 1990 marked the true beginning of the NET for me. It was the first time I saw him in a small hall; the line-up of Bob's band began to change; and the concert locations ranged from the smallest venues to large outdoor festivals. The year also saw a huge inconsistency in the quality of Dylan's shows – from drunken rambling messes to compelling art and exhilarating entertainment. All these factors, to varying degrees, were to become integral features of the NET proper as it progressed through the '90s.

The year also saw a sudden key realisation dawn amongst British fans – that 1989's tour was not merely Dylan's fifth three-yearly UK visit (after '78, '81, '84, and '87) one year early. Instead, you could begin to count on seeing him again at a venue nearby, and soon, playing a set with a greatest hits backbone that was usually filled out with surprise originals and delicious covers.

Before the first real 1990 leg of the NET, Dylan astonished everyone by booking into Toad's Place, a 700-capacity US venue, and playing four sets, across five hours from 9pm onwards, in a single night. Once word started to travel about the content of those sets, the questions began to fly: "Key To The Highway" – are you sure? "Tight Connection To My Heart"? – you must be kidding, surely? Bruce Springsteen's "Dancing In The Dark"? – are you mad? The eagerness to get one's hands on tapes of all this was incredible. The hype just grew and grew as those lucky enough to have been there talked about Dylan chatting at length between songs and the special feeling there was between performer and audience.

All this raised fans already heightened anticipation of the forthcoming Paris and London shows – due after Dylan spent a brief sojourn in South America playing for massive, six-figure festival audiences. When the Toad's tapes finally arrived, it soon became apparent that, extraordinary event though it was, that marathon night had been merely a public rehearsal. Nothing wrong with that, I wish he would do it every year, but it was ironic at the time that this most sought-after of tapes was soon blown away by recordings of proper gigs.

Two warm-up shows in the States acted as a kind of half-way house between the rehearsals and the real concerts. The first of them was, like Toad's, all-electric and found Dylan still working on "Tight Connection To My Heart", as well as making a stab at "You Angel You". Both of these held significance for the shows to come, though Dylan's recollection of the latter's lyrics at this point stretched to the title only.

The six UK dates were scheduled for the Hammersmith Odeon in West London. By a lucky coincidence I had recently moved house to the Hammersmith area, which left me a mere 15-minute walk away from both venue and box office for this residency-to-die-for. I was all set to rush there the minute Lambchop contacted me from the head of the queue.

Naturally, life did not go so smoothly. Once again I was working in Eastbourne and my pager (younger readers may need to ask their parents what this means) was going wild with so-called urgent messages. The only really urgent one was from Lambchop, telling me that those in the know were queuing all night for Dylan tickets just up the road from my flat. I was stunned and distraught at missing out. The excitement of the approaching concerts had to be held in abeyance long enough for me to dash off a letter to the Hammersmith Odeon, carefully following Lambchop's detailed instructions.

Days passed slowly. Cousin Andy phoned to say he had six tickets for various parts of the venue. Fear set in, I should have heard something by now. By this time everyone else seemed to have their tickets yet, still, I had none.

I went to the Odeon to find short tempers and confusion a-plenty at the ticket desk, with Dylan fans much in evidence. Finally, the Odeon staff located my letter. They had not sent out any tickets because I had appeared to have asked for seven in my first paragraph, one over the limit per application. They had ignored the rest of my letter, which made it clear I would accept any number anywhere at any price.

As I was breaking into a state which only the similarly obsessed can possibly imagine, along came yet another agitated Dylan fan in an identical predicament. The staff were getting a bit fed up with this, while the rest of the queue who had turned up for tickets to other events were looking on in bewilderment as various Dylan fans and members of staff were verging on nervous breakdowns.

Eventually pity welled in the breast of one member of staff at my predicament and I got my tickets; seven at that. They were dotted all round the venue and, unsurprisingly by now, none were near the front. So, after many phone calls, and much frenetic upgrade buying, swapping and buying and swapping and buying again, I had to settle for two very good seats, two in the balcony and two in the middle, plus various others spread around the hall for those I was taking along.

As the opening London show approached, mouth-watering reports filtered back from France, culminating in a call from Lambchop in a state of ecstasy at the latest Paris date. I assumed he was exaggerating in understandable post-concert excitement, but was impressed that he was so blown away by the show. The subsequent arrival of a tape proved that he was telling it just the way it happened.

Eventually the great day of the first concert dawned. My wife Pia and cousin Andy were going with me. Andy was down for the week with his usual goodies. An inspired electric "Pretty Peggy-O" on video was the last song he played for me before leaving the flat. It was the best version I'd ever heard, an opinion I would shortly have to revise.

On the way to the show, we stopped at the Novotel, which was full of people I would get to know over the next year or so, involved in a massive ticket-swapping session of quite extraordinary complexity and intricacy, all for the sake of a foot or so worth of 'advancement'. It was almost distracting enough to fill in the time before Dylan came on stage.

3rd February 1990 Hammersmith Odeon, London

1 Stuck Inside Of Mobile With The Memphis Blues Again

2 Pretty Peggy-O (Traditional)

3 Tight Connection To My Heart (Has Anybody Seen My Love?)

4 Political World

5 You're A Big Girl Now

6 What Was It You Wanted

7 Leopard-Skin Pill-Box Hat

8 All Along The Watchtower

9 Love Minus Zero/No Limit (Acoustic)

10 It Ain't Me, Babe (Acoustic)

11 The Lonesome Death Of Hattie Carroll (Acoustic)

12 Gates Of Eden (Acoustic)

13 Everything Is Broken

14 Queen Jane Approximately

15 It Takes A Lot To Laugh, It Takes A Train To Cry

16 Man In The Long Black Coat

17 In The Garden

18 Like A Rolling Stone

*

19 Mr. Tambourine Man (Acoustic)

20 Highway 61 Revisited

As show-time approached, the whole front area could hear Lambchop shouting at the top of his voice, "Bobby Bobby Bobby ... Stand up". Then Dylan took to the stage and the opening guitar lines signalled the arrival of "Stuck Inside of Mobile With The Memphis Blues Again". The screams of joy were pure teeny-bopper stuff, as was my stunned wonder that He was so close. The music pounded in my eardrums, and when Bob started singing the hall erupted all over again.

It was to be too much for some; near the beginning of the show two people actually ran onto the stage. Bob looked momentarily alarmed but then just stepped out of the way and kept playing his guitar.

The energy poured from the stage as Dylan and the band tore into the song like your favourite garage band. By the end of the first verse I could have died and gone to heaven. As the song continued, I revelled in Dylan's every word; his every facial expression; his every movement. My senses were in overdrive. I tried to tell myself that there were six whole nights of this to come, to pace myself. But such reserve was inconceivable. Then the guitar break brought another outbreak of fan hysteria.

"Stand-up for Bobby.... show some respect", shouted Lambchop as the song ended to tumultuous applause. "Show some respect! Bobby's standing for you, you stand for him..."

The clapping died down as the opening chords of "Pretty Peggy-O" emerged. Back at the flat, Andy and I had joked about how wonderful it would be if Dylan played this, and how wonderful it was indeed. This was the most heavenly part of heaven itself. My reverie was broken by Lambchop's dulcet tones:

"Fuck 'em all Bobby, fuck 'em all, they don't fucking deserve it. Show them who is boss".

"Tight Connection To My Heart" followed. Dylan slowed down enough to give a pointed delivery, making the audience actually think about what he was saying, even as they continued to act like star-crazed teeny-boppers. The coming together of these two elements is what Dylan appreciation in the NET is all about. Bob repeated the "Tight Connection" line "Has anybody seen my love?" so many times that it became the de facto title of the song in this guise, which was far removed from the *Empire Burlesque* prototype. As it drew to a close, Larry Lambchop was off again.

"Bobby, Bobby, Bobby..." he started to scream. At which point, Lambchop's voice suddenly packed in (it was amazing it had lasted so long). Then, after a pause during which it sounded like it had cracked for the very last time, he was back at full throttle:

"Too good, too fucking good for them... Bobby you are the best."

Dylan then swung into a breathless run-through of "Political World", his demeanour mercifully far removed from how he looks in the depressing, poorly-staged video that had been used to 'promote' the song. In contrast to the album version's biblical mood, this live version stressed the contemporary in the mixed modern and ancient imagery that is so typical of *Oh Mercy* songs.

An utterly classy "You're A Big Girl Now" ensued, with the phrase "singing just for you" bringing cheers from the crowd. "What Was It You Wanted" started suddenly, before the applause for the previous song had tailed off, while the insistent beat made the questions seem menacing rather than contemplative.

"ThankyouBobbyThankyouBobbythankyouthankyouthankyou", Lambchop yelled without pause for breath.

The driving intensity of "Leopard-Skin Pill-Box Hat" was beyond belief. If the 1989 version had been fine, this was pure ecstasy. The band were playing fabulously and everyone in the hall was having a ball. By the time the band abruptly slammed into "All Along The Watchtower" Larry's throat was getting pretty hoarse, but he hung in there: "Thanks for coming! Anything you want Bobby, anything you like." A woman cried "We love you" as Dylan launched into a beautiful performance of "Love Minus Zero/No Limit".

Much as singing along at concerts is anathema to me, I found it hard to decry the spontaneous crowd accompaniment to the first chorus of "It Ain't Me, Babe" – for all I know, I was joining in.

"*We're going change the title now to 'Ain't it me babe?'*" Dylan quipped at the song's conclusion.

"Thank you Bob thank you Bob", replied our feather-in-the-hat friend.

"The Lonesome Death Of Hattie Carroll" was almost perfect. Although Dylan forgot some words, he was firmly in control and his illuminating harmonica break preceded a great, guitar-driven end to the song. "Gates Of Eden" was attacked at a break-neck pace and then the whole crowd was clapping along to "Everything Is Broken". "God bless you Bobby God bless you", cried Lambchop.

Bless Bob indeed, for going into the transcendent "Queen Jane Approximately". His voice hit a high note in the song's opening, surging over the band's thrilling accompaniment, and then there was the totally wonderful Dylanesque-to-the-nth-degree vocalisation of the stretched-out line endings.

At its end we were breathless, but Dylan was not: with hardly a pause he was into "It Takes A Lot To Laugh, It Takes A Train To Cry". As he ended the lines "And if I don't make it/ You know my baby will" by stretching the last word to "willllllllllllll", a classic was reinvented in front of our eyes.

It was hard to imagine that life could get better, but it immediately did with the appearance of "Man In The Long Black Coat"; after which, a show-stopping "In The Garden" had everyone partying.

As for "Like A Rolling Stone", it had to be experienced rather than heard. We could tangibly feel we were at an Event, a pinnacle even in Dylan's peak-strewn career. Naturally, "Like A Rolling Stone" had to be the closer, and just as naturally we all went crazy.

"Thank you everybody," Dylan remarked restrainedly to the baying, happy mob as the song closed the main set for the night. The encores opened with some lovely guitar picking to introduce "Mr. Tambourine Man". Dylan's ambitious staccato delivery changed the pace of the song completely before it finished with a splendid harmonica break. Finally, a storming finale of "Highway 61 Revisited" brought this perfect evening to a close.

So many things shone out on the opening night: Dylan's mobility (in such contrast to 1989); his happiness; the hugely appreciative reception given to *Oh Mercy* songs; the brilliant recasting of "Tight Connection" into "Has Anybody Seen My Love?". "It Takes A Lot To Laugh" alone would have been more than enough to satisfy me for the entire week. Instead, the residency was to supply jewel upon jewel, night after night.

There were many highlights for me. On February 5th, I got lost on my way out of the venue, finally alighting by a side door that led straight to the waiting tour bus. I got on it and chatted to Chris Parker, the drummer. On the 6th we got one of the week's highlights: Merle Travis's "Dark As A Dungeon", performed in a dark, deep voice that croaked and crackled with emotion and emphasis.

The February 7th show featured a rapturously received "Forever Young" that brought memories of 1978 and would have made a fitting finale. Dylan began it as a benediction to the audience, but it grew into a defiant declaration of intent. That same night, there was also an oddly arranged "Tonight I'll Be Staying Here With You" (making its first appearance since 1976) – the almost shouted lyrics intimating that the narrator was moving on rather than staying. It is reasonable to assume that most people's favourite on the 7th was "Most Of The Time". "I can survive, I can endure", Bob sang, with his voice making clear that it was at a terrible cost.

Other standouts that night included "It's Alright Ma" from the acoustic set and, from the electric, the quintessential city blues, "It Takes A Lot To Laugh, It Takes A Train To Cry", which boasted additional guitar embellishment that made it even better than on the opening night. The walls of the Hammersmith Odeon seemed to vibrate as bass lines snaked and drums relentlessly pounded; above it all Dylan's vocals soared in tandem with the lead guitar. Exhilarating, exhausting, magical.

I was not alone in worrying that the last show would prove to be an anti-climax. It seemed impossible that Dylan could top his previous performances; but that is exactly what he did. As in Paris, good hands were played during each show, but all the aces were saved for the final night.

8th February 1990 Hammersmith Odeon, London

1 Absolutely Sweet Marie
2 Man In The Long Black Coat
3 Positively 4th Street
4 Ballad Of A Thin Man

5 Pledging My Time
6 I Want You
7 Political World
8 You Angel You
9 All Along The Watchtower
10 Boots Of Spanish Leather (Acoustic)
11 To Ramona (Acoustic)
12 She Belongs To Me (Acoustic)
13 Mr. Tambourine Man (Acoustic)
14 Disease Of Conceit (Piano)
15 I'll Remember You
16 Where Teardrops Fall
17 Seeing The Real You At Last
18 Every Grain Of Sand
19 Rainy Day Women #12 & 35
20 Like A Rolling Stone
*
21 It Ain't Me, Babe (Acoustic)
22 Hang Me, Oh Hang Me (Traditional)
23 Highway 61 Revisited

As the band stormed through the opening "Absolutely Sweet Marie", Dylan steered the song through the electric maelstrom. "Man In The Long Black Coat" was next, understandably similar to the opening night.

A complete mood change was wrought with a driving "Positively 4th Street". As the aisles swayed in hymnal response to this most cruel of put-downs, Dylan sounded more resigned than overtly scornful: the cawing sneer of the young man was replaced by a more mature voice, one so used to being let down that he accepts it as part of life.

"'Kyou," Bob told the enthusiastic audience and launched straight into a monumental "Ballad Of A Thin Man". Menacing, dark and wonderful, the questions pierced the thick air like stabs of lightning. A harmonica break slowed things down before Dylan had us all just staring (or dancing) in awe as he exploded through the final verses.

"'Kyou."

"Pledging My Time" made a rare and welcome appearance, as somehow Dylan conjured up a sense of intimacy in the crowded, stuffy auditorium. At the gorgeous harp break the crowd went nuts all over again.

Next was the third *Blonde On Blonde* song of the night, "I Want You", taken far too fast, but the sound of celebration in Dylan's voice made it clear he was having a ball and wanted us to have one with him.

"Political World" provided us with a needed break from the intensity, before "You Angel You", so surprisingly played in response to a request at the warm-up show on January 14th, reappeared to a roar of shocked delight. Dylan had clearly been re-learning the lyrics and gave an exuberant performance, following it with a menacing version of "All Along The Watchtower".

"Play anything you like, Bob", Lambchop wisely suggested over the ensuing hubbub of requests. What we got was a sharply focused "Boots Of Spanish Leather" that quietened everything down again.

Dylan's punchy delivery sounded simultaneously ravaged and sensuous on the following "To Ramona", and "She Belongs To Me" continued our acoustic feast.

"'Ankyou," expounded Bob at length.

Some hesitant guitar playing strengthened into the unmistakable sound of "Mr. Tambourine Man" – a fine clear version with a lovely brief harp break early on.

"Thank You", said our man, becoming positively verbose, before walking over to the piano that had remained untouched throughout the residency. A huge roar went up. All week long Dylan had been teasing us by circling the piano without ever touching its keys. As Dylan now approached the piano once again, the crowd's anticipation was tinged with apprehension that this was another put-on. The cheer redoubled when we realised that this time it was for real.

Dylan briefly went back to the front of the stage to revel in the applause, before returning to the piano for an inspired rendition of "Disease Of Conceit".

"I'll Remember You" was followed by "Where Teardrops Fall", the next glorious surprise of this week of never-ending treats. I was brought back to earth with "Seeing The Real You At Last". Even Bob in such resplendent form couldn't redeem this bombast, occasional good lines notwithstanding.

"Every Grain Of Sand" is one of those songs that should never be played live because the studio versions are so perfect. At the end of this week, however, it seemed he could do anything, and he pulled it off with aplomb.

A change of mood followed with "Rainy Day Women"; from metaphysical insight to all-out rave-up in one easy movement. The song sounded fresher in those earlier NET years and this was great fun. Dylan's voice almost gave out at one moment but he just came back with a big, bear-like roar of a "yeah-eah!" and ended the song, before instantly ripping into "Like A Rolling Stone". It was an all-out rocking climax to an entire week of euphoria. Never have such scathing lyrics sounded so celebratory. It felt as if the energy both on and off the stage could fuel a starship to the farthest reaches of the galaxy. As G.E. Smith went through his showcase solo I would never have imagined that this would be the last time I'd see him on stage with Dylan. The band just seemed so happy and so together.

Suddenly, unbelievably, the residency was approaching its end. We had reached the encores of the last show. Each passing moment was becoming ever more precious.

A strong version of the acoustic classic "It Ain't Me, Babe" opened the encores. This had grown into one of his most bonding live songs: both singer and audience aware of the irony of greeting its lyrics of denial with such a rapturous reception.

The traditional "Hang Me, Oh Hang Me" (aka. "I've Been All Around The World" or "The Blue Ridge Mountains") was sung by Dylan in a throaty but deeply satisfying growl. Deep bass lines and simple guitar strokes lent gravity. For a man who had been criss-crossing continents for the past five years, the sentiments of "Lord, Lord, I've been all around this world" seemed fitting. A hush came over the hall. It was one of the most perfect moments of my life.

Then a blistering, rip-the-paint-off-the-walls "Highway 61 Revisited" brought the whole thing to a rousing, exhausting finish. It was a long time before many of us left the hall, so reluctant were we to leave the scene of our extraordinary experience.

There was a huge over-reaction from fans in the following weeks. "The best since '75", said many; "since '66", said others. I joined in this daft game, to a slightly lesser extent, by affirming it "the best I'd seen him since 1978". Though easily dismissed by later perspectives, these heady claims certainly felt right at the time. The high standard of performance and the intimacy of the venue provoked an immediate need to elevate the Hammersmith 1990 residency over past triumphs such as the 1979 and 1980 tours, or if one was thinking of UK-only gigs the sumptuous 1981 concerts.

In any case, the experience was a transforming, uplifting one and very far from over. Hammersmith 1990 may have ended on stage but the tapes were already out and the videos, vinyl and CDs would follow. To this day, I find it hard to accept that these were just 'six more shows in the NET'. For me they were the turning point, and the beginning of a time when I could regularly see Dylan in concert at close range; when all sorts of weird and wonderful things would happen to the set-lists; when I would start to know more and more of the audience who, like me, were going to a number of shows and listening to them all. My own NET had started with a vengeance.

I had discovered the door to a magical kingdom, and felt like Charles Ryder in *Brideshead Revisited* when he first encountered the world of Sebastian Flyte.

"I went there uncertainly. But I was in search of love in those days, and I went full of curiosity and the faint, unrecognized apprehension that here, at last, I should find that low door in the wall, which others, I knew had found before me, which opened on an enclosed and enchanted garden, which was somewhere, not overlooked by any window, in the heart of that grey city."[1] This "enchanted garden" of endless touring and Bob-watching was open to anyone who wanted to step into the enclosure.

---

1 E.Waugh," Brideshead Revisited", Penguin Books, 1951, p.40

From now on I would be collecting as many shows as I could on tape, and subscribing to all those Dylan magazines I'd heard so much about. In fact I even started one myself; the first issue of that magazine, **Homer**, *the slut* came out later in 1990. Producing and distributing it would take up most of my free time over the next four years.

While we were still enthusing wildly over the Paris and London shows, Dylan popped up as a guest at some US shows, recorded a new, killer, version of "Most Of The Time" and laid down tracks for a new album of his own, as well as working on the second Traveling Wilburys record.

Then, on May 29th he picked up the NET again, starting a North American tour in Montreal. Changes had been made; most significantly the band now remained on stage during the acoustic set, providing Dylan with a sympathetic backing that allowed him to concentrate on his vocal delivery. Almost as surprising was his use of the harmonica, which resumed its status as an important element in his performances. The opening show also featured the first "Desolation Row" of the NET, a development dramatic enough to make me redouble my search for every tape. As it happens, it was a couple of months before I heard the opening night, but meanwhile I kept getting tapes from other dates. The second show, on 30th May, was one of the first and one of those I played most.

30th May 1990 Kingston Community Memorial Hall, Kingston, ON

1. Most Likely You Go Your Way (And I'll Go Mine)
2. Ballad Of A Thin Man
3. Stuck Inside Of Mobile With The Memphis Blues Again
4. Just Like A Woman
5. Masters Of War
6. Gotta Serve Somebody
7. Love Minus Zero/No Limit (Acoustic)
8. It's Alright, Ma (I'm Only Bleeding) (Acoustic)
9. She Belongs To Me (Acoustic)
10. Ballad Of Hollis Brown (Acoustic)

11 One Too Many Mornings (Acoustic)

12 Mr. Tambourine Man (Acoustic)

13 Where Teardrops Fall (Piano)

14 Everything Is Broken

15 I Shall Be Released

16 All Along The Watchtower

17 What Good Am I ?

18 Like A Rolling Stone

*

19 Blowin' In The Wind (Acoustic/Electric)

20 Highway 61 Revisited

This is the setlist, but that isn't really how I recall it. My own memories of that show only run from the middle of the acoustic set to the end of the show (not including the encores), because the second side of my tape, which became a particular Walkman favourite, began in the acoustic set with "She Belongs To Me" and ran until just before the encores. At that time my journey to work was approximately one hour, for 45 minutes of which I'd be sitting down listening to a tape. For some reason this particular tape always seemed to be with me and ready to play from that point in the show onwards. Naturally, I have listened to the whole show since and in these digital days this kind of thing no longer happens, but I want to retain the personal side to this dual tale of 'my' subjective NET and the overall objective chronology of it unfolding year by year. So, here is 'my' (truncated) Kingston 1990 experience.

"She Belongs To Me" was lovely, in spite of the crowd's determined efforts to clap along. "Ballad Of Hollis Brown", like "Gates Of Eden" in 1988, seemed to benefit from a brief foray into the electric set before returning to the acoustic. "One Too Many Mornings" was truly compassionate and the wild enthusiasm that greeted "Mr. Tambourine Man" was fully merited by its performance. The latter segued into "Where Teardrops Fall". By this point there was only "Shooting Star" from *Oh Mercy* still to be aired on the NET. It duly appeared at Alpine Valley in a tremendous version where, instead of finishing at the end of the song, Dylan returned to the last verse and repeated it after an instrumental break, building to a magnificent conclusion. Since the last verse is one of my favourite verses in the whole of *Oh Mercy* I was obviously delighted that this version worked so well. Alpine Valley was another tape I played again and again.

As for the other shows, the tapes from three nights in Toronto were also much sought-after, not just for the gorgeous "Early Morning Rain" tribute to Toronto native Gordon Lightfoot, but for yet another live debut, "One More Night", more than 20 years after he had written it. This featured a guest appearance by local rock 'n' roll warrior Ronnie Hawkins. By now Dylan had taken to chatting to the audience from the stage, and he introduced The Hawk at some length:

"Yeah, we got a friend here who's actually a hero of mine. One of my all time heroes now, Ronnie Hawkins. He's coming to the centre of the stage and sing a song called 'One More Night'. It would be awful nice if we can clap him on. If we do perhaps he'll play two. 'Cause otherwise it's gonna be up to me to sing it. All right. We did it. Here he is, oh here he comes."

That was not the only example of Dylan's new-found verbosity. Earlier in the show, he'd introduced "Boots Of Spanish Leather" somewhat patronisingly: *"There's more and more young ladies coming to my show so we're starting to do a lot of love ballads now."*

Somewhat more revealingly, between "It's Alright, Ma" and "Hang Me, Oh Hang Me" he interjected: *"Yeah! 'Put my head in a guillotine'. Actually a guillotine wouldn't be a bad way to go. Considering some of the kind of ways they got these days. Better than quittin' anyway."*

At first, I couldn't understand why Dylan had suddenly started this between-song patter, but the change could be traced to the 2nd June show in Ottawa, where he addressed two matters which had clearly upset him. First came an appeal for the return of a stolen guitar:

"Somebody worked his way in here and stole a guitar last night.... Anyway if any of you know who did it just let somebody know. Nothing's gonna happen to the thief.... We'd just like the guitar back. It was inside on the job. That's what this next song's about, something like an inside job."[2]

2 The next song was "Desolation Row".

Ottawa also found Dylan mulling over a hatchet review of the previous night's show. The critic's incredibly inapt demand that Dylan stop playing harmonica and bring back the pre-NET backing singers provoked Dylan to another extended intro:

"Well here's another song that has a lot of harmonica playing on this. There used to be a bunch of girls used to play on this instead of harmonica. But they decided they'd let me play harmonica for a while whilst they stay home. Anyway hmm. Seemed like there was an article written in the paper about me saying that the girls should come back, and the harmonica should go. Nobody showed me the article but they told me about it though. Anyway so, the girls might be back next time. But it's OK to play harmonica in this one, right?"

Unsurprisingly, there was a thunderous affirmative.

As this leg of the tour approached its climax, the shows lost a little of their sparkle. Voice and energy levels often suffer at the end of a long touring schedule, and this had been a very busy year already. Nonetheless, I think this fails to explain fully why this period is often overlooked by so many fans. My suspicion is that they were still entranced by the heights that Paris and London reached.

The first half of the year had gone marvellously well. In the NET, though, you never know what is just around the corner. It is hard to credit that a year that had gone so well was about to hit problem after problem. It is even harder to believe that the summer 1990 edition of Dylan fanzine *The Telegraph* opened with an 'Address from the Secretary', written by the late John Bauldie, that asked "Isn't Bob's recently acquired 'need to play' getting a tad tedious, even for some of the keenest of Bobcats?" Bauldie was particularly scathing about the European leg of the tour that climaxed with two 60,000-capacity festivals in Belgium, and dubbed it 'The Horrible Tour'.

This much-maligned leg had begun on June 27th in Reykjavik, Iceland. The rest of the short summer jaunt consisted mainly of festivals. Lucrative, no doubt, but far removed from the engaged performances at real Dylan shows.

"'Everything Is Broken' and 'Silvio' were delivered as meaningless babble," Bauldie complained of one Belgian festival date. "And many of the other tunes were tossed off with not a hint or a hope of subtlety or communication. G. E. Smith has turned into a heavy-handed parody of himself – all guitar-thrash and noise and none of the sympathetic interaction that made him so wonderful a sparring partner at past shows, Parker is drumming through the motions in the manner of a bored session player and Tony Garnier was always as interesting as a wet fish. Are this band played out? I mean, don't you just find yourself wanting a 'Like A Rolling Stone' without the mechanical Smith lead lines or an acoustic song without the extra guitar bashing Bob's into oblivion?"

That these comments seemed partly true at the time demonstrates how quickly the NET can change, from intimate hall and a focused Dylan to a disinterested parody in a large, muddy wasteland. However, some kind of balance should be applied; it was not that these shows were completely without merit. One of the best of these admittedly often dire summer outings was at the beautiful Stadtpark in Hamburg, and included a cover of "No More One More Time" and a curious one-off item called "Old Rock And Roller". This latter was introduced by Dylan as a song about "What happens to people like me."

As a tale about a star from the past, largely forgotten by the world he relentlessly tours, it was stunningly apt for this particular leg. Although Hamburg was one of the better shows, Dylan looked extremely the worse for wear as the show opened. If his body began to sober up, you had to wonder about his mind, and doubt the wisdom of his new penchant for chatter, when you heard him say:

"I'd like to say a lot of people in America, they're concerned about Germany reuniting. But when you think about it, why should they ever have been dis-united, really? Lot of people, they don't know that Hitler wasn't a German anyway."

Mr Bauldie's criticism[3] no doubt stemmed partially from the facts that these summer money-earners were not a regular feature back then, that Dylan had been playing so well up until them, and that we were accustomed to tours with different bands, not repeated visits from the same line-up, which was something we grew used to over the years of the NET. His remarks were very much of their time; astonishing now to look back on them over twenty-one years later with yet another leg of the never-having-stopped NET having come to a triumphant climax in London.

---

3 John Bauldie tragically died in a helicopter crash in 1996 so I cannot ask him, but I would speculate that John's editorial reflects the weariness of the hard-working editor and, indeed, the weariness of keeping up with the NET that comes and goes in many fans, as you will see as this book progresses.

Admittedly, the 1990 Belgian shows were a harbinger of the shambolic Dylan of 1991 and other depressing festival performances throughout the NET. Also, tramping through endless muddy fields, tired and hungry, and being jostled by thousands of frankly odd fans[4] of headline band The Cure, is hardly a scenario for enjoying yourself.

Festivals aside, Dylan's deterioration since February was so marked that it appeared essential he take a break. What Dylan clearly did not need was to keep touring, and drinking; and for G.E. Smith to leave, with prospective replacement guitarists being auditioned in front of paying audiences. I think you can all guess what happened next.

Dylan followed his short summer tour of Europe with a double blast in North America. Firstly, there was a month of dates beginning on August 12th in Edmonton, Canada. Fans were shocked to learn that G.E. Smith was soon to quit. Two years and some 200 concerts is a pretty fair stint by any normal reckoning, but looking back it seems way too short. Dylan believes that the 'Never Ending Tour' ended with G. E.'s departure, but for the sake of convenience fans have retained the label to refer to everything from 1988 on. Either way, many feared that the tour itself would not survive the loss of the guitarist; and things certainly did not progress smoothly. During the next month a number of new guitarists were auditioned – live on stage! John Staeheley (August 12-18), Steve Bruton (August 19-29), Miles Joseph (August 31-September 3), Steve Ripley (September 4-9), and César Diaz (September 11-12) were all given this trial.

Some of these men also took part in pre-tour rehearsals in late July and early August. The songs they covered were many and varied, giving an insight into the range of material Dylan was considering for his set-lists, despite the lack of readiness of a confirmed lead guitarist.

Despite all this chaos, late 1990 turned out to be not bad at all; although not as consistently impressive as the first half of the year, it certainly shook off the 'Horrible Tour' tag. Much like the previous year, the last leg of 1990's touring was looser and full of surprises and successes.

---

4 Yes, 'pot', 'kettle' and 'black' spring to mind, I know

There was a significant change, however; a difference so marked that one can see Dylan's point in saying *"there was a Never Ending Tour but it ended... with the departure of guitarist G.E. Smith."*

After the departure of G.E. Smith, shows that were great from the first to the last song with no filler, no mumbled lyrics, no coasting along for a few numbers could no longer be expected. Being searingly, life-changingly, on the ball for every moment of a complete performance no longer seemed within Dylan's grasp; or at least not on a regular basis.

The closing leg of 1990 produced mighty swings between the shambolic and the transcendent – sometimes happening between one song and the next. Notable moments in mid-August to mid-September included some astonishing covers. The first show featured the Beatles' "Nowhere Man", a song that seemed to have been composed under Dylan's influence. It's nice to know that Dylan covered it, but not so pleasant to actually hear it. It is hard to know what prompted these one-off covers, but the Beatles had been on Dylan's mind at the Hamburg show in Germany. Besides his inane comment about Germany and Hitler, Dylan introduced his final song that day like this:

"Thank you. It's always a pleasure to play here in this city here. Hamburg, where the Beatles started. Anybody remember the Beatles? Shout 'Yeah', if you remember the Beatles...[Nobody did]... Nobody knows the Beatles?...They started right here. This is one of their songs, which they inspired way back when." The song he actually then played was his own, "Highway 61 Revisited".

Perhaps even more surprising was his performance of Otis Redding's "Sitting On The Dock Of The Bay" on August 18th. It was another eccentric effort, with Dylan sounding somewhat drunk. This stands in contrast to another cover, one that I love unreservedly, although I have to admit that hardly anyone else seems to like it. I am referring here to Dylan's moving tribute to Stevie Ray Vaughan, who had died the night before[5],.Dylan introduced this by saying:

---

5 Stevie Ray Vaughan had played on *under the red sky*. He died in a helicopter crash near East Troy WI after having appeared as a guest at an Eric Clapton concert in Alpine Valley. Dylan was quoted in *USA Today* as saying: "He was a sweet guy. Something else was coming through him besides his guitar playing and singing...It's almost like having to play the night that Kennedy died. He'll probably be revered as much as and in the same way as Hank Williams".

"OK I guess everybody here knows about Stevie, so, this is for Stevie. wherever you are."

He then played a poignant version of the Mercer/Mancini classic, "Moon River". Given the song's history and its reference to Huckleberry Finn[6] it seems a fitting one for Dylan to cover and provided a most heartfelt and memorable tribute.

Other covers included a one-off "Stand By Me" and a swaggering version of the Grateful Dead's "Friend Of The Devil", which sounded like a song ready-made for Dylan; as did Little Feat's "Willin'", which, like the previously-mentioned song, was to reappear later and would improve with successive outings.

The shows were uneven, perhaps not surprisingly given the guitarist situation, and even a song like "Lakes Of Pontchartrain" could turn out (relatively) poorly. At Portland OR on August 21st, for example, it was painful to hear Dylan just tiptoe through that song. All the energy and glory of 1988 seemed to have dissipated in the wind.

In the month's break between tour legs, *under the red sky* (the album title was all lower case, differentiating it from the track title which had initial caps) was released to misguided, scathing reviews and disastrous sales. During October rehearsals, the band attempted several of its songs: "Wiggle Wiggle", "10,000 Men", "Under The Red Sky", "2 x 2", and "Unbelievable" (the single from the album). However, only the title track, "T.V. Talkin' Song" and "Wiggle Wiggle" would be played before the year's end.

If Dylan's 1989 casino show provoked a newspaper debate, his decision to play the military academy at West Point NY (October 13th) led to an avalanche of press. Although the set-list included "Masters Of War" and "Blowin' In The Wind", Dylan laid no special emphasis on them or on the venue; the standout track, in fact, was "Trail Of The Buffalo". For Dylan, it was just another show.

As is often the case, while Dylan drew no significance from his actions, others were more than willing to do so. *The New York Times* could not overlook the

6 Dylan is viewed by many as a Finn-like character; a correspondence he alluded to in his notes to *Planet Waves;* "I lit out for parts unknown".

irony of the man "who galvanised the 1960's anti-war movement" performing "Blowin' In The Wind" for an audience of future army commanders:

"Many hard core Dylan fans shook their heads in disbelief as they entered the auditorium," the paper's critic continued, "walking under banners for the Screaming Eagles (101st Airborne Division) and Hell on Wheels (Second Armored Division). They said the concert, in a setting they variously described as 'weird', 'bizarre' and 'the belly of a beast', had a special intensity."

Well it may have had that for them, but there is no indication that for Dylan it was any more than another show on the NET. After the West Point gig, Dylan stayed in New York for another Beacon Theatre residency, starting on October 15th. This was G.E. Smith's last stand, with John Staeheley and César Diaz being tried out onstage too.

In this five-night series of shows Dylan veered from the sublime to the ridiculous, via the successful and the awful. "He shuffled his song-deck with dizzying inconsistency," David Fricke wrote of the opening night in *Melody Maker*, "alternatively flashing aces and jokers like a schizo cardsharp – all too willing, it seemed, to play a losing hand just to upend our expectations. The Protest Prince, The Voice Of A Generation, The Folk-Rock Avenger – none of those Dylans showed up tonight. What we got was the Imp Perverse."

There were various highlights throughout the residency, as there were throughout the remainder of the year. I was collecting all the shows by now and listening to them avidly, but as the NET progressed and more and more shows clamoured for attention, I returned, perhaps inevitably, to compilation bootleg CDs when I wanted to hear late 1990.

With an average of some 100 shows a year, it was almost impossible to keep listening to all the shows (as well as all the other material that was released officially or surfaced amongst collectors), so compilation CDs became very popular. The summer and autumn US tours spawned a double-CD selecting the best or most unusual performances, while the Beacon shows were represented by discs presenting a full show plus the highlights of each night.

19th October 1990, Beacon Theatre, New York NY
(Last night of the 1990 Beacon Theatre Residency)

1 Dixie (Daniel/Decatur/Emmett) (Instrumental)

2 To Be Alone With You

3 Joey (Dylan/Levy)

4 Silvio (Dylan/Hunter)

5 Masters Of War

6 Under The Red Sky

7 Wiggle Wiggle

8 Dark As A Dungeon (Merle Travis) (Acoustic)

9 She Belongs To Me (Acoustic)

10 It's Alright, Ma (I'm Only Bleeding) (Acoustic)

11 Love Minus Zero/No Limit (Acoustic)

12 T.V. Talkin' Song

13 Shooting Star

14 Tight Connection To My Heart (Has Anybody Seen My Love)

15 Gotta Serve Somebody

16 All Along The Watchtower

17 Like A Rolling Stone

*

18 It Ain't Me, Babe (Acoustic)

19 Highway 61 Revisited

20 Maggie's Farm

All the Beacon shows started with a short instrumental, usually "Dixie", though even "Old MacDonald Had A Farm" and "The Battle Hymn Of The Republic" were tried.

The 19th October show had a subdued start with "To Be Alone With You", which was strangely at odds with the "Dixie" opening. It was a lovely choice as first song, though, and we had become accustomed by now to Dylan taking time to warm up. Warm applause greeted the song's close and also the opening of the next song, the unfairly-maligned "Joey". The fire of Hammersmith and Paris way back in February was now replaced by a more sombre shading.

An instantly forgettable "Silvio" at least got Dylan and the band going before a forceful "Masters Of War" launched the show properly; there was a good range to Dylan's vocals, from punchy to cantillating. This set him up for a powerful, deep-voiced rendition of "Under The Red Sky". Sticking with the new album, Dylan then presented us with an enjoyable, up-tempo "Wiggle Wiggle".

The acoustic set opened with the impressive "Dark As A Dungeon", sung with great feeling. "She Belongs To Me" was followed by a rapturously received "It's Alright Ma (I'm Only Bleeding)". This sumptuous acoustic set ended with "Love Minus Zero/No Limit", played with an experimentally exaggerated melody.

"T.V. Talkin' Song" live sounded more like the menacing outtakes that dwarf the released version of the song, without being as powerful as those right-on-the-edge recordings . From there it was straight into *Oh Mercy'* for a memorable "Shooting Star". Following that, there was another outing for the re-christened wonder from the start of the year, "Has Anybody Seen My Love". It was still very welcome here, although Dylan could not quite match February's control.

Things loosened up with "Gotta Serve Somebody", which saw saxophonist Karl Denham, from support act Lenny Kravitz's band, appear onstage. He remained for "All Along The Watchtower" and made a positive contribution to a chaotic, urgent version.

"Like A Rolling Stone" closed the set, but, disappointingly for a song that has changed lives if not worlds, this fell into the category of live grunge. Similarly, the encores lived up to their normal standard and function – magnificent when you are there, but less impressive on tape. On "It Ain't Me, Babe", to his great credit, Dylan made a determined effort to raise the song above a mere sing-along, but no-one told the crowd!

There was a slam bam thank you ma'am "Highway 61 Revisited" and then the evening came to a close with an even more raucous "Maggie's Farm", with Kravitz and his band onstage for a full-blast rock-out.

The last leg of an incredibly packed year saw Dylan and the band pull out many fine performances. The October 25th show in Oxford MS opened with a great rendition of ZZ Top's then current single, "My Head's In Mississippi", and he also performed, for the only time, his 1962 cry against injustice, "Oxford Town". Other treats included a moving "One Too Many Mornings", an understated "Visions Of Johanna", an interesting new take on "Every Grain Of Sand", and a surprising cover of Hank Williams's "Hey, Good Lookin'".

The year's touring ended on November 18th at The Fox Theatre in Detroit. This show opened with yet another surprising live debut, "Buckets Of Rain". This gem from *Blood On The Tracks* was a most welcome farewell present to mark the end of an exhilarating 1990.

CHAPTER FIVE

1991: "You've got to give it your all"

"You hear sometimes about the glamour of the road, but you get over that real fast. There are a lot of times that it's no different from going to work in the morning. Still, you're either a player or you're not a player."

BOB DYLAN TALKING TO ROBERT HILBURN, NOVEMBER 1991[1]

Despite a hectic 1990, Dylan was back on the road again by late January 1991. With another Hammersmith residency beginning on February 8th, we had the dubious pleasure of queuing up all night for tickets in freezing weather. After 1990's problems I was determined not to miss out but I could have done without having to queue overnight three times. This was necessitated by the way the tickets went on sale – first for five nights, then later two more shows were added and then, after that, another one. I say 'necessitated', but this was only the case if you were so obsessed that you needed to be those few extra rows closer to the front.

1 Published February 1992, *The Los Angeles Times* (Magazine)

At least the queuing gave you plenty of time to meet other Dylan fans, renew old acquaintances and make new ones. The morning after the first batch of tickets went on sale, I noticed someone joining the queue between 5 and 6 am. Within minutes he was moaning about the cold. Since I had been there for over six hours already, and in much colder weather, I kindly suggested that he should be grateful to be only three places behind me. This was my first meeting with a certain Joe McShane, with whom I am still going to Dylan shows with some twenty years later.

As the new year dawned it brought news of band personnel changes. Tony Garnier was still playing bass, and César Diaz was still around, but the main guitar duties now fell to new recruit John Jackson. Meanwhile, Chris Parker had been replaced by Ian Wallace on drums. Wallace had an approach that was so consistent it almost came to seem like he played the same on every song, every show, every time.

Still, there were encouraging noises emanating from the first leg of the year's touring. The opening show in Zurich on January 28th gave a debut to "God Knows" from *under the red sky* and featured "Bob Dylan's Dream" from his *Freewheelin'* days, which had not been performed for nearly 30 years. This alone was enough to whet our appetites and after all the queuing, the ticket swapping, the late requests, and organising seats for family and friends, the shows drew nearer, slowly (very) but surely.

Before the Hammersmith residency Dylan played two shows in Glasgow and one each in Dublin and Belfast. They did not augur well, as the band appeared under-rehearsed. To be more precise, completely unrehearsed.

"Bob Dylan shuffled onstage wearing a tartan jacket and looking like he's had a drink," Michael Gray observed in his review of the first Glasgow date. Dylan certainly seemed to be the worse for alcohol at the second Glasgow show, dropping his guitar a couple of times and wandering off stage during "Positively 4th Street", leaving his astonished band to continue without him.

"Muttering into a microphone," Gray continued, "hiding in the oblivion of the guitars and under lights so low it was hard to see him even from the front, Dylan was obviously suffering. 'God knows it's a struggle' was his most heartfelt line last night. It surely doesn't have to be this way."[ii2]

---

2 Michael Gray, *The Guardian*, "Bob Dylan In Glasgow", Feb 5th 1991.

Alas, that nevertheless is the way it was for much of this early bout of 1991 touring. Many people laud the second Glasgow show, which benefited from the most varied and interesting set-list of February. What people seemed to like most was the experience of watching a man teetering on the brink. There's an endless fascination in seeing whether he can keep going, and on the second night in Glasgow it wasn't so much teetering on the brink as slipping over the edge.

As for the Hammersmith residency, it was along the lines of the first night in Glasgow, though there were a few positives. One was that Dylan had come at all, as the Gulf War had seen a sharp decrease in any 'names' travelling from the States to Europe. Another was that Dylan wasn't sullen all the time; indeed for much of the time he was having fun, clowning about on stage. He seemed to veer from being very drunk to – well, sober might be overdoing it, but certainly well in control.

The band, though, were terrible and there seemed to be virtually no rapport between Dylan and those backing him. After "The Man In Me" on Friday 8th, I noted: "It was about then that I realised how pedestrian the band are and how it was restricting Dylan. He seems about to step up a gear and really fly but is brought back to Earth each time." However, it is probably unreasonable to have expected much else. It later transpired, according to a band member, that Dylan had accepted these shows as the money on offer was too good to turn down rather than because he had planned to start the year's touring so early. In addition he was not in the beat of health at the time and it was all done in a rush, with little or no preparation.

It certainly seemed that way to all who attended these shows. John Jackson did nothing but grin maniacally at the audience while playing the same thing on every song. I'm not at all sure what the other guitarists were doing, and the drums sounded like a drum machine with a replay button that had got stuck. Hunched up in the darkness over his microphone, Dylan offered no help, muttering and mumbling his way through the electric sets.

The acoustic sets, as usual, were better, and we got to hear "Bob Dylan's Dream". It was also exhilarating to see Dylan so close up again, with the mannerisms and the facial grimaces that are so much part of his act. Overall though, it was mainly bad memories of bad shows, and I don't mean bad just by Bob's standards. These were bad performances by any measure.

Not that you'd have known I thought so from the reviews I wrote at the time. Buoyed up by having just seen Dylan and in the full flush of running my own Bob fanzine, I wildly accentuated the positive. In addition, I chose for two of my three reviews the Saturday shows, which were the best of what I now acknowledge as a sorry bunch.

I didn't have any tapes to listen to until later the next week so I was still caught up in the 'live' experience, and the Saturday show was much better than the opening night, which I probably didn't yet rate as low as it deserved, so you can imagine that I was still very up for things on the first Sunday of the residence. Yet my notes from the time also betray a touch more realism creeping in.

"'Lay, Lady, Lay" doesn't take off," my tour diary states in black and white. "After a promising opening, the temperature is lowered and he just goes through the motions." "A grunge-rock version of 'All Along The Watchtower' gets its first London airing. Half the audience and band thought it was 'Masters Of War' at the beginning. Well, the same tune is being used for a lot of the songs this week, or so it seems. Maybe they don't know any others?"My notes betrayed other words of caution. After revelling in the "goose-pimple" delights of "Bob Dylan's Dream" I worried over how poor the electric sets sounded in comparison.

Nevertheless, there were some more highlights, such as "Man In The Long Black Coat" and "Shooting Star." I was pleased Bob seemed to be enjoying himself, but even that early in the residency, I could not help noting down "that some of the gestures and mannerisms that look so spontaneous are being repeated in an obviously predetermined manner".

These initial doubts were compounded as the gigs progressed. On the Tuesday night I was centre front row and was startled and delighted when Dylan stormed to the microphone, *sans* guitar for a handheld harmonica and vocal "Tangled Up In Blue". Except this was not a statement of artistry as it had been 1975 or was to be in 1995; instead it was just a hopeless mess. To this day I am still not sure if Dylan had deliberately set aside his guitar, or simply did not realise he had left it behind until after he started singing.

At the time I was most excited by the Saturday show on the 16th, which probably was the best of the Hammersmith run, despite the depressing rumours amongst fans that suggested Dylan had been seen that very afternoon being walked around the Odeon car park to sober him up. Anyway, the comparatively above-par Saturday raised my hopes for a good ending on the second Sunday. Joe remarked shortly before the concert that this was "Dylan's last chance to pull the series of shows out of the fire", but Dylan either did not realise this or did not care. A humdrum performance of yet another standard set-list sent the fans home disappointed and disgruntled. Comments from reviewers in my magazine include many negative comments, such as: "Desecrate ... negative ... lack of imagination ... shambles ... crushing disappointment". There were complaints about Dylan being drunk and uncaring; and unanimous agreement that the band either couldn't play at all, had never rehearsed properly, or both. It was all very dispiriting.

Another major complaint was the lack of variety in the set-lists; while Dylan's unquestionably greatest touring years of the Sixties and Seventies had also sported mostly unchanged set-lists, it was not what we had come to expect or admire about the later touring Dylan of the NET. I saw little point in the complaints at this time, however. After all, if the band were so unfamiliar with these 'standard' set lists, changing them would have been even further beyond them.

I still clung to the belief that there were some bright performances amongst the general gloom, but grim reality dawned when I played the tapes; the inevitable comparison with the previous year was highlighted in all its damning clarity.

It quickly became clear to me that my co-reviewers had been more accurate and direct than I had been. Perhaps unsurprisingly, as this was at a time when I averred, with no hint of a lie, that I would be happy to see Dylan walk on stage and read from the telephone directory.

There were defenders of the shows, as there always are of anything Dylan does (the same could be said for detractors) and a lively debate ran on for the next few issues. Most telling for me was that I stopped playing any tapes from this period soon afterwards and have never enjoyed returning to them. Allan Jones in *Melody Maker*, however, managed to find much to praise in the first Glasgow show despite listing all the problems of the tour in a review that offered more insight and creativity than Dylan managed most nights on stage:

"...The group had apparently not distinguished themselves in either Switzerland or Belgium. They had obviously prepared only a limited repertoire, and for the first time in years Dylan had been forced to play identical sets at successive concerts. Furthermore, there are sinister rumblings about Dylan's drinking. In Belgium he was allegedly pissed virtually senseless, singing off-mike throughout most of the show. When you could hear him, his singing was apparently slurred, more incoherent than ever. Those lyrics he could remember were delivered with an off-handedness that bordered on bored indifference."

Mr. Jones found himself, at the Glasgow show, unable to tell what song was being performed (it was "Stuck Inside Of Mobile, With The Memphis Blues Again"). He compared the "vandalisation" of the song to that witnessed during the 1987 UK tour, and continued:

"Dylan looks as much a mess now as he did then. The ragged comanchero look has been abandoned, however. Dylan now resembles nothing so much as an alcoholic lumberjack on a Saturday night out in some Saskatchewan backwater, staggering around the stage here in a huge plaid jacket and odd little hat. The band, meanwhile, have all the charisma of a death squad in some banana republic ... these people aren't so much under-rehearsed as almost complete strangers to each other and Dylan's music specifically. Dylan, hilariously, doesn't seem to give a f***."

Well, maybe it was hilarious that first time, but it became less so with each repeat viewing as the tour stumbled on.

To see and hear how the band looked and sounded in February 1991, you just need to view television footage of the Grammy awards ceremony from New York on the 20th, when Dylan was given a Grammy Lifetime Achievement Award. Dylan's appearance caused a media stir *par excellence* on two counts. Talking point one was his performance; number two was his acceptance speech.

Dylan performed his damning anti-war[3] indictment, "Masters Of War" – a striking choice given that the Gulf War was still going on and hawkish jingoism was rife. However, since he chose to sing it without a pause for breath, and backed by this hapless/hamstrung band, no-one who did not already know the song would have got the message. In fact, many who were familiar with the

3 Dylan has claimed in interview that the song is not, in fact, 'anti-war'; but I am going to continue to 'trust the tale, not the artist'.

song did not even recognise it. Not only did Dylan's nasal passages sound blocked (he later revealed he'd had a cold) but it seemed he had swallowed a burst of helium before starting to sing. Some observers thought he was singing in Hebrew. The tuxedoed crowd looked on in utter bewilderment. The next day's newspapers marvelled how only Dylan had performed a song with any meaning and purpose, but then, being Dylan, he had made it completely incomprehensible.

So far this was all quite funny, but pure comic genius was still to come in the form of his acceptance speech.

After taking his trophy from a deliriously happy Jack Nicholson, Dylan peered out at the lights and cameras, and hesitantly, began to speak:

"Thank you ... well ... alright ... yeah, well, my daddy he didn't leave me too much ... you know he was a very simple man and he didn't leave me a lot but what he told me was this ... what he did say was ... son ... he said uh ...."

Then Dylan paused, and the pause seemed to go on forever. Time hung still; it appeared as though Dylan had lost it completely. The crowd began to stir, a few titters were heard, then nervous laughter spread. The audience seemed embarrassed for Bob, for themselves, and for the Grammies that were supposed to go so smoothly to a pre-determined schedule of mutual back-slapping. But Dylan had not lost it: his timing was perfect as he extended the pause to a tension-filled breaking point and then concluded:

"He said, you know it's possible to become so defiled in this world that your own father and mother will abandon you and if that happens, God will always believe in your ability to mend your ways. Thank you."

With that Dylan walked off, leaving many a dropped jaw in the bewildered audience, who nonetheless gave him a standing ovation – most likely because they were relieved to see the back of him.

For me, watching this in the UK, it was a fabulous moment. Somehow Dylan had performed live on TV down to the level of his recent Hammersmith shows but, just by his choice of song, had made that noteworthy. Then, after seeming so out of it, so not in control, had pulled off another marvellous little Dylanesque wind-up with his speech. I was basking in the glow of this happy event, when my phone rang. It was someone asking me 'what the hell Bob had thought he was doing, why did he "sing" like that and what the hell was his speech all about?' Oddly enough, I knew then, for sure, that it had been a success and that Dylan had effectively stirred things up again. Once people found out what song he'd been singing, "Masters Of War" was much discussed.

It worked a treat: newspaper after newspaper carried the story along the lines of 'Want to know what Bob Dylan was singing last night?', followed by acres of print about Dylan, about the war, about the Grammies. At a time when his press was far from the adulatory fawning it was to become, it was a refreshing change that most of the comments were generally favourable. Dylan was praised for being an individual, for resisting the cloying show-business approach and for still, all these years later, being a rock 'n' roller who made you think.

The only downside to all this was that I knew that "Masters Of War" had not been made incomprehensible just for this one-off appearance; it was just one of many incomprehensible renditions we'd already heard this year. Still, the choice of song was perfect, and the timing in his speech was superb. At this point I, and nearly everyone watching, thought it was an off-the-cuff speech, another glimpse into the totally unique way he looks at life. However, someone, on the internet newsgroup *rec.music.dylan*, recognised the text as "almost a verbatim account of the commentary of Rabbi Shimshon Rafael Hirsch [the spiritual leader of traditional Jewry in Germany in the mid-19th century] on [Psalms 27:10]":

"Even if I were so depraved that my own mother and father would abandon me to my own devices, God would still gather me up and believe in my ability to mend my ways."

Now, we have no way of knowing if Abraham Zimmerman really taught this to his son or if Bob simply picked it up from a commentary on the Jewish prayer book (Psalm 27 is recited at the morning and evening prayer services during the month before the Jewish New Year), but in any case, the wording is too similar to Hirsch's to attribute this to coincidence.[4]

---

4 "By attributing the words to his father, Dylan is following a long tradition of attribution in Judaism. He can be said to be using 'father'(s) in a wider sense, meaning his heritage." Martin Grossman, *Expecting Rain* website: www.expectingrain.com

The release of *The Bootleg Series*, in the last week of March, was a major illustration of what I talked about in my introduction: the way Dylan always has to exist alongside his own past. The major Dylan 'achievements' of 1991, this compilation and the "Series of Dreams" video, occurred without his input. As an artist he cannot afford to dwell on things like this but he cannot avoid it happening, and it has recurred throughout the NET (2006 is another extreme example). The poverty of his current performances was shown up not just by the memories and tapes of the '88-'90 shows and his impressive back catalogue, but by the release of this three-CD career retrospective, consisting of out-takes, oddities and live tracks. It is a veritable feast of 'bootleg' material including some never heard on the hundreds of Dylan bootlegs released to date.

The compilation was a treat not only for dedicated Dylan fans but for anyone interested in popular music. This was especially so due to Dylan's rather strange principles that had allowed, for example, one of his finest ever songs, "Blind Willie McTell", to remain the preserve of bootleggers until this official unveiling. What for anyone else would have been a collection of cast-offs was instead a release of serious artistic worth. *Record Collector* considered it "The most important archive release we have ever reviewed. Album of the year? It seems certain. Any takers for best compilation of all time?"

It would be no exaggeration to say that the performances on this collection alone show Dylan to be the best lyricist and greatest interpretative singer in the whole of recorded popular music. At the same time it seemed an acknowledgement of the wisdom of those die-hard fans who had collected bootleg after bootleg, tape after tape; the fans who also knew that, magnificent though this collection was, it was just the tip of an astonishing iceberg. Unfortunately, though, these same fans had to endure the nadir of the NET, indeed Dylan's whole career, at the same time as *The Bootleg Series'* vindicatory appearance. The contrast between past and present seemed an unforgivingly cruel one.

Undeterred by, and seemingly unconnected to, the release of these back pages, Dylan continued the dismal start to 1991's touring with a ramshackle 15-date jaunt in America, starting on April 19th. César Diaz had left his guitar duties by now; it might have been a good idea to have had someone else replace him, but that was not to be. This best-be-forgotten period of the NET thankfully drew to a close on May 12th.

That date was less than two weeks before Dylan turned 50 (on May 24th). The welter of publicity for *The Bootleg Series* was nothing compared to the tidal wave of books, magazine articles, newspaper features and editorials, TV programmes and news clips that greeted this landmark. The coverage was exceptional, and exceptionally varied, from the trite to the ultra-serious and every shade between. If Dylan had begun to seem marginalised in the '80s, the NET, the box set and his 50th birthday were pushing him back into the limelight he appears to both detest and court.

Anyway, back to the shows, and you may think that we Europe-based Bob fans had cooled in our frantic need to see the Great Man, after bemoaning the February shows and each of the succeeding leg's tapes as they arrived. Not a bit of it: the mere mention of more dates in Europe in early summer had us scurrying about to secure tickets and arrange travel. It takes a lot to really dampen a Dylan fan's expectations, and nothing at all can dilute the hope that he can turn it around again at any given time. He had done it so often in the past and would again in the future. And, although it may sound odd now, we never knew when his last visit to Europe might be. That long gap between 1966 and 1978 was still hard to forget. This was the third consecutive summer, but we thought this exceptional, unique, even; we had no reason to think that it would continue the way it has.

June 6th found Dylan in Rome, kicking off a three-and-a-half month stint that would take him from Europe to the USA and then on to South America. In the eternal city he opened with an NET debut of "When I Paint My Masterpiece", appropriately enough, as that song also begins in Rome. We also were presented with rather lovely acoustic renditions of Paul Simon's "Homeward Bound" and John Prine's "People Putting People Down". It seemed that Dylan and the band had been working to extend their repertoire and were more focussed than on those dismal February nights. There were some stronger shows than earlier in the year and some genuine highlights; a particular standout being "Coat Of Many Colours" in Budapest. The Italian shows were comparatively strong; Dylan always seems to be raucously received in Italy and has a good time there. Van Morrison was around for a few of the Italian dates; the twosome even played a couple of 'double headers', but the only duets were in Milan, where Dylan added harmonica to two songs during Van's opening set.

Although these shows displayed a degree of improvement, disaster never seemed far away and as the European jaunt progressed, it struck on various occasions, including a dire show at Denmark 's Midtfyn Rock Festival on June 29th.

The Stuttgart show was another disaster but at least it was remarkably so, for a number of reasons. It was the first time in about 300 shows that the set-list did not feature "Like A Rolling Stone". The old war-horse was replaced in the last pre-encore slot (both on that night and for the immediate future) by that, er, other old war-horse from the same album, "Ballad Of A Thin Man". The set structure changed too: instead of six electric songs followed by the acoustic set and six more electric, it was now eight in the first electric set and four in the latter. After a catastrophic attempt at playing the piano on the first song, Dylan abandoned it.

Another exceptional thing about this show was Dylan's inane between-song patter. He introduced "Leopard Skin Pill-Box Hat" as "my fashion song". "Anybody here into fashion?" he asked us. "Like, you know, clothes." Prior to "Knockin' On Heaven's Door" the questions got even easier: "Anybody here hear of Heaven? Well here's a song about Heaven. Heaven's in the title." (I think my favourite quote to the crowd came in Ljubljana: "Thank you everybody! Well, English is my only language. Sometimes not even that." (after "All Along The Watchtower").

Stuttgart also produced one of my most loved NET fan stories. David Bristow's experience there sums up the worst of the NET, 1991 style:

"The show did not go well; the good citizens of Stuttgart were leaving by the third song. I went to a bar after the show, where many of those brave folk who had survived to the end had gathered. Next to me was a serious looking German guy writing down the track list, although one or two songs had eluded him. This was a solemn exercise being conducted by someone who took life, and such lists, very seriously. He asked me to help him fill in the blanks and seemed quite pleased that I recalled a couple of numbers that he had missed. The problem came with the first song of the night, which I informed him was 'New Morning', as indeed it was and was, no doubt, identified as such on the cue sheet given to the band. At least, three members of the band played 'New Morning', but the one at the front had some difficulty with it. As I recall, Bob tried to play the piano/organ and having failed, he decided to sing into the mic on the piano to discover that, very like this version of this song, it wasn't working. He then made his way, perhaps a little unsteadily, over to his guitar before finally arriving at the main mic to deliver a vocal performance that made any live version of 'You Angel You' sound, by comparison, word-perfect.

"Hence my German friend's difficulty in identifying the opener that night. However, when I had to insist that the song was indeed 'New Morning', or at least that is what would appear in the set-list once published, things turned a little ugly. 'But I am knowing the song "New Morning", he tried to explain in his broken English, 'and that is not it'". When I had to confirm it was, he became insistent that he was compiling an authoritative document and that it was essential only accurate information be included. He had the album *New Morning*, he knew the song and whatever else that was tonight, it was not 'New Morning'. He knew I was a fan and must therefore have thought that I was withholding this important information, the correct name of the song, as an act of spite. Hence, I had to leave a Stuttgart bar rather quickly, as otherwise I may have suffered the kind of assault that Bob had launched on the song in question. There were no survivors of that assault and I feared a repeat."

After inflicting two more festival sets on Scandinavia at the end of June, Dylan was back touring in the US, beginning on Independence Day and ending on the 27th of July. Following a shockingly lengthy break of almost two weeks Dylan then found himself playing nine shows in South America, performing mainly greatest hits to crowds that varied from under 2,000 to over 20,000. Dylan sent a "wish you were here" calling card to his regular touring fans by including "Ring Them Bells" for the first time since its botched debut in October 1989.

By the end of the summer, even Dylan was tiring and, after ending the South American jaunt on 21st August he did not resume the NET until October 24th in Corpus Christi, Texas. Exactly a week prior to that, however, he made a high-profile, filmed stage appearance at the 60s night of the Guitar Greats Festival in Seville, Spain, though without his regular NET band.

The Jack Bruce Band backed Dylan on his opening song before Bob switched to acoustic mode for the next three songs. Richard Thompson was on stage for these but seemed unsure of what Dylan was doing. Finally Dylan introduced his former Live Aid partner in crime Keith Richards for a criminal deconstruction of "Shake Rattle & Roll".

Given his poor performances in the year so far, trepidation levels amongst Dylan followers were sky-high as Dylan took the stage. In the opening song, "All

Along The Watchtower", he was clearly struggling; not particularly badly by 1991 standards, but struggling nonetheless. For a Guitar Legend event the guitar playing sounded, to put it mildly, inappropriate. No one seemed to know what they were supposed to be doing, and Dylan was having too much trouble of his own to give any directions. That very predictable choice, "Boots Of Spanish Leather",started very shakily too, and it looked for all the world as if tomorrow would once again be a day spent excusing Dylan's TV appearance.

Then, out of nowhere, something magical happened. Dylan began to find his voice and his control. The improvement continued apace with a decent stab at "Across The Borderline" and a magnificent reading of Mutterlein, Winkler, Rausch and Sigman's "Answer Me, My Love". He had suddenly rediscovered the power of enunciation and seemed engaged in his performance in a way that had been lacking previously. It was not enough to get him good reviews – and to be fair, of the four songs we'd had two poorly performed, one quite decent and one good, so that's hardly surprising - but it gave people like myself hope that the year was not going to be a complete wash-out.

After the closing, chaotic Keith Richards "duet", I spun the video back and watched "Answer Me" again, and again, and again. It was a charming harbinger of better nights to come in 1991.

Seville proved a crucial turning point. Dylan steadily improved, I am not saying it was all plain sailing but if we look at the show from Tulsa, we can see the contrast to earlier in the year, and the way he turned the November shows into triumphs.

It should also be noted that the band had transformed themselves into a much better unit. According to Olof Björner they had taken to calling themselves "the undesirables" in response to all the criticism they had received. Perhaps it was this "us vs. them" spirit of unity that inspired them to greater heights.

30th October 1991 Brady Theater, Tulsa OK

1 New Morning
2 Lay Lady Lay
3 All Along The Watchtower
4 Early Morning Rain (G Lightfoot)

5 I'll Remember You
6 Gotta Serve Somebody
7 Simple Twist Of Fate
8 I'll Be Your Baby Tonight
9 Trail Of The Buffalo (Traditional)(Acoustic)
10 Mr. Tambourine Man(Acoustic)
11 Answer Me, My Love (Mutterlein/Winkler/Rausch/Sigman) (Acoustic)
12 It Ain't Me, Babe (Acoustic)
13 Every Grain Of Sand
14 Everything Is Broken
15 Man In The Long Black Coat
16 Maggie's Farm
*
17 What Good Am I ?
18 Ballad Of A Thin Man

"New Morning" was still the opener and, even though Dylan now seemed to know more of the words than he did in the summer, it was still dreadful; even his "thanks" at the end sounded weary. On a messy "Lay, Lady, Lay", Dylan's self-parodic whining was punctuated by ham-fisted instrumentals. Dylan seemed oblivious that things sounded as bad as earlier in the year. Yet the improvement was just about to take root and grow steadily.

An impossible-to-identify intro led into a passable "All Along The Watchtower", before a throaty but stoic take on Gordon Lightfoot's "Early Morning Rain" raised the show to a new level. "That's one of my real old songs," Bob told the audience. "So old it wasn't even written by me." An acceptable run-through on "I'll Remember You" led to a "Gotta Serve Somebody" that saw Dylan having his usual fun with this song. "That's my response to, er, Arlo Guthrie's song called "Alice's Restaurant", Dylan quipped afterwards.

The audience were then treated to a wonderfully understated "Simple Twist Of Fate", enlivened by daring experiments with the line endings. The opening few bars of this magical song, even before Dylan started singing, elevated the evening and things moved on to a whole other level. Even the ending harmonica solo and band playing in this seemed to have a point as opposed to the mindless doodling evident earlier. It disintegrated at the end, alas, as a coughing Dylan excused what he called "a trick ending".

"I'll Be Your Baby Tonight" was lazy-good-time-Bob. Dylan then found an assured voice for "Trail Of The Buffalo" – "my animal preservation song". He always performs this well, but, even so, the contrast between his vocals here and on the preceding song was extraordinary. "Mr. Tambourine Man" started somewhat hurriedly, then there was a nice little conspiratorial whisper on the second line's final word, "you". Dylan seemed to play around it, eternally circling the song for further new meanings and intonations.

Still in whimsical mood, Dylan introduced "Answer Me, My Love", the song that had so impressed me at Seville, as "My new song, we've got a single coming out". Despite still being bedevilled by an intrusive throatiness he was in full expressive mode, ably abetted by some nifty guitar work. It was a good example of what going to shows on the NET is so often about: a working musician going out night after night and attempting to convey to the audience the very core of what a particular song means to him at that particular moment.

As though it had inspired him as well as us, Dylan got thoroughly into the succeeding, and lyrically contrasting, "It Ain't Me, Babe". He was now singing in an impassioned, deeper, voice. The (successful) attempt at fully communicating "Answer Me" had freed him from the tinny wheeze that had plagued the earlier material. "It Ain't Me, Babe", along with "Simple Twist of Fate", "Answer Me" and "Trail Of The Buffalo" were light years ahead of the rest of the show, and they hinted at Dylan's newly re-discovered commitment to his performing art.

This tape kicked off a period of shows which I have played and enjoyed ever since. To this day when I hear the names Ames, Wichita, South Bend, Evanston, Dayton, Wilkes-Barre or Madison, it is Dylan's November 1991 shows I think of. At Madison, Dylan gave a revealing interview about the NET to Robert Hilburn of *The L.A. Times*.

"Dylan paces impatiently backstage at the Dane County Memorial Coliseum in Madison" Hilburn began. "A snowstorm had snarled traffic, and it has taken Dylan's bus four hours instead of two to get here from Chicago. He seems anxious to get the whole evening over with. Finally, he goes back to the bus to wait out the opening act." After the show, Dylan tells Hilburn flatly, "*That was a useless gig.*" When someone mentioned that the audience seemed to enjoy it, Dylan dismissed them with a wave of his hand. "*Naw, it just wasn't there. Nothin' wrong with the audience. Sometimes the energy level just doesn't happen the way it should. We didn't invite this weather to follow us around.*" Dylan then lapsed into silence.

This is fascinating, as, far from being "useless", the gig was excellent. As for the dismissive comment "*it just wasn't there*", Dylan could hardly have been more unfair on his performance. Still, it was refreshing to hear him demanding more and more of himself. What a contrast to the shambling, uninterested figure that had visited the UK back in February.

"The night before, after the Northwestern show, he had been more talkative, and more philosophical about the ups and downs of touring," Hilburn was relieved to report. "'*You hear sometimes about the glamour of the road,*' he said then, '*but you get over that real fast. There are a lot of times that it's no different from going to work in the morning. Still, you're either a player or you're not a player. It didn't really occur to me until we did those shows with the Grateful Dead (in 1987). If you just go out every three years or so, like I was doing for a while, that's when you lose touch. If you are going to be a performer, you've got to give it your all*'."

Nineteen ninety-two beckoned, and Dylan continued to give it his all.

CHAPTER SIX

1992:
"It's hard to shut it off"

"There comes a point for everything, playing music is a full-time job you know. It's hard to shut if off and turn it off and on again like a faucet".

BOB DYLAN TALKING TO STUART COUPE, 1992[1]

The end of 1991 and the opening of 1992 were dominated for Dylan fans by rumours that the tour was going to end altogether, or that there would be a long gap before he resumed touring or, more encouragingly, that Dylan was going to get together with the surviving members of The Band for a tour of Japan. None of these rumours came true in 1992; nor have they since, despite reappearing with regularity over the ensuing years.

1992's NET legs kicked off with some 20 dates in Australia and New Zealand before Dylan returned to the States via Hawaii, playing his first shows there since 1966. Bucky Baxter, from the Steve Earle band that had supported Dylan

1 Stuart Coupe, telephone interview with Bob Dylan March 13, 1992, published in *The Age* (Melbourne, Australia) Friday April 3, 1992.

back in 1989, had joined the band, providing steel guitar and mandolin to flesh out the sound.

The opening show, in Perth, Western Australia, featured Jimi Hendrix's "Dolly Dagger"[2] and the traditional "Little Maggie", neither of which has been played live since. Another 'first' was the Grateful Dead's "West L.A. Fadeaway", which was rehearsed in February 1989 and appeared twice more in 1992 before resurfacing in 1995.

After the first show, the format for the standard 18-song set-list changed from eight electric songs followed by four acoustic, four electric and then two electric encores to a main set consisting of seven electric songs followed by four acoustic, two electric, one acoustic, one electric. The encores became two electric then one acoustic solo.

The really big news, though, came soon after, with the story that "Idiot Wind" had been played on the 2nd of April. It would be difficult to exaggerate the excitement that boomeranged around the Dylan world at this news.

The song is a central masterpiece in what most fans consider Dylan's greatest album, *Blood On The Tracks*. It was central, also, to the *Hard Rain* album and film and it seemed almost inconceivably great tidings that Dylan had decided to play it again after so many years. It is a song of such transcendent brilliance and weighty import that it was bound to be the engine room of the new shows, the song which all others in the set-list would play off.

Dylan fans were also much engaged by the news that our man had apparently "broken down with emotion" as he sang the lines "he was famous long ago" in "Desolation Row". Dylan had to stop singing and retreat from the microphone to compose himself before finishing the song. Like worried nannies, fans speculated that Dylan was overcome by the fact that he was not as famous as he used to be. Their concern mounted when he next attempted the song (14th April) and again his voice broke at the same line. Whatever the

2 Which Dylan has identified (along with the sublime "The Wind Cries Mary") as his favourite Hendrix track(s).

reason,[3] Dylan sang the song on May 4th in the United States without any problems, as he has done many times since.

As for myself at this time, I was still listening, mainly, to the tapes from late 1991. In 1992 I was not in a position to acquire tapes very rapidly from Australian shows. Technological and contact changes since then mean it would make no discernible difference today whether the shows were in Manchester, Milwaukee or Melbourne. However, back then I had to wait a bit longer. I was, though, working reasonably close to the Australian Embassy in London, and used to go there a few times a week to follow the decidedly mixed Australian press coverage of the tour.

Around the same time, journalist Stuart Coupe asked Dylan why he still spent so much of his time touring. "*There comes a point for everything, playing music is a full-time job you know.*" Dylan muttered. "*It's hard to shut if off and turn it off and on again like a faucet.*" Mr. Coupe observed:

"Possibly that's the (unlikely) key to it all – that it remains in his blood and he feels he has no choice but to continue. That doesn't however explain Dylan's extended period away from touring, some breaks punctuated by occasional performances, lasting as long as seven years. In his excellent biography of Dylan, *Behind The Shades*, Clinton Heylin suggests that this is only one of three periods in his career when Dylan has combined frequent studio activity with prodigious bouts of touring. All have coincided with periods of turmoil in Dylan's personal life, almost as if the road becomes an easy escape from the issues he must face head-on in life away from the road. If that is the case with the Never Ending Tour, Dylan certainly isn't saying anything."

The Australasian leg saw the usual number of one-offs and special performances. Tasmania witnessed a one-off "I Want You" and, perhaps not so luckily, an electric "John Brown". Sydney's shows were blessed with "When I Paint My Masterpiece", "Union Sundown", "Sally Sue Brown" and two magnificent

3 Clinton Heylin speculates that Dylan was moved by the memory of a longstanding ex-girlfriend of his, Carol Lopez, who had taken her own life' and 'apparently named Dylan in her suicide note'. Mr Heylin concludes from this that: *Though Dylan never admitted that he had received her suicide note, one night in April, 1992, when playing in Carol's adopted hometown of Sydney, he performed a rare acoustic performance of 'Desolation Row' and, most uncharacteristically, when he came to the verse about Ophelia – for whom "death is quite romantic" – visibly became moved to tears...* Heylin, Clinton *Behind The Shades: Take Two* Penguin-Viking, UK, 2000.

traditional songs, both utterly perfect for Dylan to cover: "The Lady of Carlisle" and "Delia". Bob had last sung the former in 1961 and the latter in 1960, though it was to be released a year or so later on Dylan's *World Gone Wrong* album, albeit in a different version.

The standouts were not restricted to covers, however. Another Sydney 1992 treat was Dylan in top form on "It's All Over Now, Baby Blue". As for "Idiot Wind", certain lines in it were so heartbrokenly and tenderly sung, the regret expressed could have filled the entire universe. His voice was also strong when reassurance was needed or when steelier emotions were demanded. The band was completely on top of this song and it quite gloriously echoed past triumphs in Dylan's delivery.

When emphasis was expected at the end of a line Dylan sometimes, in fact quite often, hit the middle of the line with the same emphasis instead. Somehow, he made this work and kept the same overall meaning of the original song, while highlighting new tensions and resonances.

The line: "*Blood on your saddle*", was a long-drawn-out moan that took up the same musical space as "*Visions of your chestnut mare shoot through my head and are making me see stars*", which is no mean vocal feat. An additional highlight was "Cat's In The Well" played as a low-down dirty full-out rocking blues.

However, I am running ahead of myself. By the time I did eventually get to hear these shows from Australia, Dylan was already in the States and reports and tapes from those shores were flooding in. Charlie Quintana, who backed Dylan on the David Letterman show in 1984 as a member of The Plugz, was now had joined as a second drummer, making the band a quintet and thereby allowing a wider range and a more dynamic sound. The contrast with the same period a year before was immense. Here was a band who could kick ass, then revert to a subtler, country sound and then rev things back up again when necessary. Dylan himself was singing and playing guitar with much more purpose. Some of these shows were excellent, and "Idiot Wind" was growing in stature with each outing.

The early weeks of May found Dylan in resplendent form; some of the best shows of the NET are claimed to have come from these particular dates. Most people's favourites probably include the show on the 9th at San Jose, where Dylan gave a magnificent version of "Most Of The Time" and what many feel was the best "Idiot Wind" of the year (though arguably an even better version of the latter had been performed just before, at San Francisco's Fox Warfield Theatre). The Fox Warfield show was also notable for an advance in technology, albeit one that seems quaint from a 21st century perspective. This was the first audience video I received that had been recorded on a digital camera, allowing its operator to focus in on Dylan even if quite far back from the stage. Despite still having many of the inherent drawbacks of the video medium, plus the added drawbacks inevitable with unofficial audience tapes, it was an interesting way of watching a show.

5th May 1992 Fox Warfield Theatre, San Francisco CA

1 Rainy Day Women #12 & 35
2 Lenny Bruce
3 Union Sundown
4 Just Like A Woman
5 Stuck Inside Of Mobile With The Memphis Blues Again
6 I Don't Believe You (She Acts Like We Never Have Met)
7 Shelter From The Storm
8 Love Minus Zero/No Limit (Acoustic)
9 Little Moses (Bert A Williams/Earle C Jones) (Acoustic)
10 Gates Of Eden (Acoustic)
11 Mr. Tambourine Man (Acoustic)
12 Cat's In The Well
13 Idiot Wind
14 The Times They Are A-Changin' (Acoustic)
15 Maggie's Farm
*
16 Absolutely Sweet Marie
17 All Along The Watchtower
18 Blowin' In The Wind (Acoustic)

The video opens with a garishly bestriped Dylan singing "Lenny Bruce". Unusually for this song he appears to be merely going through the motions, and things deteriorate with a dreadful "Union Sundown". They soon start to improve, however.

"I Don't Believe You" shows the first signs that it could be a good night. Dylan then tackles a fast-paced, instrumentally driven "Shelter From The Storm" with gusto. His vocals are far stronger, richer and more expansive than in the opening songs. A carefully-played harmonica leads a band running like a freight train into the song's close.

"Gates Of Eden" changes the emphasis and pace. Dylan is now the solitary figure picked out by a single spotlight in the centre of the darkened stage; strumming his guitar, hunched over the microphone, barely moving. An enduring image.

During the following song, "Cat's In The Well", Dylan gives a lovely, knowing smile when he glances back to see Jerry Garcia on stage strapping on a guitar. Garcia was certainly one of the few who could walk onto Dylan's stage and instantly be in tune to what was going on and able to add, almost immediately, something to the overall sound. The Grateful Dead man may have joined "Cat's In The Well" just for a standard blues-type jam, but it gave him time to settle in before the evening's, if not the entire leg's, *tour de force*.

As if by an act of God, the video's picture becomes clear just before "Idiot Wind" begins. The performance is so good that it overcomes even the painful sound quality of the audio track. In fact, this performance stands up well even when compared with the *Hard Rain* version. This song, clearly so important to Dylan himself, is performed with such energy and passion that it is like witnessing a wild stallion ride and wondering who is trying to buck whom – the rider or the horse. Garcia on guitar embellishes the song perfectly as Dylan is driven to ride that demon horse harder and harder.

"Idiot Wind" is clearly presented as a centrepiece. "You'll find out when you reach the top/You're on the bottom" is sung with a lived-in knowledge unequalled even by that famous, wry couplet from "Love Minus Zero/No Limit": "There's no success like failure, and failure's no success at all". Dylan then seizes the harmonica almost desperately: music just erupts through it, in marked contrast to those occasions in 1991 when he had played the harmonica simply for the sake of it. To leave that video and return to the world around you took a bit of adjusting.

The American leg finished on the 23rd in Las Vegas, where Dylan, appropriately enough, played his gangster song, "Joey". Dylan was in Las Vegas for his birthday the next day; something that was much commented on at the time.

For most of June Dylan was off the road, not that he spent the entire month resting. Instead, he found time to record some intriguing sessions with Dave Bromberg, covering a number of old standards, some of which have since appeared on the NET and at least one of which, "The Lady Of Carlisle", he had already played in 1992.

Then it was back to Europe, but not to the UK. The closest he came to Britain was three dates in France on June 30th, July 1st and July 2nd, all of which I duly attended. The last of these dates was not a full show, but rather an appearance at a festival at Belfort. These were, given the tapes that preceded them, a disappointment; Dylan and the band sounded played out. Comparatively speaking, the fire was gone from a lot of the performances, particularly the electric sets. Notwithstanding this, there were still a number of high points, including "Girl On The Green Briar Shore" from the show on June 30th, yet another traditional, acoustic classic wrought into being with Dylan's incomparable interpretative powers. The acoustic sets were the highlight of each of these shows. Dunkirk also boasted a lovely "Love Minus Zero/No Limit", and the next day at Rheims instead of "Girl On The Green Briar Shore" we got the marvellous "Newry Town" (aka "The Roving Blade").

Dunkirk marked the last time "Idiot Wind" appeared as a regular feature of the set. Thrilling though it was for me to finally witness this song live, there could be no denying that this was a poor rendition. It was no surprise that Dylan would henceforth play it only occasionally, before dropping it altogether.

At the last show in Belfort, Dylan was due to headline but he swapped places with Bryan Adams at the last minute. Apparently this was so that after he played Dylan could still get to his favourite restaurant before it closed. Dylan's Belfort set was consequently brief, but it did include a marvellous rendition of "Little Moses" in the acoustic set. Dylan referred to this as "the spiritual part of the show". Incontrovertibly, of the three shows I attended in France, the three stand-out songs were "Girl on the Green Briar Shore", "Newry Town" and "Little Moses". On the way back to our touring bus, I ranted that Dylan should restrict his sets to acoustic performances of pre-19th century traditional folk songs (or at least songs as similar to those as "Little Moses").

Although the spiritual heights of these three gems were not reached elsewhere, I remember, at Belfort, being profoundly moved during the closing "Blowin' In The Wind". Standing on a French hill, wistfully wondering when or if I would see him again. As ever, there was a tangible fear of the NET actually ending.

The 5th of July in Italy saw the first live version ever of the song "2 x 2". It clearly needed more work, but by now Dylan was running out of steam. This European leg ended on July 12th in Antibes, France at the Juan-les-Pins festival. Dylan opened the show with "Hey Joe", basing his performance on Jimi Hendrix's classic rendition and thereby sending our thoughts back to Australia and "Dolly Dagger". In this case Dylan was prompted by the previous band ending their set with that song. It was a neat idea but Dylan did not seem to remember the song too well. This was the first disappointment of many in a very depressing show. Dylan's voice was shot and the band seemed clearly spent.

If this was a sad ending to the leg, Dylan remained undaunted. After a mere month's break, August 17th found him at Toronto's Massey Hall for the start of another North American jaunt . He was back in top form, too, with a very adventurous set-list for the opening show including "Wiggle Wiggle". Dylan also treated the audience to an unexpected "Heart Of Mine" and reprised another stunning acoustic treat from earlier in the year, the traditional "Female Rambling Sailor". This was another in a long line of maritime songs, such as "House Carpenter", "Golden Vanity", "Like A Ship On The Sea", where Dylan had his audience seeing, smelling and tasting the sea air.

"Like A Rolling Stone" surprisingly reappeared after a long lay-off, before vanishing again, while one of the other highlights was an electric "I Dreamed I Saw St. Augustine". As was to become a fairly usual custom during legs of the NET, Dylan's audacious opening sets were not repeated afterwards, though some surprises continued to pop up here and there.

If the set-lists did not continue to be particularly adventurous, the performances most certainly did. Refreshed from their post-Europe break, Dylan and the band had returned to the road in fine fettle, the highlight being a marvellous five-night Minneapolis residency at the Historic Orpheum Theatre, which Dylan had once co-owned with his brother, David. Dylan pulled out all the stops, watched on the final night by both his brother and mother. Despite some sad farewells at this juncture; "Idiot Wind" was played for the last time to date during these shows, and Charlie Quintana was about to leave the band to be replaced by Winston Watson, this residency still stands as one of the high-points of the NET. Every night seemed special in its own right, but the greatest pleasure is to listen, and re-listen, to all five shows in sequence.

Twenty shows later Dylan took a four-week break before rounding off the year with a further score of shows in America, plus a short performance at an extraordinary event in his honour, held on October 16th at New York's Madison Square Garden: "Columbia Records Celebrates The Music Of Bob Dylan". 'Extraordinary' because it seemed such an un-Dylan-like affair. An air of self-congratulatory phoniness hung over the proceedings, dispelled only by a furore surrounding Sinead O'Connor, and then by the party atmosphere engendered by Neil Young.

This tribute show was broadcast on pay-per-view TV in the US and clocked in at approximately three and a half hours. During the concert, more than two dozen musicians, backed by Booker T and the MGs with G.E. Smith on extra guitar as 'musical director', sang about 30 Dylan (and two non-Dylan) songs.

Most of the guests were predictable: Lou Reed, Johnny Cash, Eric Clapton, George Harrison, Tom Petty & the Heartbreakers, Roger McGuinn and Neil Young were all present and correct. However some acts, such as O'Connor, were considerably more removed from the Dylan story, while the likes of Joan Baez, Bruce Springsteen and Van Morrison were notable by their absence.

Performances were generally worthy at best, though Neil Young lit up the event with an incendiary "All Along The Watchtower" and an impressive "Just Like Tom Thumb's Blues". Lou Reed deserves praise for his brave attempt at the difficult "Foot of Pride", though it may have helped if he had not had to strain to read every line on his autocue. At least, however, he had attempted one of only a few songs not from the '60s canon. Another was to have been Sinead O'Connor singing "I Believe In You", Dylan's song of how his faith in Jesus had brought scorn from former 'friends'. It would have been apt, as scorn had been heaped on Sinead after she recently ripped up a picture of the Pope on *Saturday Night Live*, in protest at child sexual abuse by Catholic priests.

Introduced by Kris Kristofferson as someone whose name has become "synonymous with courage and integrity", O'Connor was greeted with scattered cheers, but mostly boos. As the booing continued, the 25-year-old singer stood motionless on stage until Kristofferson tried to offer encouragement. "Don't let the bastards get you down," he said, his words picked up by the microphone. "I'm not down," she answered in a steady voice; but the hostility took its toll. Apparently too shaken to attempt the Dylan song, O'Connor launched into a defiant a cappella version of the song she had performed on *Saturday Night Live*: Bob Marley's "War," a battle cry for equality taken from a speech by Haile Selassie, the late Ethiopian emperor. Afterwards, Kristofferson again tried to comfort her as she left the stage in tears to the sound of more mixed boos and cheers.

It was a galvanizing segment in an otherwise mostly predictable event. A number of journalists later pointed out the irony of a young singer-songwriter facing a hostile crowd at, of all events, a tribute to Bob Dylan. Sinead herself bitterly complained that Dylan had not come out and defended her. This controversy and recrimination fortuitously distracted the media, for the most part, from Dylan's own performance.

Dylan took the stage dressed smartly but looking as nervous and uncomfortable as you would expect him to be in front of the cameras on such an occasion. His choice of songs was fine, if totally rooted in his pre-electric days, but his performance of them was abysmal.

Dylan's voice, at this period of the NET, took some time to warm up. It was usually only after a lung-bursting rendition of the regular third song "All Along The Watchtower" that he could shake off a rusty croakiness. One can only surmise that he had not warmed up here, as that croak was all too evident. He opened with "Song for Woody", a doubly apt choice, being his own tribute to an artist who influenced him and because it was from his 1962 debut album, the anniversary of which the night was supposedly celebrating. (That the album was released on March 19th 1962 and the celebration was held on October 16th was yet another unexplained oddity about the entire affair.) Unfortunately it was his worst ever performance of the song, his voice sounding alarmingly ravaged.

Dylan's vocals were no better on the plodding "It's Alright Ma" that followed. His verse of "My Back Pages" – various guests sang a verse each – was so poor he had to re-record the lines after the event before the 'video single' could be released. After the grand finale Dylan returned to the stage and performed a creditable "Girl From The North Country". It sounded utterly transcendent in the light of what had gone before, and at least hinted at what the whole night had been in tribute to.

Dylan's performance aside, the question lingered as to why he had gone along with the whole idea; it was surely anathema for a man famed for not looking back. He was certainly well rewarded for his efforts; to the astonishment of many this was not a charity event. Tickets ranged from $50 to $150. Pay-per-view was just under $20 and the inevitable double CD and double video soon followed. The event generated a huge profit and the main beneficiary was Bob Dylan.

It is neither my place nor my wish to begrudge Dylan the money – all the better, I thought, if it allowed him to keep touring small halls on the NET – but he could have raised similar sums from a more challenging event. An event featuring more Dylan, perhaps, or Dylan interacting with his guests more. A roster list could have been organised that properly reflected Dylan's influence and contribution over the three decades. Looking back on the event twenty years further down the line makes it look even more ill thought out. Dylan has been phenomenally active every year since then, recording, creating an inventive 'memoir', painting, producing, becoming a DJ and touring every single year. Thinking back now to this event to commemorate the first three-fifths (so far) of a career makes it all the more puzzling. The mainstream press took the view that it was a farewell event. A little research would have made it clear to them that it was not; but to be fair, it was a natural conclusion to jump to.

Obviously it would have helped too if Dylan had looked and sounded in better health. The tabloid press ventured that the event had been quickly put together before Dylan left us altogether; his press office even had to issue a denial. "It's just the way he looks after 30 years in the rock business," Bob's spokesperson told the press. "OK, he looked a bit confused, like he'd been let out of the cage for a while, but that's him."

"That's him" at events like this maybe, but Dylan's life for years had consisted of touring, rather than being in a cage, almost unable to perform. So, without pause, he was back on the NET in proper concert settings, and back on form.

For example, nine nights later in Providence RI a much more Dylan-like night opened with Muddy Waters' "I Can't Be Satisfied" and included a live debut of "Dear Landlord" from the flawless *John Wesley Harding*. For most of the rest of the show Dylan's vocals remained excellent, with "Mama, You Been On My Mind" being particularly affecting.

"The Providence tape is an absolute delight," fan Guy Borg enthused in a letter to my fanzine. "He seems to be trying to do something special with every phrase – and pulling it off! The solo acoustic slot simply knocked me out – it could've been 1962, but it was better!"

It was hard to believe that this was the same man who had croaked his way through his part at Madison Square Garden. Yet, how like Dylan it was to perform so poorly at a celebration of his career, and play so well either side of it. How like Dylan, too, to answer that bloated celebration of his incomparable writing talents by releasing an album of covers, *Good As I Been To You*, on October 30th.

The track listing and performances are worth noting, as they contrast sharply with what Dylan was doing with songs from the same oeuvre on the NET. Dylan was still able to think in vinyl terms and the LP, as released in that format, was:

Side One: Frankie and Johnny (Albert); Jim Jones; Black Jack Davy; Canadee¬i-o; Little Maggie; Sittin' On Top Of The World; Hard Times.

Side Two: Step it Up & Go; Arthur McBride; Tomorrow Night; You're Gonna Quit Me; Diamond Joe; Froggie Went A Courtin'.

Although many Dylan fans were disappointed that the album contained no Dylan originals, my first reaction was to be thrilled that he had done a whole LP of NET-type acoustic songs. Yet, one performance of "Little Maggie" in Australia earlier in the year excepted, they were all new to his repertoire.

However, my first reaction does not paint an accurate picture, as not only the content but the performances on the album were not, as one might have reasonably assumed, born of the same intent as the live covers of traditional songs on the NET

The LP, in other words, did not follow the blueprint of Dylan's live interpretations of songs such as "Eileen Aroon", "Little Moses", "Female Rambling Sailor". Instead, these album tracks saw Dylan mimicking, his inimitable tones aside, other people's versions of these mostly traditional songs. From a vast array of potential source versions, even a cursory listen left no doubts which were Dylan's models. Rather than giving us interpretations, he gave us copies: of Nic Jones doing "Canadee-i-o", of Paul Brady doing "Arthur McBride", of De Dannan doing "Hard Times", and so forth.

I have a CD of each of these 'source songs', followed by Dylan singing his take. It is uncanny, and certainly not what one would have thought from the NET's transforming performances of songs drawn from the same wellsprings of inspiration. Presumably Dylan did this in tribute to the originals. If so, though, it seemed strange that there were no credits on the sleeve notes and that the arrangements were, risibly, copyrighted as Dylan's own. This was a source of some disquiet.

None of which prevents the album itself being a fine listening experience; after all, the standard of the songs is exceptional, and they sit well within Dylan's vocal range in the period. Another sharp contrast to the NET was to be found in Dylan's brilliant guitar playing. The same man that had merely strummed his way through countless acoustic sets was now to be heard dexterously picking the guitar strings and providing effective, understated embellishments. How I wished he had played guitar like this every time I had witnessed "Boots Of Spanish Leather", "It Ain't Me, Babe" etc. (There was, perhaps unsurprisingly, a noticeable improvement in this regard in the live shows that followed *Good As I Been To You.*)

Albums and tribute shows come and go, but the NET rolls on unhindered and the year's touring continued to a formidable climax at West Palm Beach FL on November 15th. The previously discussed Providence show was only one of a series of top-notch performances. It was as though, having survived the 'tribute' night, Dylan could once again dedicate himself to giving the NET his all. Wilkes-Barre PA from November 1st remains a personal favourite, while Clearwater FL on the 11th found Dylan in fine form, with a splendidly inventive set-list.

The night after Wilkes-Barre saw Dylan perform "Farewell to the Gold", a mournful testament to the lot of the miner, which he sang with conviction. One presumes this song had once been destined for *Good As I Been To You*, as it featured on the Nic Jones album, *Penguin Eggs*, that had clearly affected Dylan around this time. Other highlights of the leg included two powerful readings of "Disease of Conceit", two outings also for the ever-welcome "I Dreamed I Saw St Augustine", and a one-off return for Lowell George 's "Willin'".

By the time he had stormed through Florida, Dylan's voice was so ravaged at that final show in West Palm Beach that he had to omit the electric encores. Notwithstanding this, he was in spell-binding form, compensating for vocal shortcomings with a *tour de force* of harmonica playing as though determined that 1992's almost ton-up of shows would come to a glorious conclusion.

CHAPTER SEVEN

1993:
"I'm still trying to figure out what some of them are about."

"The songs I recorded in my past, they're almost like demos. I'm still trying to figure out what some of them are about. The more I play them, the better idea I have of how to play them."

BOB DYLAN, 1993[1]

Nineteen ninety-three began with a live prelude to the NET's resumption on January 17th, when Dylan appeared at the Bill Clinton Inauguration Concert at the Lincoln Memorial in Washington DC. There was something moving about seeing Dylan in such a setting; so many echoes and memories resonated that one hardly had time to reflect on Dylan playing for a President younger than himself. The times sure had a-changed since Dylan had sung "Only A Pawn In Their Game" at the same venue at the climax of the March on Washington some thirty years ago.

1 Dylan talking to *The Chicago Tribune*'s Greg Kot, August 1993.

The performance, of "Chimes Of Freedom", was splendid enough in a completely Dylanesque way; that is, it did not kow-tow to the setting or the unfamiliar audience. The President seemed pleased that Dylan was there, Hillary seemed to think the whole thing was a joke (a view shared by many, I would venture) and Chelsea looked as though Bob had descended from another planet (potentially another popular view).

With Dylan's inaugural duties completed, it was time to pick up the threads of the NET. By now Ian Wallace[2] had quit and for the entire year the band comprised of John Jackson, Bucky Baxter, Tony Garnier and Winston Watson, the drummer who had replaced Charlie Quintana during the late summer, 1992 North American tour.

The year's touring began in Ireland before returning once again to the Hammersmith Odeon, which was now renamed the Apollo. You will be familiar by now with the traditional build-up to this; again a few dozen queued for front row seats. Expectation was high, especially with this series of shows coming so soon after the previous September's acclaimed Minneapolis residency.

As far as Hammersmith memories went, the glamour of 1990 offset the disappointing 1991 memories. It was an exciting time at our flat too, as again family and friends plus old and new Dylan acquaintances came to stay.

After all the seemingly interminable hype, at last it was time for the first show. Perhaps the opening minutes should have warned us that this was not going to be an easy ride. Dylan took to the stage, glowered at the microphone for being at the wrong height, adjusted it, stood back, prepared to start the opening song and stepped forward to the microphone again, which promptly fell to its lowest setting with a loud clunk. A brave roadie scrambled on to try to rectify the problem as Dylan retreated to the back of the stage.

As it turned out, this was one of the highlights of a night that, "I And I" aside, was as dull as the proverbial ditchwater. As ever the acoustic section was head and shoulders above the rest of the show, but it could achieve that elevation on this occasion by being merely passable.

---

2 Ian Russell Wallace passed away on 22 February 2007, a victim of cancer.

Winston Watson looked and, initially anyway, sounded great on drums; unfortunately he drummed the same way on every track. There was no variation between songs or portions of songs, and no acknowledgement paid to melodies. This was not necessarily Winston's fault; either Dylan purposely hired a drummer with no flexibility, or he hired a quite capable drummer and instructed him to play this way. It would appear the latter was closer to the truth. Watson was not necessarily a hapless drummer; rather, he was a drummer haplessly following orders.

This was such an unnecessary waste, especially as there can rarely have been a band member more obviously in love with Dylan's songs and singing. In the times when he was no required in the acoustic set, night after night Winston stood at the stage side and listened intently and with pleasure to Dylan's performance. He claims he never missed a single song, and I believe him. It is a great pity he wasn't allowed to express his love of Dylan's music by playing more often with, rather than against, the spirit of the songs.

The band had been crying out for a new drummer before Winston joined in September '92. It seemed then that he would be the answer; but as these shows progressed the worrying tendency to have him over-playing, or playing at the wrong time, began to surface.

Even more deleteriously, soon songs were being stretched out not just by unnecessary drum breaks but by all the instruments on stage: inane doodling and ill-timed thumping forever threatened to draw a song to a painful close, only for the musicians to go back and repeat themselves in ever-expanding loops of mediocrity. By the end of Hammersmith 1993 the only thing more stretched out than the songs was the audience's patience.

These long 'endings' were bad enough; even worse were the obtrusive 'instrumental passages' during the songs. These deadening interludes sapped any pleasure that could have been gleaned from a week of rigid set-lists. Theoretically Dylan's creative experimentation with song structure can be far more rewarding than his experiments with the set lists. However, at this stage of the NET it simply did not deliver. There's a difference between musically inventive instrumental passages transforming songs into something new and vibrant, or giving songs space to breathe in new ways, and the meaningless doodling and uninspired scratching of these 1993 dates.

Taking 8th February as an example, Dylan and the band gave us a near 12-minute "Tangled Up In Blue" and an "I And I" and a "Highway 61 Revisited" both at over 9 minutes. Plus "Simple Twist Of Fate" and "Mr. Tambourine Man" were both over 8 minutes and, really stretching things, "It Ain't Me, Babe" and "Pretty Peggy-O" were both almost so, too. Duration isn't everything, of course; a 16-minute "Simple Twist Of Fate" would do very nicely, thanks, if the minutes were spent constructing a performance that moved the listener, rather than just extending the song for no apparent reason.

"Pretty Peggy-O" started well enough; it is a magnificent song and Dylan sang it, as he nearly always does, with tremendous empathy. The first two minutes were really moving and I was totally into it. Then the band played 'doodle doodle' for a minute; which was just about acceptable, it gave Bob time enough to rest his voice before coming back with the concluding two verses. Then, at about 3 minutes 45 seconds, the song was over. Except it was not; it was back to 'doodle doodle doodle' for nearly another minute before the first verse was repeated. A further bout of 'doodle doodle doodle drum drum doodle doodle' brought the song past the 6-minute mark with all impetus lost along the way. Even then we were not finished; though by now no-one seemed to know what to do next. More arbitrary doodling took the song staggering towards an end at 7 minutes 12 seconds. Finally, each musician stopped playing at a different moment, so there was a little guitar flourish of some other melody and a cymbal arbitrarily hit to bring it to a ragged close.

From the same night, we can hear how Bob and his gang vandalised quite possibly the best song he has ever written, "Tangled Up In Blue". It started, and started, and started ... whipping the crowd into an excited state of expectation. Then still it started and started, to no effect. The build-up was over-extended and the anticipation gradually waned. There was some nice harp after a while and it sounded like Dylan was finally going to start singing ... yet still he did not. Instead, the intro began all over again.

Finally, just before 3 minutes had elapsed, Dylan croaked the first line. This is a Dylan crowd favourite and Dylan sang, albeit hoarsely, with some intensity. The crowd's excitement seemed to culminate at about the 5:40 mark, when there was an instrumental break. That was not the problem, there was every reason for it to be there. The problem was that rather than end where it should it just went on and on, sounding like the endless opening all over again. By the time Dylan eventually returned to the microphone for the epic last verse, he sung it without an iota of feeling. The song's real end came after just under 12 minutes, but it sure felt a lot longer than that.

These arrangements, and particularly the long song endings, contributed to make this the dullest residency I have attended or probably ever listened to. Not the worst; despite all my points above these were far better performances than Hammersmith 1991, but the most uninteresting. Even the actively bad has at least some kind of life-force behind it. Of course, it would be remiss of me not to add that there were intermittent silver linings in '93, such as: an electric "Under The Red Sky" and the aforementioned "I And I", but overall this was a boring week of shows. 'Boring' is simply not a word I ever thought I would have to use to sum up a set of Dylan performances.

Dylan's camp followers are nothing if not a disparate and self-analytical bunch, so I should point out that many fans thought the shows excellent; the media reviews were also mixed, and ranged all the way from hatchet jobs to stellar praise. Those who did not share the positive feeling over these shows naturally questioned whether our boredom was our fault for going every night. It is certainly a point worth considering; I am certain that I would not have minded the instrumental fooling around as a one-night experiment. Dylan has often railed against those who spend their lives going to so many of his shows, steadfastly claiming to be playing to the ones who come along more infrequently. There are times in the NET when his shows reflect the very opposite but on many occasions, as we will see throughout this book, he consciously sets out to attract a different audience and, indeed, goes as far as to denigrate and attempt to discourage the more dedicated concert-goers.

Another thing that irked we greedy fans back in the UK in 1993 was a lack of originality in the set-lists; to counter that though, as ever with Dylan, there were many more changes over the nights than you would expect from anyone else. They lacked, however, the truly surprising: a new song, one not played for years, a cover you never expected to hear.

After Hammersmith I followed the tour on to Holland where, thanks due to Willelm Meuleman's hospitality, I saw two shows in Utrecht that both featured the surprise choice of Hank Snow's "I'm Moving On" as the set opener. The following night, in Eindhoven, the opener was Johnny Cash's "Folsom Prison Blues".

I was no longer in tow as Dylan continued through Europe, ending in Belfast on 25th February. The shows were improving, though not radically so. Even better than anything on stage, though, was Dylan's arrival in Belfast the day before his show. A few precious minutes of video footage of this circulates amongst Dylan fans and collectors. In a scene that Beckett or Pinter would have given their right arm for, Bob in full 'dressed-as-a-bum' mode ambles around near a bus stop. A woman waiting for a bus looks decidedly, and understandably, worried by his appearance and demeanour. Dylan seems very confused. For one glorious moment it appeared as though the woman was going to hand him a coin.

Not one to rest for long, Dylan resumed touring in the States in mid-April, for a short run of shows leading up to an appearance on Willie Nelson's TV broadcast 60th birthday bash. Dylan, unusually for a TV programme, was in splendid form, contributing wonderful vocals on the sublime "Pancho and Lefty" and performing a sterling version of the heartbreaking "Hard Times" with his touring band.

Six weeks later Dylan was back in the UK, kicking off another summer European jaunt with an appearance at the Fleadh festival in London's Finsbury Park. Now, a day spent waiting on Dylan at a festival is not usually to my liking but this one was enlivened when I bumped into John Jackson and Winston Watson outside one of the beer tents. They were very friendly and we chatted about the year's shows so far and passed some pleasant time in the sunshine. By the time Dylan hit the stage the weather, predictably, had changed to a downpour.

Dylan played a truncated but fairly standard set. Non-Dylan fans left in fairly large numbers throughout the early numbers. Not Paul Stevenson though. Paul was my boss back in 1989 who had covered my work in Eastbourne so I could reach the Glasgow shows. Our paths had long diverged but Dylan brought us back in touch, as he does for me with so many people. Paul told me that his girlfriend thought Dylan was pretty good, though he did also tell me that the other couple he was with thought Dylan's singing was a joke and "fell about laughing". It would be reasonable to say that Dylan's unique enunciation was not at its clearest, and that the rain and the lack of any particular brilliance on stage had people running for transport home.

Years later I had another boss at work who had been at the show, and she remembered Dylan's performance as being "rank rotten", so "bad" that she "left after a few songs". I tried to explain that with Dylan, often the audience has to put in a bit of work to contribute to the occasion. She replied, not unfairly, that it was more than she was prepared to do.

This is part of the problem with these festival shows. It is one thing for Dylan to expect his experienced fans to be players in the NET's never-ending drama; but for the curious, the one-album-owning, and the Greatest Hits crowd, it is asking too much. Paradoxically, Dylan has throughout the NET built his set around a spine of classic '60s hits as though he wants to attract these people and, as discussed above, openly courted them in preference to his diehard troops. Being Dylan, the oft-named 'imp perverse', he then turns up each summer and performs those hits in a way that drives them away.

There was one saving grace at this performance, though, and it came in the last song. Just as the only good thing of Dylan's at 1992's Madison Square Garden tribute had been his closing, solo "Girl From The North Country", so at the Fleadh 1993 he only opened his true voice on the last song, a magnificent "It Ain't Me, Babe". Full of yearning, knowledge and courage, it somehow paid tribute to the need for interdependence while simultaneously declaiming the sovereignty of the individual. It was an extremely moving performance, but by now the only witnesses in the pouring rain and sodden, muddy field were those who always knew he could perform this well anyway.

The press, no doubt alienated by both the weather and Bob's performance, were merciless in their criticism. Meanwhile, as his fans reacted to the adverse reviews by proclaiming the gig to be far better than it was, Dylan was trekking around Europe again, via a few dates in Israel.

In Lyons, a back problem that had been plaguing him for years caused that great rarity, a cancelled show. Dylan has often performed shows even when quite ill, and has been known to stick to the maxim "the show must go on" even with a raging temperature. Understandably, then, the Dylan fan world was worried this was something serious. Fortunately Dylan was back on stage the next night, and the NET continued. This leg came to an end at the Gurten Festival in Berne, Switzerland on July 17th.

Dylan, however, did not fly straight back to the States. He was not finished with Europe yet and had saved one final 'performance' for Camden Town, in London, where he appeared, unheralded, on July 21st to film a promotional video. It turned out to be my favourite Dylan 'show' ever.

That was the day when I met Dylan for the first and to date the only meaningful time, the only time where it was basically a one-to-one meeting. Needless to say I was as excited as I have ever been, possibly even more so than first seeing him live in 1978 if that is actually possible.

I have decided to move the story of this meeting to the first appendix of this book. It is undoubtedly part of 'my' NET but it has nothing to do with Dylan's; on the other hand it also affected my subsequent NET experiences on all sorts of levels, from the profound to the mundane. Simply put, at the most basic level, I was not going to be as excited the next time I heard, say, "All Along The Watchtower" while being squeezed, pushed and jostled with Dylan a considerable distance away, having just had a hug from the man himself. I leave it to each reader whether they want to skip to the appendix and read that now to keep my story in chronological order, or to keep reading about the 1993 tours in order. If you choose the latter, I cannot overstress the effect it had on me, but that was mostly revealed through hindsight.

There was not time to stop and analyse its impact back then though, as I seemed to have been transported into a Bob-filled universe. Suddenly the TV news programmes, newspapers and magazines were full of his attempts to buy a house in London's unfashionable Crouch End.

We found out where his favourite Indian restaurant there was, and his favourite choice from their menu. Fans camped out on his prospective purchaser's lawn. Needless to say all the attention meant the deal never came to fruition.

I was still wandering about in a happy daze at having met the Man when he hit the road again on 20th August, for a near two-month stint in the States.

By mid-1993, Dylan's constant touring was having, what seemed then, an obvious effect on his ability to sell tickets,[3] so the trick this late Summer/Fall was to

3 Though, as we shall see later, this effect turned out to be neither self-sustaining nor, in fact, 'obvious' at all.

have a joint tour with Santana. This had a number of effects both off and on stage. Firstly, there was heightened media attention and an incredible amount of newsprint was consumed with comparing the current times to the Sixties. Also, Dylan's songs seemed tighter as he had less time to play, and when performing next to Santana no one is going to sound like they are the ones serving up the meaningless instrumental doodling.

Dylan was even roped in to do some interviews to help promote this tour. *"My whole thing has been about disallowing demagoguery,"* Dylan told *The Chicago Tribune*'s Greg Kot. *"The songs I recorded in my past, they're almost like demos. I'm still trying to figure out what some of them are about. The more I play them, the better idea I have of how to play them."*[4]

NET followers may feel, as Kot himself pointed out, that "This may explain why Dylan seems perpetually inclined to tamper with his classics, messing with chords and altering his phrasing as he turns 'Like a Rolling Stone' into a shuffle or 'All Along the Watchtower' into a dissonant rocker."

In response to Kot's musings, Dylan responded, tellingly: *"My audience has changed over a couple of times now. A lot of 'em don't even know 'Like a Rolling Stone'. They're not enchanted by the past, and I don't allow the past to encroach on the present."*

Meanwhile, Gene Stout of *The Harmony Detroit Free Press*'s attempt to find out why Dylan was touring with Santana provoked a straightforwardly honest, and therefore comically revealing, answer:

"Somebody just asked me about it one day, and I said I'd do it..." Dylan told Stout, trailing off. The obvious explanation was that it was being done to try and shift tickets. In this it was only partially successful. Some venues were half full, or less. Sacramento's Cal Expo Amphitheatre apparently had 6,000 in a 14,000 capacity. According to the reviewer, half the audience left during Dylan's set and he ended up playing to 3,000. It barely needs to be pointed out that those 3,000 would have preferred a two hour Dylan-only set in a smaller auditorium, and that this would have been a better experience for Dylan too.

4 *Ibid.*, note i

It seemed more of a touring event than a touring experience, and is not one of my favourite periods performance-wise. Dylan's constricted set time also meant there was less manoeuvrability in song choice. "It'll be difficult cutting it down to an hour," Dylan told the press.

Yet Dylan did still pull out a few surprises, such as ending a show with "One More Cup Of Coffee", or introducing, to very good effect, *Good As I Been To You*'s "Black Jack Davey". The most astonishing song appearance was "Series Of Dreams", on 8th September at the Wolf Trap in Vienna VA.

"Series of Dreams" was an out-take from 1989's *Oh Mercy* album, and how it was left out Bob alone knows. It has appeared on official releases since, firstly as the closer to *The Bootleg Series I-III,* and a magnificent video was created at that time to promote it. Dylan himself, alas, was not involved in these activities– other than appearing in a nice little cameo for the video. However, he had clearly been thinking about the song creatively before Vienna, for the version he played that night was a radical rearrangement. It was far from an unqualified success but showed immense promise. Unfortunately Dylan did not try it out again until 1994.

The Wolf Trap show also gave us another of those on-stage foul-ups that fans so love to recall. In this case it was when Dylan started playing "Boots Of Spanish Leather" as the thirteenth song; an unremarkable selection in itself, but on this occasion Dylan had already played it as the ninth song that night. Rather shamefacedly, and amidst general mirth, Dylan acknowledged his error, stopped and went on to play "It Ain't Me, Babe". Never mind, Bob, a lot of your old acoustic songs had begun to sound so alike it was an easy mistake to make.

Which is not to say they were all played by rote, the peerless "The Lonesome Death Of Hattie Carroll" brought some transcendent moments to a few of these shows; and again to the Wolftrap. Also in that stand-out Wolftrap set were notable versions of "God Knows" and "Born In Time".

Dylan's vocals on the former were fabulous, moving from fragile to menacing within a few lines. It was a marvellous and varied delivery; in places its demon edge called to mind those blistering *under the red sky* out-take versions of "T.V. Talkin' Song".

Meanwhile, the band was producing some visceral, teeth-on-edge interplay. John Jackson was never finer. This is the kind of thing defenders of Hammersmith 1993 talked about as being the point of the arrangements there. It never worked back then, but here you could hear and feel what they meant. This instrumental jam palpably benefits the performance of the song; this was superb hard-driving rock.

This was the finest performance of "God Knows" I had heard and, earlier in the set, there was the best live performance of "Born In Time", though the rejected *Oh Mercy* sessions version is unlikely to ever be bettered. Unfortunately, by the time Dylan got around to releasing "Born In Time" on *under the red sky*, he seemed to have lost the feel for it, certainly the released track is a comparative disappointment.

Dylan's delivery at the Wolftrap reclaimed the song in masterly fashion from that self-consciously 'poetic' album version, transforming it into something natural and affecting. It was a gorgeous performance and overall Vienna, 8th September 1993 was a night to treasure. In the main, though, this leg of the tour was short on shows that really sparkled.

There had been some fine song performances and some solid, if not spectacular, sets; but by September 1993, nothing in the year to date could stand alongside, say, the Greek Theatre '88, Beacon '89, Hammersmith '90, Fall '91, Spring '92, or Minneapolis '92. However, the best live shows of 1993 were yet to come.

Before that, though, Dylan was again in the news. After he finished touring with Santana, there was the release of a new album, *World Gone Wrong*. This was Dylan's second consecutive album of traditional covers, but it felt much more like a Dylan album than its predecessor. It was more cohesive. While it was also often faithful to the originals, it was not mimicry.

Dylan then returned to performing for two nights of free concerts (two sets each night, each set approximately one hour long) at New York's Supper Club on November 16th and 17th. These were shows intended to be filmed and every song was played acoustically, so it seemed for all the world that this was to be Bob Dylan's version of MTV's *Unplugged* series of acoustic shows. The idea of an 'Unplugged-type' show by the most famous unplugged artist (who became even more famous by plugging in) in popular music was irresistible; as were Dylan's spellbinding performances.

A mixture of old classics, songs he hadn't played for a while and tracks from *World Gone Wrong* were all treated to the authentic voice of Bob Dylan. Not only that but each show seemed better than the previous one and some songs, such as "Queen Jane" and "Ring Them Bells", were performed nearly as well as they have ever been. Unsurprisingly, fans could not wait to see the film and hear the released record. Unfortunately, Dylan refused to sanction the release of the film, apparently unhappy with the results. One can only speculate there must be something particular in the film that he really hates because this wonderful testament to his abiding talents as a performer would have done a great deal more to boost his reputation and credibility than the actual *MTV Unplugged* that he eventually participated in.

As a coda to these fabulous, yet sadly unreleased, performances, Dylan did appear on the Letterman Show, the day following the last Supper Club appearance, to perform a very fine "Forever Young". It was an unusually assured TV performance by a grandly be-hatted Bob, and a spectacular end to what was by Dylan's high standards, an indifferent year of touring.

As 1993 drew to an end, all Dylan fans were looking forward to the sixth year of the NET and the eighth of non-stop touring. Or I should say 'nearly all', as one of them was still looking back to a certain day in July.

CHAPTER EIGHT

1994: "You do wonder if you are coming across"

"It [Woodstock] was just another show, really. We just blew in and blew out of there. You do wonder if you're coming across, because you feel so small on a stage like that."[1]

BOB DYLAN TALKING TO EDNA GUNDERSEN OF *USA TODAY*, 1994

Nineteen ninety-four began with an announcement that disappointed many long-term Dylan fans and caused a surprising amount of press coverage. It was another of those 'Dylan sells out', 'final death knell of the Sixties' stories; this time prompted by Bob's decision to allow international accountancy giant Coopers & Lybrand to use Richie Havens' recording of "The Times They Are A-Changin'" for a TV commercial. Given all that had happened since the song's release over 30 years previously, I imagine that to most people this seemed a bit of an overreaction. On the other hand, in all the years before Dylan had never allowed such a thing. He seemed unaffected by the media

1 Edna Gundersen 5th May 1995 *USA Today*.

storm, stating that he had no problem with doing this, nor did he see anything to regret afterwards.

Stories like this made my Dylan information line busier and busier. I had to change the answering machine to a digitized one as the endless clicking on and off of the tape through the night was starting to keep me awake. I used to lie there and guess that one sudden rush of calls was people in the UK returning from the pub, later it would be commuters arriving home on the US East Coast, then move westward and so forth: expressions of the endless need to know, and to know as soon as possible. The service relied on someone getting the information to me, and there were a few regulars who did the majority of this work. Disturbingly for me, none of them was going to be able to call me from Japan, which was where 1994's opening leg of the NET was to begin.

Fortunately fan Jon Casper stepped into the breach, and thanks to him I am proud to say that the set-lists were updated on my information line as they happened. Or, as someone pointed out, due to the weird effects of the time differences it appeared that I had one set-list on before the concert had even started.

Fans soon forgot all about the Coopers & Lybrand controversy in a united, delighted, reaction to the opening two songs of the year. Dylan had begun his first set with "Jokerman", from 1983's *Infidels* album, one of his major songs of the past decade, but not played in almost as long.[2]

"Jokerman" is a key Dylan song, complex, rich and powerful. It was the single from *Infidels*, had a fine video and also featured on Dylan's TV appearance on the Letterman Show on March 22nd 1984; an appearance most Dylan fans rate as one of his best.

It suffers, as do many of Dylan's later 'major songs' from one flaw, that of being self-consciously a 'statement' carrying deep import. It is a difference in his writing that Dylan astutely noticed and described back in 1978[3] as:

---

2 It is typical of your ever hungry for novelty NET fans that it would not be long before we were desperate for him to open with anything other than "Jokerman". We were to feel the same initial excitement then longing for change in relation to "Down In The Flood" in 1995.

3 Matt Damsker Interview; 15th September, 1978 at the Senatro Hotel, Augusta ME.

"Now, in the old days, they [the songs] *used to do it automatically, but it's like I had amnesia, all of a sudden in 1966. I couldn't remember how to do it. I tried to force re-learn it, and I couldn't learn what I had had been able to do naturally, like* Highway 61 Revisited, *I mean you can't sit down and write that consciously. To do it consciously is a trick, you know, and I did it on* Blood On The Tracks *for the first time....I knew how to do it because it was a technique I learned, I actually had a teacher for it.* Blood On The Tracks *did consciously what I used to do unconsciously."*

Ironically, in *Blood On The Tracks* this appeared far from a problem; in fact the very opposite seemed to be the case, but it is an accurate depiction of a creative problem that he had to grapple with afterwards when he no longer had this "teacher".[4] This testament from Dylan's own lips on the beneficial effects of this teaching seems the only explanation for how *Blood On The Tracks* had surpassed even his classic albums of the 1960s.

However, *Blood On The Tracks* turned out to be the exception to a rule that has bedevilled him often since. As he moved away from the teacher and the lessons that had so successfully resurrected his writing skills, so the 'trick' of the 'technique' would become more visible. The 'unconscious' touch was often replaced by carefully constructed songs that betrayed or even drew attention to the craft necessary to write them.

This is not to say there was no craftsmanship before – far from it – but that the intuitive touch which led to a naturally-formed, cohesive web of imagery and symbolism that had lit those songs from within their crafted stanzas was missing. This loss has afflicted many of Dylan's best later songs. Some still stand above this reproach, if reproach it be, "Blind Willie McTell" and "Every Grain Of Sand" for example. Others, though, including some of his finest songs, such as "Jokerman", are affected by it. "Jokerman" is a powerful, majestic and magnificently crafted rock song, but it is also a too obviously carefully-thought-out explication of theological intent, drawing self-conscious attention to its meditations on the nature of humanity and belief.

4 Norman Raebun (1901-1978) was the name of the painter/art teacher who had such a profound impact on Dylan that, according to Bob, Sara could no longer understand him. More recently, Dylan has downplayed the significance of Raebun on his writing.

In concert, "Jokerman" did not need to concern itself with such considerations; instead it was a perfect, full-on introduction to a re-galvanised Dylan. It yelled that Bob was back on stage and meant business. Perhaps even more surprising and exhilarating was the second song on the opening three nights: "If You See Her, Say Hello", re-emerging nearly sixteen years after it had last been played. In 1994 it quietened things down after the explosive opener, but its presence was no less alluring and intriguing.

The live history of this breathtaking song from *Blood On The Tracks* had been brief, but one of the most dramatic in Dylan's canon. In 1976 Dylan unveiled a remarkably vicious live rewrite. No-one who knew anything of Dylan's life in the mid '70s could listen to this version without thinking it had been affected, or directly inspired, by the state of his relationship with his wife, Sara. The pivotal verse on the album version reads as follows:

"If you get close to her kiss her once for me
I always have respected her for doing what she did and getting free
Oh, whatever makes her happy, I won't stand in the way
Though the bitter taste still lingers on, from the night I tried to make her stay."

In 1976 this was changed, in performance, to the disturbing and visceral:

"If you're makin' love to her, watch it from the rear
You never know when I'll be back, or liable to appear
Oh it's as natural to dream of peace, as it is for rules to break
But right now I got not much to lose, so you better stay awake."

The song was rewritten again for the 1978 tour, though rarely performed, and quickly dropped altogether. By this point, the lyrics had returned to the same emotional area as the album version, though the crucial pivotal verse was missing.

When Dylan reintroduced "If You See Her, Say Hello" on his 1994 tour of Japan (where it had also been performed in 1978) the 'difficult' pivotal verse was still absent and he had returned to the *Blood On The Tracks* version, in the main, garnished with occasional couplets from the 1978 version.

The greatest surprise of the Japanese '94 dates was saved for February 16th, when a reworked, acoustic "Master of War" was performed in Hiroshima. This was the first acoustic performance of the song since April 12th 1963 in New York City. An apt if harrowing choice, it received a breathtaking performance. Dylan once again sounded like an angry young man: the folk singer rebelling against cause after cause. Here he was in Hiroshima, an American in the first Japanese city obliterated when the U.S. dropped 'The Bomb', singing out against the terrible sufferings of the innocent in war. I have rarely been as moved. How strange that such a blunt, unforgiving, adolescent piece should achieve that effect. Or, rather, how strange it would have been in almost any other location.

"Since Hiroshima, 'Masters Of War' has become a regular choice in Dylan's acoustic sets... but at the time this acoustic performance was a revelation," Dylan writer Robert Forryan enthused. "A gentle, haunting, melodic instrumentation; not at all angry, this time, and a voice from which the years have dropped away. This is the voice of a young man. It sounds as if for one night, and for one song, Dylan has done a deal with the Devil. 'Let me have my youth back for this song in this place – let me be inspired.' A pact with the Devil – or maybe a prayer to the Lord."

Things were moving so fast that soon local stores carrying dodgy merchandise had racks of double CD Dylan bootlegs from show after show. It was around this time that I, and a number of others, stopped collecting every show on CD or vinyl. There were just too many. Please do not misunderstand me here; we still collected them all on DAT or analogue tape, otherwise we could never have come to such a cavalier conclusion!

In all seriousness, the NET was becoming difficult to keep up with. I look back on this time in my life now, from the perspective of 2012, with utter astonishment. Although this book barely reveals it, I have many other interests in life, one such example being attending plays, especially by Shakespeare and his contemporaries.

Indeed, the next three years with Arthur Miller being added would see me attend more plays in a near-obsessive manner, needing to attend each and every play (yes, I realize you will think this out of character), than in any other three-year spell in my life. In the same time period I was attending more Dylan concerts than in any other three-year period of my life.

I have no idea how I managed this, and the addition of going to other artists' concerts and multiple football matches while working full time leaves me almost baffled. The only explanation I can come up with is that the excitement and adrenalin rush of following Dylan was fuel enough to keep me going.

In any case, 1994 was another very busy year and I found it hard when writing the first version of this book to remember exactly how I felt when the tapes came in from the opening shows of that year. So I picked a tape at random from them (12th February, Castle Hall Osaka) and placed it in the tape deck to discover how it felt listening to it in 2000, six years further down the NET. These were my thoughts when I did so:

The show starts strongly with "Jokerman"; Dylan is singing it with a sly intonation – by turns humorously and with a more meaningful edge. His voice rides over a driving beat, it is a rousing start to the show. The second song by now is not "If You See Her, Say Hello" but instead "If Not For You", and a very good performance it is too. Dylan is on top of the song, allowing the new melodic structure to portray a different side of it.

"All Along The Watchtower" opens to great cheers as Dylan gives a fabulous delivery of the opening lines. It does suffer a bit from the 1993 type of over-elongation musically, but this can work on the song as arranged here, with the heavily acknowledged ghost of Jimi Hendrix behind it.

Dylan's vocals continue to impress on "Ring Them Bells". It is, to be truthful, somewhat overly clamorous but Dylan is in command and this declamatory shouting is part of a new, more defiant version that does not completely overturn the original song's feeling.

Again we are given an extended version but at least (as with the earlier "All Along The Watchtower") this is only done at the end of the song. In any case, if Dylan is going to sing with this power throughout the show his voice will need to take the occasional breather. February 1994 sounds so much sharper all round than February 1993.

I picked this tape out by chance and it is throwing a curve ball at me, it is more exciting than I had remembered these shows being. Years of listening to hundreds of shows from the NET must have dulled my memory of this period. I include this confession as it is revealing in itself of the NET experience. The very non-stop nature of it means that all the dedicated fan can do is absorb as much as possible before the next wave hits. One is always most eager for the new shows, the new covers, the latest developments.

Next up there's a tumbling, rushed "Tangled Up In Blue". It is done as a crowd-pleaser, and although retaining some of the freshness that has so often been battered out of it in the years since it is still hurried and somewhat shrill. It is also the fifth song in a row with a long jam at the end.

"Under The Red Sky" gets us back on track, with Dylan allowing the luscious melody the room to breathe that it demands. The opening chords of "Tomorrow Night" get a very good reception, and it comes across very well. "Mr. Tambourine Man" is the next song; it is almost impossible for me to be fair to this. I now cannot help but compare it to the 1995 versions of the song. This is not Dylan's fault, nor should I allow that knowledge to impinge on my retrospective listening, yet I cannot help doing so. Dylan's performance here in the inevitable victim of his later superlative renditions of the same song. It is not as though there is anything awry with this performance as such, notwithstanding a note of insincerity in the occasional 'sobs' in the vocals.

During "Don't Think Twice, It's All Right" the audience tries to clap along, mingling these attempts with applause. It seems such a huge favourite with the crowd that Dylan has to show real persistence to keep the song on course. "Series Of Dreams" is played with a very strange syncopation. Dylan is putting a tremendous amount into his singing (as he had for the same song at the Wolftrap in 1993), changing the whole nature of the song as he veers from some kind of tonal experimentation to a shrill cry via an exercise in cantillation. All the while, the disquieting percussion plays behind him. It is a brave if flawed version which has a very unsettling effect. That is most certainly not a bad thing in itself, and even if I do not really think this version works I applaud the spirit in which it was undertaken.

In "I And I" the drums are still driving the song as they were in 1993, but Dylan's focus is not always as melodramatic as it was that year. He sounds as though he has doubts about what he is singing, and the arrangement features a discordant ending in the same experimental mood as the backing to "Series Of Dreams". "Maggie's Farm" is a cacophonous thrash, you would have to have been there to have enjoyed it; it is worth reminding ourselves when listening to tapes that the performances are intended for those there on the night, not for us listening to years later in our homes, cars or wherever. I hope the audience got up and boogied in their seats and in the aisles to this. It certainly had sounded previously on that tape as though that is exactly what they were looking forward to doing. One hopes, too, that they kept on their feet for "Ballad Of A Thin Man" before being sent out into the night with the ironically placed and touching closer, "It Ain't Me, Babe".

All in all an impressive tape, it makes me wonder if I really did pick the 12th of February by chance. Perhaps a subconscious memory of my tapes guided my hand to this particular show. I say this because I played a few others immediately afterwards and, although they all had good moments, I would have to say that none impressed me as much as the 12th had. It was, however, undeniably beneficial to return to them all, I had not done so in too long. As mentioned, one of the effects of the 'never ending' part of the NET is that there is a concomitant lack of time to spend on each leg, on each show, because there's always another leg just around the corner. After Japan, Dylan ended this Asian leg by making his first ever performing visits to Malaysia, Singapore and Hong Kong.

Then it was back to the U.S. As Dylan prepared for another American trek, he gave a journalist a glimpse into his motivations for keeping the NET going:[5]

"It seems as if you're always doing new things and reinventing yourself. What keeps you moving and motivated?" the reporter asked Bob.

"Just life itself," Dylan replied. *"There's a certain non-transparency to life that keeps me motivated. I try not to work in a linear way. That's incumbent on what's given to you at any given moment. There might be inconsistencies to that, nevertheless, it does give you a degree of independence you might not get any other way."*

This resistance to working – or, indeed, perceiving existence – "in a linear way" is something Dylan has returned to again and again in interview and, much more importantly, in his art.

---

5 *A new interview with Dylan,* St. Louis Post-Dispatch. By: Ellen Futterman, 7th April 1994

On April 5th, Dylan began a US tour in Springfield, Illinois. The shows drew widespread praise from the media. Long-term fans however were bemoaning unchanging set-lists. Tim Hardin's "Lady Came From Baltimore", at Davenport IA on April 6th, was the only song debuted live in the whole year. Still, if Dylan only presented one new song, at least he chose a particularly fine one.

The US leg had song numbers 1, 3 and 5 firmly fixed with even the 'new' opener soon caught up in the, some perceived, misery of repetition. As the US tour progressed "Señor" unexpectedly appeared as the second song, and remained there throughout. This initially caused a bit of a stir, but ultimately gave us four out of five unchanging opening songs.

Once you added the standard inclusions of "It Ain't Me, Babe" and "Maggie's Farm", my information line started to sound the same day after day. My punters were getting restless; I could feel the discontent breathing out of the answering machine. The same thing recurred in the Fall leg. Whether this is a problem for Dylan, or just for overly-obsessive fans who attend too many shows, is a question that rears its head throughout the NET

Both the argument that any criticism was just the inevitable result of jaded, hyper-critical fans who have seen too many shows and the one that insisted the only shows that were special involved changed set-lists were dealt a blow by Dylan himself soon after this leg ended.

The catalyst was Dylan's appearance at The Great Music Experience in Nara, Japan. This was a three-day UNESCO Cultural Development Project, where local artists were joined by representatives from the West including Joni Mitchell, INXS, Ry Cooder, Jon Bon Jovi – and Bob Dylan.

The entire show was the same each day, Dylan's contribution being "A Hard Rain's A-Gonna Fall", "Ring Them Bells" and "I Shall Be Released". (The last was reprised as the all-star finale every night.) For the first time ever, Dylan was backed by a full orchestra, the New Tokyo Philharmonic Orchestra. The final day was widely televised and Dylan was in magnificent form. I remember being near tears as The Voice returned in all its full, expressive, raging glory. I watched the footage again and again, transfixed at what seemed the best ever rendition of "A Hard Rain's A-Gonna Fall" and a magical and magisterial "Ring Them Bells", with Dylan filmed beneath a huge statue of Buddha.

The discipline of playing the same songs each day and marrying his vision to the backing of these accomplished musicians – who would not alter their playing just because he glared at them – had brought out the best in Dylan. For the first time in years he was being stretched. It made an amazing difference.

The Nara shows exceeded anything from the '93 and '94 legs of the NET[6]. Either unwilling or unable to pay for top-rate musicians, Dylan had become used to having a band at his beck and call. At best they could sound like a fired-up garage band, at worst like a motley crew from your local pub. Either way, they were at the mercy of the whims of their idiosyncratic and demanding lead singer. These bands have grown in time to produce some sparkling shows, but they have never been allowed to stretch Dylan, to push him to higher performance levels, to challenge him to come out and sing it.

How ironic that we fans ache for novelty, changing set-lists and debut songs, when playing the same set nightly in Nara brought the best out of Dylan. It's a reminder that Dylan's greatest years of performance – let's take 1966, 1975 and 1979 as irrefutable examples – were built on unchanging set lists (largely in the case of 1975, almost entirely for the two other years). The shows from these periods were so dramatic and intense and consummately performed that there was no need for novelty in song selection. This is not to decry the NET; those earlier tours were driven expressions of a clear artistic goal. They were presented by a white-hot Dylan on top of his game, ably backed and extended by top-notch musicians. The NET is not like that. You might get a night of searing drama, or you might be confronted with a series of standard run-throughs by a limited, cowed band and a singer who will swallow his words, sing off mike, mumble along – do anything but articulate. It is all part of the ongoing NET, and the reason one needs to sample a number of shows to become in tune with what is going on.

July brought Dylan back to Europe for his now customary summer appearances. Exceptional shows included Prague on July 16th, where the Czech President

6 With the exception of The Supper Club performances, which were also in an out-of-the-ordinary setting both physically and musically.

Václav Havel[7] (a long-time admirer of Dylan, Lou Reed and The Rolling Stones among others) joined a large and hugely enthusiastic crowd. Dylan is held in great esteem in some former Eastern bloc countries, his words and music having fuelled hope in the days of oppression. His reception here may have inspired him to start 1995's shows in the same city.

Good though Prague '94 was, the outstanding show of the summer was the second date, on July 4th, at Besançon, France, which featured an especially moving rendition of "Tears Of Rage" for Independence Day. This quite outstanding show featured a tremendous vocal performance and a set-list that included "Under The Red Sky", "Lady Came From Baltimore", "Mama, You Been On My Mind", "She Belongs To Me" and "What Good Am I?".

Sadly for me, the only two shows I caught that summer, both in Germany, at Balingen and Cologne, were not particularly memorable. Balingen was, as festivals nearly always are, more of an endurance test than an enjoyable experience.

After a short break, it was back to the States in August for a brief set of dates that encompassed Woodstock II and Dylan's 'controversial' decision to play there. Having taken the moral high ground and avoided the first Woodstock despite it being held there in honour of his residence nearby, Dylan saw no contradiction in lending his name to this corporate and phoney re-run of an event he had decried in the first place. Needless to say he was enormously rewarded in financial terms. The event took place on August 14th, and besides engendering a media blitz was broadcast around the world.

14th August 1994 Woodstock 2 Festival, North Stage, Saugerties NY

1 Jokerman
2 Just Like A Woman
3 All Along The Watchtower
4 It Takes A Lot To Laugh, It Takes A Train To Cry
5 Don't Think Twice, It 's All Right (Acoustic)

---

7 Václav Havel (1936 – 2011) was the last president of Czechoslovakia (1989–1992) and the first president of the Czech Republic_(1993–2003) as well as being a respected playwright, poet and essayist.

6 Masters Of War (Acoustic)

7 It's All Over Now, Baby Blue (Acoustic)

8 God Knows

9 I Shall Be Released

10 Highway 61 Revisited

*

11 Rainy Day Women #12 & 35

12 It Ain't Me, Babe (Acoustic)

Finnish television, in a move that was enough to make me want to return to live there immediately, showed Dylan's Woodstock set a few days after the event. The programme started with Dylan's opening words to his first song, "Jokerman", and ended when his set concluded. No other performers were shown, there was no commentary, no ill-informed presenters trotting out inaccurate and platitudinous balderdash. There was just Bob Dylan and band, performing at Woodstock in 1994.

Dylan looked in fine fettle, his trademark hair resplendent. It was good to see him in a clear light, not wearing any shades. There he was, on a massive stage before a crowd numbering in the hundreds of thousands, consisting mainly of youngsters. It was brave of him to retain his standard set opener rather than switch to something the crowd would recognise.

You would think that Dylan must have been nervous, but he and his band looked as though they knew exactly why they were there. Bob made his trademark moves and lovely little sideways glances as the crowd went mad beneath him.

Next up was "Just Like A Woman"; the crowd responded so enthusiastically that Dylan gave an almost shy smile and bent his legs in a classic guitar pose before attacking the vocal with even greater power. "It Takes A Lot To Laugh, It Takes A Train To Cry" saw the witty blues-drenched lyrics welded to snaking blues guitar lines.

This was electric city blues steeped in wise old magic. Dylan added some good guitar work and looked the part and then some. His little guitar step-dances and an occasional menacing move towards the microphone kept the audience fully engaged and ensured all-out cheering as he thundered out a blues riff, then reeled them back in with some quiet harp playing. This was then in turn built into a more aptly sinuous blues-phrase, while the drums turned up the heat and Dylan and John Jackson traded guitar solos before the song came to a close. You could see the crowd's excitement and expectancy.

"Don't Think Twice, It's All Right" elicited a cheer, but, even for Dylan, this was a big, big place to quell acoustically. He retreated into the song and, looking out above the packed congregation of heads, projected it as best he could in the circumstances.

During "Masters Of War" the crowd's enthusiasm could be heard throughout the song. Individual lines were clapped, approval was hollered. Dylan was deep within himself, singing the song with compelling conviction, as if this new generation needed to be as convinced by his rhetoric as those who went before.

He followed that with a startling, mesmeric, version of "It's All Over Now, Baby Blue". The exact thing he had been aiming for and missed in a warm-up show the week before was hit bull's-eye here, as a thousand flash bulbs popped in his face. Harmonica brought a song that had been transformed into a near benediction to its triumphant conclusion.

"God Knows" ushered in an electric guitar maelstrom and heralded full scale 'moshing' around the front of the stage in the dimming lights. Then the lights came up for "I Shall Be Released" and the spectacle of hundreds of flags being unfurled and tens of thousands of peace signs being flashed. As Dylan threw his 'guitar hero' shapes, the band was tight and loud.

A rapturously received "Highway 61 Revisited" brought the main part of the set to an end. There followed a pause filled by an American TV presenter, gushing enthusiastically, if somewhat patronisingly:

"750,000 watts of Dylan, this must be heaven. We were all kinda holding our collective breath to see how he'd be received tonight, but it was great. I feel very, very proud of Generation X tonight: showing the whole world they are full of patience, wisdom and tenderness, they are INTO Dylan big time tonight at Woodstock '94. And it looks like Bob Dylan will be returning to the microphone."

The mosh pit heaved again during "Rainy Day Woman", or "Everybody Must Get Stoned" as Americans under a certain age refer to it (the name has probably rarely been more apt, or less needed as an exhortation). Then, to close his performance, Dylan's performed a gentle, acoustic "It Ain't Me, Babe", turning the vast bowl into an intimate hall, while he gazed at the lights high above the stage, lost, it seemed, in a private reverie. When he glanced back down he was confronted by a sea of young faces, all obviously loving his performance. It was a sight that must have buoyed him, even after all the adulation he had received in his life.

Dylan, though, was later to dismiss this as just another show,[8] and though the audience was 100 times the size of the NET's usual nightly capacity this widely broadcast show is, indeed, fairly representative of the Never Ending Tour, albeit with a curtailed set. Somewhat typically, in the history of disappointing live Dylan releases, the official recorded release from Woodstock II featured only one Dylan track, and that was "Highway 61 Revisited".

Meanwhile Dylan continued to tour the U.S., passing the 600 mark for NET shows soon after Woodstock. He took a break after finishing the late summer leg, but was back on the road by October. My information line now informed listeners that my wife, Pia, and I were off to see the shows at the Roseland Ballroom in New York; but not to fear because I had a very special guest to take over the telephone news while I was away. Lambchop had agreed to deputise, proving a great success, as I knew he would. I joined about half the people I met in New York in phoning my own line just to check his latest rants on the brilliance of Dylan and his diametrically opposite views of the Grateful Dead and their fans. The Dead were appearing around the same time in New York, at Madison Square Garden. In fact, on the day prior to his opening concert at The Roseland Ballroom. Dylan appeared on stage with the Grateful Dead at the Garden and proceeded to join them in sleepwalking through a turgid "Rainy Day Women #12 and 35".

---

8 Q: Was playing at Woodstock a special moment? *A: Nah, it was just another show, really. We just blew in and blew out of there. You do wonder if you're coming across, because you feel so small on a stage like that.* Edna Gundersen 5th May 1995 *USA Today.*

18th October, 1994 The Roseland Ballroom, New York NY

1 Jokerman
2 Señor
3 All Along The Watchtower
4 Shelter From The Storm
5 Tangled Up In Blue
6 Man In The Long Black Coat
7 Mr. Tambourine Man (Acoustic)
8 Masters of War (Acoustic)
9 To Ramona (Acoustic)
10 Highway 61 Revisited
11 Joey
12 Maggie's Farm
13 Ballad of a Thin Man
14 The Times They Are A-Changin' (Acoustic)

I thought Dylan was in excellent form from "Masters Of War" on the first night onwards. Although I felt that the first electric set was not very good, Pia, who had not been at a show since the last Hammersmith date in 1993, was more impressed with this segment than she had expected to be. So, perhaps I was still judging everything in comparison to my Besançon tape and once again was allowing expectations to affect my enjoyment of the show I was at. It is certainly a danger that is ever-present for those who collect and listen to so many shows.

Notwithstanding the above, I would not swap any part of that first concert for any part of the next two, even though the shows probably got progressively better to those who could follow them properly. I find it hard to be definitive: "Masters Of War", "Knockin' On Heaven's Door", "Tears Of Rage" and "My Back Pages" thrilled me on the 18th, but the 19th was much more consistent. From the little I could hear in peace it sounded like it could have been one of my favourite shows. The show on the 20th had some peaks, but I would hazard a guess that it wasn't overall as impressive as the 19th. I don't really know, however.

The main reason I "don't really know", and that the first show is my best memory, is because the venue and crowd conspired to make the other shows more an endurance test than an enjoyable, far less a meaningful, experience. For the second show, I remember standing with Dylan biographer Clinton Heylin and NET chronicler Glen Dundas, fairly close to the stage but way out to the side.

My position had just worsened considerably in the last few minutes but I could still just about see the centre mike on the stage. Someone behind me was telling his friends what he thought of yesterday's show: "He only played for one hour 40 and his voice packed in after the first half-hour." "Odd", I thought to myself, "for me he only picked up after the first half-hour...", but this train of thought came to an abrupt end due to a sudden rush of people pushing in because Dylan's arrival was imminent.

Glen and Clinton had warned me that the crowd might make our position untenable, but still I was not prepared for what happened next. As I tried to stand my ground, a booming voice declared "COMING THROUGH" and I felt the people behind me falling back. I tried to hold on to my place, but it was not easy since any one of this guy's four chins probably weighed the same as me. There was a silver lining in this, however, as the only thing helping to keep him back was his sheer bulk: he could not get through on my left side as Clinton was refusing to budge. Alas, he boomed "COMING THROUGH" again and suddenly barged by my right-hand side, bowling over whoever had been standing there a moment before. He had a couple of friends in tow who followed through behind him. I could now only see a patch around Dylan's mike.

Dylan hit the stage and launched into "Jokerman". More people pushed forward, and it transpired that the recent interloper had a few more friends situated right behind us. They tried to push in, we refused to let them. Much pushing and shoving ensued, and eventually they decided they were not going to get through so stayed where they were. This was not the end of our problems, though. They proceeded to shout across us to their friends, whooping and talking at an incredible volume, straining to keep their conversations going over the noise of the unhelpfully intrusive band and singer on stage. It appeared they were interested in a certain band called The Grateful Dead; they most assuredly were not interested in Bob Dylan.

About three quarters of the way through "Jokerman", I vaguely sensed that Bob was in excellent voice then suddenly found myself being thumped on the shoulder. I was not being attacked, it was just that one of these people had set my T-shirt alight while trying to pass a joint forward to his friends. Helpfully, he put the flames out with considerable vigour, and nearly did the same for my collarbone. Attempts to pass the joint around were repeated interminably throughout the next two songs, my glimpses of Dylan often swiftly blocked by a spliff-holding arm. Those in front of us spent as much time facing their friends standing behind us as they did the stage. As they shouted and shoved through "If You See Her, Say Hello", I wondered if it was as fine as I imagined it sounded or if I was just presuming, with the innate pessimism of a fan, that these disruptions must be distracting from an exemplary performance; they would never happen on a relatively 'off night'.

Near the end of "All Along The Watchtower" I moved to the back of the theatre, where I discovered that the noise level was absolutely extraordinary. People were standing around in little groups, not facing the stage, bellowing to each other primarily about their sex lives and seemingly endless family problems.

The hall itself was a major part of the problem, being clearly not designed for live music. A little slope and some thought to the acoustics might have helped. By now I had walked all around the hall and found nowhere that I want to see the show from. I met other Dylan fans that I knew on my peregrinations; all were struggling to see and hear; all were frustrated by the antics of Deadheads who presumably could not get into Madison Square Garden.

The electric set passed and Clinton appeared, having given up his spot nearish the stage (things there apparently had got even worse after I left), and reported that he, too, had been unable to find a bearable spot to watch from. We resigned ourselves to observing the crowd's increasingly bizarre behaviour and catching whatever glimpses we could of Dylan.

I had, naturally, brought binoculars with me but every time I used them at the back of the hall someone bumped into me or stood right in front of the binoculars. This was somewhat irritating as it was in an area with plenty of space to move around in. I gave up trying to use the binoculars. Clinton tried to use them but the minute he did someone came up and head-butted the binoculars; good to know they were not just out to get me!

During the acoustic set's opener, "One Too Many Mornings", Dylan sounded in good voice, though it was difficult to say for sure with so much chattering going on. "It's All Over Now, Baby Blue" sounded Woodstock-ish but by now the six people directly in front of me had formed a horseshoe facing away from the stage, their conversation clearly having reached a critical point.

So the night dragged on and on; by the time Dylan got to "It Ain't Me, Babe", I was again at the back of the hall, my binoculars trained on Bob. Suddenly a Deadhead grabbed me and bellowed in my ear: "Do you think Jerry will come on?" I suspected that it was somewhat more likely that Garcia was at the Dead show, but just replied "I hope not." The Deadhead thought I was joking; he stuck his mouth right to my ear as though he was really worried that I might hear a bit of the show I had travelled 3,000 miles for: "Maybe Jerry and Bob will do 'All Along The Watchtower'?!" He is getting excited. I refrained from pointing out that this particular song had been played already, and that Dylan was about to end his show for the night. I did not answer at all, in fact, because Dylan was approaching his final words for the night. Fittingly, I did not get to hear them. Instead, the unwanted voice roared into my ear: "Wouldn't it be a gas if they played 'All Along The Watchtower' at two in the morning, wouldn't that be a blast, eh?" thus masking the last words from the stage.

End of show, goodnight.

I was luckier with the third night (the 20th); portions of the evening were almost tolerable. The majority of the crowd were there in the hope of seeing Jerry Garcia though, and I wish to God they'd stayed away, or that the Dead had played one more night at Madison Square Garden to spare us this onslaught. The one thing they did do was make tickets for the night very valuable. Which was a pity for me; I had had five spares for the first two nights and could hardly give them away, far less recoup what I had paid for them. Tonight was a scalper's feast.

I enjoyed the show as much as I could, given the ceaseless chattering and movement of a crowd who rarely seemed to care about what was happening on stage, and their continual questions of "Can you see Jerry yet?". "Jerry who?" became my standard reply.

The Roseland shows closed with extended encores as both Neil Young and Bruce Springsteen joined Dylan and the band on stage. It may have been musically forgettable, but the sight of the three together was one not to be missed.

If we fast forward to the present day, any New Yorker who has attended recent shows in London will wonder what on Earth my point is, as much the same kind of behaviour has been in evidence there, with the added 'bonus' of the ubiquitous mobile phone as video recorder/flash camera adding to the distraction. Back in 1994 it was an uncommon experience for me, however, and as you can tell took me aback.

Still, the opening night had been marvellous, because I was right in front of Dylan, with Pia by my side, at my first ever New York show. Around us were people who were there for Dylan; there to enjoy the show. We got there only thanks to the generosity of friends Andy and Michelle, who not only persuaded their friends to let us get there by swapping positions with us, but who even at one point gave us their own hard-won position right at Bob's feet.

After the shows I talked to friends from home and previous Dylan concerts. Somewhat surreally, I was surrounded by the same people in New York that I met every fortnight at Camden. I also met some American fans that I either didn't know at all or had only met briefly before. A nicer group of people would be hard to imagine, friendly, helpful, and well into Dylan. What a shame that they seemed to be in such a small minority when it comes to the shows. We had had a fantastic time in New York and knew before the week was over that we would be back to enjoy it again. The people we met were far friendlier than you would find in the streets of London, but unfortunately all those happy experiences were outside rather than inside the Roseland Ballroom, where it was a matter of enjoying what little one could from what was happening on the stage, whenever the opportunities arose amidst all the things happening off the stage.

Some fifteen years later the Roseland shows appeared on bootleg CD, from the soundboard recordings, so I finally got to hear them as I should have at the time. They were punchy shows and very fair representations of what the NET was then.

This year's touring drew to a close on November 13th. It was followed by Dylan rehearsing for, and performing in, MTV's hugely successful '*Unplugged*' show. This was a show that presented acoustic performances by leading artists from the electrified fields of rock music. It had rejuvenated or boosted the careers of many artists and it afforded Dylan a chance to build on his Woodstock success, especially among the younger generation of concert-goers and album buyers. Dylan fans, with memories of the greatness of the Supper Club and the successful TV appearances from Nara and Woodstock, thought they were in for a sublime treat. MTV Unplugged must have thought that they too were onto a winner. After all, the show had proved a commercial and artistic success for Nirvana, Neil Young and REM, to mention only three who had performed fine sets. Here, at last, was the most famous 'unplugged person' in popular music history. The scene seemed set for an out-and-out triumph.

This was not what we got. Instead, the discomfort Dylan often feels about being on TV was much to the fore. The dark glasses he kept on for most of the show kept his eyes well hidden, though not as occluded as his talent. The rehearsals were much better, because Dylan was more relaxed, but even they are not a patch on what could rightly have been expected. Nonetheless they would have been vastly preferable to the broadcast show itself. So what went wrong? Nearly everything. Who was to blame? Both MTV and Dylan, with the latter taking the lion's share.

MTV can certainly be faulted for their ridiculous insistence on putting the most photogenic, youthful fans up front, and, even more damagingly, for interfering with Dylan's proposed set-list. Dylan going along with these against his better judgement seems even more reprehensible. Unlike MTV, he knew better but just did not care enough. Edna Gundersen, interviewing him for *USA Today*, elicited revealing confessions:

Q: "Was the studio audience a typical Dylan crowd?"

A: "*I'd never seen them before. [Laughs] As I recall, they were in the polite category....*"

Q: "How did you plan this *Unplugged* project?"

A: "*I wasn't quite sure how to do it and what material to use. I would have liked to do old folk songs with acoustic instruments, but there was a lot of input from other sources a' to what would be right for the [MTV] audience. The record company said, 'You can't do that, it's too obscure.' At one time, I would have argued, but there's no point. OK, so what's not obscure? They said "Knockin' on Heaven's Door"."*

Both MTV and Dylan are to blame for allowing the TV special to omit the best of the songs played. The same could be said for the track selection on the album release. Since it is his work, though, Dylan's lack of care seems the greater fault, especially in the light of his decision not to release the vastly superior *Unplugged*-like Supper Club shows. His lack of commitment was further underlined in the following exchanges from the same interview:

Q: "Was performing before TV cameras difficult? "

A: *"It's hard to rise above some lukewarm attitude toward (TV). I've never catered to that medium. It doesn't really pay off for me...."*

Q: "Did you approve of the finished show?"

A: *"I can't say. I didn't see it."*

Dylan did not miss much. The MTV special was suffocatingly bland; there was nothing special about Dylan, no feeling that here was a major artist or performer, no excitement or invention.

Depressingly, if predictably, this safe, bland Dylan drew some positive reviews. The most misguided of which went so far as to favourably compare it to 1976's *Hard Rain*, which is a bit like preferring *King John* to *King Lear*. Even the one moment of the show as broadcast that looked natural, a bungled opening to "Like a Rolling Stone" that led Dylan to joke with the audience that the band had got ahead of him, was not natural at all. Instead this attempt to make Dylan look like a cuddly old fogey to the TV audience was the result of some trick editing. This lamentable act stands as a fitting metaphor for a programme that presented such a castrated version of the live Dylan experience. It was a poor and unrepresentative end to 1994.

Thankfully, it would not be long before the opening show of 1995 would take us from this ridiculous low to a sublime high.

CHAPTER NINE

1995: "Hey Chop! How you doin' tonight?"

"He just likes to be out there because he likes to feel young and he likes to feel that he can still do it. And out of all the people I have toured with or met, he's definitely the most constant one. He's definitely a road-type person."

CÉSAR DIAZ, FROM A&E TV DYLAN BIOGRAPHY

Nineteen ninety-five was to turn out a busy year for Dylan. He played 116 shows, more than he had ever done in a year before. By the year's end he had had a CD and video released (*MTV Unplugged*) and had made forays into the computer age with an interactive CD-ROM, "Highway 61 Interactive", and *Greatest Hits Volume 3* produced as an enhanced music CD, which, when played on a computer, brought up a variety of on-screen information.

Fans may have started the year pining for an album of new Dylan material, but the opening dates of this year's NET offerings soon drove all other thoughts out of their minds. The touring started on March 11th, a day later than scheduled, in Prague. Prague 1994 had been one of the better European shows of that year, but Prague 1995 was to prove something else altogether.

As usual a fan trip was going from London, but, reeling from the expense of European and New York shows in 1994, hassled at work and not wishing ever again to be trapped on a bus for hours on end, I decided to skip the opening jaunt. And what a one to miss!

Not that it seemed such a bad choice on the 10th, as Dylan and the band were so ill from the 'flu that the first date was cancelled/rescheduled. In all the decades he has toured and the thousands of shows he has played, this has happened extremely rarely; but there was serious danger of the next night being an unheard-of double postponement.

Dylan was so weak after his illness that he forsook his guitars and crooned his way through the night at the microphone. By all accounts this was a late decision and surprised the band, so it would appear that this inspired change in performance style came about due to illness. It seemed to work so well, though, that you feel Dylan must have been giving a lot of thought as to how he would present a show guitarless.

Perhaps Dylan had been contemplating trying this approach on some songs, and the illness had propelled him into playing all but a few minutes of the 11th March that way. On that very special night, although Dylan and the band members were still unwell, they proceeded to pull a performance of majestic splendour out of this adversity.

Anyone who has watched a sunrise over the ancient city of Prague will feel they have visited a city of magic and wonder. Anyone who has heard Dylan's performance on the 11th will have felt a similar sense of awe.

11th March 1995 *Palác kultury*, Prague, Czech Republic

1 Down In The Flood
2 If Not For You
3 All Along The Watchtower
4 Just Like A Woman
5 Tangled Up In Blue
6 Watching The River Flow
7 Mr. Tambourine Man (Acoustic)

8 Boots Of Spanish Leather (Acoustic)

9 It's All Over Now, Baby Blue (Acoustic)

10 Man In The Long Black Coat

11 God Knows

12 Maggie's Farm

*

13 Shelter From The Storm

14 It Ain't Me, Babe (Acoustic)

The shock of seeing Dylan open without a guitar might have taken some time to register on the audience, as the opening song was a huge surprise in itself; a live debut of "Down In The Flood" from *The Basement Tapes*[1].

This was a magnificent song to resurrect, and stayed as the opener for many shows. Later it became a bit of a tub-thumper, but back in March he performed a loud, deep, bassy, bluesy version with powerful vocals and a bold harp. It was a good, ballsy start to the show and the year. The second song was a much mellower number, "If Not For You". It was quite faithful to the original arrangement, though more dynamic and featured some appealing country playing and effective, if somewhat hoarse, vocals.

The audience were also being served up a visual display that was completely new to a Dylan show. Without a guitar as a prop, far less a musical instrument, Dylan stood for much of the time with knees partly bent, holding the microphone to his mouth while his other arm was outstretched, pointing outward and upwards, holding the microphone cable. Apart from pain-induced doubling over, his movements included strange, staggering dance steps and what looked suspiciously like slowed-down shadow-boxing routines.

"All Along The Watchtower" had the same basic arrangement as usual, but now Dylan could fully concentrate on his vocals. In turn, John Jackson was given leeway to express himself without worrying about Dylan's guitar lines.

1 Excepting Dylan's guest appearance at The Band's New Year's Concert at the Academy Of Music (New York) Concert 31st December 1971.

Dylan really opened up, changing emphasis all over the place, riding the song like it was a bucking, half-tamed mustang.

After this, the concert really took off and soared. "Just Like A Woman" opened with a sensuous, passionate harp while Dylan's singing saw him feeling out a new expression of the song as he went along. The band were understandably unable to keep up as Dylan created something new, live on stage. For a few lines his vocals seemed cut adrift from the backing, but he continued regardless and resolved it all in a beautiful harmonica passage. It was a stunning *tour de force*.

"Tangled Up In Blue" was not quite so successful, but featured a pointed harmonica ending. Dylan followed it with an out-of-character piece of audience interaction. "*Thanks. I was sick here last night,*" he told the crowd. "*Got the 'flu. This is a really good place to recover from the 'flu.*" As he finished speaking and headed back to his rack of harmonicas, a shout rang out above the normal between-song hubbub:

"Bobby, I love you!" Dylan paused in mid-step, smiled and asked "*Oh, could you say that again?*"

No-one did, but Dylan continued "*This is called, um, my ecology song here,*" and launched into "Watching The River Flow" which chugged along very pleasantly, ending in an instrumental jam that brought in Dylan on guitar. He raised a cheer from someone simply for picking up the instrument, and then proceeded to perform a pleasing enough exchange of riffs with John Jackson. Dylan relinquished his guitar again in time for "Mr. Tambourine Man".

Prague began a spring season full of superlative versions of this vintage song.[2] It is hard to understand how even Dylan can keep re-arranging a song so dramatically, constantly investing it with new meaning and emotion. This version had genuine warmth. There was a lovely 'echoey' sound to his voice, while the deftness and depth of the harmonica playing was quite transcendent. It was as though a Dylan of yore, the maestro harmonica player opening up our dreams

2 Actually, it extended beyond the spring, but it peaked here and in the UK where Glasgow, Manchester and Dublin especially had performances to die for.

and visions, had returned from a long absence.[3] The crowd were understandably delirious.

"Boots of Spanish Leather" was simultaneously a prayer-like plea and an emotional statement of intent. "It's All Over Now, Baby Blue" was even better than at Woodstock II, and stands with anything Dylan has ever done. Lyrics that were deeply profound to begin with took on new resonance and meaning through his delivery. It was like seeing a precious diamond being held at an unfamiliar angle under a new light, revealing yet more depth and beauty to an already treasured gemstone. Dylan then followed the lyrics with a harmonica break from heaven. Unsurprisingly, Dylan fans ache for this version to be released officially.

There was hardly time to take all this in before the darkly menacing introduction to "Man In The Long Black Coat" found Dylan in the voice of a master story-teller; a wise old prophet of the ages. A splendid version of "God Knows" followed, exploding into a rock-based rave-up about half-way through. The full-on rock sound was carried forward into the perennial "Maggie's Farm", which brought the main set to an upbeat close.

To close a remarkable evening, instead of running through a couple of standard encores Dylan returned for a magnificent "Shelter From The Storm". The song started quietly, with phenomenal care taken over the vocals, before building up to a climax infused with extensive and intense harmonica playing. It was another performance of epic stature, standing near the top of a list of performances – "Just Like A Woman", "Mr. Tambourine Man", "It's All Over Now, Baby Blue" and "Man In The Long Black Coat" – that were amongst the best the NET, or in a couple of cases Dylan's entire career, has offered us so far.

The closing "It Ain't Me, Babe" found his vocals still in stellar form. Even the crowd's clap-a-long seemed not so much an intrusion as a joyful interaction. This was the kind of show where even describing the way Dylan rolled his 'r's would get one into *Private Eye*'s "Pseud's Corner" for waxing too lyrical.

I still have tapes of the hysterical phone calls backs to my Information Line; mind you, they betray more happiness at my non-presence than at Dylan's magnificent performance. I remember being told how well I was taking all the

---

3 These past glories being the reason he is still cheered to the rafters just for picking a harmonica up and putting it to his lips.

ribbing. I would be the first to admit that a year earlier I would have been devastated. Now, though, having given up on my commitment to my magazine I was better able to deal with missing out on such trips.

I had decided that the magazine had become too important to me. I was reacting to events in the Dylan world with the fanzine in mind. I was constantly agitated about getting news on the information line as fast as possible. I was actually irritated that *Good As I Been To You* was released at such an awkward time for **Homer**, *the slut* that I had to delay sending out an issue. Eventually it became so important it stopped being fun, which was ridiculous. Dylan's work was the important thing and Dylan fandom should only be a fun adjunct to that. The minute it stops being fun is the time to change your attachment to it. I suspect, also, that meeting Dylan in Camden had a lot to do with all this, as there wasn't much further fan life could go than that.

So, I was once again back in the real world where pleasure at hearing Dylan had performed well was the important thing, and one's personal involvement was incidental. If that sounds overly altruistic, it is worth remembering that it was totally dependent on the certainty of getting tapes of the said shows. My resolve not to go to quite so many shows would not have stood a chance were it not for the knowledge that I would be receiving recordings of every gig.

As the following years were to demonstrate, I was going through a temporary period of distancing myself from the obsessive life-encompassing demands of the NET. This would probably have started in 1995, had that year's opening months not been of such stunningly high quality.

It was, as you will have guessed, another of those occasions when a tremendous current Dylan performance sparked off an abundance of extravagant claims of it being as good as the best of '66, '79, '78, '81 (name your year). Unlike most times when this happens, on this occasion you could really understand the claims.

Even more remarkably, some of those who continued on the tour thought some of the immediately subsequent shows were even better. Paul Williams picked Brussels as his favourite, while others extolled the virtues of some German shows. Then there were the other two nights at Prague itself. The 12th March show is often overlooked because of the shock and splendour of the 11th. The previous day aside, though, it was surely the best NET show since at least 1992.

Then on the final day at Prague another show of almost similar standing showcased a marvellous, probably best ever, version of "License To Kill" that liberated the great song I always have maintained lurked beneath the arrangement and production on *Infidels*.

Tapes and news of the opening shows flooded into the UK. Gavin Martin had gone to Prague to report for the *NME*, and based his extended Dylan feature around an interview with Lambchop in splendid 'Lambchop form'. Mr. Martin pointedly compared the "heroic and brazen, masterful interpretative singer homing in on his own canon" of Prague's opening night with the "polar opposite" of the *MTV Unplugged* débâcle.

"In Prague," Martin continued, "Dylan took pleasure in stretching his lyrics into new territory, making the words zing and sting again, staking his claim to greatness, laying down the gauntlet, savouring the dark truths, apocalyptic intent and visions of fiery wonder swirling in his songs. This was like no other Dylan anyone had ever seen."

Accordingly, UK Dylan fans were once again buzzing with eager anticipation of the 14-date British Isles' tour that began in Brighton on 26th March. Although I enjoyed the show well enough, I was struck by the self-inflicted curse of listening to an over-abundance of tour tapes. I spoke to people who had heard nothing from the year so far and they were in raptures. Still, it was my first live view of the 'guitarless' Dylan. I liked what I saw and heard, but felt that it was not up to the standard of the earlier shows. It is only fair to point out, though, that there were some of the all-tape-listening Dylan fraternity who rated Brighton very highly, despite their exposure to earlier 1995 treats. Nonetheless, I preferred the following night at Cardiff with its fabulous near 10-minute "Desolation Row".

After a day's break we had three shows on successive nights in London. It was no longer at the Apollo (née Odeon; this time we were at the Brixton Academy. I used to live only a mile or so from this venue back in pre-NET days, and it would never have occurred to me that I would one day see Dylan there. Brixton was usually the territory of Goths, Punks, Rastas and other tribes of the disenfranchised (or those playing at being so). The Dylan crowd included a much higher percentage of the professional classes, illustrating how far Dylan's audience had moved from being anti-establishment to themselves being the establishment.

The Brixton shows got off to a poor start. The Academy is not the best of places either physically or acoustically, but there was more amiss than that. Dylan seemed distant, a spark was missing and it all became a bit of a dull, flat night. I was beginning to worry that the early glory of the year's touring was a fast-fading flame.

Interestingly enough, on re-listening to the show I discovered a "Dignity" that was one of my favourite performances of the year. I had not really noticed this properly on the night, a superb, visceral live version. Another reminder of how complicated the 'being there' subjective experience is when trying to gauge the relative artistic merit of what one has witnessed.

The second night dispelled all my fears of a tapering off in 1995 quality. Dylan played like a man re-energised, reconnected with his performing art, prowling the stage with genuine purpose and conviction. The set-list was shaken up for the first time in the year as Dylan stretched himself in front of an ecstatic crowd. "Mr. Tambourine Man" was again exceptional and "Masters Of War" was close to the heights of Hiroshima. A flawless "Love Minus Zero/No Limit" rounded off an exquisite acoustic set. The electric songs really rocked too, and "Jokerman" followed by "Every Grain Of Sand" was a perfect pairing, particularly since "Every Grain Of Sand" replaced "Tangled Up In Blue", which previously had seemed as locked into the fifth slot as "All Along The Watchtower" still was to the third slot.

It was quite a night, as was the next, when a show much closer to the quality of the 30th than the 29th was rounded off with guest appearances by support act Elvis Costello, Carole King and Chrissie Hynde. After one night off, it was on to Birmingham where we had another tremendous set-list[4] and many highs, including a mesmerising "To Ramona". From there it was straight on to three nights in Manchester, the first of which featured a particularly masterful acoustic set. Magnificent though these acoustic segments were most nights in spring 1995, none could surpass the extraordinary one on this occasion.

As was customary, "Mr. Tambourine Man" opened the acoustic segment. As was usual this year, it was utterly outstanding, but this version was even more

4 Down In The Flood/ Just Like Tom Thumb's Blues/ All Along The Watchtower/What Good Am I ?/ Tombstone Blues/ Tears Of Rage (Dylan/Manuel)/ Mr. Tambourine Man/ Desolation Row/ To Ramona/ Highway 61 Revisited/ Jokerman/ Lenny Bruce/ Like A Rolling Stone/ It Ain't Me, Babe

so than any other night's performance. There was such a sense of time, space and movement and awareness of matters of immense import that it seemed as though all of European history was echoing through the hall. Here in Manchester, on the third of April, Dylan caught the entire essence of his spellbinding 1995 arrangement of one of his most luminous masterpieces.

There was no possibility that Dylan would lose his way after having sung so transcendently and expressively. The second song of this acoustic set, "Boots Of Spanish Leather", was graced with a gorgeous burr on his voice, plus enunciation and phrasing of the highest order.

The third in this acoustic trio was "Gates Of Eden", and it seemed many, many years since Dylan had given it a perfect reading. There were good ones, but not sustained in every verse; usually lyrics or music or both collapsed somewhere along the line. Not here though, here he got it dead on. The overly-long instrumental ending would usually detract from the whole for me but this time it worked, as though Dylan knew he had grasped a precious range of expression in this acoustic set and did not want to let it go.

All three shows in Manchester had much to commend them, and it was perhaps understandable that a dip in standards had to come. Edinburgh's two shows were much lower key; the performers seemed, relatively, drained. For those following the tour the most notable thing was that, on the second night there, Dylan spoke to Lambchop, making our friend's day (life?) by calling out from the stage:

"Hey Chop! How you doin' tonight? Where's your hat man? Hey, better put your hat back on!"

I should also point out that I met friends after the Edinburgh shows who had not seen Dylan live since 1991 or 1993, and they were completely blown away with these 1995 shows. So much so that they were highly suspicious of any reports that these were below the standard of so many others that spring. Again the importance of context was made clear to me; a 'poor' 1995 show could well be the best in half a decade, even for someone who had seen the last dozen or more shows in the UK up to that year.

Edinburgh was a mere blip. Glasgow and Dublin saw fantastic shows, played to wildly enthusiastic audiences and rewarded with rave reviews. Glasgow was the last night for me, and luckily enough it was another very special night. Paul Williams called the 15-song set – which included unforgettable performances of "Shelter From The Storm", "Tears of Rage"', "Lenny Bruce", "Mr. Tambourine Man" and "Lay, Lady, Lay" – a "doorway to knowledge".

Williams considered the cassette tape of the show to be "Intended or not... an extraordinary and durable, repeatable work of art... full of beauty and intelligence. Communicative in those very special ways reserved for great works of art... John Coltrane's *Impressions*. Monet's *Water Lilies*. Dylan's *Glasgow '95.*"

As this book testifies, tapes, CD-Rs, whatever recording means one uses transport us through time and space and allow Paul, for example, to share in the thrill of that Glasgow show. As for me, I felt I was sated. I had been having a marvellous time following this leg but 'enough was enough', or so one would have thought. At that moment, I did think so; I felt that I did not need to see Dylan again for a long time. However, that feeling, on the rare occasions it had appeared in my life, had never remained for long.

This European leg came to a suitably high-energy close with a top-quality extended show in Dublin on April 11th, where Dylan and the band were joined on the encores by Elvis Costello, Van Morrison, and Carole King.

Dylan took the next month off before taking his 1995 show to the U.S. West Coast. The U.S. audiences were ecstatic at these performances. Those who had followed on from Europe were quite blasé by comparison, having witnessed greater glories already. These were very strong shows in their own right even if not quite up to the European standard, and far from that of the year's opening shows in Prague. Individual songs, on the other hand, were still scaling similar peaks: there was at least one "Man In A Long Black Coat", for example, that was of a quality equal to the best even of the early spring shows. Dylan's tremendous vocals, brooding over an oppressive backing, created an atmosphere that was downright scary. Also, one could easily choose U.S .shows that were far superior to the 'poorer' (relatively speaking) UK nights such as the first Brixton and the two Edinburgh dates. Another boon for the U.S. audiences was that the set-lists were much more flexible. Something like the May 22nd one below would have been unthinkable at the beginning of the year:

22nd May, 1995 The Warfield, San Francisco CA

1. Down In The Flood
2. Man In The Long Black Coat
3. All Along The Watchtower
4. Most Likely You Go Your Way (And I'll Go Mine)
5. Tears Of Rage (Dylan/Manuel)
6. Tombstone Blues
7. Mr. Tambourine Man (Acoustic)
8. Desolation Row (Acoustic)
9. It's All Over Now, Baby Blue (Acoustic)
10. Seeing The Real You At Last
11. She Belongs To Me
12. Obviously Five Believers

*

13. Lenny Bruce
14. My Back Pages (Acoustic)

You may have noticed here some songs not discussed so far, in particular "Obviously Five Believers" from *Blonde On Blonde*. This song had finally made its live debut, after tantalizingly appearing as a set-list possibility and at sound-checks (minus Dylan, alas) at various shows, on May 15th at the McCallum Theatre in Palm Desert CA. During its first outing it stood up so well to live treatment that you were surprised it had not appeared before, though grateful as ever for a fresh treat.

Another speciality that same night, though a more dubious one, was a slowed down "Never Gonna Be The Same Again", appearing for only the second time, and the first in nine years. "Seeing the Real You At Last" had been a regular in these U.S. shows, so perhaps *Empire Burlesque* was on his mind. *Blonde On Blonde* seemed to be too, as in addition to "Obviously Five Believers" being unveiled on the 15th, the 17th of May saw the first "Pledging My Time" since September 1990.

That month Sheryl Crow became the latest in a long line of support acts on Dylan's NET who would go on to become a star in their own right. All in all, 1995 had been magnificent and was still going along splendidly. You just knew that Dylan was going to do something to buck the trend.

It happened in June, beginning on the 15th, when Dylan opened for the Grateful Dead for the first of five shows. Yet another ill-fated attempt to grab some Deadhead dollars found Dylan playing to a handful of Dylan fans swamped by the tiny percentage of the huge Dead following who had come along prior to seeing the headliners. The Deadheads used the time to throw Frisbees and get the joints and hamburgers in, while Dylan went largely ignored and played as though he deserved to be.

As though he knew that what he was doing in those huge arenas was a farce, Dylan played two shows at Philadelphia's tiny (800 capacity) standing-only Theatre of the Living Arts, on June 21st and 22nd, in the middle of these Dead outings. The first of these theatre dates has gone down in Dylan folklore as one of the NET's very best nights.

Certainly it was an excellent show. Dylan was clearly on top form from the opening moments, ripping into "Down In The Flood" like a man on a mission. There were also outstanding takes on "License to Kill" and "Knockin' On Heaven's Door". Dylan's warm and affectionate band member introductions give you an idea of how much he was enjoying the night:

"Thank you, thank you. Playing guitar tonight, I'm not gonna tell you how old he is though. He's from Memphis, that ought to give you some clue, J. J. Jackson. On the drums Winston Watson. I thought his name was Ice T when I hired him. Anyway it doesn't matter, he's so good we forgot about it. On the steel guitar and a bunch of other stuff, former mayor of Bluesville, West Virginia, Bucky Baxter. He was a fine looking young man when he joined me. Got a lot of years on him now. On bass guitar tonight Tony Garnier. I'm not gonna tell you anything about Tony either. I don't know anything about him. I know he once tried to milk a cow with a monkey wrench."

In spite of all this, for me the show doesn't quite live up to its reputation among the fan fraternity. Its acclaim mostly rests on the performance of two songs that have powerful claims to be Dylan's finest. The first of these was "Visions Of Johanna" in the acoustic set. It is undoubtedly a song that means a great deal to any Dylan fan. However, unlike the re-inventive Prague performances of classic songs this version does not add to the original.

The second surprise appearance was "Tangled Up In Blue" as the acoustic encore. It was an extraordinary place for such an important song, and the thought of it being played acoustically had Dylan fans around the globe salivating. Once heard, however, it was not so overwhelming, sounding rather forced and strained.

It was an impressive show, though not as outstanding as is often claimed. Such claims for both these shows are understandable; given that they came in the middle of the lamentable support slots with the Dead, the two shows must have seemed 'Prague-like' to those attending a mixture of the soulless stadiums and the intimate theatre.

The second Living Arts show deserves more of a mention too, being another fine night. It began with "Drifter's Escape", which turned out to be a fairly common alternative to "Down In The Flood" as opener as the year progressed. ("Drifter's Escape" at this point had not been played since November 12th, 1992, in Clearwater FL.)

Dylan's ill-fated stint with the Dead ended on June 25th at the Robert F. Kennedy stadium in Washington DC. Jerry Garcia joined Dylan and his band to add guitar to their last two songs, "It Takes A Lot to Laugh, It Takes A Train To Cry" and "Rainy Day Women #12 & 35". It was to be the last time the two friends were on stage together.

It was a sad setting for such a partnership to bow out. I always thought that the best time for Garcia and Dylan to play together would be sitting on a porch late one night swapping songs. It would be pleasing to imagine that they grabbed a chance to do that, far from the madding crowds, before Jerry Garcia died on August 9th, from a heart attack while attending a drug rehabilitation centre in California. The next day Dylan issued a moving statement through his press office. It gave an insight into how much Garcia had meant to Dylan:

"There's no way to measure his greatness or magnitude as a person or as a player... He really had no equal. To me he wasn't only a musician and friend, he was more like a big brother who taught and showed me more than he'll ever know.... There's no way to convey the loss. It just digs down really deep."

It was not to be the last intimation of mortality that year. In November Dylan would be a performing guest at Frank Sinatra's 80th birthday celebration. It was clear from that night that Mr Sinatra would not be enjoying many more birthdays. In December Robert Shelton, Dylan biographer and sometime New York critic who helped bring Dylan to the public's notice back in the Greenwich Village folk club days, died of a stroke.

Back on June 25th, Dylan enjoyed a few days' rest before returning to Europe for his customary summer tour. It is time for me to admit that my somewhat smugly confident remarks after the Glasgow show on April 9th, that I had overcome the extreme levels of behaviour that Bob Dylan inspires and was comfortable in the feeling that the UK shows were easily enough for me, turned out to be illusory. Come July, Dylan was playing in Germany and I felt I absolutely had to go.

I flew out on July 1st to meet again with Chris, Stephan and Daniel. When we rose early the next morning for the seven-hour drive to Hamburg I was full of intense excitement as the experience of seeing Dylan again drew ever nearer. Hamburg's Stadtpark is the perfect outdoor venue: a picturesque area enclosed by cultivated hedges and trees. The sun shone brightly throughout the evening. Dylan was due to start at seven, as there was a strict curfew at ten.

After soaking in the ambience, the great moment arrived. "Ladies and gentlemen, will you please... " My stomach muscles clenched in painful anticipation, and then there he was, the centre of all our attention.

Looking fabulously cool and wearing shades to protect his eyes from the glare, he tore straight into "Down In The Flood". It was the first time I had seen him do it with a guitar in his hands and I liked it. Suddenly I was conscious of my tense anticipation melting away. I was back in the presence of our Bob.

Next up was "If Not For You" with its pleasant country-ish backing. The acoustics were superb and Bob was in good voice. I must admit that I had no idea if he performed "All Along The Watchtower" well or not, and until it was given a long rest, or at the very least moved from the third spot, would never really care to know again. (Even obsessives have their limits.)

Fortunately the fourth song, the majestic "Queen Jane Approximately", raised everything to a higher plateau. The subsequent song sounded very like it was going to be "Watching The River Flow", but then became "I'll Be Your Baby

Tonight". After which, Dylan had greater things on his mind and went into "Pledging My Time". This was turning into a very fine show indeed. "Silvio" then brought the first electric set to an ear-shattering close, the song building to a crescendo on wave after wave of guitar attacks.

The acoustic set began with "Tangled Up In Blue". Although Dylan carefully enunciated each word, he just didn't inhabit the song. Even the first appearance, to predictable applause, of the harmonica at its climax failed to hide the fact that this just hadn't worked.

A not particularly strong "Masters of War" followed, but Dylan was clearly projecting it better than "Tangled Up In Blue". Then, suddenly, with a heart-rending "It's All Over Now, Baby Blue" the whole evening warped into another universe (where Bob is in our heaven and all seems well on Earth). This lovely, slow version, first unveiled just before Woodstock II, was to prove my favourite single performance of this particular trip. The audience were spellbound and totally attentive, the only interruption was the singing of the birds above in the treetops, as Dylan poured himself into a glorious rendition of a magnificent song on a balmy evening in Northern Germany.

'Slam, bang, thank you ma'am' guitars led us into the second electric set with "Stuck Inside Of Mobile With The Memphis Blues Again". For me this had peaked at the Hammersmith Odeon in 1990, one of my favourite memories of the song. By 1995, after countless turgid renditions, I could no longer connect with it. Fortunately, he followed it here with an excellent "She Belongs To Me".

The highlight of the encores, and the second best performance of the night for me, was a beautiful, acoustic "My Back Pages". After the closing strains of "Rainy Day Women #12 & 35", I wandered around the park, meeting lots of friends from Germany and the UK. Then it was time to find a telephone to call Lambchop and get him to update my information line.

After a few hours sightseeing in Hamburg, the 3rd of July found us in Hanover in plenty of time, around about half past six. As Dylan was back to the more customary 20:00 starting time, there should have been no danger of us being late. Indeed, we were planning what to eat pre-show as we arrived in the city.

We drove in circles. We stopped to ask directions. We drove in circles. Time passed. We stopped to ask directions. We drove in circles. By now it was approaching 19:30. We were told to follow the signs. We couldn't see any signs to follow. We looked in increasing desperation. At 19:48, we saw a half-obscured sign. This led to our discovery that all "Music Hall" signs had been covered by a poster campaign; thankfully, not quite 100% successfully.

Ten minutes later we caught sight of the venue. Bob was due on in two minutes. All three of us bravely waited in the anteroom as Stephan parked the car. Meanwhile, the band struck up the opening to "Down In The Flood". Stephan was astonished to find us all waiting for him.

We had missed all of 34 seconds of Dylan. I explained later that it was a sacrifice worth making for a friend, especially one who had driven us, albeit in circles, to the gig. Though if the opening song had been "Drifter's Escape", which I had yet to witness live, it would have been a different story.

Dylan's relentless touring schedule, and the resulting effect of supply and demand forces, meant that there was no problem walking straight down to the front, even when arriving so late. I had a perfect view from about the third row. What a contrast this was to the pre-NET days.

It was another excellent show, 1995 was full of them. My highlights from the first set were "Positively 4th Street" and "Jokerman". The majority of the audience, as at the other two shows, were far more enthusiastic about "All Along The Watchtower" and "Silvio". The acoustic set was the usual delight, with "Mr. Tambourine Man" absolutely stunning yet again. Later highlights included "Tombstone Blues", "Leopard-Skin Pill-Box-Hat" and "Rainy Day Women #12 & 35", all of which were pile-driver party pieces.

Next up for us was an overnight drive to Berlin. We stopped at the first opportunity for refreshments. Later that night we discovered that we had missed Dylan and his entourage at the same stop by a matter of minutes. Ah, well......

We made the most of the day in Berlin. It was my first visit and the centres of the old West and East formed our forward path. There was a fascinating exhibition of the proposed reconstruction of Berlin centre.

"Berlin 2005" said the poster; "2005? – the acoustic tour", I murmured. It was as we left this exhibition that major concert-goer and Internet tour agent

Ray Webster[5] came out with a comment that I think sums up all of the more besotted Dylan fans, and illuminates the way the NET has come to dominate their lives. Ray was deep in discussion with Stephan about previous German Dylan dates he'd attended, and made a slip of memory by calling Frankfurt '87, "Frankfurt '89". When Stephan pointed this out, Ray said, straight-faced and with due gravitas, but in a startling indication of how we measure our history in NET years:

"Ah, yes, of course, the Berlin Wall came down in '89, Dylan in Frankfurt was '87."

After a visit to the Reichstag we took a bus back to the venue, still with plenty of time before the doors were due to open. We alighted to hear the strains of "The Lonesome Death Of Hattie Carroll" being soundchecked. We followed the sounds: "It is alright, it isn't Bob singing..." I began to say, but Stephan was over the road and far away already.

We stood outside the gates. There were intermittent breaks in the soundcheck, so during one I shouted greetings to John Jackson. Ever accommodating, he returned them with a big smile. We saw Winston and Tony too. The soundcheck, since we first heard it, had consisted solely of different versions of "The Lonesome Death Of Hattie Carroll".

This was more than enough to keep us where we were, particularly as we were standing where Bob's bus would be most likely to arrive. Dylan's road manager Victor Maymudes[6], a man whose features are carved out of a material even older and more seasoned than those of Keith Richards, walked up to the security gates which had remained unlocked but under close surveillance all this time. He could not find his pass and fumbled for it in every pocket. He

5 Ray Webster, a Dylan follower par excellence and a great friend of many Dylan and Cohen fans, groups and forums passed away in February 2010. He was and is widely mourned.

6 Victor Maymudes (often spelt Maimudes) was Dylan's road manager-come-buddy in the early '60s and returned to be Dylan's personal manager from 1986-1996. Their relationship turned sour and Victor spent his last years penning a book that was alleged to be a shocking expose of his one time friend and employer. (It was to be called "The Joker and the Thief"). Victor Maymudes died in January 2001, a year before his book was scheduled for publication. As this book was going to print the first two 'interviews' that were to form the basis of Maymudes' book appeared, for a brief time, on YouTube.

eventually found it, not that anyone was waiting on it, as he was immediately recognised anyway. This was a diverting little sideshow but more was to follow.

The only person who had more trouble with his pass was Bucky. He had his Bob Dylan access badge round his neck and walked through the guards showing his card to each one. They all completely ignored him (because he's recognised too, I supposed). Bucky clearly felt that someone should nod to him or open the gates or give some acknowledgement of his status, so he made a very firm point of showing his pass to the last person at the gates. This was our companion Daniel, who was intently reading the sports pages in his German paper and would only lift his head when Dylan himself arrived.

Consequently Daniel also completely ignored Bucky, who was left to wander inside in a rather aimless fashion. Minutes later the German paper – which included the splendid line: "Watching Dylan perform 'Like A Rolling Stone' is like hearing Goethe reading *Faust*", was discarded as THE (pronounced theee) bus arrived.

It was only now that anyone paid attention to us and we were asked to move, asked quite firmly as it happened. However, there was no way we were going to miss Dylan's appearance, so we ignored the requests and surrounded the bus.

Dylan emerged pretty quickly, before even more rapidly disappearing into an enveloping throng. Nonetheless I got a lovely glimpse of him, dressed in a hooded sweatshirt with jacket on top in the height of summer. When I returned to the UK I was asked more questions about this brief peek than about all three shows combined, which is a slightly worrying indicator of what Dylan fans can be like. Then again, as David Bristow remarked to me, "Those are the moments we live for."

So, with Bob in place, it was time for us to join the queue at the doors to the Berlin Tempodrom. This was an unusual venue, resembling a big circus tent. Nonetheless, it turned out to be a pretty good way to see Dylan, with the massed foot soldiers at the front and well-raised seats around. Highlights included "I Want You", "Under The Red Sky", "Girl From The North Country" and driving versions of "Lenny Bruce" and "Cat's In The Well". "Knockin' On Heaven's Door" and "The Times They Are A Changin'" were pretty special too. During the latter's fabulous harmonica climax, I felt overwhelmed with sadness that I would not be seeing Bob again for months as far as normal gigs were concerned. I did, at least, have his appearance at The Phoenix Festival at Stratford-upon-Avon still to come, or I would have been feeling even worse. Further depression was to follow when I saw the original set-list, with acoustic alternatives which included "Visions Of Johanna" and "Desolation Row", and "Tears Of Rage" as an electric alternative.

Of my fellow travellers, Marion and Giovanna had Glauchau to look forward to, Chris, Daniel and Stephan had Dortmund and Stuttgart, Ray had Stratford and Spain. I only had Stratford and that really did not seem nearly enough. As it transpired, it was an even bigger let-down than I was already fearing; when the time came for it, that show was to be the low point in a year of so many highs.

The Phoenix experience began when we arrived at an airfield packed with thousands of Suede fans. After an unsavoury 'ego-spat' between Dylan and Suede, Dylan was billed as the headline act, while Suede were to close the show.

Dylan was out of place and so were we. There was even a rumour Dylan wouldn't appear but he did, and he looked fantastic when he took the stage: 'Supper Club' jacket, shades, that hair. Unfortunately the giant video screen that had been showing previous acts such as Van Morrison and Tricky in close-up was switched off for the duration of Bob's set.

At least I finally got to hear "Drifter's Escape", though that claim is more in theory than practice. This opening thrash bore virtually no resemblance to the song I had cherished for so many years. "I Want You" made an overwhelming, joyous contrast. However, during another unwelcome third-song appearance of "All Along The Watchtower" my view was obscured by a steward. I was left to wonder at the manic security that tries to block videos and photographs of our man. The giant screens bore blanked-out witness to this nonsense.[7]

After a solid "Tears Of Rage" and another unsuccessful "Tangled Up In Blue", things began to improve with "Mama, You've Been On My Mind", and really took off with its climactic harmonica playing. The highlight of the night was a beautifully paced, vocally rich "One Too Many Mornings". However, it was

7 In case you are wondering, yes, I did complain and asked them with increasing lack of manners to move out the way and no, the 'security crew' did not take kindly to these complaints and requests.

all over far, far too soon, and "Seeing The Real You At Last" and "Rainy Day Women #12 & 35" finished off what seemed a let-down of a set after the three German shows. Shows are always subjective experiences, as we know, and here I was watching in a toxic combination of bad sound, horrific venue, shortened set and, finally, the heavens opening and torrential rain lashing us as we left. There was no shelter from this storm.

I might have finished attending shows, but Dylan was only in the middle of his busiest touring year to date. The European trek ended on July 30th, and by the end of September Dylan was out on the road in the States, yet again. The shows, while not reaching the heights of the spring, were enthusiastically received by fans and press alike. In addition, they were bookended by two more events that were broadcast on TV.

The first of these was on September 2nd, when Dylan made a high-profile, though musically merely competent, five-song appearance at the opening of the Rock and Roll Hall of Fame and Museum in Cleveland. Bruce Springsteen joined him for the final song, "Forever Young".

The TV episode at the other end of this leg was at the previously mentioned Frank Sinatra 80th Birthday Tribute on November 19th. All the guests were to perform one song associated with Sinatra. Dylan however sang one of his own songs, allegedly at Sinatra's request, the long-neglected "Restless Farewell".

Intriguingly, the quintessentially Dylan ending we have to this song, which signalled the end of both an album and an entire phase of his career, echoes the sentiments of Sinatra's signature tune. "So I'll make my stand", sings Bob, "And remain as I am/ And bid farewell and not give a damn". It is a far greater "My Way", even though it is from a near-forgotten, half-formed, hastily written back page.

I should not leave the autumn of 1995 without remarking on a special show on September 23rd, at a tiny club called The Edge in Fort Lauderdale FL. Another 'live rehearsal' in an intimate setting, the show stirred memories of 1990's Toad's appearance. This was no four-hour marathon, but the normal-length set was dominated by eight covers:

23rd September 1995 The Edge Club, Fort Lauderdale FL

1 Real Real Gone (Van Morrison)
2 Friend Of The Devil (Hunter/Garcia/Dawson)
3 Maggie's Farm
4 It's Too Late (Chuck Wills)
5 Silvio (Dylan/Hunter)
6 Confidential (Dorinda Morgan)
7 Willin' (Lowell George)
8 That Lucky Old Sun (Haven Gillespie/Beasley Smith)
9 West L.A. Fadeaway (Garcia/Hunter)
10 When I Paint My Masterpiece
11 Key To The Highway (C Segar/Big Bill Broonzy)
12 Tangled Up In Blue
13 With God On Our Side
14 Highway 61 Revisited

After one of the covers Dylan is clearly heard to say that he is tired of trying to "turn bullshit into gold". This is one of his most peculiar remarks, considering that he has spent many nights of the NET making "gold" from his cover versions. We also know from numerous interviews just how important these songs are to him, which makes the "bullshit" comment even more mysterious. John Dolen of *The Sun Sentinel* managed to get a telephone interview with Dylan soon after and tried to prise an explanation out of Dylan, but the response raises more questions than it answers:[8]

John Dolen: "At the Edge show Saturday, you did a lot of covers, including some old stuff, like 'Confidential'. Was that a Johnny Ray song?"

Bob Dylan: *"It's by Sonny Knight. You won't hear that again."*

---

8 *Fort-Lauderdale Sun Sentinel* 29th September 1995 'A Midnight Chat With Bob Dylan by John Dolen'.

John Dolen: "Oh, was that the reason for your 'trying to turn bullshit into gold' comment at the show? Were these covers just something for folks at the Edge? Does that mean you aren't going to be doing more material like that on your tour, including the Sunrise shows?"

Bob Dylan: *"It will be the usual show we're used to doing on this tour now, songs most people will have heard already."*

There was a most surprising ending to 1995, as Dylan broke with his own tradition of not touring through the Thanksgiving-Xmas-New Year holidays. This year, rather than spend all that time with family members, as was customary, he lined up ten dates in December. This was a special tour with the particular purpose of helping Patti Smith get back on the road and her career on track. It turned out very well for Patti, but as far as Dylan was concerned it was a depressing end to what had hitherto been a magnificent touring year.

Dylan's voice was wasted and he and the band sounded like they needed a well-deserved break. The shows were high-energy enough, consisting of a blanket of loud rock to cover a poverty of subtlety and inflection. Nonetheless, to my surprise and dismay, these performances were as warmly greeted by some fans as those earlier in the year. The more discerning wrote them off as a good thing for Patti and forgettable for Dylan.

There were some highlights though; Dylan chronicler Clinton Heylin is particularly fond of "Desolation Row" at Bethlehem on December 13th. By the time you got to the same song on the last night at Philadelphia on the 17th, Dylan's voice was so strained that it is painful to listen to. Which is something it shares with the appalling performance of "Tangled Up In Blue" before it. The gulf between these pitiful acoustic set openers and the vocal splendour of the spring sets was so vast that it was beyond comprehension. There were, however, a few redeeming features, such as a fine "Every Grain Of Sand", a burst of stellar harmonica on "It's All Over Now, Baby Blue" and, the big talking point of this mini-tour, Bob and Patti duetting on "Dark Eyes". Patti was the one who had brought this magnificent song back into circulation.

Unfortunately, the first time Bob and Patti attempted the duet her talents were all one could admire. Dylan's memory of the lyrics seemed to stretch only as far as the title phrase. Given the wretched state his vocal cords were in, one could be forgiven for wishing that had eluded him too. Suitably chastened, Dylan relearned the words from his own lyric book and his performance of it improved.

A final footnote to 1995 is to mention that our old friend G.E. Smith joined Dylan on stage for the final song on December 14th. It reminded me of just how many shows had passed since G.E. had departed, and that the current line-up had lasted some three hundred shows unchanged.

Would 1996 bring any line up changes? *Would there be new Dylan material*? These were the questions that dominated Dylan fans' minds that Xmas, as well as the perennial *When's the first time I can see him next year*?

CHAPTER TEN

1996: "...it looks like I'm moving, but I'm standing still"

"I was born here and I'll die here against my will
I know it looks like I'm moving, but I'm standing still
Every nerve in my body is so vacant and numb
I can't even remember what it was I came here to get away from."

FROM "NOT DARK YET", RELEASED 1997

Though there were about 30 fewer shows in 1996 than in 1995, they began only in April so the touring year seemed hectic enough once it had started. Apart from one-offs, the 1996 shows took place in three bursts: April-May saw 27 shows in the USA and Canada, then it was European summer time again with 28 shows through June and July, followed by the same amount in the USA in October and November.

It is not a year remembered with great fondness by most long-term fans. In contrast to the innovation and stellar performing levels of most of 1995, it was all too predictable; same band, same set structure, and not many song debuts. Overall the shows were solid enough, but, as in late '93 and periods of '94, just not particularly special. More alarmingly, some of the overlong, uninspired, unproductive guitar instrumentals were reappearing too.

By 1996 there was a change in my own situation. I was still obsessive by normal standards and I still went to shows in both the UK and Germany, followed the news daily and collected tapes and CDs and videos. Nonetheless there was a palpable lessening of intensity, especially when I eventually stopped my telephone information service later in the year.

It is inevitable that there will be such 'peaks and troughs' within one's own personal energy, time and enthusiasm. Perhaps, too, there was still an after-effect of having met Dylan in Camden. It was not as though I would ever get that close again, nothing was going to top that. Also, the sheer longevity of the Never Ending Tour was energy-sapping for a dedicated fan, so goodness only knows how much more so for the band and their singer. However my relatively diminished obsession with the NET was also partly down to the fact that so many shows by now had featured the same personnel and utilised the same basic set structure. How I longed for a return to half acoustic/half electric shows. Or more keyboard playing, or a saxophone or a violin. One of these wishes was to come back to haunt me in later years, but that was far in the future at this stage.

Not going to so many shows did not, however, mean that I was unable to follow the tour in other ways. The beginnings of what was to be an explosive growth in the availability of CD-Rs aided me in enlivening a palate jaded by tape after tape of similar-sounding shows, and the rise of the Internet was playing a larger and larger role in my experience of the NET. With its swift dissemination of information and unparalleled global communication capability, the 'Net seemed tailor made for the NET.

Much as fanzines had helped to create communities out of disparate and geographically separated Dylan fans in the 1980s, so the Internet facilitated this, at an exponential growth rate, in the 1990s. Apart from the ease and speed of e-mail itself, the 'Net soon furnished Dylan-focussed newsgroups, chat rooms and Web pages. Back in 1996, the only newsgroup was rec.music.dylan. This had started at the turn of the decade, and I had been participating in it for around four years. The newsgroup had many spin-offs where people would help others get to shows or upgrade tickets, and even spawned a dedicated team of 'agents' whom one could write to for help and information on their specialist subjects. These covered everything from tickets and civil rights to tape decks and tour parties. Like all popular internet newsgroups the postings varied: from someone dropping in to ask "What album is 'Blowin' In the Wind' on?" to long, erudite lyrical analyses and in-depth concert reports. Unfortunately, too, like all unmoderated newsgroups (on any topic, it would appear) the occasional 'nutter' would be attracted to the site and try to spoil it for everyone else.

In addition, a number of dedicated Web pages had sprung up around Dylan, including a still extant one begun in autumn 1995 and run by Bill Pagel which includes an entire area dedicated to the NET. As soon as possible after the show the set-list is posted, perhaps with a picture of the list that had been pinned up on the stage, and sometimes with photos of the event. Reviews are posted too, though these are nearly always written from the point of view of a fan in the full flush of joy at having just been at a show, so one tends to get a larger proportion of raves than anything else. There are by now thousands of "this has to be one of the best shows ever".

In any case, it was easy to stay well and truly informed of all that was going on in the NET even without waiting for one of the Dylan fanzines to pop through the letterbox. As the technology and software behind the internet developed, this became more and more true with each passing year.

My touring for 1996 was restricted to the following dates: June 26th and 27th, Liverpool, June 29th (shortened set) Hyde Park and July 1st-3rd in Germany, at Münster, Mannheim and Konstanz. I found the two nights at Liverpool to be contrasting; the first I thought was competent without being exciting, but the second was better and included a fine acoustic set. For these dates Dylan was joined by Al Kooper on keyboards. As Michael Gray picked up on in an article for U.S. Dylan fanzine *On The Tracks*, this evoked thoughts of the mid-60s and the contrast with the last time he played in Liverpool, 30 years before. Unsurprisingly, the 1996 shows did not do well in the comparison:

"The band is 1/10th as good as The Band; Bob Dylan isn't 1/10th as energetic or innovative or communicative or accurate or acute; only the ragged rapture that greets him is greater than it was. Ironically, now that Dylan has got so much less to say, and cares even less how he says it, he's knee deep in Lifetime Achievement Awards and disproportionate adoration. This time half the audience comes to both shows, and the Bobcats who descended from all corners of the land occupy all the front rows; the usual 18 faces peering up at Bob's (how very dispiriting is must be for him). They spend the whole show on their feet, whooping at every number in the usual ritual way, regardless of how well or badly Dylan sings it.

"There is nothing healthy in this ballyhoo of over-reaction; nothing to tell the Bob Dylan of the 1990s what he knew instinctively 30 years ago; that just one new, thoughtful song, with words unfamiliar to the audience – but fresh and invigorating for their creator – and delivered directly from the calm centre of the artist, would be an infinitely greater treasure and thrill than any number of patchy re-visits to the obvious hits of the past."

In spite of Liverpool's local papers praising Dylan for his professionalism and his inspirational performing art, for the jaundiced regular NET-goers it was inevitably "just another show", albeit one that they may have whooped their way through.

The very title for the Hyde Park event showed it not to be "just another show" but something far less worthy. June the 29th was the date for Dylan to play at 'The MasterCard Masters of Music Concert for The Prince's Trust' which probably tells you all you need to know about the occasion, however admirable the cause. Also on the bill was the hugely successful newcomer Alanis Morrissette, plus Eric Clapton, The Who and, for some strange reason, the subsequently disgraced Gary Glitter[1]. Most of the crowd were there to see The Who. Dylan performed only nine songs. Al Kooper was still on board and was now joined by Ron Wood. Depending on where you lived you would get either three or five Dylan songs shown on a TV broadcast of the event.

In the end, Dylan at Hyde Park was not as bad as I had feared, though the day itself was as gruesome as its title and location imply. "The Who plus Bob plus Eric Clapton plus no booze in a bleak, mid-summer Hyde Park equals one damp squib," *The Independent*'s Andy Gill quipped in his review, continuing:

"It was all dismayingly corporate, and the only way around the Royal Parks' alcohol ban was to pay £200 to enter the VIP area, where Royal tradition was washed away in a sea of free champers. From my wind-swept eyrie in row ZZ of the seats, I could see the VIP tent, over whose entrance was strung a banner bearing the corporate sponsor's logo and the mystifying claim 'Palace of Rock', wherein slavering rock beasts like Virginia Bottomley and the charity's distinguished patron – to whom I overheard one plummy voice refer, with

1 Gary Glitter (real name Paul Francis Gadd), prominent glam-rock star in England in the early 1970s. In later life he was found guilty of a string of paedophilic offences in the UK and Vietnam.

overweening familiarity, simply as 'Wales' – could refresh themselves and rattle their jewellery away from the hoi-polloi. With no equivalent means of warming up from the inside out, the bulk of the crowd was dependent on the show itself raising the temperature, and this remained steadfastly tepid."[2]

While Dylan managed to avoid living down to the worst trepidations of long term fans, one has to admit that his set was far from inspired. As Andy Gill pointed out, Dylan spent "much of his time onstage subverting his own material, rendering some of the most well known of rock anthems virtually unrecognisable, both to the audience and, at times, to his own musicians, who follow gamely wherever Bob's boot-heels may be a-wanderin'." Gill sympathised with an audience stuck playing 'Spot the Intro'. "Even spotted correctly," he continued, "the songs were impossible to sing along with, Dylan twisting his delivery in the most tortuous fashion, flattening most of the melodies in a manner that sounded utterly dismissive of the songs."

However, three less than special shows was never going to be enough to deter even my new 'not quite so obsessive' self from continuing on to Europe for another Dylan-led visit to my good friends Chris, Stephan and Daniel.

1st July 1996 Halle Münsterland, Münster, Germany

1. Drifter's Escape
2. Shake Sugaree
3. All Along The Watchtower
4. Simple Twist Of Fate
5. It Takes A Lot To Laugh, It Takes A Train To Cry
6. Silvio
7. Boots Of Spanish Leather (acoustic)
8. John Brown (acoustic)
9. Mama, You Been On My Mind (acoustic)
10. Maggie's Farm
11. Ballad Of A Thin Man

2 *The Independent* Section 2, Monday 1st July, 1996

12. Obviously Five Believers
13. Alabama Getaway
14. It Ain't Me Babe (acoustic)
15. Rainy Day Women #12 & 35

Some people seemed to love this show; I was less impressed, placing it somewhere between the first and second Liverpool shows. It kicked off with a chaotic "Drifter's Escape", cocked up as only Bob can cock things up. He was all over the place, beginning verses just as Jackson's guitar was ending them. I really liked "Shake Sugaree" though, and not just because I had never heard him sing it before. It was entrancing, but the mood it engendered quickly passed as the concert continued. I knew, though, that it would be a song I would return to. I cannot remember anything about "All Along The Watchtower" or "Silvio", but in between them we had a tender "Simple Twist Of Fate" and a fine, rocking "It Takes A Lot To Laugh, It Takes A Train To Cry". Although these were very good indeed, this was as good as it got.

The acoustic set was passable, they are never less than that. Dylan usually performs "Mama, You Been On My Mind" better than he did here, however, and it now seemed to be sung to the same melody as "Don't Think Twice, It's All Right". In fact, I was starting to think that Bob was gravitating towards having one acoustic and one electric song and just giving them different names.

The acoustic song could have the same melody and still be any one of: "Mama, You Been On My Mind"/ "Don't Think Twice, It's Alright"/"It Ain't Me, Babe"/ "Girl From The North Country" etc. And the electric could be a standard live run through of one of: "Maggie's Farm"/"Ballad Of A Thin Man"/"Leopard-Skin Pill.- Box Hat"/"Tombstone Blues"/"Highway 61 Revisited", the encore then would be an amalgam of "Silvio"/ "Alabama Getaway" and then the acoustic song again. The disappointments of many repetitive shows had made me paranoid. I was becoming NET stir-crazy.

"Maggie's Farm" passed by and then Bob started "Ballad Of A Thin Man" which I thought had been one of the few electric successes in Liverpool, where Dylan seemed to be inventing a whole new version as he went along. I was sure he was going to attempt that same version but, unfortunately, he lost the words and went into a sulk, with the song bearing the brunt of his mood.

"Obviously Five Believers" picked things up slightly before the all-too-predictable encores. I felt like the year since I had been in Germany had not passed for Bob; I was witnessing more or less the same show, except that now it had lost its sparkle. What had been fresh and innovative the year before was now merely a professional procession, night after night. It was still enjoyable, but that special spark, that great rush of mental and emotional discovery that Dylan can inspire, was missing.

2nd July 1996 Mozartsaal im Rosengarten, Mannheim, Germany

1. Down In The Flood
2. Pretty Peggy-O
3. All Along The Watchtower
4. I'll Be Your Baby Tonight
5. Man In The Long Black Coat
6. Silvio
7. Ballad Of Hollis Brown (acoustic)
8. Gates Of Eden (acoustic)
9. To Ramona (acoustic)
10. Everything Is Broken
11. What Good Am I?
12. Seeing The Real You At Last

*

13. Alabama Getaway
14. My Back Pages (acoustic)
15. Rainy Day Women #12 & 35

Designed for opera and ballet, this hall is outstanding both acoustically and for ease of viewing the stage. Thankfully, Dylan made the most of this opportunity. It was a pleasure to hear so many variations from the night before, and took someone as churlish as myself to pine for the as-yet-unheard "This Wheel's On Fire".

A chaotic opening song was again followed by a great choice for the second: "Pretty Peggy-O". There were many other highlights, principally a magnificent acoustic set (even though the last verse of "Gates Of Eden" began with "the motor-cycle Black Madonna" lines) and a moving "What Good Am I?". "Everything Is Broken" was instantly forgettable, and I only wish "Seeing The Real You At Last" had been too. Still, it was my favourite show so far that I had attended in 1996. A strong "My Back Pages" redeemed the usual uninspiring encores. (It also featured the only harp solo of the night – a good one too, so much more effective than just throwing them in all over the place.)

3rd July, 1996 Zeltfestival (Tent Festival), Konstanz, Germany

1 Down In The Flood
2. I Want You
3. All Along The Watchtower
4. Shelter From The Storm
5. Watching The River Flow
6. Silvio
7. Mr. Tambourine Man (acoustic)
8. Masters Of War (acoustic)
9. One Too Many Mornings (acoustic)
10. Maggie's Farm (dma)
11. I'll Remember You
12. Everything Is Broken (dma, dmb)

*

13. Alabama Getaway
14. The Times They Are A-Changin' (acoustic) (dma)
15. Rainy Day Women #12 & 35 (dma, dmb, dmc)

(dma) Dave Matthews' violinist played on this song
(dmb) Dave Matthews on guitar
(dmc) Dave Matthews' horn player played saxophone on this song

In the intimate setting of a tiny tent perched on a beautiful lakeside, this was one of the strangest Dylan shows I've been to: a boring set list, a very indifferent performance from Dylan for most of the show, but immensely entertaining and fun by the end.

Back to the beginning, though, and there was a promising start as Dylan and the band actually played the same song for the opener. This was followed by a very pleasant "I Want You" and an as-good-as-it-can-get-under-the-circumstances "All Along The Watchtower". All this augured well, but there was something wrong with his voice. I am not sure if he had a cold or was hoarse from over-touring, but he could not pull off the tender version of "Shelter From The Storm" that he was attempting. Then the show dipped alarmingly with a turgid "Watching The River Flow" and a worse-than-normal (if that is possible) "Silvio". The weakest "Mr. Tambourine Man" I could ever remember hearing, making such a depressing contrast to the year before,was followed by the most boring "Masters Of War". I was glumly thinking that it would probably be my last show for about a year and I hadn't liked anything apart from the second song.

Fortunately, on "One Too Many Mornings" Dylan finally began stretching his voice, hesitantly at first then with more confidence. Things were looking up, though my interest was dimmed by the opening chords of "Maggie's Farm". I should not have despaired, help was at hand, albeit from an unlikely source. I am as anti guests on stage with Bob as it's possible to be. I was even furious when Dylan fans cheered George Harrison when George joined Bob on stage at Wembley Arena in 1987. I thought he should have been booed for causing a distraction from Dylan.

Nonetheless, it was a guest who saved this show, someone I did not even know the name of: the electric violin player from the supporting Dave Matthews Band.[3] This tall, muscular, distinctly cool black man bounded on stage with a

3 I later found the following piece of information from the Dave Matthews Band Web Site: "Boyd Tinsley: (violin, vocals) finds it strange sometimes that he abandoned the reserved precision of classical violin for the spontaneity of contemporary musical performance. 'This was an area I hadn't explored before,' says Tinsley, who has been playing popular music since 1985. 'When I'm really into the music, my whole body, my whole soul is into it.' In fact, one of his trademarks are his 'jams' with Dave Matthews. The best thing, though, he says, is how much it matters to the audience, and to the players. 'People are drawn to it,' he says. 'There's a passion here'."

huge grin and a presence to match, and suddenly Bob had to wake up. Here was someone on stage who was not only drawing the audience's eyes away from Dylan, but who could also play like fury and had no inhibitions in showing it. "Maggie's Farm" really took off and ended in a duet/duel between Dylan's guitar and the tall dude's manic violin. The sheer joy on Dylan's face was something to behold and the audience responded with passionate enthusiasm.

At the song's conclusion Dylan high-fived the violinist and we were into a run-of-the-mill "I'll Remember You". A grim "Everything Is Broken" followed, with Dave Matthews himself now on guitar but probably as unfamiliar with the song as Dylan appeared to be. However, halfway through it was transformed when the violinist returned to the stage. A huge grin split Dylan's face and they were off again, Dylan revelling in having a musician on stage who played for playing's sake and, although clearly admiring Bob, deferred to no one. A typically God-awful "Alabama Getaway" was played next, but was then succeeded by the highlight of the night as the violinist reappeared for a stunning "The Times they Are A-Changin'".

After a verse or so to familiarise himself with the arrangement the violinist upped the ante. Dylan responded with vocals and guitar, the two of them egging each other on. Then Dylan grabbed a harmonica and started his walk around the centre stage. The violinist took this as a cue to circle Dylan, playing ever louder and faster. Dylan responded by redoubling his harp playing while moving to the violinist's (previously John Jackson's) microphone as the demented fiddler now took centre stage. The two then came together, warily at first like two nervous fencers, before meeting up again at the centre microphone for a blistering end to the song. By this time the crowd could probably be heard in about five central European countries.

The whole thing ended with a completely over-the-top "Rainy Day Women #12 and 35", with both bands on stage and crashing guitars competing with sax, violin and Dylan's voice in a wild orgy of sound. Rarely have I seen Dylan so happy on stage; more hugs and high fives followed for the guests. My set of shows in the UK and Germany that had given so little in the Dylan scheme of things ended up leaving me smiling and content after all. As I ever, I metaphorically doffed my cap to the departing Dylan and thought: "Until next time, thanks again, Bob".

I mentioned above that it was a shame that the visual spectacle of Bob duelling with Dave Matthews' violinist wasn't preserved on video. However, in 1996 two NET shows were captured on film: the previously discussed Hyde Park show, and a gig at the so-called House of Blues – a temporary venue set up in the Olympic Village as part of the Olympic Games celebrations at Atlanta GA. Sadly, both turned out to be wasted opportunities, with Dylan just going through the motions and his voice extremely the worse for wear. They were representative of the NET at its least inspired.

The House of Blues, which is not yet on general release[4], was little better than the nine-song Hyde Park outing. You do not see or feel any sense of Dylan's presence, not because of the limitations of the video medium but because he simply was not present to any meaningful degree. There was no fire, no passion, no engagement with the songs. It was "just another show". Of which there were becoming far too many that could be referred to so dismissively.

A measure of how poor the House of the Blues show was came when even "Under The Red Sky" sounded dull and, in the acoustic set, "Love Minus Zero/ No Limit", a song Dylan usually performs at the very least to a high standard and often raises to an exquisite level, just passed by in a blur. As for the long guitar jams on "Watching The River Flow", I cannot imagine what this inoffensive song had ever done to deserve such a fate. I think the closing guitar instrumental was probably longer than the original song itself. Dylan seemed happy enough though, nodding and waving to the audience who, as usual, lapped up "Silvio".

If little of value was preserved by the professional television crews, the dedicated tapers provided high quality tapes of most shows. As I mentioned at the beginning of this chapter, however, I, like many others, had grown weary of listening to whole shows in 1996. The same band (until October), the same format and the perpetual recurrence of songs that had been done to death caused this weariness. Fortunately, bootleg-industry-transforming technology meant that by 1996 one could get a show on CD-R rather than on tape, with all the convenience that brings. Heard "All Along The Watchtower" too many times? Simply press the "skip" button. Want to locate the new song played for the first time? Press the requisite track number.

4 There were two nights at the House of the Blues but I have only seen the video from one.

Then there were compilations. Fans had always made and shared compilation tapes. 'My favourite acoustic songs in 1988'; "Best of 1992", '15 NET versions of Maggie's Farm' (no, I am only kidding with that one) and so forth. The same concept on CD-R was even more attractive, given that format's flexibility and programmability. Stack a number on a multi-player and you could programme all kinds of tailored NET experiences.

While something is certainly lost when one is listening to a song without the proper context of an evolving show, this was a marvellously convenient way to keep some kind of track of over eighty shows coming in three two-month bursts. In addition, if certain performances sounded particularly fine, one could always then listen to the whole show. I may have stopped listening to entire shows from every night but it was not as though I had stopped collecting them; the thought would never have occurred to me in those days. One way or another I heard much to enjoy in 1996, and some of the highlights are worth pointing out to balance the rather jaundiced overall impression I am presenting.

Far and away the finest performed song of the year was the NET debut in Berlin of "Shake Sugaree". This is credited to Elizabeth Cotton, but this version came via Fred Neill. I was entranced by this at the Münster show. I could not immediately grasp the full significance of the words but I felt their poetic depth when Dylan sang them. It is a sumptuous song, and although Dylan did not write it, it feels like he should have. It has just the right mixture of simplicity, mystery and discontinuity to not be out of place on *The Basement Tapes*. In Berlin, Dylan's performance of it was transcendent, an authentic piece of consummate artistry amongst the nightly slog. Triumphs like these are more than enough reason to keep following his touring schedule as long as it continues.

Speaking of *The Basement Tapes* and song debuts where Dylan got it absolutely right first time, the first show in Madison on April 13th saw the live debut of "This Wheel's On Fire". "Gonna try something new," Dylan began to audience cheers, "new for us anyway...." I cannot imagine that anyone would have guessed what it would be, though it seemed an apt follow-up to 1995's first-show unveiling of the contemporaneous "Down In The Flood". As with "Shake Sugaree", you feel there must have been some serious rehearsing going on: both debuts of these marvellous songs were given proper readings, and in both cases the first performances have not been bettered since. Other debuts included an acoustic take on the Grateful Dead's "Friend Of The Devil", which unsurprisingly was a vast improvement on the electric version. The song's lyrics tell a banal tale of absurd macho posturing, yet you find yourself drawn to the old loveable rogue of a narrator rather than despising him. Dylan's voice inhabits the song and makes you side with him, just like he makes you empathise with the protagonists of the old traditional songs he performs so compellingly.

"To me each song is a play, a script," says NET guitarist (plus guitar and amplifier technician) César Diaz[5], "and he'll be that guy from the song for that moment, but [then] he'll change back to Bob....It took me a while to realize that. But he actually convinces you that yes, it is me who is talking to you, and I'm being sincere about it." My favourite version of this song, taped in magnificent quality, is part of a CD-R collecting the best performances in the best quality available. Alas all tracks are undated, so in this case I do not know if the song is representative of a particularly good show, or a standout in an otherwise ordinary affair. Actually, I quite like the mystery, perhaps there's a really good show out there that I have still to come across. There was another Dead connection in the debut of a song called "New Minglewood Blues", a version of which Garcia and company had long been playing under the title "New, New Minglewood Blues". Confusion abounded as to which version Dylan was playing. Unlike "Shake Sugaree", however, once one heard "Minglewood Blues" one didn't really care too much which version it was.

It was not just covers that made their NET entry during this '96 trek. "Seven Days" had its NET debut too. This song, a minor hit single for Ron Wood, had previously enjoyed four Dylan live outings, back in 1976. This is not one of Dylan's 'deep' or 'majestic' songs but it is fun, has a strong melody and is clearly the work of someone who knows what rock and rock 'n' roll hooks and internal rhymes are. It might be a throwaway, but it was still good to hear. In addition to debuts and covers, my 'Best of the NET 1996' included such delights as a towering "Disease Of Conceit". Once again Dylan brought the best out of an *Oh Mercy* song on stage. There was also a beautifully paced, wistful "Pretty

---

5 César Carrillo Díaz is described in his Wikipedia entry as "a Puerto Rican born guitar amplifier technician and guitarist". However it is not a description he would have liked. I had described him similarly in *Razor's Edge* and when that was published, I gave a talk at a Dylan convention. César was also giving a talk there and was most upset at not being described firstly as a guitarist and secondly as a guitar technician. I promised him I would put 'guitarist' down first if it were ever updated. César quickly went from threatening to stab me to sharing stories of the tour and giving me one of Dylan's guitars to strap on for a few minutes. Yes, he was quite a character! His talk drew a standing ovation and he played guitar also to great acclaim at the end of the event. Sadly, only about a year later, he passed away at the age of 51.

Peggy-O" showcasing Dylan's wonderfully deep, dark *World Gone Wrong* tones, and a funereal but gripping "Positively 4th Street" from Berlin on June 17th, where Dylan's magnificent regret-steeped vocals turned this well-known piece of vitriol into a wholly new song. This was the same night that featured the sparkling "Shake Sugaree", and it also boasted a fine "Friend Of The Devil".

In general, as in so many years, it was in the acoustic sets that Dylan most regularly pulled out the stops. One compilation I have features a version of "The Lonesome Death Of Hattie Carroll" which is truly dazzling. Listening to such highlights is both exhilarating and cautionary. It is so easy to get lazy, to write off whole legs of Dylan's touring years because they do not match up to some of his stellar periods. It is important to remember that even the dullest runs on the NET can harbour such gems.

One of the biggest events for long-term fans was an acoustic "Visions Of Johanna" on June 24th in Luxembourg. As with Philadelphia in 1995, much of the fuss was down to the choice of song rather than the performance, especially among the travelling fans that saw many shows but missed this one. Nonetheless, while the performance may have not been superlative it was very fine indeed. As I said, many of the travelling caravans of Bobcats missed Luxembourg, but most were in Utrecht on 21st June to hear Dylan once again address Lambchop. After Edinburgh the year before they were becoming quite chatty:

Dylan: "*Thank you. Thanks everybody!*"
Lambchop: "Thank you, Bobby. "
Dylan: "*On this side, gentleman playing the guitar, from Memphis...J.J. Jackson! Also we wanna say to our good friend the Chopper, who's down here. Hey Chopper, how come you never made it to Cincinnati, you were supposed to come over there, supposed to come down to Atlanta, you never showed up there.*"
Lambchop: "I didn't know about it, I wasn't invited."
Dylan: "*On the drums tonight, Winston Watson, give him a big hand. And on steel guitar, Bucky Baxter, he's playing the mandolin too. On bass guitar tonight, Tony Garnier. We'll be seeing you Chopper. All right! Ha-ha-ha! Hey! We've been missing you. We've been missing you the last hundred shows. Listen to what he is saying...*"
Lambchop: "You're the guv'ner – you always have been and you always will be, play what you want to play – You choose!"

Dylan: *"That's it! That's it! Ha-ha-ha. How about giving the Chopper a hand! He's seen more shows than me! He-he-he. He's seen me play more times than me!"*

I have mainly been talking about the first two legs of the tour, as that's where the debut songs appeared and where I saw him myself. The last bout of touring for the year was a return to the Southern States for the Fall. By now the long absence of original Dylan songs had begun to assume as 'endless' a feel as the NET itself. Throughout the year rumours continued to grow that we were indeed about to get a new album of such songs. By September '96 those in the know were telling us that Daniel Lanois was working on a set of Dylan acoustic demos, and that the songs were masterly insights from a mature artist.

The anticipation was now at dangerously high levels, and some fans even hoped that the Fall 1996 shows would feature some of these songs. Nothing could have been further from Dylan's track record on such things, and this tour was no exception. The Southern shows were all very similar in what was, for Dylan, a routine year; the songs themselves might change but you had to pay close attention to notice which mid-sixties 'classic rocker' replaced which from the night before, or which old folkie he was singing to the tune of "Boots Of Spanish Leather". There were no new songs debuted; the nearest thing to a surprise selection was the first appearance of "Man Of Peace" since 1991. In contrast to the leg at much the same locations five years previously, this was no Fall tour to revive the year.

Nonetheless, some seeds of future change were evident. First of all there was a change in band personnel. Drummer Winston Watson was replaced by David Kemper (formerly of the Jerry Garcia Band, thus keeping the Grateful Dead connection going.) Fortunately, unlike the hapless Watson, Kemper did not seem to have been given the same instructions to just keep bashing away whatever the song. His contributions would be part of a new sound, though this was not noticeable at first. This was partly because Kemper needed time to bed in, and these shows comprised mostly guitar-dominated standard run-throughs of old hits punctuated by longed for and much appreciated acoustic sets. A very public on-stage falling-out with John Jackson saw him temporarily replaced mid-tour by the excellent Charlie Sexton.

It seemed certain that Jackson's time was running out, and so it would prove early in 1997. Charlie Sexton's appearance on the NET was not to be his last, though. While Charlie's 'guest' appearance was rather out-of-the-ordinary, 1996 was a year full of more conventional such appearances. The roll call of those who joined Bob on stage during the year included Nils Lofgren, Ray Benson and James Burton, Roger McGuinn, Jewel, Paul James, Al Kooper, Amie Mann, Ron Wood, the Dave Matthews Band, Leroi Moore and, of course, Van Morrison.

Before the year's touring came to a close on November 23rd, the '60s were once again officially pronounced over, when Dylan allowed the Bank of Montreal to use "The Times They Are A-Changin'" in an advert. An unmemorable end to a relatively unmemorable year. "Give us something new", "It's time for a dramatic change" were the wishes of the fans. As the saying goes, you should be careful of what you wish for.

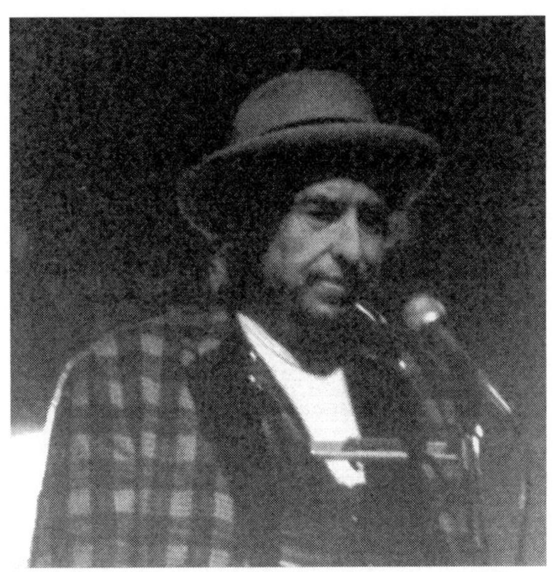

GLASGOW 1991, DYLAN AMIDST THE DARKNESS

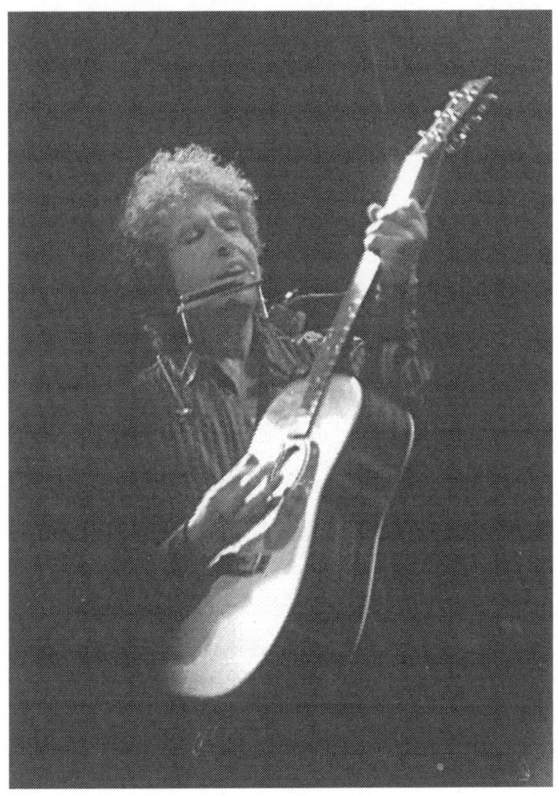

LYON 5TH JULY 1994

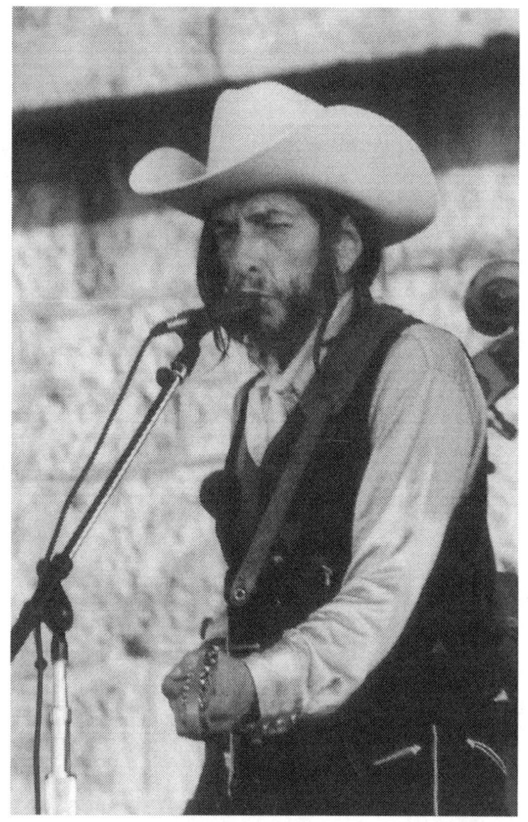

NEWPORT 2002, A NEW LOOK FOR THE SPECIAL DAY.

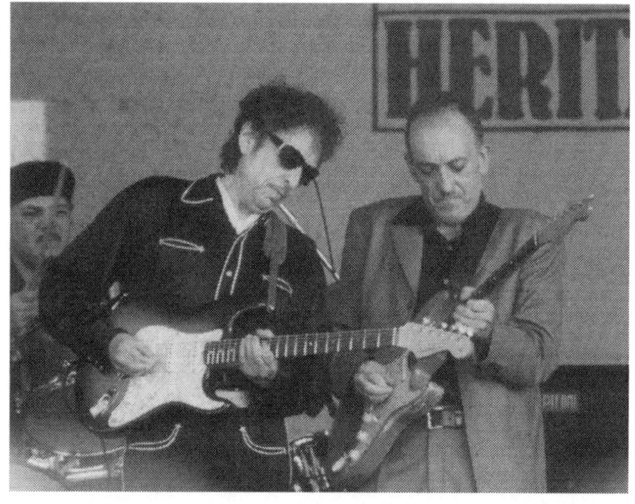

NEW ORLEANS 2003, WITH FREDDY KOELLA

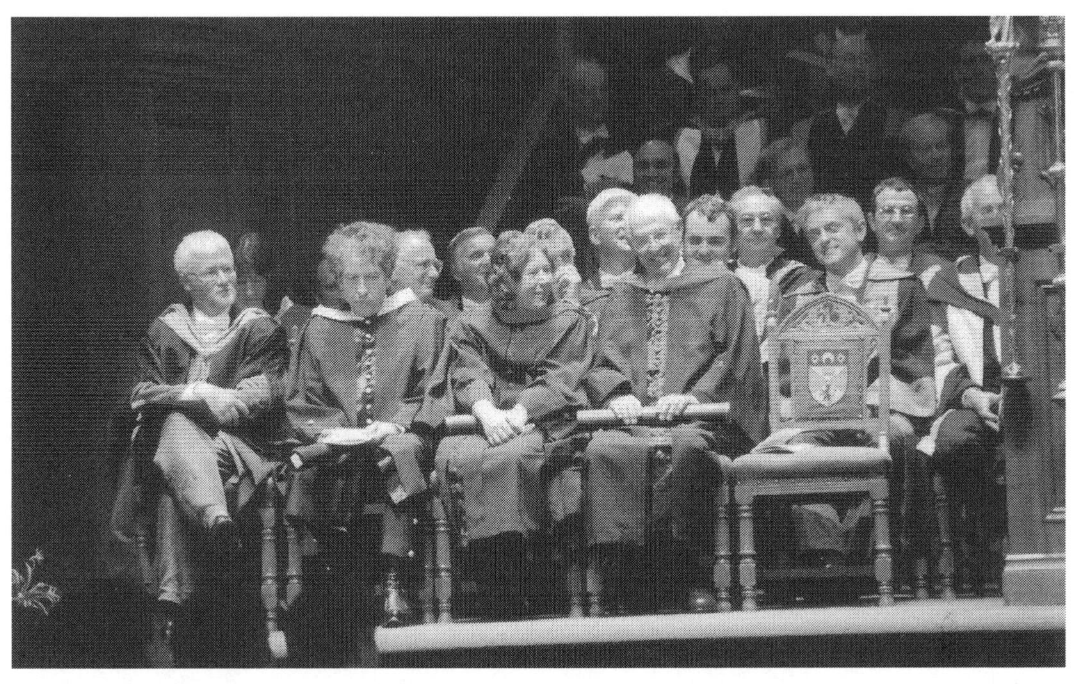

ST ANDREWS 2004. A TIRED DYLAN DURING THE LENGTHY CEREMONY

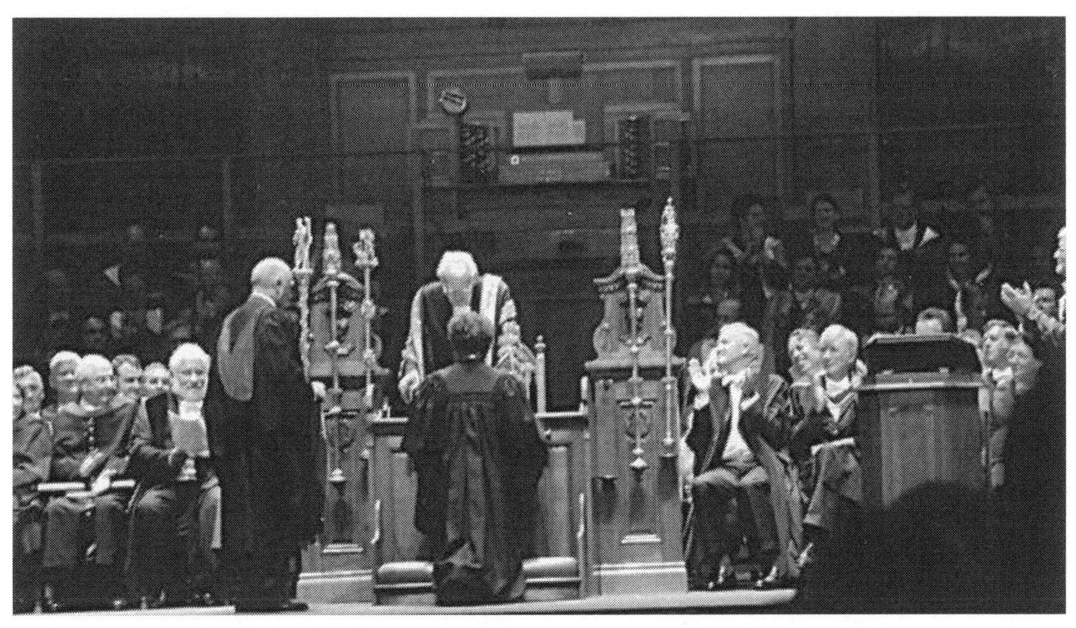

ST ANDREWS 2004, RECEIVING THE DOCTORATE

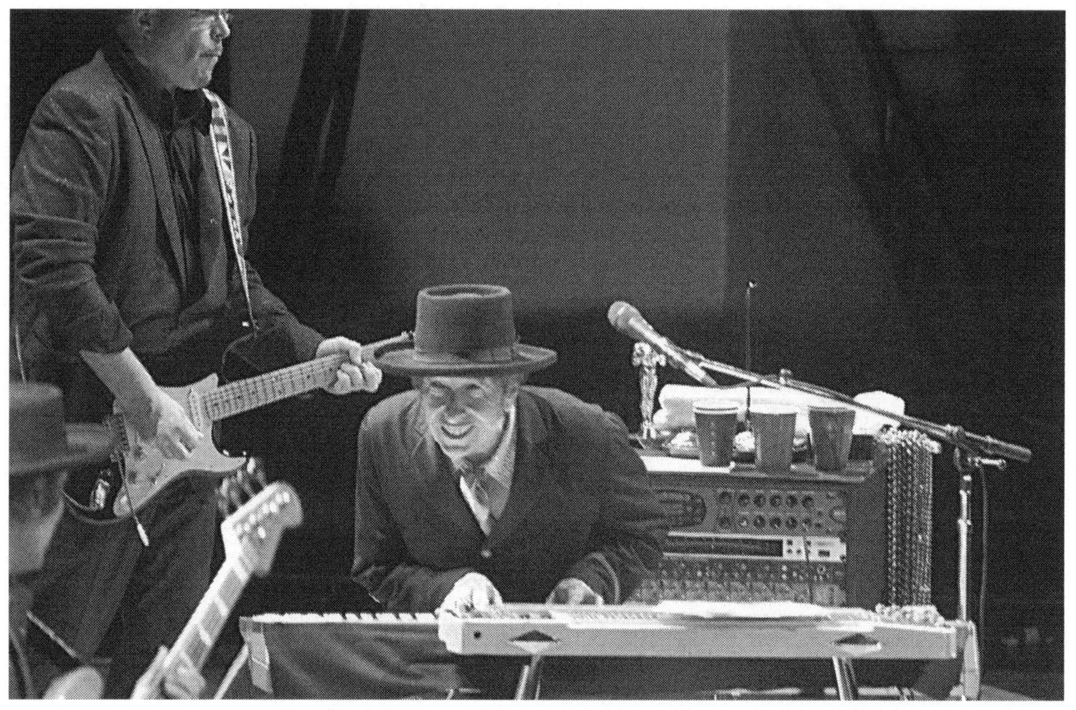

BOSTON 12TH NOVEMBER 2006, DYLAN BEHIND THE KEYBOARDS

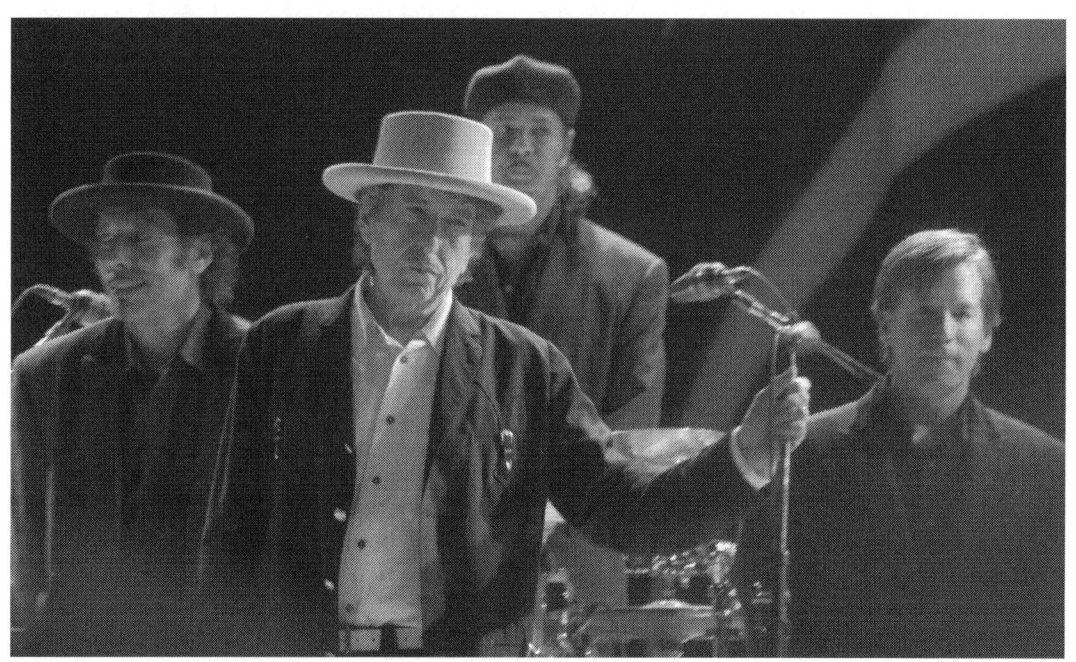

THE FORMATION, BIRMINGHAM 2007 – NO LAUGHING IN THE RANKS!

CHAPTER ELEVEN

1997: "I really thought I'd be seeing Elvis soon"

"When I was a little kid in La Jolla we had a parade on the Fourth Of July, and I remember clearly the sight of civil war veterans, marching down the main street, kicking up the dust. The first time I heard Bob Dylan it brought back that memory and I thought of him as something of a civil war type, a kind of 19th Century troubadour, a maverick American spirit. The reediness of his voice and the spareness of his words goes straight to the heart of America."

GREGORY PECK, 1997

If 1996 had been a largely uneventful year, 1997 was chock-full of incident. The three most startling of which sent news scurrying around the world: first, Bob Dylan was hospitalised with a 'potentially fatal" illness; second, Dylan met, and performed for, the Pope; third, and not least, "All Along The Watchtower" was moved from the number three slot and then dropped altogether.

Before these dramas unfolded, January saw Dylan record a new album of original material. The year's touring then began on February 9th in Tokyo. The shows on this short Japanese tour followed on directly from 1996, with few changes in the set-lists. There was, however, a one-off version of Noah Lewis's "Viola Lee

Blues" at Sapporo on February 24th. Yet another song heavily associated with the Grateful Dead, "Viola Lee Blues" was a delight to hear. Its classic blues riffs paved the way for the one-off version of Dylan's own "Pledging My Time" that was to follow a couple of months later.

Japan also saw Elizabeth Cotton's "Oh Babe, It Ain't No Lie" introduced to the set-list. It was a perfect melody for Dylan, and he gave lines such as "Stop telling all those lies on me" an added resonance. This really was a highlight in Japan and through the upcoming Spring shows. It was also reprised twice later in the year, so more people could enjoy the aptness and execution of Dylan plaintively singing: "Been all around this whole wide world".

In general, however, Japan 1997 was very much a continuation of the Fall/ Winter 1996 shows. It appeared that the relationship between Bob Dylan and John Jackson had not improved; the atmosphere between the two was reported by concert-goers to be verging on a breakdown. It seemed inevitable that a run of six years and near seven hundred shows for Jackson was approaching its end.

By the time Dylan headed off for another bout of touring on March 31st, Larry Campbell was on board as Jackson's replacement. While Campbell was more versatile and could also play violin, he would take some time to settle in, and these Spring '97 shows continued in much the same vein as Japan, and by extension, as in 1996. There were, though, a number of interesting developments in the band's playing, and a few more set-list surprises to augment the impressive "Oh Babe, It Ain't No Lie".

This leg also saw a rare postponement of a couple of shows when a Nova Scotia ferry transporting the band's equipment from the opening night venue – St John's, Newfoundland, Canada – got trapped in packed ice. The shows on April 3rd and 4th were both put back by two days as a result. Once the gear was recovered, the leg's rescheduled second show on the 5th began a seven-night run without a break, during which the new guitarist was obliged to find his NET bearings.

April 5th 1997 was also the date that Allen Ginsberg died of a heart attack. He was 70 years old. That night, Dylan dedicated "Desolation Row" to his old friend. "That was one of his favourite songs, the poet Allen Ginsberg," Dylan told the crowd afterwards, "that's for him". It was a splendid version that would have made Ginsberg very proud.

While the latter half of the '90s saw CD-R technology encroaching on the larger bootleggers' territory, early 1997 saw those nefarious fellows pull out one of the best examples of why fans will search out their illegal wares: the bootleg double CD *Bathed In A Stream Of Pure Heat* showcased the 1997 NET from Japan right up until a special one-off show on May 22nd. This was obviously the work of fans with an intimate knowledge of the NET, as it not only collected the rarities, the one-offs and the covers but also provided an overview of the best of the shows played during the period.

From it you can hear, amongst many other things, how Dylan continued to spice up his Never Ending Tour sets with covers. The 19th of April show in Hartford CT featured the first version of "I'm A Roving Gambler" since the marvellous South Bend show, back in November 1991. This version was effective enough, and the song would grow to become a valuable visitor to NET sets through this and future years.

That same night in Hartford saw Buddy Holly's "Not Fade Away" open the set. While it would take the most besotted fan to actually describe this attempt as 'good', it was much better than most of the desecrations that have been inflicted upon the poor song since it was moved into the 'rave-up-encores' slot. It is a pity Dylan has not covered Buddy's magnificent songs with the same excellence he has brought to so many other artists' work.

The night before, in Albany NY, there was a notable "Pretty Peggy-O". Yet another different arrangement for this ever-welcome traditional song. Here the lines 'caught up' with succeeding ones, almost as though they were running on too fast. Consequently, it was not always the last word of a line that was stressed, resulting in a different, and mixed, pace to the melody. Dylan's semi-wasted voice sounded appropriately like that of a soldier fading away through illness or injury.

Even more welcome, and better performed, was the 28th April appearance of "Long Black Veil"; a perfect song for Dylan to sing during the NET. Though created in the modern age in a conscious attempt, as lyric writer Danny Dill recalled, "to write an instant folksong", this beautifully-constructed, heart-breaking ballad sounds like one of the classic old-time songs, reeking of guilt, crime, punishment, stoicism, bravery, lust, love lost and death. I had wanted Dylan to tackle this for about as long as I could remember; I still semi-dream that there is a *World Gone Wrong* outtake of it (in pristine quality, one Dylan hasn't 're- engineered'). Now I could lay aside the wonderful versions from people such as Dylan's one time support act, BR5-49, from his one-time backing band, The Band, from his great fan, Nick Cave, from his friend, Johnny Cash, and luxuriate in the definitive article. Like "Delia" and "Stagger Lee", this dark elemental ballad was perfectly suited to Dylan's withered old prophet delivery.

Not every cover was as successful. The trite lyrics of "Friend Of The Devil" could not carry the weight that Dylan's Spring '97 version demanded of them. Dylan may have sounded genuinely like a man at the end of his tether, but the effect was more one of unsettling mystification than anything more meaningful.

If the covers were a mix of the great, the good, the merely curious and the poor, then this was a fair reflection of the shows overall. There were, as this trusty compilation showcases, very splendid versions of Dylan originals ,such as the ultra-bluesy "Pledging My Time" from April 22nd, and the marvellous, mysterious angst of "This Wheel's On Fire", where Dylan's yearning take on the doom-beckoning lyrics became a fearful query by the end of the song. You cannot but be awed at Dylan's powers of 'acting out the part' when presenting us with these compelling visions. The very second this song ended, he snapped out of the mood and into a laconic "Thanks everybody", followed by whimsical band intros. It was as if a switch had been flicked.

Other notable Dylan originals included a brave, if unsuccessful, attempt at "John Brown" featuring understated backing that meant the focus was all on, unusually for Dylan, lyrics which do not stand up to over-scrutiny.

Some other songs didn't work at all. "Every Grain Of Sand" on the 9th of April was hampered by Dylan's vocals all too clearly enacting the "dying voice" in the song's lyrics. It was inescapably clear that Dylan's voice was shot. And when Dylan debuted "You Ain't Goin' Nowhere" at Portland ME on April 10th, the narrator's call for an "easy chair" seemed imperative considering the pinched, strained voice the demand was sung in. Undeterred, the bold Bob continued on, with good reason as in the very same leg of the tour there were times when not only were Dylan's vocals strong enough to carry "Shooting Star" and "Born In Time", but he also ably performed the harmonica parts in heartfelt versions of "You're A Big Girl Now" and "Love Minus Zero/No Limit".

The *Bathed In A Stream Of Pure Heat* bootleg was obviously intended to show this NET leg in the best light, and this it does. It successfully interspersed the nightly routine of croaked vocals and rock guitar work-outs with short bursts where his voice and lungs seemed to find renewed power. As it happens, the capabilities or otherwise of Dylan's lungs were about to become the main talking point of the year.

Prior to that, this leg of touring came to a halt on May 3rd. There was a one-off appearance on May 22nd when Dylan and his band, excepting Kemper, played three songs as the headline act at the Simon Wiesenthal Center benefit dinner at the Beverly Hilton Hotel in Los Angeles. Jonathan Dolgen, chairman of Viacom Entertainment Group, received the Center's Humanitarian Award and requested Dylan as the main entertainment. "He's the poet of my generation without question," Dolgen told the press.

Dylan played three songs, all in band-backed acoustic mode. The last two, "Masters Of War" and "Forever Young", were both relevant to the extremely worthy occasion. The opener, Ray Pennington and Ray Marcum's "Stone Walls And Steel Bars", was completely surprising. Like the sublime "Long Black Veil", this is a carefully crafted ballad about the tragic consequences of pursuing "the love of another man's wife".

After the show, Dylan took a break to celebrate his 56th birthday at home in Malibu. Everything seemed to be going along as normal when Dylan announced a joint UK tour with Van Morrison for June. Dylan fans groaned in anticipation of the shorter sets dictated by a double-header and the inevitable extra hassle caused by vying for tickets with the loyal followers of another 'big name'. However, such mild complaints soon became totally irrelevant.

On May 25th, the day after his birthday, Dylan was admitted to hospital in Los Angeles with chest pains. The papers were quick to print scare stories of heart attack and near death. The truth was, Dylan had contracted histoplasmosis – an infection of the sac surrounding the heart – which, though potentially serious, is rarely fatal. Dylan was released from hospital on June 2nd.

"Doctors are continuing to treat him," a record company statement informed the world's media, "and are confident that Mr. Dylan will make a full recovery in four to six weeks." When asked about his plans for his recovery period, Dylan was quoted as saying, "I don't know what I'm going to do. I'm just glad to be feeling better. I really thought I'd be seeing Elvis soon."

The record company also announced that Dylan had cancelled a European tour scheduled to begin on June 1st in Cork, Ireland, though he planned to fulfil his later US concert commitments. Concerned fans, however, had gone from worrying about set-lists and set lengths to facing the prospect of the Never Ending Tour actually ending, and for the worst of reasons at that.

I remembered fellow NET traveller Ray Webster asking me in Germany once what I would do if "anything happened" to Dylan[1]. I had not been able to answer; I found the concept of the NET finishing difficult enough to imagine, never mind Bob's demise. And I was sure I wasn't alone. That spring there were many anxious Dylan fans around the globe, though the more news that came out the better the situation became. The main thing was that Dylan was going to be all right. Dylan later recalled, "The pain stopped me in my tracks and fried my brain." There were "no illuminations", just six weeks of being bed-bound and staring at the ceiling as his body struggled to overcome the sickness.

However, nothing seems to stop Dylan in his tracks for long. Amazingly, he resumed the NET on August 3rd and kept going all the way to the end of the year, to complete ten more shows than in 1996 and, once again, play almost 100 shows in a year. August 3rd's 'comeback' show, at Lune Mountain in Lincoln NH, will always retain a special place in fans' hearts. Press attention centred on Dylan in a way it had not been for years. The media interest was nothing, however, compared to the ferment the fans were in. My friends from Germany were among the large number of people who flew over from Europe. I got a phone call straight after the show from Stephan to tell me that Dylan was in fine voice though looking, understandably, very tired and a little bit shaky.

It was tremendous to hear that he was back on the road and well enough to do a show. There was, though, a genuine fear that he was pushing himself back too soon, a fear not allayed by his need to sit down for a rest between songs, nor by the fact that his latest touring leg started with shows on the 3rd, 4th, 5th, 7th and 8th. Dylan assured Edna Gundersen in her interview for *USA Today* that

1 As noted earlier, Ray never had to face the moment he so dreaded. I thought of our conversation when news reached me that Ray had passed away.

the doctors had told him it was fine to proceed with the tour. However, more than one night off in the opening six might have been more prudent. Dylan, though, was not in a cautious mood. Running at about 20 minutes shorter than the spring tour, and without any harmonica, Dylan managed his 22-date stint between the 3rd and 31st August with aplomb and no little daring. Not only was he on the road again, but he was also still experimenting with the set-list.

He opened with an infectious, good-time "Absolutely Sweet Marie", the mood of which quite belied its cynical lyrics, the gorgeous upbeat pop melody seeming to be a celebration of Dylan being back on the road. Then came "I Want You", with the "took his flute" verse restored. You could hear Dylan forcing himself, you could almost feel his physical exertion, in his determination to ensure he put on a good show for this 'return' gig.

The next song was, astonishingly, "Tough Mama", which had not been played since the year of its release on 1974's *Planet Waves* album. The melody was faithful to the original and, if Dylan's vocal and lung power were sadly diminished in the interim and by his illness, he gamely carried it as best he could. For those who haven't noticed, "Tough Mama" was the third song of the night. Its selection would have been remarkable in itself, but Dylan's illness had clearly caused a rip in the space-time continuum. For the first time in hundreds and hundreds of shows and many, many years "All Along The Watchtower" was not at number three in the set list.

Planets did not fall out of orbit, however, as it was played as the next number. Nonetheless, it was the first thing that was reported to me after the fact that Dylan was "looking alright if a little tired". It was mentioned before anything was said about "Tough Mama" or the introduction of the wonderful "Cocaine Blues" in the acoustic set, a traditional song Dylan had last played in 1962, and one which was to become a welcome addition to many an NET set-list.

The next day, August 4th, saw this rip in the space-time continuum become a tear that threatened existence throughout the galaxy. For the first time in seven years and approximately 700 shows, "All Along The Watchtower" was nowhere on the set-list. Having earlier that year, on April 7th, become the first Dylan song to have been performed live over 1,000 times – it was gone. Worldwide, Dylan fans receiving tapes of the show must have thought that they had been given an edited version. "Watchtower" made a brief return about six days later at Montage Mountain and was then dropped for the rest of the year. Regular touring fans were delighted to see the back of it, and probably even more elated, if that's possible, with the live debut of "Blind Willie McTell".

"Blind Willie McTell" is one of Dylan's finest-ever songs. While it lay in a vault, officially, at least, unreleased, between 1984 and the release of *The Bootleg Series* in 1991, it acquired a mythic stature amongst Dylan fans. If you had asked a group of us which songs we would most like to be played live, "Blind Willie McTell" would have been very high on that list. After all these years, Dylan blessed Montreal on August 5th with this 'lost' touchstone.

It was as if Dylan was going out of his way to make this post-illness return to the stage as memorable as possible, an impression strengthened by the appearance, a week later, of "One Of Us Must Know" for the first time in 19 years. Dylan's massive back catalogue of songs allowed him to keep the surprises coming without upsetting the standard set-list construction that had held for so many years of the NET. For example, even that August 3rd set list that caught everyone by surprise had a very predictable 'spread' amongst its fifteen songs: ten songs from the 1960s, three from the 1970s, one from the 1980s and one cover.

This was an exciting and rewarding time of the NET, but it was shadowed by one particularly negative development that would have a lasting effect on Dylan's choice of song and style of performance in future years. Dylan's vocal powers were already damaged from continuous years of touring and his recent illness had clearly further ravaged them further.

At the time this was hardly a fan priority. It was a miracle that Dylan was up and touring so well, so quickly. However, from this point on Dylan has seemed physically unable to sing in certain ways. His vocal range was narrowing, and the possibility of fully expressive vocal inflections night after night, month after month now appeared unattainable. This is something that an ageing, and only human, Dylan would probably have had to face eventually in any case; it is not as though the difficulties first appeared at this point of the NET. The illness, however, accelerated the inevitable.

Dylan would deal with the problem by choosing songs and arrangements more suited to his restricted vocal range, and by finding a way of performing that was not so taxing night after night. This was to particularly influence shows from late 1997 onwards. On this leg, and for obvious reasons, the vocal problem appeared almost randomly as far as type of song was concerned. You could get a "Man In The Long Black Coat" performed with a despairing whine rather than a yearning keen, or a "Tough Mama" that musically excited you but was painful to listen to, so enfeebled was Dylan's voice.

Even songs that should come comfortably to him at any stage of life, like "Stone Walls and Steel Bars" and "Oh Babe, It Ain't No Lie", were laid to waste by a raw, pinched voice that simply had nothing more to draw on. Yet Dylan's vocal strength would return intermittently. On another night, or at a different time in the same show (especially later in the month), he produced a powerful "One Of Us Must Know (Sooner Or Later)", an assured "Blind Willie McTell" or (as on 18th August) a masterly, mournful "Pretty Peggy-O".

You just never knew what was coming next; a mangled and wheezy "Tangled up In Blue" could be followed by a clear, dramatic reading of "Cocaine Blues". There was even a show where I found "Under The Red Sky" for once unappealing, due to Dylan's vocals, and then during the following song, "Silvio" of all things, everything changed: though raspy, Dylan was doing something effective with his voice. This was a strange and unique time in the unfolding drama of the NET.

It should be remembered too that, Dylan, on form, can turn even his hoarseness to great communicative effect, as he did on the 23rd of August with "I Want You". A broken and despairing voice was quite fitting for lines like "Cracked bells and washed out horns". He paced it perfectly that night, growing a bit more defiant by the end of the song.

Dylan's illness meant that both fans and press would feel an extra significance to many of his lyrics that late summer. On the opening night, no one present could fail to hear special meaning in lines like "You knew that we would meet again" from "This Wheel's On Fire" or "I'm still on the road" from "Tangled Up In Blue". Reviewing a Vienna Wolftrap show in *The Washington Post*, Mike Joyce was startled by how, during the encore "Don't Think Twice, It's Alright", "...each time [Dylan] sang the chorus, the song seemed transformed, as if it had been inspired not by a lover's farewell but by a friend's recovery."

Indeed, the press responded warmly towards the shows and especially Dylan's performances. The media's former scorn appeared to have dissipated with the realisation that Dylan was a treasure that we might have lost earlier that summer. A sea-change occurred in media coverage of Dylan and ever since he has received , in general, a very favourable press. Of course, there would be exceptions to this rule, and an event which would provoke Bob's critics was just around the corner.

The NET's first post-illness leg ended in Kansas City on August 31st, but Bob's restless spirit saw him back on stage again within a month, in truly unexpected circumstances. Dylan's already high press profile went into hyper-drive when it was announced that he was to play the satellite TV-syndicated World Eucharistic Congress in Bologna, Italy on September 27th, sharing an audience with the Pope. The event was a Vatican attempt to convince Italian youth that the Catholic Church was modern and relevant. However, Dylan aside, the show was a bland mixture of anodyne native pop and watered-down gospel.

The press that seemed so delighted Bob was still with us could not resist weighing in with references to two "tired old spiritual leaders, revered by a multitude of followers". The Pope was in far from the best of health, but most writers seemed to think that the 77-year-old Pontiff looked in better shape than his 21-year-younger star turn. Dylan did look frail, and given that he was due to play a very short set and that he normally takes a few songs to warm up, I feared the worst.

Dylan took to the stage in full 'riverboat gambler' mode with his embroidered suit, white shirt, crossed leather black tie and cowboy hat proving quite a counterpoint to the Pope's white robes and somewhat smaller headgear. He opened with "Knockin' On Heaven's Door", a song to launch a thousand post-hospital newspaper headlines, playing it straight while Tony Garnier beside him guarded his master like a dutiful spaniel. Even Bucky was concentrating.

During a very short pause before "A Hard Rain's A-Gonna Fall" a wide-angle TV shot revealed a distinctly unimpressed Pope on a raised dais. Dylan's performance appeared to have sapped John Paul II's will to live.

After just two songs, the legendary iconoclast of "don't follow leaders" fame climbed the dais steps to meet the Pope. After stumbling on the first few stairs, an ill-at-ease Dylan recovered his composure in time to remove his hat as he approached the Pontiff. The Pope rose from his seat to greet Dylan and in a touching if somewhat surreal scene the two men shook hands.

John Paul II then stepped forward to speak, and in an instant the frail old man came alive in front of the microphone. Eyes that had seemed asleep were suddenly alert and darting around the audience. Here was someone else who lived for an audience, for putting his message across. His speech went down well and he revelled in making the crowd laugh by saying:

"You say the answer is blowing in the wind my friend," – presumably addressing the audience, rather than the composer of the line – to warm laughter and applause. "And so it is, but it is not the wind that blows things away, it is the wind that is the breath and the life of the Holy Spirit. ...."

The Pope also had an answer to that song's thorny question of "How many roads must a man walk down?"

"One," he told the rapturous audience, "there is only one road for man and it is the road of Jesus Christ."

By now Il Papa was really enjoying himself, though he appeared bemused at the football-terrace style reception he got when he finished his speech and retired from view. It was quite an act to follow. Had even Bob Dylan ever experienced a crowd so in awe of a 'performer', one wondered. It would be interesting to know if the same question crossed Dylan's mind, or what other, very pertinent questions were raised by the sight of such blind devotion from a massed audience to a preacher pontificating platitudes. The echoes of the Dylan of 1963 and 1979 were surely inescapable to at least one of the two main men here.

With his hat still off, Dylan played a delicate, heartfelt "Forever Young" – a song that was appropriate for a youth festival and that was alleged to have been requested by the Pope himself. Rumour also had it that the Pope had asked for "Blowin' In The Wind", which had more credence as it tied in with his speech. This song's absence from Dylan's set was rectified, at least in terms of the Pope's oratory, by its performance by a number of local singers. "Forever Young" brought Dylan's performance to an end, his three-song set falling considerably short of the half-hour that had been promised in the press.

Most Dylan fans I know disliked Bob's performance. There were negatives, undeniably, and as I had feared his voice never fully warmed up. However, Dylan tried hard to do himself and the songs justice in front of a very untypical audience, and I found that quite moving. Nonetheless, nothing Dylan could have done on stage could have competed with the overpoweringly odd symbolism of the whole event.

When quizzed over his motives, Dylan insisted "You don't say no to the Vatican." He was handsomely rewarded too. Press estimates put the Papal promoter's pay cheque at $350,000. The event also generated a huge amount of publicity, with reports of the event and photos of Dylan shaking the Pope's hand splashed across newspapers around the globe.

Certainly not everyone saw the coming together as a 'marriage made in heaven'. Ten years later the succeeding Pope released a collection of memoirs which included the unsurprising news that he had tried to stop Bob Dylan playing at the event. Unsurprising because this Pope viewed rock music as "anti-Christian", and he also conferred on Dylan, in a fatuous and inaccurate sound-bite, the title of "self-styled prophet of pop". To be fair, however, it is hard to disagree with Pope Benedict's remarks on the 'show' itself:

"The Pope appeared tired, exhausted. At that very moment the stars arrived, Bob Dylan and others whose names I do not remember. They had a completely different message from the one which the Pope had. There was reason to be sceptical – I was, and in some ways I still am – over whether it was really right to allow this type of 'prophet' to appear."[2]

Three days later, on 30th September 1997, the long wait for an album of new Dylan-penned material ended with the release of *Time Out Of Mind*. The massive wait since 1990's *under the red sky*, in addition to Bob's recent brush with mortality, ensured that anticipation among fans and other observers was acute.

For the Never Ending Tour, the implications were profound; a new album was exciting in itself, but one of the greatest joys it brings is watching the development of the new material in live performance. This had been especially true of the first real such album of the Never Ending Tour, *Oh Mercy*. Now that *Time Out Of Mind* was officially released, Dylan would, it was hoped, play some tracks at his upcoming four UK shows; then again, being Dylan, having an album so acclaimed might well mean he would just shun it. We did not have

2 *John Paul II, my loved predecessor*, Pope Benedict XVI, published by Edizione San Paulo 2007.

to wait long to find out, as these four shows started in Bournemouth the very next day.

As Dylan took to the Bournemouth venue's smoky incense-filled stage on 1st October, the day after *Time Out Of Mind*'s release, it was an emotional moment. For most of us present that night, it was the first time we had seen him on stage since his illness. In contrast to the Papal audience, Dylan looked completely at ease. His lively expressions of sly humour in the first song, "Absolutely Sweet Marie", were to be repeated throughout this and the following shows. The ovation that greeted this opener was rewarded by the opening chords of "Man In The Long Black Coat". This show provided me with two magnificent Dylan songs, "Tough Mama" and "Blind Willie McTell", live for the first time, as well as a very affecting "Cocaine Blues", a simple song that was nevertheless one of the highlights of the period.

None of this was enough though to detract from fans' greedy need for the new. As the concert progressed without any *Time Out Of Mind* material, it seemed more and more likely we would not hear anything off the new album. As usual, tapes of the album had been circulating for some time before the actual release, so hardcore fans were already familiar with the entire record. Our hope was finally rewarded, in the encores of all places, with "Love Sick". Although not one of *Time Out Of Mind*'s 'big four', this is unquestionably my 'best of the rest' of the tracks from that album. Notwithstanding this, I had two problems with it as released. One was Daniel Lanois' trademark swampy, soupy production. The other was the banal lyrics and obtrusive, forced rhyming of one verse:

"Sometimes the silence can be like thunder.
Sometimes I wanna take to the road and plunder.
Could you ever be true?
I think about you
And I wonder."

I knew my problem with the production would be overcome in live performance, however I was even more delighted when it later appeared that Dylan himself had realised how clumsy that problem verse was. After giving it a straight reading for its debut, Dylan went on to sing that one stanza with a sheepishness that developed into swallowing the word "plunder" or deliberately singing it off-mike. Eventually he took the rather more sensible step of rewriting the words and thus eliminating the infelicitous effect.

Lyrics aside, Dylan performed "Love Sick" so well at Bournemouth that I cannot think of a later performance that bettered it. The band were magnificently menacing, the clock the tormented narrator hears ticking in the lyrics was incarnate in the drums we heard beating as they relentlessly drove Dylan, and all of us in the audience, towards the end of this love that he is/was so sick of.

As I recognised opening chords to "Love Sick", I had involuntarily spun right round in sheer glee only to then realise for the first time that I was standing right beside two friends, and well-known Dylan fans, Phil and Alison Townsend. It was such a special moment to have my excitement reflected by the delight on their faces that I can recall it, all these years later, as though it were yesterday. This is quite a testament to that moment as I am now of the age when recalling yesterday itself is a struggle. There was a tangible feeling of being somewhere special, among friends, when Dylan, back from his illness, first debuted a song from his long awaited album.

I was back at Bournemouth the next evening but only after another personal nightmare of a tortuous NET journey that seemed doomed to end in failure to arrive at the gig in time. This time I was travelling from a badly-timed work assignment in Paris. I got stuck in a taxi, in rush-hour traffic on my way to the airport to return to the UK. I only made it on to the plane with the help of my boss at the time, who deliberately delayed the steps being removed so I could clamber up them. After landing it was on to the south coast via a mad and hugely expensive taxi dash from Heathrow. Bribing the driver got me there in record time, but even then I was about fifteen minutes late and Dylan almost always starts on time. I rushed into the hall, amazed at the lack of booming speakers and Dylan's voice. I piled forward to find various friends staring at me as though it was my fault the show was commencing late. It took me a long time to convince them I had not phoned ahead and provoked a 'bomb scare' to delay the opening. Actually, some still remain unconvinced to this day. As I caught my breath, Dylan and the band appeared on stage and the show began.

I had made it there just in time, sure in my deeply held belief that had I not done so it would be a sensational performance to be lauded for years to come. However, make it I did, against all the odds and, therefore, somewhat inevitably, it turned out to be a very predictable show.

The songs that you would think would stand out did, while the rest were a routine run-through. "Love Sick" appeared in the same place in the set-list (it would retain that position throughout the rest of the year) and though it was not as excellent as the previous outing, one could now admire it with more composure than the night before.

The Cardiff date was impossible for me to make due to work commitments, but I was soon back at a show at Wembley Arena to catch a strong Dylan performance with a rewarding set-list that featured a transfixing "Blind Willie McTell" and a tender "One Too Many Mornings". Yet for all the show's strengths we still pined for more songs from *Time Out Of Mind*.

A couple of weeks later, on October 16th in New York, Dylan was honoured with yet another award, the Dorothy and Lillian Gish Prize accompanied by a $200,000 cheque. Bob said "Thanks", adding that he "wished [he] had made a movie with her".

Four days later, rehearsals were under way for another bout of touring in America. Showing no signs of weariness, Dylan began another leg of the NET at the Humphrey Coliseum, Starkville MS. The soundcheck tantalizingly included a run through of *Time Out Of Mind*'s epic closing track, "Highlands". Although it was not played that night, three more *Time Out Of Mind* songs were added to "Love Sick": "Cold Irons Bound", "Can't Wait" and "'Till I Fell In Love With You". Shortly afterwards, "Make You Feel My Love" was also unveiled, so that with the exception of "Million Miles" and the ill-fitting "Dirt Road Blues" all the songs from the new album had been played live – except the four standout pieces.

Not that many in the American audiences were complaining; these were auspicious times when the nature of the shows went through a transformation. The set list from 2nd November, at the Township Auditorium, Columbia, South Carolina, for example, went as follows:

1. Maggie's Farm
2. Pretty Peggy-O (Traditional)
3. Cold Irons Bound
4. Born In Time
5. Can't Wait
6. Silvio (Dylan/Hunter)

7. Stone Walls And Steel Bars (Acoustic)
8. Tangled Up In Blue (Acoustic)
9. Tomorrow Is A Long Time (Acoustic)
10. Friend Of The Devil (Hunter/Garcia/Dawson) (Acoustic)
11. Make You Feel My Love
12. 'Til I Fell In Love With You

*

13. Like A Rolling Stone
14. My Back Pages (Acoustic)
15. Love Sick
16. Rainy Day Women #12 & 35

What a change from what came before! As well as the extra song in the acoustic set, the split of songs was now radically altered. Here we had five songs from the '60s; one from the '70s; two from the '80s (I include "Born In Time" here as although it was released on 1990's *under the red sky* it came from the 1989 *Oh Mercy sessions*); five from the '90s and three covers. Quite a contrast to the 1960s-based sets that had dominated for so long.

Certainly the new songs were all written by a man conscious that his voice was more restricted. Songs from *Oh Mercy*, *under the red sky* and *Time Out Of Mind* suit his NET range. Traditional folk pieces, by their very nature, suit anybody's range. With these kinds of more balanced set-lists Dylan can exploit his current voice and limit the amount of times he needs to stretch to hit the notes of his younger days. Experiments with changing set-lists would continue over the succeeding dates.

In general terms, the *Time Out Of Mind* songs were still finding their feet. Dylan was working on how best to present them and how they should sit in the set. "Cold Irons Bound" particularly benefited from escaping the cold, clangy production that drowns it on the album, while "'Til I Fell In Love With You" live implied a deeper meaning than on record, though it has to be acknowledged that this was hardly a difficult achievement. Perhaps most surprising of all, "Make You Feel My Love", a song so mawkish as to make "Emotionally Yours" sound like "Visions Of Johanna", became something quite moving. It was to assume the position of 'big, overblown ballad' in many a set-list in years to come, and really it should not have worked.

The number had already been recorded by Garth Brooks and Billy Joel, and would soon be by many more, and is exactly the kind of meaningless, clichéd pop you hear on a hundred radio stations and never think twice about. How it became so central to Dylan shows is a startling testament to his live powers; I swear there were shows in 1998 where it was the best thing played. More importantly, the majestic "Not Dark Yet" made an appearance on October 30th. It was, at the time, a one-off, but it hinted at what was to become a major NET song in the succeeding years.

Having survived his illness, and now touring to acclaim, Dylan suddenly found himself so popular that he could play a private corporate party for the company Applied Materials without attracting too many cries of "Sell-Out". Dylan and the band played it as a normal NET set. Closed to the general public it may have been, but you cannot stop Dylan fans from getting in to see and record their man that easily. It was not long before collectors were listening to this, along with all the other shows.

Dylan repeated his 1995 surprise of touring in December. That one had been brought about by Patti Smith's situation, this one by Dylan's long summer illness. Even that could not deter this road warrior from packing in as many shows as he could. Consequently, he ended the year with a headline-grabbing, so-called 'club tour'. The thought of Dylan playing to audiences of a few hundred in very small venues caused a rush of excitement for the fans and attracted a lot of publicity. Given all that had happened in 1997, the idea of seeing Dylan in such intimate settings had fans clamouring for tickets and the shows sold out almost instantly.

On December 1st and 2nd Dylan played at the Roxy Theatre in Atlanta and set the scene for this welcome tour by mixing up covers ("Shake Sugaree" and "The White Dove", for example) and originals. Not all of these December shows were triumphs, but the best were to be savoured and club dates became something Dylan would return to as the NET continued over the next few years, zigzagging its way between huge stadiums and tiny theatres, via soulless arenas and ice rinks.

Dylan ended 1997 with an exhilarating run of five sold-out shows at Los Angeles' El Rey Theatre, from 16th to 20th December. The shows also featured notable opening acts each night, including Joan Osborne, with whom Dylan recorded a version of "Chimes Of Freedom" for a TV show the following October. Sheryl Crow not only opened on the 19th but joined Dylan onstage for the first two of the encores. The following year would see her present Dylan with a Grammy Award and delay the release of her new album to include "Mississippi", an out-take from the *Time Out Of Mind* sessions that Dylan thought would suit her.

"Rock's most celebrated songwriter was alternately playful, arbitrary, purposeful and, as always, unpredictable," Robert Hilburn enthused in the *L.A. Times*. "And he only did four songs from the widely hailed new eleven-song album – and not the four that most people would agree are the most memorable. Yet, there wasn't a moment in the fast-paced affair that didn't seem like a special occasion."

Support act Beck opened the five-night extravaganza with the words: "Let the games begin, this is the opening of the Bob Dylan festival." And the festival proved a great pre-Christmas treat not only for ordinary fans, but also for some of the stars of the neighbourhood including Ringo Starr, Eric Clapton and Andre Agassi. The guest that seemed to most please Dylan though was Gregory Peck.

It was Peck, himself an honoree, who presented Dylan as one of the four Kennedy Center Honorees on December the 6th. Dylan was inducted along with Lauren Bacall, Charlton Heston, Jessye Norman and Edward Villella. I am sure he was pleased to be following in the footsteps of Johnny Cash, who had been similarly honoured the year previously. There was not only the Gala event itself but also a reception at the White House, where President Clinton said of Dylan: "He probably had more impact on people of my generation than any other creative artist. His voice and lyrics haven't always been easy on the ears, but throughout his career Bob Dylan has never aimed to please."

This presidential recognition came only five days after former President Jimmy Carter and his wife attended the opening show of the 'club tour' and witnessed not only "Shake Sugaree" but also the live debut of "Million Miles". Popes and Presidents: "Phew! Rock 'n' Roll".

"When I was a little kid in La Jolla, California, which is a very small town, we had a parade on the Fourth Of July," Peck told the Kennedy Centre audience.

"And I remember clearly the sight of civil war veterans, marching down the main street, kicking up the dust. The first time I heard Bob Dylan it brought back that memory and I thought of him as something of a civil war type, a kind of 19th Century troubadour, a maverick American spirit. The reediness of his voice and the spareness of his words goes straight to the heart of America."

It's an interesting portrait, and it shows how far Dylan's image had come from the fiery, drug-fuelled, verbose *Blonde On Blonde*/1966 tour days. Gregory Peck then recounted how wonderful it was for him to buy a Dylan album years later and hear Bob sing about watching a Gregory Peck western (in "Brownsville Girl" from *Knocked Out Loaded*.) Peck explained that the song referred to the film *The Gunfighter*, and that all through the movie the townspeople kept telling his character to get out of town before the shooting started. "Bob Dylan's never been about to get out of town before the shooting starts," Peck added, while Dylan looked genuinely moved.

In an attempt to answer his own question, "Who is this fellow 'Bob Dylan'?" Peck concluded: "He is surprises and disguises; he is a searcher with his songs. In him we hear the echo of old American voices: Whitman and Mark Twain, blues singers, fiddlers and balladeers. Bob Dylan's voice reaches just as high and will linger just as long."

This is the Romantic side of the NET Bob Dylan – the troubadour who is still out there, still searching, still touring. While so many of his contemporaries have gone to ground or appear stuck to forever repeating the same shows from their golden pasts, the NET sees Bob constantly lighting out for the territories, exploring frontiers both artistically and geographically, changing directions and changing shapes, all the while as contradictory as Whitman's *Leaves of Grass* persona.

Musical tributes followed Peck's opening address, with Bruce Springsteen first on the grid. Springsteen's opening eulogy was the highlight of his performance: "The yearning for a just society in America just exploded," Bruce told the audience. "Bob Dylan had the courage to stand in that fire and capture the sound of that explosion. This song remains as a beautiful call to arms. The meaning of this song and the echo of that explosion live on in the struggle for social justice in America that continues so fiercely today."

It was a great pity Bruce didn't stop there, instead of proceeding to murder "The Times They Are A-Changin'". Dylan spent most of this song with a furrowed brow and bitten lip, looking worried for Bruce who seemed so lost in this stage of his career, so removed from his muse, that Dylan's 1980s wanderings from the creative well seem like a momentary blip in comparison. Thankfully a creative resurgence lay ahead for "The Boss", just as it had done for "The Bard".

David Ball followed onstage, thanking Bob for writing "Don't Think Twice, It's All Right", calling it "a country classic" and played it as though it was. President Clinton clasped Hillary's hand and sang along. Everyone was a-toe-tapping to this irresistible song. The best was still to come however, with the final number by Shirley Caesar. Dylan may have liked Bruce just for being Bruce, and enjoyed "Don't Think Twice, It's All Right" because it was so "nice", but his delight at Caesar's speech over the opening chords of "Gotta Serve Somebody" was obviously deeper and heartfelt. She gave a fabulous performance, ad-libbing and inserting her own words without detracting from the song – "I heard Bob Dylan say it," she sang as the whole place moved to a full gospel onslaught. Dylan's mother, Beatrice, seemed as 'into it' as Bob so clearly was.

The Dylan segment of the evening ended with the President, First Lady and Lauren Bacall leading the applause for a bemused, little-boy-lost Bob with his mother sitting behind him. The entire evening ended with all the honorees present on stage as President Clinton gave a speech, the concluding words of which were "America The Beautiful". In a triumph for crass commercialism run wild, this was overplayed, I kid you not, with an advert for Continental Airlines. The advert cleared *just* in time to reveal Dylan, standing shoulder to shoulder between Lauren Bacall and President Clinton, singing the anthem for all he was worth.

What a strange old trip, indeed.

CHAPTER TWELVE

1998: "I've found a different audience"

I've found a different audience. I'm not good at reading how old people are, but my audience seems to be livelier than they were 10 years ago. They react immediately to what I do, and they don't come with a lot of preconceived ideas about who they would like me to be, or who they think I am.

BOB DYLAN, *GUITAR WORLD* INTERVIEW[1]

You would think Dylan would want a break and a nice easy start in 1998 after the December tour in 1997, which brought the final tally of NET shows in the year of Bob's illness to 110, but not a bit of it. He was already playing shows on 13th and 14th January, in New London CT, to warm up for some East Coast U.S. dates with Van Morrison. Dylan and Morrison alternated as headliners on the tour, which ran from January 16th to 21st at New York's Madison Square Garden Theatre, followed by two shows in Boston on the 23rd and 24th.

1 This *Guitar World* interview was not published until March, 1999.

The press praised Morrison and Dylan for playing in the small, intimate confines of the Madison Square Garden Theatre, while the Rolling Stones strutted their stuff in front of capacity crowds in the Garden itself. In comparison to the size of the venues the Stones were playing the Garden Theatre was intimate, but compared to the venues the NET had become accustomed to in the 1990s it was a large arena.

Bob's proximity to the Stones led to a plan that Dylan would leave the Garden Theatre one night and go and join the Rolling Stones at the Garden itself for "Like A Rolling Stone". Although it is believed Dylan got to the side of the stage in time, he was never called on. Unfortunately for lovers of the song everywhere, he was to play it with them later in the year. Dylan is hard enough to control on stage when he is totally in charge, far more when he has to interact with other stars.

Given Dylan's recent high profile and the success of *Time Out Of Mind*, this was his first chance in years to fill arenas (though at this stage this was only as long as he had another big crowd-puller with him). Dylan also continued to play smaller shows of his own throughout the year, refuting any claims that he was 'selling out' the NET.

After the Van Morrison dates Dylan continued to tour, his appetite for the road seemingly as insatiable as ever. He even argued with the doctors over a decision to postpone one show due to influenza. He did concede in the end, accepting that it was unwise to push his luck too far. Notwithstanding this 'flu, January 27th found Bob in Poughkeepsie NY, starting on six dates that would take him through to February 2nd. Then, after a 12-day break, he picked up for another six shows before it was time for the Grammy Awards. Since Dylan's August 3rd return from illness he had maintained a relentless pace.

The most exciting set-list news for long-term fans was the frequent appearance of "Not Dark Yet", the integration of "Million Miles" into the 'standard numbers' and the occasional duets with Van Morrison, such as "More and More" on January 18th, though these were strictly for curio hunters only. Van and Bob did produce one duet of intrinsic merit with their rehearsed cover of "Blue Suede Shoes". This was played as a tribute to the great Carl Perkins, who had died aged 65 on January 19th. At Perkins' funeral, in what was becoming a depressingly regular occurrence, Dylan issued a stately tribute. Wynona Judd read it out: "*[Perkins] really stood for freedom. That whole sound stood for all the degrees of freedom. It would just jump right off the turntable. We wanted to go where that was happening."*

Days later, I would catch my first 1998 glimpse of Dylan via a TV broadcast of the Grammy Awards, where he played the song that had thrilled us so much back in October at Bournemouth, "Love Sick". One of Dylan's three nominations was for "Cold Irons Bound" so, being Dylan, you could not expect him to play that. The other nominations were for album of the year and 'best contemporary folk album', both of which *Time Out Of Mind* won. (Incidentally, Dylan's son Jakob won two Grammies the same night, for 'best rock vocal' and 'best rock performance by a duo or a group with vocal'.)

Despite the risible nature of some of the Grammy categories, the main award for Album of the Year is seen as a big thing. Certainly, American record buyers take the award seriously; sales of the album subsequently increased dramatically and the album leapt almost a hundred places back up the charts to number 27. The artistic merit of the awards might be somewhat more dubious given that when Dylan was putting out the likes of *Highway 61 Revisited* and *Blonde On Blonde* the winner was *Hello Dolly* or something like 'The Tijuana Toastmasters Rock Cole Porter'. For all his ground-breaking albums, Dylan had never even been nominated for an Album of the Year Grammy before, excepting a one-of-the crowd nomination for *A Concert For Bangladesh.*

If you could ignore this overly commercial setting, Dylan's performance itself was splendid, in spite of a rather bizarre distraction. In the middle of Bob's set, shirtless, self-styled 'almost-vegetarian-multi-genre mastermind-artist' Michael Portnoy jumped on stage with the words "SOY BOMB" written in block letters on his body. Dylan and the band just kept playing, though the expression on Dylan's face spoke volumes. Still, at least Portnoy's complaint injected some spontaneity into the Grammies . "Soy is protein and life and energy, and bomb is explosive and propulsive," the stage invader explained to the press. "All art should be soy bombs."

One of the evening's highlights came when Dylan began his walk to the podium to collect one of his awards for *Time Out of Mind*. At that point, the TV shot of the audience captured high priestess of hip Patti Smith shouting "Bob" with the demeanour and all the intensity of a teenage pop fan.

By April 4th, Dylan was back on the road for a rather strange little South American jaunt which took in two small venues and four dates as support to the Rolling Stones. The support slots brought the added trauma of the previously mooted Bob and Stones collaboration, with a joint performance of "Like A Rolling Stone" each night. These were even worse than expected. Dylan appeared not to know what to do on stage, and the Stones appeared not to know what to do with Dylan. The audiences, however, usually clapped wildly. Clearly it was being at the 'event' that mattered, not the performances. Some of the photographs from the shows let us see that Dylan and Jagger appeared to be having great fun, so maybe you 'just had to be there', as the quote to cover up a multitude of performance sins, puts it.

Next it was back to America for a further stint on the road with Van Morrison. However, Van pulled out and Joni Mitchell stepped in to fill his place. Van then did a U-turn, so the tour now comprised three 'singer-songwriter legends'. Dylan and Van alternated as headliners, with Joni remaining in the middle slot on each of the seven nights.

Having all three veterans on the same bill once again led to acres of newsprint about "the old days". NET followers were less impressed, aware that when faced with a large audience, many of whom are not there just to see him, Dylan normally plays safe. Dylan did indeed stick to conservative sets, breaking the habit only on May 26th when he performed "Restless Farewell" as a tribute to the recently deceased Frank Sinatra.

"I played at the Frank Sinatra Tribute show a few years back, and I played the next song," Dylan told the audience. "We had it all worked out and everything, but then they said they wanted to hear this one instead so ... I hadn't played it up till that time and I haven't played it since, I'll try my best to do it."

It was time for another on-the-mark obituary note from Dylan, and he provided the following:

"Right from the beginning, he was there with the truth of things in his voice. His music had an influence on me, whether I knew it or not. He was one of the very few singers who sang without a mask. It's a sad day".

With Dylan's energy levels apparently fully recovered from 1997's scare, on May 30th he embarked on a long summer tour of Europe. This leg took him all the way through to July 12th with hardly a night off. Unfortunately, Bob brought Van Morrison along for some of the dates, resulting, again, in fairly unadventurous set-lists.

There was a change to the set structure in Leipzig on June 2nd, however, when the crowd refused to vacate the hall after the show. Dylan fans have often tried to win further encores with this tactic, but to no avail. I am not sure what was particularly special in Leipzig, but when over 10 minutes after Bob's last encore, with the house lights on, the enthusiastically applauding crowd had still not dissipated at all, Dylan and the band returned to reward them with an extra encore of "Blowin' In The Wind". This extension of the encores obviously pleased Dylan because he retained this format for the forthcoming shows. However, the biggest change to the set-lists' structure was to come after I saw him that summer.

In June '98 I was regularly travelling back and forth to Europe for both work and pleasure. I was also preparing to move house. The Dylan tour found me having to squeeze the shows into a frenetic itinerary. I did manage, with the aid of yet another taxi dash from the airport, to make Hamburg on 12th June, once again at the Stadtpark. The venue was as lovely as ever but the Dylan I saw in 1998 was a travesty compared with what I had witnessed there before.

By the time Dylan elected to sing into his microphone, rather than away from it, one wished he had not, though at least it left us under no illusion as to what a foul mood he was in. To make matters worse, the band were lacklustre and the sound was appalling. I later heard various explanations for this, ranging from lack of accommodation the night before to a broken sound system and illness. Whichever the reason, I felt I had not yet really seen him at all.

Following the NET was immensely tricky that summer. The World Cup meant that every mode of transport to France, and every hotel in France, was fully booked. There was a knock-on effect in neighbouring countries, and since I was both going to the World Cup in France and working there and in London while Dylan toured elsewhere it was going to be hard to fit in another show, especially as I was also preparing to move away from London that July. Somehow, with much manoeuvring, I managed to get to Rotterdam for the show on June 15th .

Hamburg had really hit me hard, and the unexciting way the year had being going had reduced my customary over-the-top anticipation of seeing Dylan to something more resembling curiosity. It may also have had something to do with the longevity of the NET itself; back in 1998, ten consecutive years seemed a lot. I had first seen Dylan live when I was 19, and having then got used to seeing him every three years I now found myself approaching forty and my tenth consecutive year of seeing him live. At the beginning of the NET there was always the thought that it was going to end soon, which created a nervous energy and a certain desperation to miss as little of it as possible. Perhaps I was just struggling to become accustomed to its ongoing nature. Whatever the truth of the matter, I felt a little distanced from my usual total immersion in the upcoming show. So to try and get in the mood I played a couple of tracks from *Time Out Of Mind* before heading to the airport. It kind of worked but felt a little forced, a staged re-enactment of what once came naturally.

At this point I still did not have a ticket. Despite all the years of going into concerts with enough tickets to cover an extended family and despite always seeing concert-goers (far less touts) selling spares, this situation always worries me. The nearer I got to the venue, the more worried I got. I took a taxi from Rotterdam Central to the arena, which was in a godforsaken wasteland some distance away. Heavy machinery, rather than touts, greeted me.

As ever, I met up with people I knew. Both Carsten from Germany and Josh from America were following the tour around, as usual, and both told me that Dylan played a much better show in Bremen than in Hamburg. I was relieved that they thought Hamburg was as bad as I had. If that show had been held up as typical of what was going on in the summer of 1998, the outlook would have been bleak.

Encouraged, I wandered around the tout-free zone looking for someone selling tickets. Finally, when I was just about to give up, a fan sold me one at face value. It was 'up in the gods' but at least it was a ticket, and there was still some time to go before Van, far less Bob, was due on stage.

At this point I had no intention of watching Van's set, but I wanted to go in and have a beer and a chat with Josh. After a couple of stewards refused to let us go in together, because our tickets were for different parts of the venue, I poured out a series of 'sob stories' regarding why it was imperative I talked to Josh immediately. These, coupled with my vehement, and frankly heartfelt, explanation that I would leave the minute I thought Van was coming onstage, got me past security.

I had also promised not to steal anyone's seat, a promise I managed to keep rather easily as the snack bar offered a remarkably clear view of the stage. Once there I knew I was going to stay even though it meant going back on my word and, worse still, enduring Van's set. A glance up the steep sloped seats to the third tier where I was supposed to go was all the proof I needed that this little bar was the place for me. A seat for an absent attendant for the adjacent lavatories completed my comfortable little perch. It was all reminiscent of the show at the Tempodrom in Berlin in 1995 where my best view of the night came from a spot near a bar, an upturned litter-bin providing an added height advantage.

Van Morrison was distant and uninterested; standing centre stage, moving one arm in time to the beat, but otherwise motionless. Even "Cleaning Windows" and "Tupelo Honey" were poor. I have seen a number of Van shows over the years, ranging from the so-so to the exhilarating; this was the dullest I had ever seen him. The ninety-minute set dragged on interminably.

As Bob's set approached, I felt, self-indulgently, I had suffered so much that I needed a good Dylan performance to reaffirm my wavering commitment. When Bob finally appeared, I was just happy to see him rip into "Leopard-Skin Pill-Box Hat". After a pretty neat "You Ain't Goin' Nowhere" a hard-rocking "Cold Irons Bound" was next, and it was clear already that Dylan was much more pumped up than he had been in Hamburg. It was just a shame for me that I had to listen to this instead of, say, "Tears Of Rage" from the previous set-list.

In contrast, a dazzling "Just Like A Woman" redeemed things before "Silvio". I thought back over the last three songs and how the beauty of "Just Like A Woman"' was highlighted by the torpid thumped-out hard rock on either side. "Does Dylan not notice this contrast?" I wondered to myself.

"Silvio" received a football-terrace-like acclaim then, as with "Just Like A Woman", "Desolation Row" invoked a great cheer of recognition. So did "The Times They Are A-Changin'", particularly from the back and sides of the auditorium, as opposed to the front, which was much more demonstrative for "Silvio".

The ovation for "Times" was oddly contradicted by the bar suddenly getting busy, so much so that for the first time my spot looked like a bad choice. Luckily for me this was the only time during Dylan's set that this happened. I found it hard to comprehend why there was a busy bar during "The Times They Are

A-Changin'" after it had been empty during "Silvio". The answer seemed to lie in the different responses to songs from the various sections of the audience.

From my further-from-stage-than-normal position I could observe what Dylan's songs mean to people, particularly the older songs. The people around the sides of the auditorium and up where I should have been had clearly come to hear Dylan perform the classic songs they had listened to throughout their lives. They would have been paying rapt attention to "The Times They Are A-Changin'", unlike the throng nearer the front who saw it as a reason to rush to the bar. Dylan sometimes views these folk as his audience, and at other times feels he is playing to people who always embrace his newest work. He also often seems to confuse the two, both in terms of their constituents and their preferences, as we shall see. It probably is confusing, however, if you always apprehend the audience from the same place. At this show I had a vantage point that allowed me to see almost two different audiences in the one hall.

Suddenly it was time for Dylan to mangle "Tangled Up In Blue". As Dylan ran through his 1998 desecration, I survived by casting my mind back to the original recording, a 1978 version, and a snatch of Barcelona 1984, or was I thinking of Brussels? Never mind, he was nearly finished and it was time for me to pay attention again.

Except that the next song was the dull, unmelodic "Can't Wait". Appropriately, large chunks of the audience agreed with the title's sentiment and headed to the toilets in an exodus reminiscent of Earls Court in 1981 when Bob played a 'religious' song. In 1981 I thought it sacrilege (towards Dylan, I mean), but I found it hard to condemn in 1998.

Time Out Of Mind was mined again for the next song, "Make You Feel My Love". However well performed, this remains an overblown ballad. Why could it not have been "Standing In The Doorway" or "Tryin' To Get To Heaven"? Not that the crowd seemed to be worried, they were showering the song and Dylan with acclaim. As for the coolest man the planet has seen, he was playing up to his front row groupies like the hammiest of hams. The grandeur of the arrangement for "Make You Feel My Love" had stretched his voice, and "It Ain't Me, Babe" found his fractured vocals now sounding imbued with grace and even a hint of majesty; like a ruined cathedral, its beauty and magnificence still was present in the shards that remain.

It was extremely moving and I was once again in the palm of Dylan's hand. "Highway 61 Revisited" found me down at the front bopping away and gaining a good viewing position for "Love Sick", which sounded as good as it had back in Bournemouth in 1997. Bob stood bathed in red light: Ah, those curls, that profile; what a powerful image he still presented. This visual side to a Dylan show is hugely important to many fans.

The chorus of "Rainy Day Women #12 and 35" was belted out by the occupants of the land of the 'coffee shops' and it was all over. I faced a trek back to Amsterdam and a couple of hours sleep before heading off to Bordeaux for the football.

Whilst admitting that the amount of time, energy and enthusiasm one has to put into touring as an audience member is influential, there were still a number of developments that made 1998 a low point of the NET for myself and for the majority of my long-term NET-going friends. As ever, there were many who loved the year, indeed many who liked every show.

In re-listening to the shows for the purpose of this book I began to see why. Although I did not find any show I liked all the way through, I could see someone having a good night at the show in Stockholm, for example, where both "Desolation Row" and "Every Grain Of Sand" were performed with a mixture of dignity and vulnerability, and where the despairing chorus in "Forever Young" truly reflected the impossibility of the verses' altruistic pleas. The inner contradiction of a song that exhorts someone to grow up true and strong and yet to remain forever young has rarely been voiced so movingly. "Love Sick" was as powerful as ever, and even "All Along The Watchtower" was given a different arrangement.

For me, though, Dylan had become quite distanced from his audience and detached from what had, until comparatively recently, driven the NET. Many elements that I had found concerning as they began to surface in previous years seemed to come to a head in 1998. For me, these combined to render a Dylan gig less of an event in the sense of something magical and special and more of an 'event' in the sense of a deliberately calculated stage show. The staged duck-walks and rock guitar hero poses that had initially seemed endearing were growing stale. Once you realised that it was all pre-planned, like Bob's increasingly premeditated tease of picking up harmonicas and putting them down without playing them, the appeal rapidly diminished. It was as if Dylan was constantly checking his watch to see if it was time for another imitation of Chuck Berry in need of the toilet.

Worse by far was the increasing North American trend for carefully choreographed crowd invasions, keeping people back from the stage until a pre-set time or signal from the stage and then letting them flock forward, thus creating a false sense of sudden heightening of audience excitement. Then it developed further; in certain songs, like "Rainy Day Women #12 and 35", for example, people would get ready to invade the stage. If the time was right, security was given instructions to let them do so. Not all of them, though, just a select number of young, preferably good-looking women. It must be good fun for Bob to be surrounded by all these young babes, jiggling their assets in front of his face and planting the occasional smacker on him, but since it is all pre-planned it has a tawdry look. Following on from Woodstock '94, it appeared that Dylan's courting of a younger audience was threatening to run out of control.

If you look at the hand-picked audiences at *MTV Unplugged* and the 1998 Grammies, you are faced with the stench of manipulation and false representation of what Dylan's audience actually looked like at the time. These 'spontaneous' crowd rushes were just more of the same thing. How much of this was Dylan's idea, I do not know, but he must at the very least have agreed to it. I know that this is a stage show, but does it have to be such a staged show? Dylan shows, and especially Dylan NET shows, had always been something far more spontaneous and meaningful, involving a more direct communication between artist and audience.

Dylan and his band's performances all seemed too similar to me too. Each show sounded much like the one before. Naturally, he kept changing songs around but they were usually like for like and "Girl From The North Country" replacing "Boots of Spanish Leather" or "Maggie's Farm" replacing "Highway 61 Revisited" did not make for a different 1998 NET experience.

This was probably necessitated by the amount of double and triple headers Dylan was playing, but again these are not what the NET was meant to be, or had been, in my eyes. Dana Parsons, of *The Times Orange County Edition*, pointed out all the expensive cars in the car park at one Dylan show, and captured the appeal of the triple-header show to many of the audience: "We've all come a long way, I guess, and these three superstars aged right along with us. They all wrote much of their best material while we were going to high school, graduating college, getting married, having first babies, signing for first mortgages, taking first jobs. It's a powerful bond many baby boomers have with the rock stars of our generation." "He's representative of the culture I grew up with, he's inside me," fan Elizabeth Cumming told Parsons. "I love Van Morrison, too, he's exceptional in his own right. It's one of those things. If we don't do it now, when are we going to get the chance to see Van Morrison, Bob Dylan and Joni Mitchell together? It's an epic moment. How many more epic moments are we all going to get? So I want to take my epic moments when I can get them."

This was a viewpoint as different from mine as could be had between two people wanting to see Bob Dylan. I want to see a Dylan gig, not some travelling nostalgia show. These shows were deliberately designed, with cold-hearted commercial rationale, to cash in on the burgeoning economic power of a generation that was 'born in the fifties'.

Looking back on the period from mid-1997 to mid-1999, John Scher, president of New Jersey's *Metropolitan Entertainment*, explained to *The Philadelphia Inquirer* the change in the way concerts were being packaged and sold:

"There are a lot of baby-boomer artists seeing the end of their careers who are less sensitive to appearing greedy ... If you have to pay $200 for a pair of tickets ...you will if you feel a strong emotional connection to your favorite artist ... And the artists are saying, 'They're giving us so much money, how can we turn it down?'"

Nineteen eighty-eight and that opening one-hour rush of primal rock suddenly seemed far away. The other highly sellable qualities of these shows were the ages of the artists and Dylan's recent illness. Dana Parsons quoted another fan as saying: "With this kind of line-up, and with people dropping like flies ..."

What is perhaps most remarkable is that these shows attracted the very fans, like those cited above, that Dylan specifically claimed to have finally freed himself from.

"I've found a different audience," Bob told *Guitar World's* Murray Engleheart in 1998. *"I'm not good at reading how old people are, but my audience seems to be livelier than they were ten years ago. They react immediately to what I do, and they don't come with a lot of pre-conceived ideas about who they*

would like me to be, or who they think I am. Whereas a few years ago they couldn't react quickly.

"I was still kind of bogged down with a certain crowd of people. It has taken a long time to bust through that crowd. Even the last time I toured with Tom Petty, we were kind of facing that same old crowd. But that's changed. We seem to be attracting a new audience. Not just those who know me as some kind of figurehead from another age or a symbol for a generational thing. I don't really have to deal with that any more, if I ever did."

What Dylan said here was true for the majority of the normal NET audience. He has toured so often now that the 'tick-seeing-a-legend' masses have had chance after chance to see him. However, with these big co-headliner shows, and the following year's double-headers with Paul Simon, Dylan was appealing to those very audiences he claimed to have happily lost, and to keep them satisfied he had to play in a different, more 'professional', for want of a better expression, way, which made him more detached from his material.

There is clearly a difficult balancing act needed between spontaneity and a premeditated show. In early 1991 I complained about the complete lack of professionalism, while in 1998 I complain of too much professionalism. In 1993 I objected to the sloppy, long-drawn-out endings, in 1998 I began to object to the band being too polished. I am aware of how hard to please I seem and how difficult it is to pitch a series of shows so that they avoid such problems, but these 'complaints' tell only part of the story. They come from me comparing them to more successful stints for one thing, but for another they are not by themselves the cause of a less-inspiring run of shows. For example, the elements I disliked in 1998 would still be present in the following two years, yet those years would see me return me to the NET fold, and would renew my faith in Dylan's ability to still perform killer shows.

Back in 1998 Dylan was on his way, *sans* me for once, around the UK. Before the Newcastle show he made a change to the long-standing set structure, extending the middle acoustic set from four songs to six. It was a most beneficial change, and one that stayed in place for the remaining double headers with Van the Man. Other than this the UK gigs, interspersed with a quick return to the European mainland, were more of the same; mainly greatest hits sets plus *Time Out Of Mind* selections. There were some enjoyable enough shows, with certain standout individual song performances, but all in all it was generally very safe and predictable.

Most reviewers spent their time marvelling that the combined age of the two "old buzzards" was in three figures and compared their relative abilities to still perform at this stage of their lives. Like most critics, *Hot Press*'s Stuart Baillie placed Bob firmly on top.

"You want extraordinary?" Baillie asked his readers. "Look at Bob Dylan on the stage up yonder, blowing at his mouth harp, bucking at the knees, shaking those ancient hips. It's a wonderful testimony to the life-fizzing power of music, especially since old Bob was dangerously sick a while back.... tonight, he looks great in his western cut tuxedo and his white boots, the scratchplate of his battered Fender flashing in the sun, his voice rejuvenated ...

"On tonight's evidence, it may be debatable whether Van is still 'the man'. But thankfully, Bob's yer uncle after all these years. In a harp-blowing, blues-wailing, gut-bucket, soul-believin' kind of a way."

The Guardian's Pat Kane was one of the minority of reviewers who begged to differ, praising Van as a "magnificent old bastard": "The truth is that Dylan stands much, much closer to that mausoleum moment than Morrison," Kane opined. "Dylan was a man desperately fighting against what the passing years have done to his talent and ambition and only occasionally winning through ...

"Mr Zimmerman's two-note guitar solos and gingerly executed rock poses suggest someone who's doing this music for therapy as much as artistic statement. And the trademark vocal drone – which once spoke truth and authenticity – has now permanently split between a frog-like gurgle and a thoroughly shattered falsetto scrambling the words of songs ..."

One of the many rumours that has reappeared virtually every year of the Never Ending Tour is that Bob Dylan would appear at the Glastonbury Festival. This rumour is about as frequent as the one that the NET is about to come to a close. I am not sure which of the two rumours worried fans more. The idea of having to go to Glastonbury because Dylan was there was all too much for some of us oldsters. However, 1998 was the fateful year that Dylan did work on Michael Eavis' farm, and his brief festival set was very well received by the massive Glastonbury crowd.

After a short break, it was time to tour again: beginning on August 19th in Melbourne, Australia, Dylan started a run of shows with Patti Smith supporting, though no longer singing duets, that ran until September 12th, finishing in Christchurch, New Zealand. On the second night of this leg, Bob made me a happy man by dropping "Silvio" from the set for the first time since September 27th, 1995. Not content with these Australia and New Zealand dates, Dylan returned to the States via Hawaii where he played on 17th and 18th September and then, starting on the 22nd, played six more dates in the United States.

On October 13th the world finally saw the official release of the most famous bootleg of all time, *Bob Dylan Live in 1966*, for many years erroneously known as 'The Royal Albert Hall Concert'. This most celebrated of gigs, where a defiantly electric Dylan responded with fury to a folk Luddite's "Judas" accusation, was in keeping with Dylan's high media profile of the previous eighteen months. It also gave him an enormous amount to live up to; Dylan was at the height of his powers in 1966, not only when playing with the Hawks but also in the stupendous acoustic set.

Two days after that release Dylan hit the road again, touring Canada and the northern U.S. through to November 7th, and taking in a November 1st Madison Square Garden show with Joni Mitchell as support. To celebrate the occasion he unveiled a one-off gem, a sublime rendition of Charles Aznavour's "The Times We've Known" ("Les Bon Moments").

"*I want to try something here from a guy playing off the streets that I've always liked, Charles Aznavour*," Dylan told the crowd. "*I usually play these things all by myself, but I feel I am all by myself now.*" In a poignant performance, Dylan invested the words with deep feeling.

A mere two days later, at Rochester NY, "I Believe In You" returned for the first time since I saw it in Cottbus, Germany, July 14th 1996. It was joined in the set-list by "Across The Borderline", which had not been played since the wonderful interpretation at Ames, seven years and one day before.

After 110 shows, the same number as in 1997, the year's touring ended on November 7th in Atlanta GA. It was a prodigious number of shows for Dylan to perform two years running, especially as it included a period of enforced rest and recuperation. My own uncharacteristically low attendance rate did not stop me keeping in constant touch with what was going on. I did this not just through Bill Pagel's website, plus the fanzines, the tapes, the CD-Rs and so forth, but also from the official Sony Bob Dylan website, www.bobdylan.com.

From August 1997 onward, the official Bob Dylan website developed into a goldmine for fans. In addition to its many other attributes, including an impressive on-line lyric service, it featured live recordings of Dylan performances old and new. As Dylan was playing his early 1998 shows, bobdylan.com was featuring songs from his recent performances, as well as some of the Supper Club songs, for example, and superb recordings from the 1997 December club tour. It was an act of immense largesse, at odds with the tradition of live Dylan material being hard to come by without resorting to the bootleg market.

In January, when Dylan was running through a standard set in a huge arena before Van Morrison took the stage, I was sitting at home revelling in things like the 16th of December 1997's "The Lonesome Death of Hattie Carroll".

Listening to this you felt that his voice was still so needed. Dylan's history is behind this song by now, as much as Hattie Carroll's painful story. The fact that you are at a show in the NET hearing this song sung by its author, as only he can, and that you listen to it knowing that, sadly, its relevance has scarcely diminished makes it all the more moving. By being at the show or listening to the song via this marvellous new service from the official Bob Dylan website, you were, as Jack Nicholson had said at Live Aid, being presented with "one of America's great voices of freedom".

Here Nicholson's words rang true and suited so much better than at that sad performance, where a befuddled, bloated and sweaty Dylan seemed far removed from any purpose in life. The NET has given him back this purpose and relevance and has given Dylan back to us, his lucky audience.

The on-line munificence included many highlights from the current year. From the 17th January show we were presented with "Tears of Rage". This is such a special song, such a magical, majestic, gut-wrenching meld of melody, lyric and vocal delivery, that to have a live performance available in perfect quality from a line recording seemed almost too good to be true. It reawakened in me a feeling of how precious and powerful Dylan's presence is in this world. How lucky one is to be alive and have the opportunity to go and witness something like this.

Imagine you had lived in the early 17th century and could have made it to a public oration by John Donne, you would have gone, wouldn't you? You might have hankered for an inspired author's reading of "The Sun Rising", a poem that had so moved you when you were growing up, or perhaps some other masterpiece that had changed your views on life and love. Yet you may have been offered a gloomy treatise based on "The First Anniversary" instead. Then again you just might have got the best, most passionate exploration of Donne's thoughts and emotions you could ever have imagined. You might also get an entirely new work of insight and imagination; fused from the experience of a life that had soured the earlier optimism and grand vision into a fatalism bolstered by dark cynicism, and yet still shot through with wit and insight. You might, with Dylan, get all three in a row with "Tears Of Rage", "In The Garden" and "Not Dark Yet". In either artist's case, if you were never to take your chances to go and hear a master at work, it would be your loss.

"Girl From The North Country" from January 20th came with a wonderful Mexican flourish in the guitar playing. "Make You Feel My Love" from Los Angeles on May 21st proved that, for all I have said about Bob's ravaged voice after the first decade of the NET, he could still bring out a vocal that tore the stars out of the very sky.

"You ain't seen nothing like me yet,"
"I could make you happy, make your dreams come true
Nothing that I wouldn't do
Go to the ends of the earth for you
To make you feel my love."

These words neatly summed up what Dylan was doing for his fans year in, year out on the Never Ending Tour.

From Leipzig, Germany, on June 2nd, we were given a magnificent "A Hard Rain's A-Gonna Fall". Another standout was "Mama, You Been on My Mind" from Brussels, June 17th; a superb vocal performance on a song that gets me every time. I may, in general terms, feel that 1998 was a comparatively poor year, but vocals like this and "Tomorrow Is A Long Time" at Glasgow in June are outstanding.

Although that last performance was not on the site, Glasgow was present in the form of "Boots of Spanish Leather". The extended acoustic sets gave Dan Levy, who ran the website, a plethora of riches to select from. Levy had an almost impossible task, albeit a hugely enviable and enjoyable one. Luckily for Dylan fans everywhere, he was fully up to the task.

Best of all was an outstanding rendition of Gordon Lightfoot's "I'm Not Supposed To Care". This was Dylan as 'Uncle Bobby' rather than the cool Big Brother of the mid-sixties. We now know for ourselves what the world is like, we do not need him "to sit behind our eyes and tell us how we see". What we have instead is a travelling musician, singing his heart out in this song of a hopeless romantic (with a small 'r'). This most affecting of performances ended with what could almost be taken as a message to dedicated followers of the NET:

"If you need somebody, somewhere
You know I'll always be there
I'll do it, although
I'm not supposed to care."

All these covers transformed by Dylan's interpretative powers year after year in the NET made me think that somebody should gather them altogether and put them out as a multi-CD box set. 'Ask and thou shalt recieve'; this is precisely what happened soon afterwards and it was as amazing an experience to listen to as I had imagined. What Dylan has always known is that there is the strength in, what we might roughly refer to as, 'popular music' to move men's hearts, to shift mountains, to open up the better side of ourselves that we too often keep hidden away.

In a way this sums up why the cover versions in the NET have had such a prominent place in this book. Despite my love of and admiration for Dylan's magnificent lyrics, he never had to write a single one of all his phenomenal words to be the most influential artist in my life. His voice reaches higher and speaks even more deeply than all those linguistic triumphs.

Yet, for all my praise of the covers, most fans feel a special bond when seeing Dylan sing songs he has authored, especially recent ones. It was clear from the very first playing that "Not Dark Yet" was not only one of the best songs on *Time Out Of Mind*, but also a bona fide masterpiece. Bob's vocals on this live version were, as on the album, exemplary; the perfection of the way he sings "gay Paree" is one of the reasons we all get so excited by new Dylan material, and by his singing. The epic grandeur in this one song was enough to indicate that my relative estrangement from the NET would be just a passing phase for now, though I did not realise this at the time.

1998 had ended with me having only caught a paltry two shows, the same as in 1989. However, while back in '89 I was starving for more, this year I was sated, I did not need any more live shows. There were many reasons for this: the amount of times and the regularity with which I'd seen him, the predictability of it all in 1998, the ready access to top-quality recordings just in case anything great did go down. All of this notwithstanding, 1998 had marked the lowest point of my interest in the NET. I was on a downer; the only way to go now, Bob willing, was up again!

CHAPTER THIRTEEN

1999: "Right now, I'm enjoying it"

Touring is something you either love or hate doing. I've experienced both. I try to keep an open mind about it. Right now, I'm enjoying it. The crowds make the show. Going onstage, seeing different people every night in a combustible way, that's a thrill. There's nothing in ordinary life that even comes close to that."

BOB DYLAN, *USA TODAY*[1]

I could have realized as early as January that 1999's shows had massive potential, but I failed to listen to the testimony of my friend Nigel Simms, who reported back from the opening Florida dates with news of a great performance, including a fascinating (Daytona Beach, 29th January) debut of Lefty Frizzell's "You're Too Late". Cynical old me just thought "Yeah, yeah", and made no effort to track down the tapes, so I did not hear Bob's Florida performance until later in the year. My mistake, Nigel was spot on! The Frizell number saw Bob's voice erupt into a country-tinged melody like a damaged but

1 "Two titans on tour Dylan and Simon mix and match" *USA Today*; Arlington; Apr 5, 1999; Edna Gundersen.

beautiful diamond, sending shafts of emotion through the ether into one's very soul. Thus began another year of exceptional covers.

Due to my tardy awakening to what was going down, my NET year was not at all the same as Dylan's. I heard far more from the spring European tour than from the January to March US dates. I remember the double set at Atlantic City on February 27th causing a bit of a stir; but before I was really fully 'on board' listening-wise, Bob was swinging into the April shows. Perhaps this was a good thing, an enforced period of restricted listening meaning that I was relatively 'fresh' when I finally caught up and once again plunged into the tour.

My early attention may have been restricted, but it was far from non-existent. Consequently, I did pick up on a number of individual performances. I was really glad to hear "Blue-Eyed Jane" in February and enjoyed his rather strained attempt at it, despite the crowd's incessant chatter. As the background intrusion receded, Dylan's just-about-to-go-but-just-hanging-in-there vocals guided us through this pop-country treat of a love song. There was also that magnificent Hank Williams' song, "Honky Tonk Blues". In addition to the sterling covers, early highlights included a rare outing for "Ring Them Bells" and Brian Setzer's horn section guesting on "Ballad Of A Thin Man" on 13th February. The horns were inspirational and their presence seemed to push Dylan to greater heights.

My early 1999 NET consisted of sporadic bursts from the aforementioned website, www.bobdylan.com, and tour compilations. While listening to "I Don't Believe You" from one such compilation, I realised it was time to start paying full attention and plan my return to the concert trail.

Meanwhile, there was yet another triumph of new technology for this Dylan watcher. Bob was one of many who contributed a song to a Johnny Cash tribute broadcast on TV. Dylan sang "Train Of Love" while rehearsing in Spain and his contribution (taped April 6th) was beamed to the event and therefore broadcast on April 18th. When I got up the next morning there was a video of this in my E-mail inbox; it was astonishing to see it so soon after it had taken place. Compared to my early days of Dylan following and collecting the modern world seemed a fan's heaven. The only thing better would have been to be in Spain for the April shows. By now I was really getting into this year's NET, but due to time constraints I was still reliant largely on compilations.

One of the tracks I rushed to play, as did all Dylan fans, I am sure, was "Fourth Time Around". A surprise choice, this: an NET debut and a very agreeable one at that. The music here was much more understated than the original's delicious pop and blues confection, but it had an appealing swing to it. Dylan growled gorgeously enough for one not to feel overly wistful for the past glories that *Blonde On Blonde* songs inevitably bring to mind.

There were other treasures, too. "Not Dark Yet" just seemed to get better and better, and the acoustic standards were unfailingly well sung. By the time I heard Málaga and Granada, two of a number of standout Spanish shows, I was no longer declining the kind offers of full shows on CD-R. No matter how busy I was, I simply had to make time for them all. The long-awaited change of set structure had made a dramatic impact on the NET. The hitherto dominant 5-6 electric songs, 3-4 acoustic, 2-3 electric and then encores had become 5-6 acoustic songs followed by up to 6 electric songs and then the encores. Now we had classic Dylan acoustic songs and covers followed by electric rockers, paced so as to build, and then subside into a more please-pay-attention-to-this *Time Out Of Mind* selection or a one-off, a rarity or a new arrangement. The sets would then build up to full-on, rave-out encores.

I could not get enough of them, and so you find me scurrying across Europe in late April, once again caught up in the excitement and whirl of following Dylan on tour. As war and atrocities raged in the ongoing break-up of the former Yugoslavia, there was something profoundly moving in Dylan singing songs like "Masters Of War", "Blowin' In The Wind" and "A Hard Rain's A-Gonna Fall", especially as he was singing them with a passion, clarity and engagement I had feared was lost forever. Dylan was clearly pumped for these shows, and after the reflective brilliance of the acoustic sets was looking for a party atmosphere to propel him to ever greater rock-outs in the electric sets.

Now there are many Dylan fans, especially among the older ones, who do not like this side of the modern Dylan shows. They prefer the idea of the audience sitting in rapt attention and only moving and clapping in between the songs. While this would certainly make for better tapes, it is undoubtedly not what Dylan usually wants. Having had the pleasure of hearing his carefully presented and perfectly delivered acoustic sets, if Dylan wanted an all-out rocking second half to the night that was fine by me. It was like getting two concerts in one.

There was one problem: arena security guards. After a spellbinding opening set in Vienna, Dylan lit into "Cold Irons Bound" and a heartfelt "Make You Feel My Love". At the end of each of these songs he peered below the front of the stage to see how everyone was reacting, and his disappointment was palpable when he saw no one there. His "thank you kind folks" comment after the latter was a mixture of the routine and the ironic.

The problem was that the security guards at Vienna's Stadthalle were stopping anyone moving forward. Dylan enticed the fans to come to the front by extending the beginnings and endings to songs that normally found the front-stage area full, but the guards wouldn't let anyone move down to the front section, which was inhabited by less demonstrative members of the audience. I was sitting to the side watching a cat-and-mouse game develop as Dylan kept trying to pull people towards him with extended guitar playing. Vienna, unsurprisingly, became the longest Dylan concert I had been at for many a long year. Something had to give, and give it did during the damn-the subtlety-get-up-and-party noise of "Stuck Inside Of Mobile With The Memphis Blues Again", which brought a forward crowd surge from behind the front section.

Then a big guy, who had already been removed from the front a few times, had finally had enough. He defiantly walked straight down the centre aisle with arms extended above his head, clapping along all the way, and planted himself in front of Bob. He was dragged away on more than one occasion but kept returning, exhorting those at the front to sit up and cheer. They did not. A few others were also playing cat and mouse with the security guards, trying to get down first one aisle, then another. Both they and our now-retreating hero were wildly cheered by the rest of the crowd, so kept going back down one aisle after another. The cheers increased, and the song just kept going on. A couple of other people tried to get down the front, then a few more, then the trickle became a flood that the guards could no longer repel and the cheering got even louder.

Not being too shy at coming forward at times like this, I joined the 'front of the stage' storm troops. For all the world it was like the 1970s at football games in the UK all over again. I used people who were being held by guards as my decoys and gained remarkable speed for one of my advancing years. The first two guards were dead easy; as they seized another fan I ducked around them. I was close to the stage now and I could have stayed put as others filled in behind me, but the magical barrier was only a stride or so away so I tried the same trick one more time. This last guard was up to it. Holding one fresh captive with one arm, he caught me with the other; impressively, if distressingly, enough, he held us both while shouting something in German. But through no fault of his own he was on a loser; hundreds had caught up with us and I could feel them pressing me forward and him backward. I made a break for it and the crowd heaved forward, allowing me to squeeze under his arm and onwards.

I hit the barrier just to the left of Dylan's centre microphone position. The delay had been costly but not disastrous and the extra few places away would make me less self-conscious about using my binoculars from so close to the stage. I should say that the last I saw of our erstwhile captor was him being helped over into the moat by his comrades, who had given up what was, after all, a situation they were never going to come out of on the winning side.

During all this the auditorium rang to the crashing sound of the guitar-driven "Mobile" and huge cheers from the crowd who had made it to the front. Some of the audience further back didn't make it all the way, but were clearly there in spirit. Meanwhile Bob's sudden realisation that the vast majority of the crowd were loving his performance and wanted to share the joy of the night with him brought out his inner showman. The exaggerated dancing, facial expressions and guitar flourishes that had gone before seemed pale now.

Rather than a hooligan pitch invasion it suddenly seemed like our team had just won the cup, and we had streamed onto the pitch to be thanked by our captain for helping cheer him to victory. It was a terrific moment, but the whole thing was by now so cranked up that it was as though we were at the last two songs of the encore already. It was hard to imagine where Dylan could take it from here without losing momentum. However, Bob carried it off with aplomb by quietening things down for a bit with a spellbinding "Tryin' To Get To Heaven". My cynical 1998 persona completely evaporated as I stood, once again, misty-eyed at the feet of the maestro.

As for the song itself; Dylan was putting a lot into the vocals. The way the second half of the show was arranged left the audience in no doubt which songs they were to party to, and which to pay attention to. Unfortunately, Dylan became miffed by some of the band's playing and Bucky got 'the look', the like of which I hadn't seen since John Jackson's or Tony Garnier's early days. It happened after two different verses at the same musical moment, and both the unplanned discordant note, and Dylan's expression of anger with it, caused me to fear that he may not have continued to play the song live (certainly, it boded ill for Bucky's future in the band). Dropping the song would have been a cause of great regret, it was very atmospheric: dark, smoky and yearning – and it sure sat well in the same set-list as "Not Dark Yet".

The song ended with a mumbled apology, explaining this was something they had been wanting to try out, and when the song reappeared in Munich two days later it was back in the acoustic set. In between the Europe shows and the summer tour of the States, Bucky Baxter (over 700 shows behind him) left the band. He was replaced by Charlie Sexton, a guitarist held in high regard and one who could bring, amongst many other benefits, a cutting edge to the increasingly blues-dominated sound. With Sexton on board the band could Roll as well as Rock; swinging from a plaintive country sound to a howling blues at the flick of a switch. It would take a while before Sexton bedded in, but it was well worth the wait.

As a critic of Bob's double and triple headers with Van Morrison *et al*, I was especially depressed by news of the summer plans, an extortionately priced joint arena tour with Paul Simon. Art was losing out to Mammon as the promoters chased baby-boomer bucks.

After recent big money tours by the Eagles, Fleetwood Mac and the Rolling Stones, Bruce Springsteen was also touring that summer. Meanwhile, Crosby, Stills, Nash & Young, Tom Petty, Steely Dan, John Mellencamp, Rod Stewart and James Taylor were amongst others chasing older rock fans' dollars. Gary Bongiovanni, editor of *Pollstar*, was quoted as saying: "The baby boomers typically don't go out to more than a couple of shows a season ...t o appeal to that audience, you have to do things that reach 'event' status, in their minds at least."

"It's the summer of the outrageously priced concert ticket," *The Philadelphia Inquirer's* Dan DeLuca bemoaned. "Nationwide, prices for premium seats are going through the amphitheatre roof, particularly for superstar acts favored by baby boomers ... Bob Dylan and Paul Simon are getting $100 for tickets to their July concert at Camden's Waterfront Entertainment Centre ... Industry buzz has it that Dylan and Simon will split $525,000 a night."

However, Once In A Lifetime Event or not, it seemed a hundred bucks for a ticket might be too much. "A study in contrasts, Dylan and Simon have indelibly shaped and broadened pop's musical landscape", George Varga reflected in *The Union Tribune*. "[They] had never performed together before ... making their unlikely-to-ever-be-repeated tour even more special, as do the on-stage duets ... So why are the ticket sales lagging for this historic tour? In a word: money .... For those fans who can afford it, hearing them together may be worthwhile at any price. But for many more, this tour may be remembered more for its prohibitive cost to attend than for its music."

Dylan, as you would expect, played the line of "I'm just a travelling musician, I'll play for anybody, I'll do what it takes to get on stage." More shocking were Bob's comments that implied he considered Simon to be on an artistic par with himself.

"I consider him one of the pre-eminent songwriters of the times," Bob commented. *"Every song he does has got a vitality you don't find everywhere."*[2]

Robert Hilburn, a writer convinced of Dylan's pre-eminence in the song-writing field, concurred. Elevating Simon above such celebrated Dylan concert partners as The Band, Joni Mitchell and Van Morrison, Hilburn concluded, "Simon deserves a place alongside Dylan on the list of the half-dozen most enduring songwriters of the modern pop era."

As it turned out, my fears re the Paul Simon double headers were not fully realized, Dylan turning in high-level performances despite relatively unchanging set-lists. He was in better voice in many of the joint shows than in the much-lauded 'Tramps' New York show on July 26th. This show quickly passed into legend among Dylan fans because of its appealing set-list (including "Every Grain Of Sand", "Visions Of Johanna" and an extra encore with special guest Elvis Costello), the more intimate venue and, most of all, its lack of Paul Simon. Hardly reasons I'd disagree with, but on hearing the show I was disappointed. Dylan's voice was thin and reedy and he was straining for effect. Naturally, I'd love to report that a Dylan-only show with an inspired set-list showed up the money-making Simon shows for the rip-off they were, but I just don't hear it.

I should also point out that all those at the 'Tramps' show found it to be amongst the best they had ever witnessed. Given that most who were there

---

2 "Two titans on tour Dylan and Simon mix and match" *USA Today*; Arlington; Apr 5, 1999; Edna Gundersen.

would be faced with Madison Square Garden the next night, I can understand their enthusiasm for the location. For the record they were treated to a "Visions Of Johanna" that repeatedly spoke of "visions of Madonna", for some reason known only to the man himself.

Despite the Simon shows sounding better than I had feared, I did not want to listen to all of them. As a long-term Dylan listener I had heard too many of the songs too often in their current guise. "Tangled Up In Blue", "The Times They Are A-Changin'", "Silvio", "Seeing The Real You At Last", "Ballad Of A Thin Man", "Tombstone Blues", "Maggie's Farm", "Highway 61 Revisited", "Like A Rolling Stone", "It Ain't Me, Babe", "Not Fade Away", "Blowin' In The Wind" and "All Along The Watchtower" could no longer hold my interest in these incarnations.

One of the 'selling points' of this tour (of which there was another leg in September) was the nightly cringe-making duets of "The Sound Of Silence", "I Walk The Line"/"Blue Moon Of Kentucky" (medley), and "Knockin' On Heaven's Door". The whole idea of these duets was silly in the extreme, but the contrast between the two singers was illuminating. It was instructive for us Dylan fans bemoaning the rigidity of the set-lists night after night that Dylan was praised for the variations in his performance over Simon's bland professionalism. Where we see predictability by Bob's standards, the standard reviewer sees a wealth of creative exploration in Dylan's attitude to performance compared with the 'professional' approach of someone like Paul Simon. These particular duets were 'fairly nice' in a very bland way. Amusing too for their very awkwardness, but not too obnoxious. Or at least not until a reggae-lite "Knockin' On Heaven's Door" was jarred by the monstrous perversion of incorporating some lines from a Simon song into the Dylan original. This nearly cost me a CD player and a replacement window.

Nonetheless, as I say, I liked these shows more than I thought I would. Especially one I listened to repeatedly, from June 16th at Sacramento CA. That night's opener, "Cocaine Blues", is a song he always does well, but I particularly loved the Sacramento version. Another song that regularly fully engages Dylan is the superlative "My Back Pages" and the Sacramento show was no let-down here. The "younger than that now" phrase here became a howl of independence and the band's playing was splendid, as was Bob on the harmonica.

Sacramento also featured a very fine "Don't Think Twice, It's Alright". Here was a song he performed as well as when he was much younger. This served as a reminder that I (and 'we all', I suspect) take great versions of songs like "Don't Think Twice, It's Alright"/"Girl From The North Country"/"Boots Of Spanish Leather" etc. for granted when often, despite being 'not exciting' in terms of the set-list, they are amongst the best-performed songs in a show. "Masters Of War" followed it and was equally impressive.

In fact, throughout 1999 this song was brilliantly played time after time. Dylan's somewhat aged and ragged voice perhaps perfectly expressed the appalling never-ending relevance of the blunt unforgiving words. When I heard it again, live, that year in Europe with the bombs, bullets and torturers at close quarters, it was chilling. As Robert Hilburn wrote of the performance he witnessed four days later at Arrowhead Pond in Anaheim CA: "This version of 1963's 'Masters of War' carried the urgency of a news bulletin."

"Tangled Up In Blue" was the next song to be delivered. It was ever present again in 1999, be it a 'greatest hits' night like this or a one-off club date with an otherwise more adventurous set-list. Dylan was struggling to overcome a hoarse voice as the run of acoustic songs reached its climax, with a performance of this magnificent song that added absolutely nothing to the transcendent versions of yore. It was as close to boring as such a masterly song sung by the master could ever be. The crowd loved it, naturally.

Then "All Along The Watchtower" appeared, or 'old number 3' as I think of it, with a reasonably understated opening. The unmistakable melody is still a foot-tapper and still an audience favourite. "Positively 4th Street" was taken slowly; Dylan sang it with a warm rasp, sounding more understanding than vindictive. "Stuck Inside Of Mobile With The Memphis Blues Again" was given a passable rendition, although the vocals developed a 'whine' by the song's conclusion. "Not Dark Yet", on the other hand, was a flawless reading of a song that was consummately performed more than once in 1999.

After the introduction of the band it was into the slam-bam rock encore of "Highway 61 Revisited", which sounded fresher than it often had been. "Love Sick" sounded much as it had on its debut back in Bournemouth, UK '97; still atmospheric and film noir-ish, still marred, though not for much longer, by the calamitous "thunder/ plunder/wonder" triplet.

Then it was time to please the audience with that greatest of greatest hits: "Like A Rolling Stone". I must admit to preferring "Love Sick" in these 1999 end-of-show settings. Although it is an immeasurably slighter piece of work it was consistently performed with a commitment missing from the 'done-a-thousand-times-and-more' other electric encores.

As had become common, the best of all encore performances was to be found in the penultimate slot, reserved for the last acoustic song of the night. In Sacramento, it was "It Ain't Me, Babe" that reminded us of Dylan's power and glory with words and music before he and the band attempted to destroy any similar memories of Buddy Holly's gifts by trashing the life out of "Not Fade Away".

Dylan's interview comments that the Simon shows would be the same as he would normally play can be easily disproved by comparing this show with those performed in the upcoming November leg. However, although I was not representative of the target audience I found it had much of merit, and I obtained a great deal of enjoyment from my repeated listenings. You may well wonder, given my antipathy to this leg, why I ended up playing it at all, far less repeatedly. It was all down to luck.

I was sent Sacramento by one of those lovely people who like to send on rarities the minute they get them. In this case the rarities were to be found as 'bonus tracks' at the end of the Sacramento show. As one of these tracks was much sought after, I inevitably ended up copying the discs for many friends. Out of curiosity, I listened to the show itself, in addition to the extra tracks, and found myself drawn to it from the first listen.

The 'surprise' songs and covers included, for example, "Down Along The Cove". This was from July 10th at Maryland heights, Missouri. Sadly, hearing about this one being played was much more exhilarating than actually hearing it. "Somebody Touched Me" was also on my double disc. I know it is a trifling piece but I thoroughly enjoyed it. This made you want to 'slap your thighs', get out that banjo and join in the shindig. It was a joyful, religious celebration of a hands-on experience from the Lord Himself. However the greatest of summer buzzes, and one in which the headiest of anticipations were met in full, was the stunning live debut of "Highlands" on 25th June.

This was why I was repeatedly copying the CDs for friends. It is hard to describe the excitement amongst Dylan fans when we heard he had done this song, though this excitement, it must be said, was tinged with a fear that he'd not do it justice. Many of us have never recovered from hearing that he had sung "Brownsville Girl" in 1986 only to discover on playing it that although he had indeed sung "Brownsville Girl" a few more words certainly would not have gone amiss. There were no such problems with "Highlands" on 25th June. Anchored to a steady beat Dylan sang it with panache and, praise be, he remembered the lyrics! The performance is a bit jauntier than that on the album, the humour and the fun elements more stressed. The 'Neil Young' verse and the superb waitress interlude were particularly effective. They are also so on the studio track, but they seemed to stand out even more here. All in all it was fabulous, "worth all of 1998 on its own" was my immediate, perhaps jaundiced, reaction.

After a break, September saw Dylan continuing to tour with Simon for another ten dates. It was more of the same with the most surprising song selection being a one-off cover of Dwight Yoakam's "The Heart That You Own" on September 2nd at West Palm Beach FL. It also included the novelty of having a guest on for the entire Dylan half of the show. This happened on September 8th at the First American Music Centre in Antioch TN. The guest was country multi-instrumentalist and singer Marty Stuart, and so inspired was Dylan by his presence that he turned in a performance which Dylan chronicler for the last five decades, Paul Williams, described as: "quite possibly the best Dylan concert I've ever seen". That is quite a quote from a man who'd seen Dylan at his peak in the 60s and 70s, even allowing for the rush of enthusiasm one gets from catching Bob on a hot night.

Notwithstanding such shows as the 8th and 16th of September, the best of 1999 was still to come. After another short break, Dylan resumed touring in October, sharing the bill with Phil Lesh. Yes, the world-famous Phil Lesh. If you are wondering who he is, think ex- Grateful Dead bassist. Think then on Lesh being so much more popular than Dylan that he would end up headlining the shows. It speaks volumes for the pulling power of the Dead's surviving members, and of the diminished appeal Dylan's non-stop touring had led to at that point in time.

The Worcester Phoenix's concert previewer was suitably astonished and dismayed by this turn of events. "Hey, we like Bob Dylan just as much as the next lopheaded freak, right on up to *Time Out Of Mind*. But lately we're starting to wonder about the crowd he's hanging with. First there was his cameo on

Dharma & Greg. C'mon – 30 years of reclusiveness and the guy comes out of his shell for these retards? And now he shows up on tour with that dreaded spectre of post Grateful death, Phil Lesh. And Friends. Wooga. Choke us with an ankh, but we'll wait for the VH1 Special."

Notwithstanding the validity of these catty remarks, the shows themselves blew any depression out the water. We were in NET wonderland; you could pick almost any of them and remain impressed. The quality was as consistent as the set-lists were full of surprises. Dylan, freed from the restraint of performing greatest hits for the baby boomers, shook things up with ever-changing set-lists and arrangements. It was a rewarding time for those who follow the tour night after night.

For example, on the 8th of November at Baltimore the set included: (acoustically) "I Am The Man, Thomas", "Mr. Tambourine Man", "Visions Of Johanna", "Ring Them Bells", (electrically) "Big River", "Joey", "Down Along The Cove", "Man In The Long Black Coat" and "Tombstone Blues" amongst others. The following night had none of these but did boast (as well as an extended encore) (acoustically) "Hallelujah, I'm Ready To Go", "The Lonesome Death Of Hattie Carroll", "Boots Of Spanish Leather", "A Satisfied Mind", "Mama, You Been On My Mind", (electrically) "Folsom Prison Blues", "Man Of Peace", "I'll Be Your Baby Tonight" and "Shooting Star" amongst others.

On 26th October Dylan played another small club gig at Atlantic City; two shortened sets in the one night, announced only a few days prior to the event. The two sets augured well for the upcoming leg with Phil Lesh. Even songs like "Tombstone Blues" and, a differently paced "Like A Rolling Stone" benefited from a freshness and renewal of energy. You know when a throwaway number like "Everything Is Broken" is enjoyable that Bob is really on song. After the October Atlantic City shows, the next I heard was 13th November, East Rutherford NJ. I played these tapes repeatedly. Half a dozen of East Rutherford's finest tracks were put on the official website in the year 2000 (and remain there at the time of writing). Both shows featured warm, avuncular stabs at "Visions Of Johanna". You could tell when he drew out the line endings it was to please the crowd; this was not the incandescent 'wild mercury' performance of *Blonde On Blonde*, after all it would be odd if he still sang lines like "the ghost of 'lectricity howls in the bones of her face" exactly as he did then.

In the month or so following, we had a run of consistently high-standard affairs. As ever during good spells of the NET there were interesting covers and oddities, including five cover debuts (the aforementioned "A Satisfied Mind", "Hootchie Cootchie Man", "Money Honey", "Duncan and Brady" and "This World Can't Stand Long") and a stellar outing for Johnny Cash's "Big River". This last was on the 8th at Baltimore, where Bob paid his dues near Miss Mary's house with a notable performance. This was a show I quickly fell in love with. All the good elements of this run were in place for a night that found Dylan and the band in top form from beginning to end.

Then more shows came in from November, and I was listening to whole shows again. The Baltimore show remained my favourite, but listening to the 3rd of November I had to question whether my preference was swayed by the intrusive crowd noise on the tape of the 3rd. Dylan's heartfelt singing in the opening acoustic numbers had to compete with loud shouts, talking and repeated attempts by someone to cry "Woof! Woof!". In an attempt to draw attention to what he was laying down, Dylan addressed the crowd: "We're gonna slow it down just a little a bit...." Unfortunately his attempt to make them pay attention was fruitless. So the Baltimore show remained my most-played, but the important point was the non-stop high standard of these shows; the 7th and 9th that surrounded my Baltimore choice could make loud and long claims for being the best. .. and so it could go on.

Dylan and his band pulled out all the stops night after night, and not just on the covers and 'oddities'. Dylan songs from throughout his career were also showcased to great effect. Standout performances included "Ring Them Bells", "My Back Pages" (repeatedly), "Highlands" (at Worcester MA on the 14th), "Señor", "To Be Alone With You" and so on. Sexton's presence was really beginning to tell, and the band were flying; playing as well as they had in a very long time. The effective harmony singing on "Tears Of Rage" spoke of a team working in, well, yes: 'in harmony'!

For all the splendours of earlier in the year, this last leg was the most consistently triumphant. By the time Dylan brought the year's touring to an end, with an extended set on November the 20th, he had played 121 shows – the most in a single year of his entire career. It had been a very good year, the best since 1995. While it never reached the superlative heights of that year's Spring shows, it was more consistent in that it ended so very strongly, while the glory of '95 had dissipated as the year progressed.

CHAPTER FOURTEEN

2000: "We're playing over here with a lot of pride"

"We're playing over here with a lot of pride, it's a big honor to play in this country, Great Britain. When I grew up, they used to tell me about the Battle of Britain, RAF, Winston Churchill, all that stuff. Now, we all know that Britain stood alone and without any allies; and that always meant a lot to me and everybody that I grew up with."[1]

Suddenly years began with a '2' and not a '1'; still the world kept turning and Dylan kept touring it. What was to prove a bumper year of goodies opened with two sets in Anaheim. The first, on March 10th, included a number of surprising song selections, a tight band and Dylan in authoritative voice, willing to radically experiment with and, once again, reinvent his back pages. The reworked "Dignity", alone, could bear eloquent testimony to this.

The biggest surprise was the first live performance of "Tell Me That It Isn't True" since it appeared on *Nashville Skyline* at the end of the 1960s. Brilliantly

1 Onstage, Wembley Arena, London, 5th October 2000.

sung, it was the standout song in a remarkably strong set. The following show at the same venue featured the almost equally unexpected "We Better Talk This Over". However, unlike "Tell Me That It Isn't True" this was not an entirely successful version and, sadly, has not been played again.

These extremely impressive opening shows kicked off a spring tour packed with highlights. Overall, however, the high standards of Anaheim were not maintained throughout entire shows. As the weeks passed I therefore found myself drifting back to compilations rather than complete shows. This, though, is not really a detrimental comment on the shows themselves; after all it is inevitable that compilations bring together a 'best of' collection, and the shows were all more than fine in themselves. It is not really common in the popular music field to go to concerts and have every song be a 'highlight'; indeed it rather defeats the meaning of the word.

Nevertheless, it was indicative of something I mentioned in the chapter on 1997, which was that Dylan had to develop a way of performing that allowed him to put on around one hundred shows a year, notwithstanding his age and the ravages of illness, hard living and (perhaps) over-touring on his vocal capabilities. One way to do this was to pace himself; to hold back from giving his all on every song, every night. He didn't stop trying, but he came to rely on an increasingly polished band to help him put on a 'good show' even when he was not entirely on top of his own game.

Rather than the more extreme variance of the earlier NET years, when Dylan's performance seemed to be a mirror of his mood of the moment, we now had years of consistently 'fine' shows. I say 'consistently fine' because that is how they were viewed by the majority of press and fellow fans at the time (the same scenario I describe here has been repeated since then too). Other than at certain times (especially in parts of 1999), I am not so convinced. I tend to see them as shows 'containing some fine performances' (some outstanding ones come to that), rather than shows which hit the heights all the way through.

To me Dylan is often coasting, 'fine' though he sounds. He achieves this by over-burring his 'r's for a strong, masculine tone and extending the 'i' sounds for a light, feminine touch. He drags out vowel line endings in a parody of his *Blonde On Blonde* vocals, with inevitable crowd-pleasing results. All the other switches he flicks to get Pavlovian responses from the aisles, as mentioned in the chapter on 1998, are also still present.

When he is fully engaged all the above devices sound and feel genuine, because they *are* genuine in that strange way where something being performed takes on an aspect of being genuine despite its obvious theatricality. The artist, be it a singer inhabiting a song or an actor onstage inhabiting a character, has entered into this performance area deep inside themselves, given themselves over to the truth of what this area holds and projected it out to us in the audience, the fortunate recipients of their transforming artistic gift.

Shows have come to seem to me either 'good' or 'bad' (it should be remembered that I am judging by Dylan's own high standards here) depending on how much 'coasting' they have in them. Obviously ones like Anaheim on the 10th, where I feel he is totally switched on throughout the night, his vocals fully engaged, are my very favourites. Other nights range from me enjoying most of the songs to only liking a few; on the occasional bad night I feel he never gets into it at all.

A lot of these feelings were clarified for me as I wrote *Razor's Edge* and listened and re-listened to so many shows. They came to a head just before I finished it, in the autumn of 2000 during yet another European tour. However, I am getting ahead of myself, so let's return to earlier in the year. Dylan had once again toured Germany and I managed to catch a couple of the shows, the first being an interesting night in Cologne.

May 11, 2000 Kölnarena, Cologne, Germany

1. Roving Gambler (Traditional) (Acoustic)
2. The Times They Are A-Changin' (Acoustic)
3. It's Alright, Ma (I'm Only Bleeding) (Acoustic)
4. Mr. Tambourine Man (Acoustic)
5. Tangled Up In Blue (Acoustic)
6. Gates Of Eden (Acoustic)
7. Country Pie
8. Things Have Changed
9. Down Along The Cove
10. Every Grain Of Sand

11. Cold Irons Bound

12 Leopard-Skin Pill-Box Hat

*

13. Love Sick

14. Like A Rolling Stone

15. Forever Young (Acoustic)

16. Not Fade Away (Buddy Holly/Norman Petty)

17. Don't Think Twice, It's All Right (acoustic)

18. Rainy Day Women #12 & 35

I must say that Dylan looked fabulous as he opened with a run-through of "Roving Gambler", classy, cool and in control. "The Times They Are A-Changin'" was next, and to begin with the lyrics were all over the place. I suddenly saw Dylan with extreme clarity, he was sweating heavily and he looked terribly frail. Nonetheless, his voice began to open up, he sorted the song out, even getting the right words for the second half, and it turned into an affecting rendition.

Most noticeable to me was the crystal clear sound. It was years since I had heard Dylan's singing so clearly via the sound system. The difference this makes is startling; and it also puts him under a much more intense spotlight. Now you knew for certain when he was fluffing, because you could hear everything. The considerable upside being that you also knew when it is a beautifully modulated aside rather than a fluff. In a similar fashion you realised almost instantly whether the harmonica solos were the real thing or Dylan just hamming it up.

Another huge change was that Dylan was restricting his guitar playing to the odd stab. There were two main benefits that arose from this. Firstly, it allowed the band to play and marked the end of long pointless Dead-like jams. Instead, we got real music played by craftsmen taking pride in their jobs. Sexton was exceptional and Kemper, Campbell and Tony also could now shine. Secondly, it allowed Dylan to concentrate on his singing, as evidenced by a riveting "It's Alright, Ma (I'm Only Bleeding)". Things were looking up for a good show when a fine "Mr. Tambourine Man" found Dylan's soaring voice move me to tears. Little did I realise it at the time but the playing or non-playing of the guitar was to become a dominant theme of shows in the 21st century.

The highlight of the whole night was then presented in the form of an extraordinary "Gates Of Eden". After a brief wrestle with his guitar Dylan stopped playing, making way for a Prague '95-type delivery. This time there was an added piquant twist: as Bob crooned a delicious and involved reading into the mic, he kept hold of the guitar neck with his right hand and used it to punctuate his delivery. It was magical, a bit like the crossed arms at the wrists delivery of "Isis" in Rolling Thunder days. I was in Heaven, far less Eden.

"Country Pie" was fun, if limited, while "Things Have Changed" was streets ahead of the studio version, he really sang it so well. An enjoyable "Down Along The Cove" poured over the audience in wave after wave of sound, building and building to a climax that seemed never to come. Then the mood changed again for the other highlight of the night, a passionate, crafted "Every Grain Of Sand".

After that, my interest faded: a female fan (Lola) was onstage with an *acoustic* guitar, not that you could hear her at all, playing on a ritual desecration of "Like A Rolling Stone". The rest of the electric songs were just 'party animals' but "Forever Young" was moving and "Don't Think Twice, It's Alright" was magnificent.

In characteristic NET roller-coaster style, the next night at Hanover was not nearly as good – it was a terrible hall acoustically and Dylan kept forgetting lyrics and mumbling half lines to disguise the fact. On the other hand, it had a very lovely "Tomorrow Is A Long Time" and a fine "Ring Them Bells". In addition, "Like A Rolling Stone" was much better than in Cologne and there was a surprise highlight in "Leopard-Skin Pill-Box Hat" which was performed with gusto and tour-de-force harmonica playing.

Most other songs were only partial successes; "It Ain't Me, Babe", for example, had one great verse, and "Tombstone Blues" started horribly but ended well. If the concerts had happened the other way round, it would have been the excitement of Cologne that lingered in my mind as I made my way home from Germany, rather than the disappointment of Hanover. Of the concerts I had personally attended Hanover was probably better than any I was at from 1996 to 1998, but because Cologne was so special Hanover seemed a bit of a let-down. This is just an 'occupational hazard' of the NET. You follow the tour as best you can and you take the cards you are dealt; only snatching two shows from a leg is bound to leave you with an even chance of preferring the former and leaving the latter feeling a little let down, unreasonable though that be.

As it transpired, Cologne was partially a fluke, benefiting from technical problems with Dylan's guitar. Guitar playing was not his forte this year, in contrast to his generally splendid singing and harmonica playing. Yet, in quintessential Dylan manner, as the year advanced he played more and more guitar and with more and more eccentricity. Larry Campbell and Charlie Sexton would have to stand around idly while Dylan took the leads.

Even with US and European legs already behind him Dylan was not for slowing up. Back to the States he went to tour with Phil Lesh again before returning for another European jaunt, this time taking in a number of gigs in the UK that were rapturously received by the majority of fans and press. To me they were a mixture of the detached Dylan putting on a show and the genuine spine-tingling excitement of Dylan really getting into it. Most, the Portsmouth shows for example, were a fairly even mixture; others tended to one extreme or the other. Sheffield was an example of Dylan at his most detached, while the following show at Cardiff found him at his most engaged.

Not that the reception Dylan received varied with the quality. He gets the same reception in the UK whatever he does. I was very disappointed after the Sheffield show but found, on leaving the arena, that most people were enthusing wildly about it. I began to wonder if I'd been at the same show as everyone else. I did eventually hear some comments that were more in line with my own views, Michael Gray being as deflated by the show as I was, and Clinton Heylin dismissing it as the worst Dylan show he'd ever seen. The much travelled and multi-hundred show attending Andrew Goldstein concluded simply that "It sucked". This was one of those shows that really split reactions in the touring fraternity.

In stark contrast, at the next show in Cardiff Dylan was fully engaged throughout and everybody agreed it was a splendid show; one of, if not the, best of the time. The overall consistency of the show was remarkable. There was a brilliant "Ballad of Frankie Lee and Judas Priest": Dylan's knowing voice, with no backing, drew us in until we were completely mesmerised. This is what ensures the NET remains an engrossing and exhilarating experience. Dylan, the great live experimenter performing one of his most loved songs with a completely different arrangement. All my disappointments at Dylan's 'coasting' are made irrelevant by performances like these. Though much derided by casual fans, and certain critics, this constant recreation is his strength rather than a weakness.

As the Scottish broadsheet, *The Herald*'s Ian Bell put it: "Had he been a jazz musician no-one would think twice that he takes old songs and breathes new, startling life into them ... there is an aspect to all this that appears to elude most commentators on Dylan's work. The idea of him as a poet of the page was never plausible. Listen to him shape the phrasing of something like 'Rolling Stone' or 'It Ain't Me, Babe', however, and you realise that performance never the same twice, never final and perfected – is the very point, the end in itself. Is any production of a play ever definitive? Is there only one way to perform Brahms? Dylan, playing in the same league, appears to think not."

This acute insight stands in stark contrast to an e-mail sent to www.bobdylan.com after Dylan's Santa Cruz shows in 2000. This correspondent asked for a refund on the basis that Dylan had not played enough 'hits' and that when he had performed familiar material, the arrangements had been so altered from the original that this poor audience member could not 'recognize and sing along to the songs of his youth'. Ian Bell, in the same piece, had anticipated and rebutted such nonsense with these words:

"... the ever-changing arrangements, long his habit in any case, are also part of the argument over ownership ... Dylan was challenging the audience even to attempt to 'sing along' with songs they thought they knew. As a believer in corporal punishment for lachrymose community singing, this writer, for one, owes him a debt."

This writer makes it two, barring exceptional occasions, which are made all the more special because of their rarity. Routine "lachrymose community singing" is extremely off-putting: only once or twice every thousand shows is it special and extremely moving. Dylan is well aware of the problem his performing style poses for a portion of his audience. In the Hilburn interview quoted in earlier chapters (post Madison show, November 1991 – published 1992) it is a problem he views as being mainly consigned to the past:

"*Older people – my age – don't come out anymore,*" he says. "*A lot of the shows over the years was people coming out of curiosity and their curiosity wasn't fulfilled. They weren't transported back to the '60s. Lightning didn't strike. The shows didn't make sense for them, and they didn't make sense for me. That had to stop, and it took a long time to stop it. A lot of people were coming out to see The Legend, and I was trying to just get on stage and play music."*

To return our focus to the Cardiff 2000 show, it also featured the new, slow and heartrending arrangement of "Trying' To Get To Heaven".[2] Another song from *Time Out Of Mind*, the much lesser "Cold Irons Bound", was given just as experimental a reworking. In this case, the reworking involved replacing its near non-existent melody with something Lou Reed would have cavilled at including on *Metal Machine Music*. If the magical spell of "Tryin' To Get To Heaven" had to be broken for the show to continue, this dissonant blare and Dylan's swaggering vocals sure broke it. It was good to see him still experimenting with the *Time Out Of Mind* songs.

There were, in truth, too many highlights on the tour to recount; but special mention should be made of two distinctly different, yet both triumphant, outings for "Fourth Time Around". After an exhilarating electric interpretation at Portsmouth (the first time that both it and "Visions Of Johanna" had been played in the UK since the legendary 1966 shows[3]) it appeared in acoustic guise at Wembley. There it was sung with a tenderness that evinced a different kind of life-knowledge than that which infused the gorgeous, incomparable *Blonde on Blonde* version.

There was also a return to surprising onstage remarks, represented by a somewhat rambling speech at the Wembley show in between "The Wicked Messenger" and the band credits:

We're playing over here with a lot of pride, it's a big honour to play in this country, Great Britain. When I grew up, they used to tell me about the Battle of Britain, RAF, Winston Churchill, all that stuff. Now, we all know that Britain stood alone and without any allies; and that always meant a lot to me and everybody that I grew up with.

---

2 You can get a feel for this from an official release, of the same song at Wembley on October 5th. This was included on *Tell Tale Signs: The Bootleg Series vol. 8 rare and unreleased 1989-2006*, Columbia CKC 735797, released 6 October 2008.

3 Robert Forryan, chronicler of both Bob Dylan and his beloved Nuneaton Borough FC, rocked me with his carefully timed comment as I left the show: "Fourth Time Around" and "Visions of Johanna". Well, I haven't seen them both in the same night since Leicester '66."

Now, this is far from those infamously strange comments we noted earlier in the NET such as "Hitler was not a German, not many people know that" and "I'm descended from Vikings" from Hamburg and Oslo respectively. However, it was odd to hear, given how many times Dylan had previously played in the UK in general and in London in particular. The reason for it being spoken this particular night lay in a back-stage gift from Jim Callahan, a photo-laden account of London during the Blitz.

The excitement around this tour was increased even further by another of those 'impossible to miss', 'intimate' gigs. This one was held at Vicar Street in Dublin, on September 13th. Sean O'Hagan wryly reported that: "THE 800 TICKETS for this suddenly announced 'intimate' show supposedly sold out in 15 seconds. For the select multitude, then, this was a night of almost impossibly high expectation, but Bob Dylan, for a long time now the most erratic of live performers, did not disappoint...."

The set-lists continued to change and included more than a few surprises. Anything seemed possible. Dylan writer John Stokes even mused, on our way to Portsmouth, that maybe he'd get to hear his all time number one concert wish, "If Dogs Run Free". This completely untypical song (from *New Morning* some 30 years previously), replete with scat singing no less, seemed to me to be just about the most unlikely performance choice imaginable. I confidently stated on September 24th that "If we live to be a million, he'll never play that song."

No-one was likely to disagree, except Dylan. After all these years, I still had not learnt this well enough. The song duly debuted a week later in Münster, Germany. I saw it at Paris on October 3rd when I just happened to be there 'on business'. This was the last live show that I saw before *Razor's Edge* was sent to the publisher. It was a splendid show, mostly high-energy, with Sexton's guitar more prominent than it had been earlier in this European leg. At the same time, it was laced with subtle and impressive readings of "Standing In The Doorway" and "Tryin' To Get To Heaven".

Looking back to the European shows I saw in 2000 from a later perspective finds me judging them far more highly now than I did then. The following two years were to see the US enjoying the best legs, by quite some distance, and although 2003 and 2004 saw me witness some remarkable shows in the UK they were exceptions. I was not to witness anything like the same standard, quantity or consistency as 2000 in future years. I slowly came to realise that I had taken it too much for granted. Back then, I was soaked in listening to the late 1999 shows and saw the 2000 ones as a natural extension. I still do, come to that, but it meant that although I knew the shows were full of magic, this was merely what I expected, what I had always expected. Maybe my standards were too high, maybe I was repeating the old mistake of comparing Bob with Bob rather than enjoying the shows for and of themselves. I was not following the advice I propose in these very pages.

Perhaps knowing I was writing and coming to the end of *Razor's Edge* also had an effect, though I find it impossible to judge that now. Whatever the influence of each of these factors, to look back now is to honestly say that I have seen nothing to come even vaguely close in Europe since the tours of 2000, and I should have been (even) more appreciative at the time. Still, that is my loss, no one else's. In addition, it was not as though I did not enjoy them; I loved them, it was just that everyone else seemed to *adore* them.

Although October marked the end of my live shows for the year, Dylan was far from finished. On he went to the US for strong shows with some riveting individual song performances. However, I felt that overall the last leg was a notch down on the rest of the year,. This was only reasonable as the late legs of the following two years, also in the US, were to prove far and away those years' highlights. Back in 2000, despite still being impressive, the quality suffered a dip compared to the years' previous legs due to the aforementioned increase in Dylan's guitar playing at the expense of the cohesion and quality that Sexton and Campbell had been providing. Ed Masley picked up on this in his review of an early November show:

"And *boy*, did he play guitar, an instrument he plays at least as well as Master P plays basketball. But hey, it's his name on the ticket. If he wants to get some leads in when they could have gone to Campbell and/or Charlie Sexton, both of whom were just amazing, I suppose it's up to him."[4] That aside, the show Mr. Masley reviewed was clearly akin to those we had just witnessed in Europe:

"'Standing in the Doorway' proved an early highlight, greeted by a cheer as Dylan took on the opening line with a fire he could have used on 'Like a Rolling

---

4 *Concert Review: Dylan brilliant even when less than perfect.* Ed Masley, *Post-Gazette Pop Music Critic* Tuesday, November 7th, 2000.

Stone' and other songs he's more than likely sick to death of singing. It was Dylan at his poignant best as a vocalist ... And in the end, as always, it was worth it sitting through the remedial solos and the screwed-up versions of the classics just to get to all the moments that found him redeeming himself: 'Forever Young' 'awash in aching harmonies; a lazy nightclub jazz arrangement of 'If Dogs Run Free'; a breathtaking 'Just Like A Woman'; and a gently-rocking, smile-inducing version of 'Leopard-Skin Pill-Box Hat'."

His review ended with a line that most NET followers could relate to and which would be echoed in a review of the year's last show. "In closing, no, the night was not without its flaws, but it was brilliant all the same."

November saw a continuation of songs not played for many a year ("Chimes of Freedom"), a new cover ("Blue Bonnet Girl") and a Dylan original being played for the first time ever ("10,000 Men").

The last show fell on November 19th at Towson State University in Maryland. The setlist was extended for the occasion and ran to nearly two hours. Those who made the sensible choice of going to the last few shows of the year would have found a whopping eleven songs played here that they had not witnessed in the penultimate show of 2000.

19 November 2000 Towson Center Arena, Towson State University, Towson MD

1. Oh Baby It Ain't No Lie (Elizabeth Cotten) (Acoustic)
2. Mr. Tambourine Man (Acoustic)
3. Desolation Row (Acoustic)
4. One Too Many Mornings (Acoustic)
5. Tangled Up In Blue (Acoustic)
6. Searching For A Soldier's Grave (Johnnie Wright, Jim Anglin, Jack Anglin) (Acoustic)
7. Country Pie
8. Blind Willie McTell
9. Seeing The Real You At Last
10. Tryin' To Get To Heaven

11. The Wicked Messenger
12. Cat's In The Well

*

13. Things Have Changed
14. Like A Rolling Stone
15. If Dogs Run Free (Acoustic)
16. All Along The Watchtower
17. Don't Think Twice, It's All Right (Acoustic)
18. Highway 61 Revisited
19. Blowin' In The Wind
20. Rainy Day Women #12 & 35

The reviewer for this show from the *Washington Times* had a very similar response to that of Mr. Masley earlier in the month, again finding the word 'brilliant' the most apt concluding adjective, albeit laced with a bit of ageist slander:

"The set list ranged through different styles he's sampled through the years; blues, country, folk, rock. Mr. Dylan played enthusiastically .... For his final encore, he launched into the crowd-pleasing 'Rainy Day Women No. 12 and No. 35,' whose 'Everybody must get stoned' chorus must have been pretty rebellious when the song was released in 1966. Now the song is like Mr. Dylan. A little dated, a little jaded, but brilliant all the same.[5]

5 *Washington Times:* 'Aging Bob Dylan's brilliance intact', Tuesday, November 21, 2000.

CHAPTER FIFTEEN

2001: "Nobody has to ask me what I think about this town"

BOB DYLAN, MADISON SQUARE GARDEN ARENA, NEW YORK NY, 19TH NOVEMBER 2001

I was in a semi-divorced state from the tour at this point. Firstly, after finishing *Razor's Edge* I was concentrating on another book. Secondly, I had a feeling that a bit of distance from the tour might be a good thing anyway after focussing on it for so long. I say 'semi' divorced because I was still deeply involved in the 'Dylan world', and in any case the continuing technological advances and expansion of the Internet made keeping up to date and receiving recent recordings easier than ever. In all truth, you would actually have to work hard *not* to keep up to date in 2001. What a complete turnaround from twenty years earlier.

The same band that ended 2000 kicked off the new year with thirteen dates in Japan. A new balance of electric and acoustic songs was settled on after the opening three dates. Individual shows could vary, but generally Dylan now opened with three acoustic followed by three electric songs, then the same pattern again before a set format of encores with a mixture of four electric and three acoustic songs. The term 'acoustic' had become somewhat meaningless by now, the old solo acoustic Dylan was long gone. String-based band or semi-band backing had taken over and electric instruments were now heard in what we still, for the sake of convenience, refer to as the 'acoustic' slots. The opening songs were all covers, as they would be throughout the year.

Naturally, I kept in touch with general developments and especially noted the oddities, such as one-offs of "Chimes Of Freedom" and "In The Garden", as the tour continued through Australia and on to the US. The innate NET craving for novelty will never leave any of us. I noted, too, that by the US spring tour Dylan was in stronger voice and the shows more upbeat.

I suspect this was at least partly due to the thrill Dylan got from being awarded an Oscar for "Things Have Changed". Having already won a Golden Globe award in January for this nearly ever-present live song, Dylan 'joined' the 25th of March awards ceremony via a broadcast of him performing the song in a Sydney TV studio. It was fun to see, especially as it allowed the hard-working touring band exposure to such a vast audience.

In the 14 shows of the US spring tour 62 songs were played. Indeed, the three US tours of the year featured an impressively varied song selection, particularly as the last leg of the year found the set list radically altered due to Dylan heavily featuring songs from his new album, *"Love And Theft"*. However, I run ahead of myself.

Before then, there was the summer tour of Europe. As we knew by then that Dylan had recorded a new album, there were excited thoughts of previews of the new songs. Had I known then how brilliant the songs in question were, I suspect the anticipation would have been too much to bear.

As it happens we did not hear the pre-release tapes of the new album until the tour was over, and the sane view prevailed that there was no way Dylan would play any songs from it. Dylan's interview comments made clear that he was paranoid (justifiably, it has to be admitted) about bootleggers putting the new songs out before his record company could. How tragic, though, that inspirational new works were kept under wraps. How strange and frustrating that must be for the artist, bursting to share his new visions but instead being forced to trot out the same old stuff.

All in all, then, summer was not in the end an auspicious time for my own 2001 NET live experience. Still there was, as ever, much of interest. On the 28th of June in Langesund, Norway, the opening song was "Humming Bird". This debut song was, in 1958, the biggest hit for Johnny and Jack. The teenage Dylan would have heard this duo playing the song whilst in Minnesota. In 2001 the near sixty-year-old Dylan had taken another musical track of theirs ("Uncle John's Bongos") as the backing of "Tweedle Dee & Tweedle Dum", the opening song of *"Love And Theft"*. With the benefit of hindsight, it appears that Johnny and Jack were much in Bob Dylan's mind that May and June.

May had also seen Dylan's 60th birthday and the newspapers and magazines went to town again, just like they had for his 50th; one was left worried for the Amazon rainforest as career retrospective after career retrospective appeared. Naturally, all this proved good advertising for the upcoming dates.

There were only to be two UK dates that summer, but they seemed so appealing. Stirling Castle with all its significance in Scottish history providing a spectacular backdrop for the one, and Liverpool, home of the Beatles, and with so much musical history intertwined with Dylan's for the other. This was heartland UK, real people, real humour, real love of music, both traditional and popular; the music that has fed into so much of Dylan's career and indeed the American music tradition he has been excavating and highlighting for most of his career.

In Liverpool for the summer pops festival at the home of the Beatles, 18 of Dylan's 21 songs were from the 1960s. The first thing somebody said to me at the end of the show was: "I didn't come here to hear a Sixties show". It would seem that whatever Dylan does, it upsets some portion of his audience.

The Sixties' dominance could not seem bad to me, not when Dylan was wearing a polka dot cravat and bringing back memories of his shirt when he 'went electric' in 1965, the heyday of that holy triumvirate of Beatles, Stones and Dylan.

July 12, 2001 King's Dock, Liverpool, England

1. Oh Babe, It Ain't No Lie (Elizabeth Cotten) (Acoustic)
2. To Ramona (Acoustic)
3. Desolation Row (Acoustic)
4. Maggie's Farm

5. Just Like A Woman
6. This Wheel's On Fire
7. Visions Of Johanna (Acoustic)
8. Fourth Time Around (Acoustic)
9. Boots Of Spanish Leather (Acoustic)
10. Stuck Inside Of Mobile With The Memphis Blues Again
11. Positively 4th Street
12. Cold Irons Bound
13. Leopard-Skin Pill-Box Hat

*

14. Things Have Changed
15. Like A Rolling Stone
16. Knockin' On Heaven's Door (Acoustic)
17. All Along The Watchtower
18. I Shall Be Released (Acoustic)
19. Highway 61 Revisited
20. Blowin' In The Wind (Acoustic)

*

21. Rainy Day Women #12 & 35

Heralding the apocalypse as only Dylan can, he lit into "This Wheel's on Fire" abetted by some fearsome blasts on his harmonica. It augured well but was not really built upon, though I seemed to enjoy Liverpool more than most I spoke to afterwards. Perhaps my expectations were not as high as theirs, or maybe it was due to factors nothing to do with the show itself (the importance of which were about to be shown in spades the following night at Stirling).

As Dylan was due to hit the stage, I still had not heard from Joe McShane and other friends whom I had been due to meet earlier, other than that they had passed on a message that they were "stuck in a horrendous traffic jam" due to some motorway pile-up. While I plead guilty to being as keen as the next man on *Schadenfreude*, the idea of them all missing a Dylan show is going too far, even for me. So, the empty seats either side of me were causing me some discomfort when, glory be, Joe arrived out of breath just as Dylan began the show, not quite so out of breath. The feel-good factor this generated perhaps allowed me to enjoy the show more than others I spoke to, who at best were calling it a 'standard show'.

Everyone agreed that the night's highlight came at the end of "Things Have Changed". As the song had progressed so had Dylan's engagement with it; lines became stronger, words became clearer as he sang the second half into the microphone with verve and gusto. The song ended to a thunderous ovation as Dylan moved to the back of the stage near the amps, as he often does to locate a mischievously hiding harmonica, something else he needs, or just to scratch his head, gather his thoughts and come back with a new song. This time he came back with something else too, he clambered up and brought his Oscar down from on top of the amp. Half shy and yet fiercely proud, knees bent, like a little boy with a new toy he held it aloft to the cheers from the front rows of the audience.

Another thing that makes me think reasonably fondly of Liverpool was the show that followed at Stirling Castle. Even having checked in advance that it was the Castle car park rather than the Castle grounds themselves, the show sounded very romantic.

Reality, however, was another matter; the car park had the stage at one end and a not particularly imposing partial view of a small bit of the castle at the other end. You looked down on the stage with the castle mostly obscured behind you. It was all rather moot in any case as the sheets of rain *de rigueur* for an open-air Dylan concert in the UK were out in force. They were putting on a spectacular show of drenching one and all and keeping us all terrified of what seemed the imminent occurrence of a torrent of water from the stage roof hitting Dylan's guitar as he got more and more into the electric songs.

Other occurrences conspired to make this miserable occasion hard to bear, far less enjoy. Arriving at around the time that normally affords a good view, we found ourselves instead joining a very, very long queue that doubled back on itself but still stretched for miles. So long indeed did it stretch that after hours of queuing we had to sprint to make the opening song. The reason for this torturously slow process was that everyone was being checked for alcohol. This was done by large numbers of police, none of your security staff stuff here. Football matches between Rangers and Celtic could hardly command more man (and dog) power than this, as the force ensured this event would be as 'dry' as an event can be when the clouds above are unloading on the assembled hordes. I have not even mentioned the so-called acoustics yet, but I am sure you have got the idea by now: this was a washout in every sense.

The delay caused by the queue left me standing at the back of a car park with lots of people who had never seen Dylan before. People who were wondering when he was going to come on stage and play a song they knew – or rather, recognised – or wondering when this strange fellow would get off the stage and the man who sang on *The Freewheelin' Bob Dylan* or *Blonde On Blonde* or *Blood On The Tracks* would come on instead. This was definitely a show that I would have to get to know from a recording.

The town of Stirling itself, however, put on a fine performance, with various hostelries offering Dylan-named drinks and cover bands and generally ensuring a good time was had by all after the show. I was at a very well-run event myself, the highlight of the night being a rather marvellous rendition of "Romance In Durango" by Scottish singer-songwriter Sandy Watson. 'Oh, to hear Bob Dylan playing it and playing it well', we all laughed, never imagining that "Romance In Durango" was to feature in an NET show a couple of years later. Poor Sandy has now to settle for having performed this millennium's second best version of it.

The leg ended in Taormina, Sicily, with a pyrotechnic display to make the most outlandish rock stage show look like a damp squib as Dylan's show went ahead with the Etna volcano erupting in the background. There were other fireworks that summer, also in Italy, but in these cases it was Dylan who was erupting.

While in Rome, Dylan gave an interview purportedly to promote *"Love And Theft"*, though you would be forgiven for thinking that the real reason was to launch an ill-founded attack on the very people that had made the NET possible – his loyal fans. Variously reported in a number of summaries and mistranslations (I quote below what Dylan actually said, taken from the circulating recording of the interview), Dylan talked about NET fans, shedding insight into his sometimes bored or angry behaviour on stage. In response to a question about whom he felt he was relating to when he was on stage, Dylan said:

D: I usually play to the people in the back. I disregard the people in the front because usually these people have come to quite a few shows and they are gonna be there anyway, like what they hear one way or another, so we are not trying to reach them. We are trying to reach the people in the back who might not have been there ever before.

Q: So you don't think about the people who follow each and every show?

D: No we don't think about those people because they are always there, we think about the people we have never seen.

If we think back to Rotterdam in 1998, the audience at the back wanted to hear old songs and protest anthems; which is exactly the kind of expectation Dylan has so often spoken out against. On the other hand it is an expectation he has fulfilled night after night, year after year – if often seemingly against his wishes. It seemed then that he actively disliked playing "to the people in the back".

Or cast your mind back to my chapter on 1994 and the Roseland shows. Here the back of the audience were not there even just to hear the 'old anthems from their spokesman' or, indeed, anything else. Here they were out to socialise with their friends. If Dylan was really playing to the back of the crowd at those shows, then he was playing to people who had not the slightest interest in what he was doing (other than that he was a bit too loud at times, almost interrupting their conversations) and would not have cared what he played or how he played it.

Another point on the audience split between front and back would be one of age. The front by now tended to be a mixture of young and old; the back virtually all from the older camp. Something that Dylan again seems not to understand, given his comments in reply to *La Repubblica*'s question: "It seems like your audience is growing. Are there many young people at your concerts along with your old fans?"

I don't think there are many old fans. The fact is that people of my age die, or change their lives. At a certain point in your life new problems arise. Family, children, priorities change, entertainment becomes less important.

His point is a general, and sad, truth; but the very people he now claimed he was playing to at the back of the hall were his older fans, who probably do not go to many rock shows in a whole year, far less more than one by the same person. These people want to hear Dylan play all the old 'hits'.

I should add that all these comments are generalizations; some fans at the back (or front) will be the opposite of what I write, but we are forced to deal in generalities here given Dylan's polarisation and misrepresentation of 'back' and 'front'. I should add that there is absolutely no way that Dylan was playing to the "people at the back" in Stirling; he is completely deluded if he thought he was reaching them. Meanwhile the hard-core fans he was about to further decry were whooping it up in front of the stage. It is a pity, too, that the remarkable growth in the number of younger fans attending Dylan's concerts was misinterpreted and confused with other, also misunderstood, crowd tendencies.

An even greater pity is the detrimental effect his relationship with the front rows has on his shows. It should be pointed out that Dylan's actions often are counter to what he is saying; it is only by playing to and interacting with a boisterous front few rows that his shows take off, although clearly he would like these to be different faces each night. Perhaps because, completely contrary to what he says in the interview, the front row people are actually the most demanding and acute section of the audience and much more likely to know when Dylan is having an 'off night'. Or perhaps there are particular people who annoy him. That was certainly the case in Milan, as Rock journalist Paolo Vites recalls:

"What happened in Montreux was that, as is usual for years now, this guy was in front of Bob Dylan, right under his microphone. The small venue and the small stage made it possible for him and Bob Dylan to be in eye contact throughout the show. Actually, this man, as he had been doing for a long time, was showing his disgust for what he thought was a poor performance. While the people around him were clearly acting like an average audience, yelling and cheering for the performer, he was standing, moving his head and visibly making facial expressions disapproving of Bob Dylan. At one moment, Bob Dylan was obviously annoyed by the man and went almost down the stage to express his anger. *"Fuck you."* said Bob. *"I don't want to see you! I don't wanna see ya anymore at MY shows."*

The other, quite serious, problem occurs when Dylan decides to punish the loyal fans by muscling them out of their rightful positions. By the time of his 2000 tour of Europe his pre-emptive strikes against his most faithful fans plumbed ridiculous depths when he ordered the front stage to be cleared of those who had queued to get those prime positions. They were to be replaced by others chosen by the security guards.

The injustice of this was breathtaking; I often wonder at the legality of it, but have never been in a position to test that out. There were letters in the mainstream press from people who had been moved on after queuing up for the only concert they could get to. I remember one from a single mother in Glasgow who had saved up for a long time to pay for the show and a babysitter and she was determined to get near in her one chance to see Dylan up close. After going through all the expense, time and effort to get to the front she was chased away and replaced by someone else who had only come for a casual night out. One does not need to stretch one's imagination to guess the age, looks and gender balance of the people that were selected for the front by the security guards.

Of course this only worked where there was standing in front of the stage, they were not yet actually taking people out of seats and resettling them in some faraway part of an auditorium. How much this restriction on replacing the front rows with hand-picked people irritated Dylan was made clear by his demeanour on taking the stage at Sheffield 2000 and looking at the front rows.

However, this sorry state of affairs obviously did not come about just on a whim. Dylan no doubt feels he has to disregard the front rows to prevent his performance art from stagnating. There is undoubtedly something disturbing for him in seeing the same rows of people each night, year after year. It even started to depress me as an attendee, far less the performer. Meeting the same people show after show in an almost regimented seating pattern made each show seem part of a rock revival type yearly event rather than the rolling ever onward unpredictable NET. On the other hand, the most important thing is the effect on Dylan's music and performance. For example, the shows in Edinburgh 1995 and Sheffield 2000 were relatively poor in relation to the shows surrounding them. If this was due to Dylan's disgruntlement at seeing the same old faces, perhaps we have to put up with the injustice and accept it as an inevitable outcome of the situation.

Yet there is an unpleasant taint of hypocrisy about all this. This recent antipathy, or mere indifference, to those at the front has come mainly with Dylan's star on the rise. There was a time when he both needed and courted these very followers.

I remember back to the 1991 Hammersmith shows, which we have been told 'were giving Dylan too much money for him to turn down', that went ahead despite his illness, the lack of a rehearsed band and other problems we are not supposed to comment on[1]. It was the regular fans who go to every show and who try to get down to the front as often as possible who filled the hall on the eight nights.[2] Only these now-to-be-disregarded people would have kept going that year and refused to let the experience of those lamentable gigs be the final leg of a tour that seemed to have lost all meaning. Most people at Hammersmith were at the previous United Kingdom shows. I wasn't, though I did, like many other foot soldiers, continue on after Hammersmith to Holland.

Undeterred, two years later the same people filled the same now-renamed venue for another residency. My fanzine and information line were in full swing by that time so I was heavily involved in getting people tickets. The demand from the same people never wavered, nor the desperation to get nearer the stage, even one or two rows were crucial to them (and me). Of course you can think that risible to an extent, and Dylan can now afford to do so, but back then it was those people who kept the halls full enough for the tour to keep coming back. Over and above that, the stage was so poorly lit that if you were not near the front you could not see Dylan at all. If Dylan was playing to the back of the audience in those days, it was an audio-only show. His comments make him seem oblivious to the important visual nature of his performances; everyone who has seen him from close up for the first time remarks upon how it transforms the experience of seeing him play.

Perhaps the worst thing about Dylan's attitude to those who "usually ... have come to quite a few shows" is that he seemed to have forgotten that, back at the beginning of the NET's extraordinary peregrinations, he spoke of how he knew he needed to hit the road and yearned to have a travelling group of fans like those that followed the Dead. Here he is, back in the NET's early days, enthusing over the exact same audience and explaining why he was changing the set-lists so much:

---

1 Dylan in yet another interview, this time in *Rolling Stone*, got angry with people who made comments about him being very drunk on stage. He claimed it makes no difference to his performance.

2 It was because of the same people buying tickets for every show that they kept adding dates. There were 3 sets of ticket sales, 3 sets of overnight queuing in freezing temperatures.

"There are a lot of people that come to our shows lots of times. So, just for them, it's a good idea to do different things. It's not as though they just come and see me once."[3]

Be careful what you wish for, Bob, you just might get it.

Around the time of the Rome interview there had been events that brought all of this to a head. Paolo Vites was again in attendance, here is what he remembers about the events at the Brescia show:

"... before the Dylan show started, people from the unreserved section of the audience (the show was in a big, long, but not very large open square) were trying to remain standing in front of the stage, in front of the numbered seats. There were protests by the people who purchased the seats. The security came and made those people go back. When Bob Dylan came on stage, there was a big rush from the people in the standing only audience. A riot started in front of the stage between those people, the seated people and the security people. Bob Dylan was obviously aware of what was happening at his feet, because he was acting in a very nervous way, going back and forth during the songs. He clearly let his arms down, stopped playing and kept looking backstage as if he were searching for someone, the local promoter or the police. At one point, the security decided they could do nothing to send those people away. Those in the seated area were standing on their seats while everyone was standing in front of the stage. It was quite a mess. It was at this point Bob Dylan started the most vicious and angry Positively 4th Street I have ever heard (with the possible exception of the original), spitting the words of the song in a rage, clearly to the audience, or at least to part of them."

Perhaps this explains why Dylan seems to have very contradictory thoughts on his NET fans, at one point in the interview claiming that:

"Oh, I don't really feel like I have any hardcore fans, you know, I just don't. There's some people who do, I really just don't. We have a few people who see an abundance of my shows, but we don't think of them as hardcore fans."

3 Interview, Peter Wilmoth, *The Age*, Melbourne, 3rd April 1993

In the time between the group interview and the private one given to *The Times*, Dylan had changed his mind about having 'hardcore' fans. Talking of bootlegs, he said:

"And have been bought up by so-called hardcore fans of mine (a sneering tone here), whoever they might be – those folks out there who are obsessed with finding every scrap of paper I've ever written on, every single outtake. These so-called connoisseurs of Bob Dylan music ... I don't feel they know a thing, or have any inkling of who I am and what I'm about. I know they think they do, and yet it's ludicrous, it's humorous, and sad. That such people have spent so much of their time thinking about who? Me? Get a life, please. It's not something any one person should do about another. You're not serving your own life well. You're wasting your life."

No doubt there is validity to his main point, many of us do spend an unhealthy amount of time thinking about him. We are not unaware of that ourselves, however, and you cannot help but feel like retorting, albeit with a deal more grace, that he has just emphatically proved that he does not 'have any inkling of' who his fans are nor 'what they are about'. The effects of this misunderstanding were to continue to be felt as the NET progressed, but were mercifully absent from what was to be a successful and fulfilling concluding tour, showcasing songs from his new album amidst the terror and horror of an America feeling threatened and vulnerable in a way it had not since around the time the young Dylan wrote 'A Hard Rain's A-Gonna Fall'.

It is also worth remembering that Dylan's generosity to such fans has been demonstrated previously in this book, such as to me in 1993 and to Lambchop in 1995, when Dylan realised he had been unjust, for just two examples. In addition, he has played shows he knows to be full of the front-row travellers he was now so scornful towards and seemingly sometimes, at least, given special sets to reward this faithful following. As someone has said before "there are so many sides to Bob he's round", and as he himself has remarked, his moods change so quickly that the next time you ask the same question you may well get a completely different answer from him.

In any case, Rome's sour approach to fans was offset by the generosity of genius that spilled forth from the wonderful new album *"Love and Theft"*. Despite having the usual dosage of Armageddon, woman troubles and other blues, the overriding feelings were of warmth, humour and generosity; so much more life-enhancing than the tone of parts of *Time Out Of Mind*. Dylan sounds alive; enjoying life, seeing through and laughing at the absurdity of it all, while still giving the serious side its fair due. The rest of the world, those listeners who do not get advance tapes of new albums, would have to wait to find out about that though; the despised 'connoisseurs', on the other hand, spent August marvelling at its many-layered delights.

Naturally this meant that the US summer tour passed by in an excited blur of awaiting songs from the new album. Dylan tour chronicler Glen Dundas, who started his NET attendances the same year as me, summed up the mood of some of us when he wrote about attending the opening show of this leg:

"This was one of the very few times I've sat in the audience and wondered why in the name of hell I'm doing this. Somewhat typically for a tour opener, Dylan was going through the motions (maybe he wonders why in the hell he's starting another round of this incessant touring), the sound system sucked, the set list (except for 'I Threw It All Away') was typically mundane, and I couldn't help but wonder how the people at the far reaches of the grandstand (across the racing track from the stage) could possibly see Dylan at all...the long drive back home on Sunday left me with doubts on the advisability of spending that much time and money on something that just maybe had lost its flavour."[4]

Still, at the end of this leg, we were all looking forward to the official release and the introduction of the new songs with an anticipation that cannot be overstated. Their importance seemed paramount and beyond question. Then on the day of the album's release, 11th September 2001, the world changed.

No amount of disaster movie viewing could help prepare you for the pain, suffering and horror broadcast worldwide that evil day. The scale of the atrocity was beyond comprehension, the knowledge that this would change the world immediate, though at first you felt it was about to end, not just change. Somehow the world did keep going; and commentator after commentator noted eerily apt lines from Dylan's new album.

These were all written well before the attack on the Twin Towers, but seemed uncannily to evoke that fateful day. Music may seem a trivial thing to talk about

4 *Judas!* issue 1 April 2002

at such a time, but it is not; rather it brings strength to many. The last Dylan tour leg of the year in the US assumed vital importance, not just for Dylan diehards waiting on live *"Love And Theft"*, but also for mainstream rock fans with any liking for Dylan. It was a time when people with Voices were needed, and no one's voice resonated deeper or carried more weight than Dylan's.

Reviewer after reviewer mentioned songs such as "Masters Of War", "John Brown" and a whole host of "civil rights' protest songs" as being Dylan's none-too-subtle responses to the American Right's reaction both abroad and at home in the wake of the terrorist attack. In fact these songs had featured in the set-lists for years, though they certainly seemed to be taking on a new significance for many at these shows. Not that it was only what passes for left-wing views in America that latched on to them; the vicious lines glorying in others' deaths in "Masters of War" were sometimes cheered with a disturbing relish, and Dylan photographer Duncan Hume came back from a November show reporting that crowds who cheered Dylan were doing so with a mix of "Thanks Bobby" and "God Bless America". Complex emotions and responses were clearly in play, recalling the contradictory responses Neil Young evoked on his tour at the time of the 1991 war (that time under UN auspices to expel an invader from Kuwait), with his yellow-ribbon-adorned microphone and powerful version of "Blowin' in The Wind".

What did the songs signify for Dylan in this time of turmoil? He wasn't saying; his on-stage comments were restricted to a moving moment at Madison Square Garden on November 19th. Stephen Scobie recalled that special night in an interview with myself for *Judas!* magazine[5]:

"I was at the November 19th show in Madison Square Garden in New York which was the first time that Dylan had played New York after September 11th. As a concert it was a fairly standard set list, but there was an atmosphere in Madison Square Garden which was just incredible. There are good bootlegs of the concert but I don't think they can capture the kind of feeling in the audience of welcoming Dylan to New York two months after September 11th, and there were two moments especially when this became very clear. He started singing "Just Like Tom Thumb's Blues" and it was as if the entire audience just drew in its breath until the final line, going back to New York City, and when it got to

5 *Judas!* issue 9 April 2004

that final line there was just this huge cheer that moved all over through the audience, it clearly at that moment had very, very special meaning for everyone in there. Then there was this weird very strange moment when he got to the band introductions, he said this wonderful dignified and beautifully restrained line, he said: *most of the songs we've played tonight were recorded in New York City, so nobody has to ask me what I think about this town*, and that was all he said, and again you could sort of feel the huge wave going round the audience."

19 November 2001 Madison Square Garden Arena, New York City NY

1. Wait For The Light To Shine (Fred Rose) (Acoustic)
2. It Ain't Me, Babe (Acoustic)
3. A Hard Rain's A-Gonna Fall (Acoustic)
4. Searching For A Soldier's Grave (Jim Anglin) (Acoustic)
5. Tweedle Dee & Tweedle Dum
6. Just Like A Woman
7. Just Like Tom Thumb's Blues
8. Lonesome Day Blues
9. High Water (for Charlie Patton)
10. Don't Think Twice, It's All Right (Acoustic)
11. Tangled Up In Blue (Acoustic)
12. John Brown (Acoustic)
13. Summer Days
14. Sugar Baby
15. Drifter's Escape
16. Rainy Day Women #12 & 35

*

17. Things Have Changed
18. Like A Rolling Stone
19. Forever Young (Acoustic)
20. Honest With Me

21. Blowin' In The Wind (Acoustic)

*

22. All Along The Watchtower

Many other attendees reported similar feelings. While accepting it is not the same as 'being there', the show was superbly recorded and much of the atmosphere does come across. "Forever Young" sounds like a benediction on the self-healing residents of the suffering city. "A Hard Rain's A-Gonna Fall" and, especially, "Blowin' In The Wind" with its line "and too many people have died" have a special feel to them; a feeling that you can sense is being supplied almost as much by the audience as the performers. "Searching For A Soldier's Grave" and Fred Rose's song "Wait For The Light To Shine" cannot help but do the same, and the carefully-controlled lighting effects all added to the ambience.

Dylan's vocals were strong and affecting throughout the show, even on what had earlier in the year seemed tired old run-throughs ("It Ain't Me, Babe" and "Just Like A Woman", say). Almost inevitably, given the attention paid to this particular show, it attracted a backlash from some Dylan fans. Fans who had not been at that particular show, or ones who had been to it and to others that they liked equally, or more, began downplaying Madison Square Garden in comparison with other shows from around the same time.

Without agreeing with this retrograde, comparative denigration of Madison Square Garden, I can understand why it happened. There were many other fine shows, some of them at surprisingly large venues for someone who has toured so often in the same places. The attraction of a peerless artist still able to produce a masterpiece like *"Love And Theft"*, still out there on the road, at this of all times was palpable. Dylan's 35-show, 689-song stint, nearly always with a moving Christian cover to open, was a popular and critical success.

Before the world was knocked out of kilter, I had been anticipating the introduction of *"Love And Theft"* material and had confidently predicted in my first review of that album that the material would be able to go straight into his show and provide the spine of a set-list. So it proved; Dylan merged in the new songs right from the opening night, October 5th in Spokane WA. The four debuted there were "Honest With Me", "Sugar Baby", "Summer Days" and "Tweedle

Dee & Tweedle Dum". The next night in Seattle brought "Moonlight" and as the tour progressed all bar "Bye And Bye" appeared.

At first I was so excited by the new songs that I made a CD of those live songs only and played and replayed that. Unlike *Time Out Of Mind*, however, it didn't really work. The studio album sounded so good in this case and it seemed that – fine though many of the performances were – Bob's ageing vocals could now inspire more magic in the studio than live, with these songs at any rate.

In fact that 'seeming' was only partly to do with Dylan. The songs were immediately integrated into the set-lists as I had forecast, and were best heard there *in situ* rather than as an album substitute. Show after show I was listening to in full again as the joy of playing the new material spilled over and rejuvenated old warhorses. The shows flowed with purpose, crackled with energy. Audience anticipation of and regard for the new songs was impressive, a song like "Sugar Baby" met with a reverential hush as Dylan, in a throwback to the old acoustic days, stood in front of the band bathed in light with them in darkness; just Bob in the spotlight singing to the audience.

I say reverential silence, but this song was often ruined by male whooping and hollering after the lines about women bringing trouble. It sounded more like a reaction of a crowd to ice hockey players clashing violently than anything else, a sad thing to hear in the midst of Dylan's intense concentration on singing this sublime and complex work.

Still, it was *mainly* listened to in hushed tones and a hush descended also for the tender "Moonlight". Reworked arrangements of "High Water" (the song signalled by the appearance of a banjo onstage) and "Lonesome Day Blues" added to the heady mix, with the *tour de force* being blistering rave-ups of that homage to the Rockabilly era "Summer Days", where nightly Dylan and the Sexton-driven band "raised a glass to toast the King".

The band, who seemed to be revelling in this leg as much as the audience and Dylan himself, should be commended for their intuitive flexibility as Dylan moved from country to bluegrass to folk to rock as the inspiration took him. Sometimes the change was from song to song, other nights a particular genre took on the overall tone; all the while Charlie Sexton funnelled Dylan's intent into the arrangements, with Larry and Tony anchoring every move without skipping a beat. It really was a considerable step up from the rest of the year, but if we Europeans were feeling jealous of the US audiences at that time, and we were, it was nothing to what we would feel a year later.

There was a humorous episode, too. Glen Dundas, in Judas! Issue 1, recounts that: "From Oregon, too, came the wire services' story of Dylan, because of the added security now enforced at many venues, being denied admission to the theatre because the guard there didn't recognize him. The stories painted a picture of a spiteful Dylan then demanding the guard's dismissal. The tale seemed apocryphal, and 1 later talked with someone who witnessed the incident and who described a playful Bob, who joked through the entire seven seconds it took for the scene to unfold. The security person, a female, had just then been stationed at the entrance, and as Dylan did not have a backstage pass, she tried to block his passage. When asked if a nearby roadie could identify him, he smiled, saying 'No, but my drummer could'. Simply moving on, he then remarked that the guard would probably 'do a good job at the front door searching people'."

And there was more terrible sadness when, in this year of shocking death, former Beatle, Wilbury and Dylan fan, friend, collaborator, George Harrison passed away on November 29th. Dylan released the following statement:

"He was a giant, a great, great soul, with all of the humanity, all of the wit and humour, all the wisdom, the spirituality, the common sense of a man and compassion for people. He inspired love and had the strength of a hundred men. He was like the sun, the flowers and the moon and we will miss him enormously. The world is a profoundly emptier place without him."

CHAPTER SIXTEEN

2002: "In the middle of the stage, where Bob ought to be, was an electric keyboard"

"My friend Renée always likes to rush the stage, and find a place in the front row, literally at Bob's feet ... she was making a bee-line for her favourite spot, she stopped dead. What the fuck? There, in the middle of the stage, where Bob ought to be, was an electric keyboard."[1]

STEPHEN SCOBIE

As 2001 became 2002 the NET rolled on, the year's first leg being in the US again, from 31st January to 24th February. It was more or less the same show as the previous autumn, except that the drummer had changed. Dave Kemper had been replaced by George Receli, and the immediately noticeable difference was a changed arrangement of "It's Alright, Ma". Receli's influence would become more apparent as he settled into his role, and the whole

1 Stephen Scobie *Judas!* Issue 4; January 2003

band set-up was to undergo a radical transformation by the end of the year, but more of that later.

Back then, as we Europeans who were unable to travel to the US waited impatiently to hear the *"Love and Theft"* songs live, the US press revelled in this tour, more so than diehard Dylan loyalists, it has to be admitted. In the mainstream press, fountains of praise had replaced the rivers of scorn from a decade previously. Playing shows from the first half of 1992 and the first half of 2002 and reading the attendant press reviews is an interesting, if very disturbing, experience.

The European spring tour kicked off with a show in Stockholm, and the Dylan fan world was immediately plunged into controversy as esteemed critic Michael Gray penned – for the right-wing UK national broadsheet, *The Daily Telegraph* – a scathing review of: the show, Dylan fans, the locale, the venue, just about everything in fact, though he was highly positive about *"Love And Theft"* at least.

Michael's almost Swiftian attacks on Dylan fans' appearance, both physical and sartorial[2], diverted attention away from what he was saying about the show itself, and by implication the ongoing NET. Of significance to this book was the way Michael tied what he saw as a "painfully poor", ("by the very standards of imaginative integrity that Dylan himself threw out into the world"), performance to Dylan's sourness towards his most loyal fans, bringing back to mind the Rome interview from 2001:

"Until recently, if you were close enough to see, Dylan's face was ceaselessly expressive of subtle emotion and savvy. Now it seems reduced to a handful of clumsy, self-parodic grimaces. Where his concerts were events, in which an artist of genius lived in the dangerous moment, now he plays safe and seems to have no reason to be there. Where he didn't care what the audience thought because he had his own vision and was ahead of us, now he doesn't care what the audience thinks because he thinks it's a gullible rabble ... No wonder he's given interviews in which he's said that he dislikes the long-time fans almost as

2 "Among the customers for trainers and cosmetics I begin to see blokes with moustaches, wounded eyes and unclean skin, sporting bellies and grubby jackets, walking in twos and threes. If these men look like poachers, their women look like game old birds."

much as he hates critics. He wants fresh meat: young people who don't remember how incomparably better he once was."

The main problem many of us[3] were having was with Dylan's voice. In an effort to convey emotion without further damaging his already fragile and torn vocal cords, Dylan was ever increasingly 'singing up' at the end of every line. This kind of vocal trickery does not go down well with those who remember his voice from the past when he was always the indisputable master of timing and phrasing. Dylan showed on *"Love And Theft"* that he was still totally adept at this, so, as Michael's argument would have it, he could still do it when he *cared* to. Another vocal 'trick' was also causing considerable disquiet. Mr. Gray observed that:

"Most of the time it seems to me that the real Bob Dylan is largely missing and he's busier faking it than trying his best. Where once he was so alive, communicating so much quick creative intelligence so alertly and uniquely, now he snatches at showbiz clichés from which he once recoiled: like repeating half a line en route to the end of it – 'Gave her my heart: gave her my heart but she wanted my soul' – a device so crudely portentous it's always been the preserve of the world's Vic Damones."

When this "crudely portentous" device was first introduced there was at least some meaning to it; in "Tryin' To Get To Heaven" at Cardiff 2000, for example, the repetition signalled the struggle to get to the door. By now, though, it was just being used to fill up any old line.

The songs I had downloaded from Stockholm, and a long conversation with Michael when he returned from that show, meant that I travelled to my two German shows (Berlin and Leipzig) with very low expectations. Perhaps this was a good thing, and the best way to go about it, because the shows were unexpectedly impressive. Many positive things were happening onstage that I felt had been missing recently, and there was a noticeable absence of many things I had grown to dislike.

---

3 This was most evident among (some of) the older fans; there was by now a largish number of younger fans who loved the second half of the Never Ending Tour more than anything else in Dylan's career. [Us oldsters would pick pre-1996, not post, as our favourite NET period]. There is always, too, the constituency that likes everything Dylan does without reservation.

To begin with the latter, gone, for example, were the meaningless grimaces that he had been throwing out at set times as if by rote. There was a lot of smiling on the second night, but it was between songs to his fellow musicians, and patently genuine rather than the 'lets get a roar for showing my teeth at a supposedly emotional peak of the song' play to the audience. Also the rock 'n' roll poses that had seemed so inappropriate when they were not genuine expressions were transformed when demonstrating the joy of having fun onstage.

Most importantly there was less 'fakery' in his voice. He really tried to sing, with the exceptions of standard encore fare like "Not Fade Away", and a truly dire "Tangled Up In Blue" in Berlin, which was particularly disappointing as longtime Dylan commentator Ian Woodward had enthused about this song when he witnessed it in Copenhagen.

However, back to the successes; the best single song of the two nights was a lovely take on "Boots Of Spanish Leather". I had forgotten just how sweet the melody is and Campbell played it quite brilliantly, forcing Dylan to attend fully to the lyrics. It was a shimmering reminder of glories past, so much so that it was near the end of the next song ("Solid Rock") before I recovered. I can only recall the last verse of that, even though it was the song I had most admired from listening to Stockholm and had consequently been very much looking forward to hearing live. Nonetheless, I was more than pleased that Dylan could still so easily wrong-foot me and usurp my expectations, even with so oft-played a song as "Boots of Spanish Leather".

Nothing in the two nights bettered that, but there were careful, clearly rehearsed versions of "Visions of Johanna", "Fourth Time Around" and a host of others, especially the *"Love And Theft"* songs. Of these the highlight was a joyous "Summer Days" in Leipzig, where this time Sexton's brilliant guitar work forced Dylan to be at his (current) best. The first night may have had better highlights but the second was more consistent; Dylan seemed to be revelling in his band's playing and was concentrating on his singing. The early tour 'rustiness', that had so terrified me in the songs I heard from Stockholm, was gone.

This trip provided me with two other highlights. Firstly, it was in Leipzig that Dylan saw his first copy, hot off the presses, of my then new magazine, *Judas!*. Less personally and more significantly, the reaction that "Blowin' in the Wind" got in the venue, near the Berlin Wall, was astounding; people who had been on their way out flooded back in to the hall to join in a clearly sincere celebration of a song that had meant the world to them. I thought I should mention that for the next time 'seen-it-in-too-many-shows' gig-goers turn their noses up at this still exceptional song, due to over-familiarity with it[4].

My next two shows from this leg turned out to be nowhere near the standard of the first two. This may just have been bad luck, or may have had something to do with a distressing incident that took place in Milan, usually the scene of boisterous crowds and hugely good-natured events. This one, unfortunately, was an exception to that rule. Paolo Vites is again able to provide us with a first-hand account of what happened:

"As the familiar introduction begins, I see Charlie Sexton and the other boys in the band going on stage. They start playing 'Humming Bird', Bob Dylan follows behind them a few seconds later. As soon as Bob Dylan's feet hit the stage, I clearly see a cigarette flying from the first row of the audience to the stage. At the same moment a thousand camera flashes explode... Even though I'm quite sure Bob Dylan noticed the cigarette, I cannot say whether what happened next was because of that or because of the flashes or something else, but he refused to go to the mike. Sexton and Campbell continue humming the melody of the song. They keep playing and keep watching Bob, wondering what they should do. Bob Dylan is going back towards the stairs, as if he wants to leave the stage, then he comes back to the microphone, but not to sing. He takes the microphone back, almost behind the drummer, in a move that seems to say: 'Fuck off' to the audience. He looks mad and he says something to Sexton (probably 'Keep playing') then he speaks with the road manager. After this instrumental 'Humming Bird' ends, all the stage lights are turned on, toward the audience. People are wondering what is happening and hoping the lights will be turned down soon, but song after song the lights remain on. Meanwhile, after a couple of songs, Dylan takes his microphone to the normal position. People are getting angry: the lights are very disturbing. I'm not disturbed by the lights because I'm near the side of the stage, but the rest of the audience can hardly see Dylan and the stage. During the first part of "Visions of Johanna", the audience explodes into an angry protest: 'Turn those fucking lights down', but nothing is happening. The lights stay on for the entire show."

4 There is another fantastic version of it from Santa Cruz Civic Auditorium, Santa Cruz CA on March 16th, 2000 at the end of Dylan's 2003 film *Masked And Anonymous*.

Dylan's management were to make pleas for no flash photography for the rest of the European tour. To say both Dylan and his security staff were disturbed by the events in Milan would be an understatement. Dylan was reported to be in a bad mood following this night, but this was not in evidence when I next saw him, in Paris; though he did seem to glare a few times at the idiot standing right in front of him who kept his binoculars trained on his face throughout. Well, sorry, but I just could not help myself.

Also I am not sure how pleased he was at the ovation that greeted drummer Jim Keltner's name in the band announcement (Receli being temporarily replaced for health reasons). It was an OK show, nothing dramatic or particularly memorable. Highlights were an intriguing "I Want You" in the 'interesting' second slot and "Not Dark Yet". There was an interesting moment or two during "Visions of Johanna" when someone nearby me, bearing an uncanny resemblance to the photographer for this book, tried to get Dylan to sing one of the verses he most often omits. He partly succeeded, Dylan did actually start the verse, but then realised he didn't know the words and stumbled on to the next one.

The last show I was at of this leg was in Cardiff. I left it a bit late to go into the hall, going for a 'slightly hung back but near enough the front to strike forward if something exciting happens' position. It was, as ever, an animated crowd near the front but I couldn't see or hear why they were so enthused. All the things I had grown to dislike in recent years seemed to come to a head in the one show. After a while, we worked our way out of the main throng. I slumped against a wall where I could still see passably well and certainly could hear well enough, although that did not feel particularly beneficial. A couple of songs later Nigel Simms wandered out from the front with a disconsolate look on his face. He gave a wry laugh at my own demeanour: "Welcome to the worst show of the leg", he said as he passed.

So, we end my personal experience of the year on a bit of a downer. Yet all this does is underscore, yet again, the danger of judging legs from only the shows one attends. After all, I had attended just four out of the 29 shows in this leg (in a year of 108 in total). Additionally, imagine how differently I would have felt if I had seen 'my' four shows in reverse. After the first one I would have been desperately disappointed. The second one I would have thought was better than the first one without being too exciting. The third one I would have felt was a great night out, with some very fine music. And after the fourth one I would have been enthusing about some sublime music topped off by the cultural, historical affirmation of Dylan's worldwide appeal and the communal love for his classic 'protest songs' that one particularly tends to find in or near East European countries. Instead I felt in limbo, and Michael Gray's post-Stockholm misgivings seemed more apt to me now than they had at the beginning of the tour.

Dylan was continuing in the United Kingdom, but I was not. The only other date I could make was in London and there is a problem with some of the venues there. I had said I would never go back to the London Wembley Arena and although Dylan was now playing in the Docklands Arena, I found that prospect just as unattractive. From all reports my fears for the venue were justified. The problem I had back then was that if Dylan were to have stopped touring, Cardiff 2002 would have been the last show I would actually have attended. I cannot tell you how much this worried me in the forthcoming months.

It seemed to many, though by no means all, that a change was desperately needed in the Never Ending Tour. That change was coming, not quite yet, but soon, and it was more dramatic than anyone could have predicted. Prior to that there was an August tour in America. Given the seismic shocks that were to come in the last leg of 2002, this, preceding one is easy to overlook. Of particular note was the surprise appearance of "Quinn the Eskimo", which in a normal year would probably have been the main talking point. It was played for the first time since the Isle of Wight in 1969. Dylan chose to unveil it on the 18th August at, a 100th anniversary celebration of Harley Davidson.[5]

A number of less obvious changes included an expansion of the year's earlier trend for electric songs turning up in acoustic guise: "If You See Her Say Hello", "Señor", Man In A Long Black Coat", "I Want You", "Things Have Changed" and "Just Like Tom Thumb's Blues", of all things, among them. Meanwhile, moving in the opposite direction, the previously part-acoustic arrangement of "High Water (for Charley Patton)" was altered to a full blown electric one.

5 This spectacularly named venue was the Pimlico Race Track, Baltimore, Maryland and it was a celebration of the "Harley-Davidson 100th Anniversary Open Road Tour". Names like these let you see the extent of Dylan's NET 'go anywhere, play anywhere' attitude. The last three venues on this leg, for example, were: 'Sundome For The Performing Arts', 'Hard Rock Hotel & Casino' and 'Antelope Valley Fair'.

Talk of 'acoustic versus electric' was very much in the air, as the second date of this leg was at the historic Newport Folk Festival. Cue an avalanche of media reports on Dylan 'going electric' there in 1965. The same old stories were retold in the same old magazines. The buzz surrounding this performance was yet again a testament to Dylan's overarching significance and cultural importance, something that is completely out of proportion to his actual record sales. A fact that must puzzle the Sony marketing department responsible for the *Bootleg Series* that documents, amongst other things, these much-hyped historical shows.

Dylan's response to all the media excitement was to wear a ludicrous wig and a ridiculous false beard. There was a reason for this, he had been wearing them to tape a music video for a Civil War film – *Gods and Generals* – but nevertheless even with that explanation it was quite a bizarre appearance. This did mean that, handily enough, although Bob was for once open to photographers taking his picture, they could only take a snap of a man in a false wig and a false beard. Dylan played a mundane set as mundanely as he could, Completely ignoring any historic importance attached to the venue, he did not alter his set one iota. Nonetheless, the way modern 'reporting' goes, it was guaranteed that after the huge build-up there would be a remarkable amount of praise for this very dull set. This duly followed and the NET was then left to continue on its way.

Another happening of note during this period was a rather curious one. For many years and over a thousand consecutive shows, fans had been informed that Dylan was about to appear on stage with the words "Ladies and gentlemen, would you please welcome Columbia Recording Artist, Bob Dylan". Now at first these words seemed somewhat demeaning; the best one could think of them was that they were cutely self-deprecating, not that there was any hint that this was the intent. As time passed, however, they became ingrained as an integral part of the ritual of going to a Dylan show. They called you from the bar, if you were so blasé as to leave it late to find your place, they ended your pre-show conversation, or, if you were in the happy position of being pressed against the front barrier, they set your already pumping heart valves into overdrive. The words merged memories of favourite shows with the one you were about to witness. They were a call to arms, an immovable part of the event itself. Or so it had seemed.

All that changed at the Erie County Fair in August 2002. Here, Dylan's entrance was preceded by a whole new slew of words preceding the normal invocation for the festivities to begin:

"The poet laureate of rock 'n' roll. The voice of the promise of the '60s counterculture. The guy who forced folk into bed with rock, who donned makeup in the '70s and disappeared into a haze of substance abuse, who emerged to 'find Jesus', who was written off as a has-been by the end of the '80s, and who suddenly shifted gears and released some of the strongest music of his career beginning in the mid-'90s."

These words were written by journalist Jeff Miers, who was present at the show and was unsurprisingly shell-shocked upon hearing a passage from his pre-concert preview read aloud.[6] I thought this story most amusing when I first heard it but I did not for a minute expect that this elaborate intro would remain, yet it has. I cannot say that I enjoy this hackneyed career summary being repeated each night ,and it seems most un-Dylan like to allow, or even insist upon, it. I presume it is a joke of some kind but on what level of satire or irony I cannot fathom, nor do I know whether it is well-intentioned or, as Mr Miers fears, malevolently meant.

Whatever, just by dull repetition it too became part of the NET ceremony for around the next ten years. This is an aspect I have perhaps not mentioned enough in these pages thus far, believing it to be so much a part of touring life for me and the expected readers of this book that it did not need stating. The build-up to a show: the ever-present smell of incense from the burning buckets of Nag Champa[7], the Copland music, the pre-show announcement(s) all conspire towards the customary feel of the event. Dylan seems aware of this ritual aspect and in this century introduced a further ceremonial item, one that fans term 'the Formation'. This occurs at the end of the show. Dylan and the band stand, as though to attention, in formation and stare out at the audience; Dylan's face an impassive mask as he surveys the cheering crowd. The band are sometimes impassive too and one suspects are meant to remain that way, but

6 Mr Miers recounts the tale in a humorous follow-up piece for *The Buffalo News*, August 23rd 2002 available for a small fee from their archives at http://www.buffalonews.com/newslibrary/.

7 http://www.ancientwisdom.biz/nagchampa/.

Tony Garnier, for one, has often broken out into a wide grin, a natural reaction to the adulation from the audience.

Meanwhile, back on the music front, the media blanket on the Newport Folk Festival notwithstanding, it seemed to me that the tour had simply run out of steam. This was one of my lowest points in the entire history of the NET. I needed the injection of something new, or for Bob to cease the proliferation of the alarmingly insincere styles of singing that had begun to take over whole shows. Again, I stress these were *my* NET feelings, shared by many though disputed by others.

Prior to this leg there were the usual rumours, stronger than normal, that the Never Ending Tour was about to end. Allegedly Dylan was to stop touring altogether or change his approach radically; these by now repetitive and tiresome rumours were based on the leaked news of the departure of very popular and talented guitarist Charlie Sexton. This time, though, the rumours were partly ahead of the game. A radical change was coming and this was to be Sexton's last stand, *pro tem*, and what a last stand he made.

The same band for now, then, took the stage at Seattle on October 4th to continue the Never Ending Tour, but if we thought another normal leg was about to transpire how wrong we were. In *Judas!* magazine Steven Scobie captured the shock:

"My friend Renée always likes to rush the stage, and find a place in the front row, literally at Bob's feet. In Seattle she got a head-start on the crowd, and was into the venue ahead of anyone else; so she was making a bee-line for her favourite spot, front row centre, when, half-way across the floor of the Key Arena, she stopped dead.

"What the fuck? There, in the middle of the stage, where Bob ought to be, was an electric keyboard. What was going on? Was Larry moving to centre stage? Where was Bob's mike? Surely he couldn't be playing keyboards? Was there a new band member? Should she move to the left or the right? Was she even in the right place on the right night?

"For a long moment Renée stood there, trapped in an existential dilemma only a truly fanatic Dylan follower can appreciate. Then the rest of the crowd appeared behind her and pushed her forward, and yes, she held her line, ended up front centre, at the foot of whoever it was who was going to be playing keyboards ... Which turned out to be Bob ...We were all amazed."

And the amazement did not end there, the following set-list reverberated around the world as the Internet spread the well nigh unbelievable news that Dylan had just played:

October 4, 2002 Seattle Center Key Arena, Seattle WA

1. Solid Rock (Acoustic) (Piano)
2. Lay, Lady, Lay (Acoustic) (Piano)
3. Tombstone Blues (Piano)
4. Accidentally Like A Martyr (Warren Zevon) (Piano)
5. I'll Be Your Baby Tonight (Piano)
6. Brown Sugar (Jagger/Richards)
7. Don't Think Twice, It's All Right (Acoustic)
8. It's Alright, Ma (I'm Only Bleeding) (Acoustic) (Piano)
9. Love Minus Zero/No Limit (Acoustic) (Piano)
10. Boom Boom Mancini (Warren Zevon)
11. Searching For A Soldier's Grave (Jim Anglin) (Acoustic)
12. Mr. Tambourine Man (Acoustic)
13. Honest With Me (Piano)
14. To Ramona (Acoustic)
15. High Water (For Charley Patton) (Piano)
16. Mutineer (Warren Zevon) (Piano)
17. Floater (Too Much To Ask) (Piano)
18. Summer Days

*

19. Like A Rolling Stone
20. Knockin' On Heaven's Door (Acoustic)
21. All Along The Watchtower

Not only was it the first time Dylan had a piano on stage in over eleven years, but he played it on no fewer than eleven songs. In addition to that bolt from the blue, there were five covers, four all-time debuts and a complete change of the normal order of acoustic/electric based songs. You could almost forget "Solid Rock" had never been 'acoustic' before. Nonetheless that *was* the opening shock; a piano-based 'acoustic', yet also a hard enough version to live up to a secular interpretation of those words 'Solid Rock'. So stunned were the lucky attendees that they clung to the standard line-up of encores (yes, those very things normally dismissed as 'same old boring finale') as though they were shipwrecked sailors about to drown espying a raft.

The visual shock also cannot be overstated, the whole shape of the band on the stage and, most importantly, Dylan's own position there dramatically changed the show as *spectacle*. The fact that Dylan was spending much, if not most, of each night on the piano was a huge change to the band's set-up. Regular concert-goers were astounded, and given the general public's view of Dylan as someone with an acoustic guitar and harmonica and no band at all, to see him fronting a full rocking band as a centre-stage pianist must have been a surprise of huge proportions.

Nevertheless, I want to concentrate for now on the music. Three of the five covers were Warren Zevon songs, the obvious reason for this tribute being the sad diagnosis of terminal illness that had recently been passed on the vibrant and witty Zevon[8]. Yes, other Dylan friends had been under similar sentences without being so acknowledged, but George Harrison, to pick a near contemporaneous example, is known to all rock and pop fans in the world, whereas Zevon forever laboured in the region known as 'cult artist'; that is, he was given lots of respect but was not widely heard. Dylan was doing his bit to help rectify that situation in Zevon's last months. Dylan's magnificent tribute to George Harrison would come in time, as we will see at the end of this chapter, and it is possibly the only thing that can be construed as being as affecting as his astonishing renditions of two of the four Zevon songs he played on this leg. Both of the sublime Zevon covers were present in Seattle on that opening night.

8 After a cheerfully courageous and hard-working spell under the cloud of his own demise, Warren Zevon died in September 2003.

The first, "Accidentally Like A Martyr", hit me like the proverbial large railway vehicle moving at high speed. The vocals conveyed an astonishing depth of feeling and insight and an immense gravity. You could not fail to understand immediately that this was a song of import. That is even without taking into account its title, reminiscent of mid-sixties Dylan, the extended vowels on "accidentaleeee" and "so loneleee" that also evoked that era and the oh-so-redolent Dylan song and album title phrases "abandoned love" and "time out of mind" embedded in its lyrics.

It seemed that nothing could bring more pleasure to a Dylan NET fan than this and yet there was – unbelievably – an instant contender in another Zevon song, "Mutineer". Magic once again bestrode the stage; all of humanity was present here, in Dylan's vocalisation and the band's playing of Zevon's words and music, all our hopes and dreams, our strengths and weaknesses, everything. It was and remains an awesome testament to the human condition and spirit. When I say 'remains' I mean both in this debut version on every re-listen and in later performances, some of which even transcended this seemingly untranscendable rendition. At Berkeley, a week later, the fragility of Dylan's vocal on "here" at the end of the bridge, reworked to evoke Dylan's own history, begs for descriptions that would fill the pages of satirical magazine *Private Eye*'s *"Pseud's Corner"* column for decades to come:

Thunder rolled and lightning followed
It could never find us ... here

Amongst Dylan fans, those that heard "Mutineer" first thought it the finest of all the Fall 2002 treasures, while those who, like me, were first exposed to the wonders of "Accidentally Like A Martyr" thought the same of that. What we were all agreed on was that both were beautiful and achingly moving; as much if not more so than anything we had heard from Dylan in some seven years. I refuse to separate them, were a loaded gun put to my head with a demand that I chose only one to hear ever again I would still simply be unable to choose. I need both. The numinous, luminescent beauty of "Mutineer" encompasses all of humanity's desires and frailties, and yet for similar reasons "Accidentally Like A Martyr" is equally indispensable.

These two songs came to dominate despite, as we are about to see, a plethora of other surprises and highlights. "Accidentally Like A Martyr" was played 22 times (always as the fourth song of the night) and "Mutineer" 31 (always as the 16th).

Boxing enthusiasts seem to love "Boom Boom Mancini", the other Zevon cover from that opening night. It is certainly more honest to find fight fan Dylan singing this than his scathing indictment of that sport, "Who Killed Davey Moore?". Nonetheless, for all it is a piece of near-juvenilia brimming over with the self-righteousness of the innocent, I much prefer 'Davey Moore'. "Boom Boom Mancini" does little for me; not least, though not only, because I cannot hear:

When they asked him who was responsible
For the death of Du Koo Kim
He said, "Some one should have stopped the fight
And told me it was him."
They made hypocrite judgements after the fact
But the name of the game is be hit and hit back

Without immediately recalling:

Who killed Davey Moore,
Why an' what's the reason for?
"Not me," says the man whose fists
Laid him low in a cloud of mist,
Who came here from Cuba's door
Where boxing ain't allowed no more.
"I hit him, yes, it's true,
But that's what I am paid to do.
Don't say 'murder,' don't say 'kill.'
It was destiny, it was God's will."

"Lawyers, Guns And Money", yet another Zevon song that Dylan unveiled the next night, was also not at all in the same league as the first two discussed here. However it is only fair to bear in mind that the bar those two covers set is dizzyingly high. "Lawyers, Guns And Money" is worthy enough, a very Zevonesque piece of enjoyable satire which Dylan tried again a few times before it slipped out of the set-lists.

More surprising in the circumstances than even the Zevon covers was Dylan suddenly singing the Rolling Stones' "Brown Sugar". Hard to believe but glorious to hear, Dylan was really singing the lines "I ain't no schoolboy, but I know what I like" with all appropriate relish. The band also deserve tremendous credit for their faultless Stones take-off, though no doubt the sheer, obvious, pleasure in doing so was thanks enough for them. Hearing this as a Dylan fan, you could not help but recall his whole history with Mick Jagger.

Inevitably one remembered Bob needling the vacuous Jagger by saying he could write "Satisfaction" but Jagger could never write "Desolation Row". This message was no doubt conveyed to their lead singer by the musicians that make the Stones what they are and who have always befriended Dylan. Jagger's eventual, and inelegant, riposte about how he would like to hear Dylan trying to sing "Satisfaction" was answered by this other prime slice of Stones real estate played in 2002 with a verve, swagger and genuine panache that the preening one had long lost the ability to conjure up.

I say this in all sadness; thirty years earlier the Stones's barnstorming tour across the US was, and remains, one of my all-time favourite rock tours. However, listening to the nearest contemporary performance of theirs of "Brown Sugar" to the ones Dylan and his band played shows the Stones in a very sorry light indeed. I realize one could do the same with, say, a 1996 performance by Dylan compared to a 1966 one, but even at his most formulaic Dylan was still then far less *intrinsically* formulaic than this sorry travesty of all the Stones once stood against. "Brown Sugar" live was once something to celebrate and now, praise be to Bob and his band, it was so once again.

Glorious fun though that was, the depth of spirit captured in the finest two Zevon covers was understandably absent. It reappeared on Van Morrison's "Carrying A Torch", a stately, hymnal and explicitly religious song that nonetheless shares with Dylan's own "I Believe In You" a delicious possible ambiguity in the "you" referring to a divine being, or a divine body that has just "torched up the night" in his bed. Certainly "I can make it on my own" sounds like Dylan singing "I Believe In You" and then the caressing of "baby" brings back that song's duality as does the intonation on "... keeper of the flame" and the ecstatic, elongated "Yes" in most versions. It is worth noting that by the time of the Elmira show Dylan was performing another interpretation entirely of this song, albeit this being only its fourth outing, yet another testament to the renewed artistic fire breathing through him at this time.

Something you might have imagined having as deep as resonance, on a humanistic level at least, was Neil Young's "Old Man"; the multiple connections between Dylan and Young are too many for me to recount, but it's fair to say that Young is one of the artists most Dylan fans 'are into'. Indeed, only Bruce Springsteen has more followers amongst the Dylan legions. Over and above that, though, was the implicit irony of the song's title; here was an old man singing a song written by a (relatively) young man named Young that was addressed to an old man. The possibilities seemed endless, but, in truth, the performances themselves were perfunctory at best, with only the odd flash of what could have been.

Two other covers from this leg went from the clichéd extremes of 'the ridiculous to the sublime'. Don Henley's "The End of the Innocence" may have the best of intentions at heart, but melodically and lyrically plumbs the depths you'd expect from an ex-member of the Eagles. This ranks for me as one of Dylan's more inexplicable selections to play.[9] There was yet another cover, one of unsurpassed beauty and emotion. Before we get to that, however, I wish to point out a general NET experience exemplified at the beginning of this leg and briefly look at some of the Dylan originals that also lit up this period.

The general point is that quite often a particular show comes to represent a leg due to some special significance, or due to the speedy circulation of a high-quality recording of a specific show. The latter happened here with Red Bluff CA, the third show of this leg, on October 7th. This was a pity; not because there was anything wrong with Red Bluff, quite the opposite, but because other shows just as fine tended to be overlooked. It was, though, an understandable general reaction, which is not to say it was true for everyone. There were many people who were listening to show after show. However, there were so many rich banquets being served up by Dylan and the band that no one could digest them all at once. This encouraged many people to concentrate on just the one show, at least initially; time has shown that this was a leg to bear repeated revisits.

I am not claiming that every single show was equally stellar. Some nights the total magic was not present. Nor am I saying every song in every set list was

9 There is a further connection however, in that Henley and Zevon worked with Andy Slater, who in turn managed The Wallflowers, Dylan's son Jakob's band.

transcendent – but, then again, you would have to go back to at least Prague in 1995 to think of making that claim – but the overall standard was excellent, and consistently so. There were nights where runs of songs, over five or six, were of a remarkably high standard and power. It should be noted that Dylan was rocking in a way that took us right back to the beginning of the NET. Charlie Sexton leading the band in the storming versions of "Summer Days" was one of the heaviest things you'll ever hear. This song had grown into a quite monstrous show-stopping fun-stomper that blew the roof off many an auditorium. The *"Love And Theft"* songs continued to play a large part in the shows and the debut of "Bye And Bye" at Los Angeles on October 17th meant that every song had now been played live from that album.

There was much fine singing from Dylan, the piano effect changing the emphasis totally in many songs, whether Dylan just played in a quiet, "plinkety plonk' style rather than hit savage chords on a guitar, or used the piano to completely rework the arrangement of a song. "It's Alright, Ma", for example, was transformed into an effective blues-based number. "When I Paint My Masterpiece" had a new tempo to go with reworked lyrics. Most striking, though, were the affecting vocals on phrases like "hell of a climb"; there was a plaintive, almost disbelieving tone to them.

Dylan's vocals evinced a strength and subtlety that had been missing for some time. "In The Summertime" (first since 1981) featured some such vocals, Dylan even on one occasion turning a verse 'nasty sounding' to give this delicate song another angle. The 'tricks' of doubling lines and 'panting' were still occasionally present (they appear, respectively, in the two songs just mentioned) but they do not dominate and often are completely absent, allowing songs like "I'll Remember You" to blossom so effectively that you could hear echoes of past performances of "Covenant Woman". In the aforementioned "In The Summertime", Dylan's vocal presence imbued the song with a depth and grandeur belying its slight lyrics.

Perhaps the most surprising of all Dylan original songs was the live debut of "Yea! Heavy And A Bottle Of Bread", recorded as part of *The Basement Tapes* in 1967 but never performed live before November 11th at Madison Square Garden, over 33 years later. After the song Dylan said he had played it as a request; speculation was rife about who it was for, Al Gore being one of those suggested, but the most popular assumption was that it was for writer Greil

Marcus, who was sitting in the front row and had recently written a book based on *The Basement Tapes*.

Whoever it was done for it was fun to hear. What intonation, what a surprise! I loved it, not as much as I loved "Accidentally Like A Marty" or "Mutineer", but then it would be completely unrealistic to hear anything that transcendent again, surely. Well, one would think so but you should never doubt Dylan's ability to confound or to rise to an occasion. There was another performance of the standard of the two Zevon songs, another cover as it happens, and one played for the saddest of reasons: to commemorate the death and celebrate the life of the 'quiet Beatle', George Harrison. On November 13th, at the end of the second show at Madison Square Garden, Dylan introduced an extra song to ecstatic acclaim, with the words:

There's a tribute going on, I guess it is next week or the week after, over in England for George Harrison. You know, all kinds of people are in it, I'm not quite sure who, but we can't make it and I just want to do this song though in remembrance of George because we were such good buddies..."

It all sounded so strangely offhand, the very opposite of the song that followed. It was a bit like the terrible joke after the affecting statement about New York at the same venue the year before; the switch of emotion was as extreme, the change of tone from the shy introduction into the song itself all but unfathomable, as are the depths of emotion this performance evokes.[10] Following that hesitant introduction, at the venue where they had performed together at the Concert for Bangladesh all those years ago, Dylan played Harrison's classic love song, "Something". It is an odd experience to hear a new performance of a so familiar song with a so familiar voice; it is something both new and known at the same time.

Dylan's performance stands as an outstanding tribute, one that would make George Harrison so very happy and proud were he around to hear it. That is the problem with such tributes, they come too late for the deceased. Though you hope against hope that somehow it could be that George Harrison was hearing this. After all, a man who could so perspicaciously understand the beauty of

10 Someone handed Dylan a set of the lyrics and he told them in no uncertain terms to 'get it out of here'.

Dylan's singing on "Nobody's Child" would weep at the brilliance of the vocals here.

Fall 2002 was a time not just for fantastic live shows from Dylan. Mutability and mortality stalked the stages, individually this time, as opposed to the collective tragedy of the previous year. Every time I listen to this requiem I think of Jimi Hendrix, Janis Joplin and Brian Jones; Dylan's singing evokes in me memories of those young people, bright lights too soon extinguished. Even though, overwhelmingly, it is George Harrison, and, naturally, Warren Zevon that I most specifically think of, among many others who have passed away. I can also hear in my mind that other astonishing tribute to a fallen musician, "Moon River". You cannot listen to Dylan singing "Something" and not think of death, specifically musicians' deaths; you are listening to a song being performed as a tribute to a recently deceased musician, a 60s icon like Dylan, like Jimi and Janis and Brian.

Yet that is only the beginning of where the song takes us. Far more importantly it also sings, ringingly, of an overwhelming love and in praise of achievement. The achievement of Harrison and all other musicians, artists and other gifted people who have brought joy, insight and love into our existence; anyone and everyone, that is, who has 'moved us like no other'. In memoriam.

Thank you Bob, for this goodbye to George, whom we did not 'want...to leave us now'. Here, as the fondest of farewells, is his beautiful love song, given the most moving of performances in salute to its creator.

CHAPTER SEVENTEEN

2003:
"It showed me where my future was"

"When I got into rock 'n' roll, I didn't even think I had any option or alternative. It showed me where my future was, just like some people know they are going to be doctors or lawyers or shortstop for the New York Yankees".[1]

DYLAN IN INTERVIEW, 10TH NOVEMBER 2003

It was always going to be difficult for the first leg of 2003, in Australia and New Zealand, to follow the extraordinary end to 2002. This difficulty was exacerbated by the long-anticipated loss of Charlie Sexton.

Sexton was replaced by Billy Burnette, who has quite some pedigree, born as he was in Memphis into a musical family headed by legendary rockabilly heroes Dorsey and Johnny Burnette, his father and uncle respectively. Billy Burnette is not, though, remembered fondly by most Dylan fans. However, for a number of reasons, you cannot help but wonder if this is a fair judgement.

1 *Rock's Enigmatic Poet Opens Long Private Door.* By Robert Hilburn, Amsterdam, Holland interview. 10th November 2003. Published in April 2004 *LA Times.*

Firstly, Burnette was playing for this one leg only. Most musicians find it problematic to come to terms with Dylan's onstage behaviour, it takes nearly everyone some time to adjust. Even at his most predictable, one of the complaints about the music on this leg, Dylan is still far more unpredictable and idiosyncratic than they are used to. Secondly, you cannot help but wonder how much rehearsal time Billy Burnette was given and, thirdly, what and how he was instructed to play.

It is not just Billy but the whole leg that is not held in high esteem by fans; except, somewhat pertinently, by those who actually attended it. Part of what counted against these shows' reputation, ridiculous as this may sound, was a geographical bias. Dylan fandom is dominated by American and British websites and magazines. Even in these days of 'travel anywhere to follow Bob', Australia and New Zealand are accessible only to a small percentage of non-native fans. There was definitely a touch of 'out of sight, out of mind' about some of the comments.

It is true that I am not a big fan of this leg either, but as we shall see this is not just to do with the shows themselves. I would, though, be willing to wager that this leg would have a higher reputation had it taken place in a heavily populated area of America or Europe. As it stands, the fans who did attend saw a unique band and as varied song lists as in some other legs. Granted, NET followers' never-ending craving for novelty was left unsatisfied, as alternates came from a 'standard pot' of replacements. There was *one* bolt from the blue, though.

The opening show, on February 6th 2003, featured, very surprisingly, "Saving Grace" for the first time since the 'Christian' tours of 1979 and '80. It was asking a lot to expect Dylan to be able to sing this song properly, demanding as it does a sweeping devotional vocal to convincingly convey the depth of feeling and intent behind the simple words. Asking too much, as it transpired. Dylan's trademark elongated endings sounded strained almost to the point of parody.

It was, it should be remembered, the opening night of the year. His voice would get stronger and it is, in any case, affecting to hear someone sound vulnerable and struggling while singing a song that proclaims:

By this time I'd-a thought
I would be sleeping
In a pine box for all eternity.

Whether this evocation of pity was the intended effect was another matter entirely. Dylan's voice, although resolute at times, was to remain an on-off problem in 2003. It did gain power as the year progressed, culminating in a miraculous recovery one late November evening in London. The rest of the year's problems were foreshadowed here, in the seventh song of the first show of the year, not least in Dylan's ever-growing need to repeat words to make lines fit: "all, all I'm seeing" and "so many, many times".

Nonetheless, there was a touch of magic in the way he sang "I'm only", followed by a long pause and then a voice full of impish glee for "*livin'*" before finishing the line: "By the saving grace that's over me". It truly was a *devilish* piece of pronunciation. My blasphemy is half intended here, Dylan makes the word sound so full of the enjoyable things in the world that the joys of being alive sound distinctly fleshly to me. Overall though, "Saving Grace" was less a musical triumph than another pointed answer to those with the temerity to ask about Dylan's religious beliefs. Dylan seemed to be saying: "If singing songs such as 'Rock of Ages', 'I Am The Man, Thomas' and so forth isn't a clear enough message, then cop this."

Both Dylan's voice and Burnette's integration into the band improved throughout the Australian dates. This can clearly be heard by comparing the later shows in Australia and then the shows in New Zealand to the opening ones. However, the improvement was only relative and my overwhelming worries regarding Dylan's 2003 voice did not abate as he launched into his much more positively received spring American tour.

Although the shows were greeted with the now customary media goodwill, it was accurately, if somewhat patronisingly, noted that Dylan hardly played the piano and had developed some distressing vocal mannerisms. Nonetheless, most fans found songs to like and gave a generally thumbs-up view of the shows.

A number of my close friends went to New Orleans to enjoy the hospitality of one of our 'crew' in that fascinating city. So, you would presume I could give you an accurate report of what those shows were like, yet I am afraid I cannot as the descriptions from the various attendees were violently divergent. This was a trend that dominated 2003 and which had, by the time of Birmingham in the UK, on November 21st (mere days before unanimity of views was achieved by the re-emergence of the Real Deal), reached ludicrous proportions. My year consisted of receiving detailed first-hand reports from Dylan veterans of much NET experience that indicated nothing more or less than that they simply could not have attended the same show.

For example, the performance of "A Hard Rain's A-Gonna Fall" at the first of the two New Orleans shows was described to me as everything from a masterpiece to a travesty of performing art, both extreme points of view being argued with remarkable passion. Clearly something was going on here with the power to move people, albeit in completely opposite directions.

In truth, the differing views in this single song instance are more understandable than the later ones regarding entire shows. Those who loved this version of "Hard Rain" were responding to the daring of a performer not afraid to completely rework one of his classic songs and give his all in a powerful performance. The scorners were reacting to the inconsistency of Dylan's vocals which encompassed the odd bit of strong vocal but also extreme examples of the 'panting' effect previously described and the horrific 'end of line upsinging' that had so bedevilled recent years of the NET. Up the octave Dylan went, again and again, line after line; like a salmon leaping except that the salmon's repeated, graceful leaps are a striving towards a challenging and arduous goal that is, just, attainable. While Dylan's vocal here, I am afraid, was a sham, it wasn't ever going anywhere.

To compound these felonies, for most of the song, and alarmingly large stretches of the spring and summer, Dylan threw in a third 'voice', one born in Australia but 'ripening' as 2003 progressed. Someone, somewhere on the Internet dubbed this the 'wolfman' voice. Whoever that was clearly hit the mark as the term stuck, and every fan knew exactly what to call it when hearing the desperately hoarse, gruff growl. So ugly was it that one would not have been surprised if the lycanthrope community had felt defamed by the term and sued for compensation.

I think everyone can agree it was an 'extraordinary' performance and perhaps it is best I leave it at that. The following night in New Orleans, played not outdoors at the Fair Grounds Race Course in daylight but at the Municipal Auditorium in the evening, had the welcome addition on most songs of sax played by distinguished local musician Dickie Landry. This was not only apt for the New Orleans Jazz and Heritage Festival it formed part of but also seemed to re-energize Dylan, making this show a highlight of the year for many fans.

It sparked some interest in me too, but only a flicker of the fire that the NET once engendered. I was again feeling estranged from the tour, for the same basic reasons as a year previously. I kept up with what was going on, but felt little enthusiasm. In 2001 *"Love And Theft"* had given my NET listening a huge boost, and I engaged deeply with the late 2001 shows, reinvigorated as they were by the new material. Despite this, I spent most of that time and the following months listening to the album itself over and above everything else, as that is such an overwhelmingly rewarding experience.

The late 2002 tour, full of glorious performances, had changed all that but those shows now seemed the exception, a creative oasis in a desert of relative tedium, and although I knew many people who were as 'into it' as ever, the NET for me had moved from being central to my life to being something of a side issue. Yes, I realize this is a shocking admission, but my role in this book is to tell you how it felt for me throughout the NET so it is only fair to record these thoughts, harbingers of a personal 'touring crisis' that hovers ominously, not far in the future.

Back in 2003, this process of disenchantment was exacerbated by another ill-considered fling with The Dead. A Dead now without Jerry Garcia at that, and therefore making even less musical sense than ever before. Culturally, too, it seemed an even stranger combination than in earlier years.

Dylan playing to Deadheads in the hope of swelling his own fan base is an odd concept. The dedicated travelling Deadheads are exactly the kind of fans Dylan had grown to treat with varying shades of indifference and contempt. And this is something they are not used to, Deadheads are encouraged to record their experiences, even given special taping areas; Dylan on the other hand instructs security guards to confiscate whatever they can get their hands on, especially cameras.

Just to make the concept even more bewildering, Dylan yet again performed to the least of his abilities in front of the hapless surviving Dead members. The only people who could have enjoyed any of this would be the Profaci-Colombo family, who would surely have approved of another ritual torturing, dismemberment and burial without honours of "Joey".

There were other Dylan shows, too, without the Dead; sometimes supported by the well-received Waifs. As the tour progressed it garnered more enthusiasm from regular listeners, Gilford NH, on August 21st, in particular exciting many followers. Not me, alas; despite hearing things that were comparatively better than the perfunctory performances that had so depressed me, I was still unmoved to any real degree.

You would think reading this that by the time Europe 2003's autumn tour came around I would have given up completely. On the other hand, it was a mere year earlier that "Accidentally Like A Martyr", "Mutineer" *et al* had stirred my soul in that way only Dylan can. Being on a roller-coaster of emotion is part of the NET experience. My trepidation was, however, exacerbated by an astonishingly poor performance by Dylan just before I headed off to Sweden to see him. This was when Dylan 'sang' "Highway 61 Revisited" as a guest at the end of a Bruce Springsteen show at Shea Stadium in October. Dylan performed the song abjectly even by the standards of some of his previous lamentable guest appearances. Much later, on seeing a video of this event I realised better what the impish Dylan was up to, and he certainly looked the part, but going on audio alone it sent an ominous warning for the upcoming leg.

As it happened, my own tour started earlier than planned due to an unmissable opportunity to speak at a convention in Stockholm, run by the Swedish Dylan group, 'Love And Theft'. *Judas!* publisher Keith Wootton and I went over for the convention, which turned out to be a fabulous event, and two shows. On the Saturday of the Stockholm show we went with Pelle Kassman to see the legendary Izzy Young. I thought I would take him a book and maybe get a photo taken with him and, if the opportunity arose, shamelessly pump him for stories from the old days. To my double surprise he knew me and was very pleased to see me. After he took the book he started showing us all manner of treasures. We had a marvellous afternoon there and then it was time for the show.

Would all my nagging worries about Dylan's voice come true, or would he prove them unfounded once again? Alas, it was the former. I did, however, enjoy watching him walk about the stage doing ... well, nothing but walking. He looked neither at the band nor audience, he was not singing or carrying a guitar, he just went for idiosyncratic little walks in an odd gait and made the occasional strange hand gesture.

The stage layout was intriguing, I did not understand the point of it but the sheer novelty factor was engaging. Dylan, mainly on keyboards throughout the show, was on the left hand side of the stage as faced by the audience. This meant those on one whole side of arenas would be watching Dylan's back. Beside him was post-Billy Burnette guitarist Freddy Koella, who hovered over Dylan in an alarming mode something akin to a vampiric praying mantis. Freddy's influence would grow throughout the leg and caused a split amongst Dylan fans, some being venomous detractors and others enthusiastic supporters. This may have constituted one of the main reasons for the extreme split in fans' views of shows this year.

It is hard to sum the show up; it was not as actively 'bad' as some of the summer shows I had heard or the horrendous effort at the Springsteen show, but it was, to use a word I never thought to attach to live Dylan, rather dull.

Still, it was just the beginning of my trip and the next day found us heading off to the kind of place that is so surprised a name like Dylan is appearing that the papers run special features, the media covering the event as though a UFO had landed. Come to think of it, they may have had a point. The train taking us there was, in effect, a 'Dylan special'; full of touring Dylan people all heading for Karlstad (or, as it now seemed to be called 'Karlstad: The-Beatles-and-Hendrix-played-here-in-the Sixties-and-now-Bob-Dylan-is-too').

A quick walk from a TV interview to join the pre-show throng was suddenly halted by the sight of a very familiar bus. By pure chance the pre-arranged meeting place was next door to a hotel which just happened to contain Bob and the band. A nice little game then developed, many of you reading this will know the game, and we eventually saw nearly everybody leave the hotel and go to the gig. The one person we did not get to see was Dylan. Presumably he had been taken out by some back way to avoid us. Still, Larry seemed in very good humour which was something not at all apparent the night before, ostracized, as he was, so very far from Dylan onstage.

On to the show and it became apparent early on that this was going to be very different from the previous night. Dylan was actually trying to sing rather than the hiccuppy, sing-song thing that ruined the shows that I had been listening to before the leg started. 'Trying' was the operative word here, it seemed, to be honest, more a case of hoping for a triumph of will over physical possibility. Still, it was encouraging to see him engaging with the songs and trying to wring something from them. It was also good to see Dylan so happy, he was undeniably enjoying himself and keen to interact with his audience.

Unfortunately, as he looked out to the crowd all he saw were mute shapes, glued to their seats as though in church. The more enthusiastic fans were all further back. Striving to remain undeterred, Dylan then launched into a performance of "Desolation Row" that was full of drama and depth. It was so captivating that I only half paid attention to what verses he included, though one could not help but notice the rare appearance of the 'Dr Filth' passage. By 2003's standards it was a triumph and I found more enjoyment and worth in this one song than in the entire Stockholm show.

Dylan was understandably pleased with himself too; he walked toward the crowd to accept anticipated and deserved acclaim – alas, though, there was no one there to greet him, he was faced instead by our churchgoers. Dylan's disappointment led to a couple of the stage guards moving off, whether intuitively or under instruction I cannot say. I had just finished whispering to Keith that it was about time for the stage rush, when it started. I cannot recall the row I started out in, but I was one of the first to the front. A half-hearted effort to block my progress by an uninterested security guard did delay me by a few seconds, enough to stop me reaching the very front; I ended up one behind the barrier.

Suddenly Dylan had an enthused crowd in front of him and the pace of the show picked up as Bob showed his obvious delight that his efforts weren't being ignored after all. It is instructive to contrast what happened here, and how the situation was allowed to develop, with Dylan's comments in the Rome 2001 interview. Contradiction, thy name is Bob!

So, with Dylan getting right back into attempting to vocalize as well as he can and being now almost as close as possible to him, we settled down to enjoy ourselves. Somewhat oddly the security guards then reappeared and told us to go back to our seats. There were hundreds of people all crammed together so I thought it was just a token gesture on their part (that may well have been what it was); unfortunately the guy leading them was one of the scariest and largest people I had ever seen. Whether due to his physical presence, or just down to some Scandinavian reserve, the people in the 'row' in front of me actually left when asked to. Now the only person between me and the barrier was said guard and his cohorts who started to push us backwards before realizing there was simply nowhere to push us to. After a short period of this impasse, they all melted away and left us to it. Later it emerged that they had been told to leave the people at the front on Dylan's express instructions.

I was now on the barrier and could see how just how pleased Dylan was with the ovation he received at the end of the song. He proceeded to really let rip and enjoy himself. The interaction with the band was back and they, too, could revel in the atmosphere and Dylan's sudden, presumably unexpected, encouragement. The show built into a celebratory party, and by the time of the encores though not exactly a musical treat everyone was having a ball.

All of this should not be taken as claiming the show was, in the grand scheme of things, musically or vocally a triumph. It was more to do with the instinctive realization that Dylan was not just going through the motions but beginning to put a new stage show together. "Desolation Row" and "Boots of Spanish Leather", the highlights of the night, had, in hindsight, only the odd flash of real Dylan vocals rather than being sustained performances.

Nonetheless those 'flashes' alone were enough to excite us all at the show and soon did the same to the wider fan community via the Internet. It may seem risible to read that for weeks afterwards people were seriously getting terribly excited by the phrasing on "Cain an' Abel", well it *is* risible in the normal world, yet that is what happened. I cannot poke a finger of fun at it because that very phrase lifted me out my somewhat blasé attitude and seat, left me poised to rush to the barrier and was all we talked about for about an hour after the show. A moment's reflection when the thrill had died down betrayed what this was saying about the rest of the vocals that night and in the shows leading up to it. Nonetheless, it gave reason for hope.

From that moment in Karlstad, Europe was to witness an intriguing battle between two Dylans: one with the authentic voice laced with the subtleties of his incomparable phrasing, the other playing the 'wolfman', 'gaspy' or 'upsinging' cards in lieu of real delivery.

Therefore you could get excited by a blistering opening in Leipzig, say, until about twenty minutes in the 'trick' singing re-emerged, you could hear rave reports of "Desolation Row" in Berlin, "Boots Of Spanish Leather" in Hamburg, "Hattie Carroll" in many a place and play them in isolation and get rather excited. The excitement never lasted for a whole show though, you might get just the odd song or, on a good night, a run of consecutive songs before the vocals switched back on to one of the automatic settings. Incidentally, the two Hamburg shows further highlighted the subjectivity issue. Of the people who went to the two nights most praised the first far above the second. When the recordings of the show arrived, the second sounded a far superior show to the first. Live music appreciation is, indeed, a mass of subjective responses.

By the time Dylan hit the UK, all kinds of mixed emotions and expectations were at play. There were four London shows, starting at Wembley before returning there after Birmingham (where the year's touring had been originally scheduled to end) for three added dates. The venues for these extra nights encouraged fans to hope for something special. Dylan's debut appearance at Shepherds Bush Empire was to be followed by returns to the Hammersmith Apollo (*neé* Odeon), of mixed NET heritage, and Brixton Academy, scene of a 1995 three-nighter.

I had sworn never to return to Wembley Arena after 1997, and had stood firm until 2003. Keith Wootton was to blame for this collapse of my resolve. It is impossible to say 'no' to someone who generously offers you a ticket and door-to-door transport. Keith's kindness aside, it is not a night I remember with any pleasure. First we suffered horrific traffic problems and delays which resulted in us arriving too late to see the people we had arranged to meet. Then there was a re-immersion in the soul-destroying venue. However, our seats gave us a perfect view and the opening song was an exhilarating "Maggie's Farm" that promised great things; a promise that went unfulfilled as far as I was concerned. A mere three dates into a leg, I felt I had already been to one too many. Though a sizeable number were of the same opinion as myself, it was by no means a unanimously accepted view.

On the contrary, for many Wembley was a favourite show. I could share in the fun at the novelty factor of seeing Dylan spending whole songs on keyboards. I can agree that, as well as the powerful opener, 'Cry A While' was strong and "Desolation Row", "It's Alright Ma" and "Hattie Carroll" were passable, if not as worthy as in some of their earlier outings in Europe. I could not agree, though, with the avalanche of praise these attracted from some quarters, and speculated that maybe it was as a result of their close proximity to truly distressing versions of "It's All Over Now, Baby Blue" and "Mr. Tambourine Man" and a 'gasping' "Boots of Spanish Leather".

The more I heard back from people the more marked the divergence of opinion grew. Two of my friends, Catriona and John Kennedy, respectively big Bruce Springsteen and Miles Davis fans, were at their first ever Dylan show and were highly enthused by Wembley. That's understandable, I thought, it is their first show, Dylan is always incredibly striking the first time you see him if you really appreciate live music in any form. Springsteen and Davis fans were bound to find first exposure to Dylan to be to their liking. Yet it was not that easy for me to wriggle out of my dilemma. A voice I think comes with more than a little authority, Nigel Hinton enjoyed Wembley thoroughly despite being 'trapped' on the left hand side and mostly facing Dylan's back and despite being a man who expects the highest standards. Given that Nigel and I were in total agreement over the other shows on this leg that we both experienced, why we should be in complete disagreement over Wembley, especially with the one of us in who was in the better position in the Arena liking it very little and the other liking it very much, mystifies me. The 'it-was-his-first-piano--performance' argument seemed too flimsy to explain it.[2]

Even those who had been to a number of shows and, broadly speaking, normally agree were at opposing ends of the spectrum. I was again beginning to feel we had all been at the same concert only in theory. I was determined to get to the bottom of this and on three separate occasions before and after later shows convened 'debates' between tables full of people who had been there and gauged their immediate reactions to what they had witnessed.

My intention was for this to clear things up but instead they grew ever murkier. Not only did the split in the view of the Wembley show grow ever wider but the Birmingham show (a mere few days earlier at the time of the debate) became embroiled in the same controversy, with the result that the contradictory views became even more extreme.

Michael Gray, yes, he of Stockholm 2002 total disparagement fame, found much to enjoy in the Birmingham show. Long-term fan Mark Carter also enjoyed it. In both their cases it was the only show they went to in this leg and their first experience of Dylan's piano based performance. I clung to this as the reason they enjoyed it while simultaneously the likes of Alan Davis, who usually can find beauty in any Dylan performance, were sending me messages of despair:

"I'm not sure I'll ever recover my respect for Bob after this. It was nothing like anything I could ever call music. It was not like anything I could ever call entertaining. Someone might be able to argue that it had value as some kind

2 Nigel, by the way, is also the author of a sublime novel, *The Heart of the Valley*, as well as of many other books including the famous 'Buddy' series for teenagers. Official site: http://www.nigelhinton.net

of anti-art statement I guess. But personally, I'd have had more fun spending 2 hours in the most dangerously deafening corner of a steel foundry." Alan's view was corroborated by scathing comments from Joe McShane who thought it 'even poorer' than Wembley.

Although Dylan was apparently still visibly unwell the worry was that Wembley was as good as it could get, Birmingham was the result when he was off-colour. Nick Hawthorne was extremely downbeat in *Judas! #8*:

"At the end of the show in Birmingham, Dylan gave one of his shortest-ever curtain calls, a few seconds and he was gone. He couldn't get off the stage quickly enough. And that was the most engagement with the crowd he had. He never looked at them, never interacted, just seemed to be hanging on for grim death until the whole thing was over. Him and us both."

Yet multi-show attendee Tim Price agreed more with Michael Gray and Mark Carter, saying it was 'fine as far as arena shows went, nothing wrong with it'. I respect their opinions; then again I respect everyone's that I have mentioned here. I endeavoured to find a pattern to explain the chasm between these views by attempting to correlate the various Wembley and Birmingham reports, following on from Tim's "arena" comment. I found no joy here either. Some who loved Wembley hated Birmingham and vice versa while others loved or hated both. There were, interestingly enough, virtually no 'so-so' views.

Ultimately, I achieved no resolution; the extremely subjective nature of one's response to live music in general and Bob Dylan's in particular is acknowledged upfront in this book. Nonetheless, such a powerful demonstration of it would have shaken me to the core had a counter-blow for a degree of objective standards not been struck by the man himself as I stood side by side with Nigel Hinton at Hammersmith, more of which later.

The night before that, the Shepherds Bush Empire's show had seemed to set a plateau of unimpeachable excellence for 2003. This was partly due to a designed-to-please-the-faithful set-list and partly to the beginning of a consistent re-emergence of the authentic Dylan voice and live experience. The night prior to Hammersmith, this was more than enough; a show featuring most of the good elements of the war that had been going on between the 'two live Dylans'. Suddenly, a miraculously younger and fitter looking Dylan was delivering a show of vigour and fire.

Fans had been hoping that, if there was one time Dylan would shake things up, it would be here in Shepherds Bush in front of approximately 2,000 camp followers; the smallest London venue for Dylan since the pubs and clubs of 1962.

On the other hand, they knew that similar thoughts for the extremely intimate venue of Vicar Street in Ireland in 2000 resulted in nothing more dramatic than a reasonably rare "Ring Them Bells" and a show that although fine enough was not significantly different from any other.

Notwithstanding this, in the true NET follower's heart 'hope springs eternal'. And this time hope was fulfilled, and then some. Where Birmingham had seen a very predictable set-list of:

November 21, 2003 NEC Birmingham

1. To Be Alone With You
2. It's All Over Now, Baby Blue
3. Tweedle Dee & Tweedle Dum
4. Love Minus Zero/No Limit
5. It's Alright, Ma (I'm Only Bleeding)
6. Bye And Bye
7. Highway 61 Revisited
8. Can't Wait
9. Boots Of Spanish Leather (Acoustic)
10. Cold Irons Bound
11. The Lonesome Death Of Hattie Carroll (Acoustic)
12. Honest With Me
13. Every Grain Of Sand
14. Summer Days

*

15. Cat's In The Well
16. Like A Rolling Stone
17. All Along The Watchtower

On November 23rd Shepherds Bush Empire witnessed:

1. Cold Irons Bound
2. Quinn The Eskimo
3. Down Along The Cove
4. It Takes A Lot To Laugh, It Takes A Train To Cry
5. Just Like Tom Thumb's Blues
6. Most Likely You Go Your Way (And I'll Go Mine)
7. Million Miles
8. Tough Mama
9. Under The Red Sky
10. Positively 4th Street
11. Dear Landlord
12. Tombstone Blues
13. Jokerman
14. Silvio

*

15. Tweedle Dee & Tweedle Dum
16. Like A Rolling Stone
17. All Along The Watchtower

These two dates were preceded by a cancelled gig in Ireland. The official reason given was 'severe viral infection', but trusted sources advised that 'fatigue' was the more likely cause. Whatever had made Dylan ill, his recovery medicine or techniques should be made available to all health services immediately. Though it should include a note about 'delayed effects' as the mystifying restoration they effected appeared to take a few days to kick in, leaving a tired Dylan struggling through the Birmingham show.

By the 23rd of November, though, it was as though Dylan had undertaken one of those complete blood changes you hear about from the seamier side of the athletic world. Re-energized and resplendent in white shirt and black bow-tie Dylan took to the stage.

The band's positioning was also much changed from when the tour had started. Now a tight-knit group of comrades-in-arms faced their piano-playing leader in a mini-horseshoe. Koella now was playing with the kind of intuitive abandon that Dylan himself brings to live performance. When it came off for both of them simultaneously it was electric, when it didn't it was wild enough to be a riveting spectacle in any case.

As for the songs themselves, surprising selection after surprising selection was approached with a buccaneering swagger that recalled the best periods of the NET, all the way back to 1988 when he launched these never ending peregrinations with force and more than a hint of anarchy. The hesitant, gimmick-filled vocals had been replaced by a confident voice able to be as venomous as "Positively 4th Street" demanded, as vigorous as "Jokerman" needed and as bluesy-rock 'n' roll as the double from *Highway 61 Revisited* in slots four and five screamed for, abetted by coruscating work from Koella in particular and the band in general.

"Phew! Rock 'n' Roll" indeed! Perhaps, though, it is a time for a little perspective. Had Shepherds Bush been the final show of the year it would have been my favourite, but not, set-list aside, *inconceivably* better than what had preceded it. There were individual performances or segments of other European shows that one could place beside it. I would have still been astonished by Dylan's physical reinvigoration, but I would not be looking upon it as some kind of miraculous restoration, I would probably have surmised it was the effect of knowing he had a long rest to come and was determined to go out with a BANG! Well, he gave us the 'BANG!' but he didn't go out with it. The wonder of the ending to the year was that he used Shepherds Bush as a stepping stone, he built upon it to provide an even better show the following night in Hammersmith. This scene of various previous NET triumphs and disasters hosted another triumph .

Using a set-list that cleverly balanced the experimentation of Shepherds Bush with oft-played selections from the leg thus far, Dylan hit the perfect note for the evening, sustaining a level of excellence and authentic singing unmatched in years. Without losing any of the previous night's edgy excitement, this show added the swaggering, assured control that we used to always take for granted. To top it all off, Dylan performed one of those songs you think you would never get to hear no matter how long the NET continued . These occasions constitute the high spots of the NET experience for hard travelling and multi-show attending fans. It was one thing, and quite a thing, to realise that in front of us was

Dylan playing "Romance In Durango" for the first time since 1976, but he more than just 'played' it, he genuinely *sang* it. The vocals were reminiscent of those glorious 2002 last leg covers.

The moment of realisation still sends chills down my spine, almost a decade later. There was a hush around the hall when the fifth song started. 'Durango' starts so suddenly that Dylan and the band could virtually play anything they liked before hitting the opening lyric line. No one knew what was being played in those first few moments. I was later told that the band were all grinning at this point but I only had eyes for Bob. Then he started singing and somewhere in that famous first line:

Hot chilli peppers in the blistering sun

I was sure enough, though still utterly astonished, to delightedly mouth "DURANGO!" to Nigel Hinton, but I stopped at "D...." as I could see from his eyes that he had just realised too. Attention has never been more rapt as Dylan gave a virtuoso vocal to a melody very reminiscent of the album version. Given the huge difference in musical backing and setting it seemed simultaneously familiar and yet different, and it sounded like pure, heavenly magic.

As the song drew to its conclusion Dylan returned to the microphone and re-sang the first two lines; a lovely gesture to all those who had gone into neural shock and missed them first time around. The feeling afterwards was that Dylan can say whatever he wants about his fans in interviews as long as he keeps treating us so generously onstage.

Athough 'Durango', was, understandably, the song we would talk about for some time afterwards this show had far more to it than that. All the songs that were repeated from the night before were even better. Unsurprisingly, it took a recording to make me realise how good "Dear Landlord" had been; coming as it did as the sixth song, it could have been virtually anything and gone unnoticed.

Dylan looking even finer and fitter than the night before, fully realizing the new arrangement of "Girl From The North Country" at last. All those attempts that had seemed without purpose suddenly blossomed into a version that made dazzling sense. "Million Miles", of all songs, was a towering triumph and "Jokerman" a dynamic joy. Despite all these individual triumphs it was the overall consistency of the singing and playing that was the show's crowning glory. Nearly, though not quite if one is being harshly truthful, banishing the trick voices for a whole night.

All this and there still was a night to go. Almost inevitably Brixton came as a slight anticlimax, though such an appellation is a harsh and unfair inevitability. If it had not been for Hammersmith, Brixton would have been vying for the title of 'show of the year'. The build-up from the previous nights and resultant hope for an even more resplendent set-list and performance was increased tenfold for those of us who were hoping that Dylan would not end the year's touring without debuting one of his own compositions. To top "Romance In Durango" would have taken such a thing, and it would have had to be a notable song at that.

As it transpired, Dylan did not play anything for the first ever time; but he came as close as possible to that by presenting "Yea! Heavy And A Bottle Of Bread" for only the second time. As this came as the second song of the night the hugely excited crowd's expectations went, if this were possible, even further into overdrive. In the end there were no further surprises, but it was still a very fine show and there was a marvellous 'last night of the year' atmosphere with love and support for the man at the piano descending from the auditorium to the stage in waves.

"Jokerman" was again outstanding, "Blind Willie McTell" another highlight and yet in some ways "A Hard Rain's A-Gonna Fall" was the most compelling performance of the night. This one song could stand as an emblem for the whole year. It started all over the place and all attempts to get it back on track seemed doomed to failure until the last verse where a Dylan reborn appeared in total command and bestowed upon his audience a spellbinding new delivery. The year's touring ended in a passionate climax of searing encores.

The press that had been so supportive of what I, ultra-critically perhaps, been so unmoved by at Wembley, struggled to convey the magnitude of what had happened:

"The London shows underlined Dylan's claim to be regarded as one of the great creative forces of the age. It's no longer sufficient to discuss Dylan in the context of other popular musicians. Comparisons with pop-rock contemporaries – the Beatles, say, or the Stones, or the army of superannuated hoofers still peddling heritage entertainment to eager nostalgics – do Dylan a disservice.

"Dylan should be judged, instead, by reference to the musical giants from all genres - Mozart, Bach, Miles Davis, Louis Armstrong, Callas … And against the great writers, in all media, from all eras – Shakespeare, Joyce, Goethe, Cervantes … Bob Dylan's writing and performance art bridge the gap between popular entertainment and high culture."[3]

Still, three shows does not a year make; this was not as triumphant a *leg* as the concluding one of a year before. Nonetheless, Hammersmith in particular did show that he could still do it. I mused that if the reinvention of acoustic songs with a less melodic, almost punky approach was deliberate and an artistic way forward to utilise his current voice rather than rely on gimmickry, it augured well for 2004.

On the other hand 2002 and 2003 started disappointingly in comparison to the last leg of each preceding year, so it was impossible to predict if 2004 would see the development of the good new trends, a relapse into treading water or a new, unexpected route forward on the never ending road. I did not know which it would be, but once again I could hardly wait to find out.

---

3 Music for Grown-Ups. http://www.spacemonkeylab.com/mfgu/.

CHAPTER EIGHTEEN

2004: "Listen to me"

"Listen to me: you are the best singing audience we have ever had. We've played that song 1000 times and nobody could sing with it...."

DYLAN ONSTAGE, 24TH JUNE 2004

By the time Dylan took the stage at Cain's Ballroom in Tulsa OK, on February 28, 2004 to kick off another year of touring, a great deal of revisionism had taken place amongst some of the merry party people I was with at the end of 2003. At the one extreme there was a group whose view was summed up by Raymond Landry, who had travelled from New Orleans to witness the final three shows of the year. He commented that: "The shows were a blast to be at, but they don't stand up on CD at all." At the other, there were those who agreed fully with the first half of that statement but still loved playing the recordings. As usual in Dylan circles, these extreme positions were more heavily populated than anything in-between.

Arguments had raged over the whole of the European tour, come to that. Were the closing shows in London really any better than those that had preceded them, or was the only difference the 'surprise songs' being performed?

Also, the eternal problem Dylan has with competing with his past was thrown into sharp relief for me as I was exiting the Hammersmith show. Collector 'Street Legal' asked if I had enjoyed "the worst 'Romance In Durango' ever". A sharp and harsh lot, these Dylan audiences. He had a point, it undoubtedly was, and remains, the weakest performance of it that we know of; nonetheless it was still, to use Raymond's term, a blast to be there and hear it. One can have enjoyed the night and treasure the memory while still agreeing with critic Michael Gray's later remarks that: "... yes, it was great to hear him throw that in, a marvellous surprise: but in truth it was a poignantly less certain vocal performance of the song than any on the Rolling Thunder Revue."[1]

Overall, the year had not ended as strongly as 2001 and 2002; however, the fact that Dylan could still pull something as surprising as "Romance In Durango" out of the hat, and yet again could end the year with a leg that was far superior to what had gone down earlier, gave people a much-needed shot in the arm. Confidence was relatively high that Bob could still produce something very worthwhile on the Never Ending Tour in 2004.

For the opening leg the band was augmented by a second drummer, Richie Hayward[2] of Little Feat fame. This leg took Dylan north; there is always something touching about Dylan returning to Minnesota, and it often is blessed with stand-out shows. St. Paul on March 10th was again home to one of the year's strongest gigs. As his tour wound its way there, the press were, as was now customary, overwhelmingly positive. There were some quibbles, however, and the Chicago *Sun-Times* headline caught the mood of many fans when it proclaimed "Confound it, Bob, give up the keyboard."

Still in March, Detroit saw consecutive nights of extra encores. Firstly, Bob Seger's *Get Out Of Denver* was added on the 16th as a tribute to the Detroit musician being inducted into the Rock And Roll Hall of Fame that very day. This made it an instantly collectible show, and the same became true of the following night. This was because the widely lauded and much loved Jack White of The

---

1 Michael Gray, http://bobdylanencyclopedia.blogspot.com/2010/06/photo-from-padova.html 25/6/2010

2 Richard Hayward, drummer, singer and songwriter was born in 1946. He died from complications of lung disease at a hospital in Victoria, British Columbia on August 12, 2010 while awaiting a liver transplant, following diagnosis of liver cancer.

White Stripes guested on his own song, *Ball And Biscuit*, which provided that evening's bonus encore.

While Dylan was touring the US, tickets went on sale for the UK. This dual activity of following the tour while it is far away and frantically making plans for when it is next in your neighbourhood was by now very familiar, and yet it remained an exciting one. Before Dylan reached these shores, the fan community was enthusing over an especially clear recording that circulated worldwide, seemingly instantaneously, of the Gilford NH show on June 4th. This was the first of six US dates immediately prior to the European leg (I should note that Richie Hayward had by now left the band, as had guitarist Freddie Koella, the latter being replaced by Stu Kimball).

While not sharing fully in the excessive praise lavished upon the Gilford show, I found it very rewarding and noteworthy in the way it seemed to get progressively better. Perhaps not in an absolutely straight progression, but it felt almost like that. So much so, in fact, that the over-performed "Like A Rolling Stone", of all things, was one of the highlights; a slow, careful rendition compared to most I had heard in recent times. "Floater" was a treat, a very pleasant version with Larry's violin working nicely in counterpoint to the vocal. For many in Europe it was their first chance to properly hear the new arrangement of "It Ain't Me, Babe". Undoubtedly the highlight of the set, however, was a dark, brooding "I Believe In You". This song was to appear in various guises throughout the year, almost always being one of the night's standout tracks when it did so.

However, the high-energy "Summer Days" was perhaps more typical of the show overall. The contrast between these two songs, so divergent in approach and tone, bears shining testimony to how much variety Dylan was bringing to the stage that night. A local paper reflected the excitement of the occasion:

"As Dylan sang 'sometimes the silence can be like thunder', he swayed and swerved. He sang classics like 'Highway 61' and 'It Ain't Me, Babe' while mixing in some of his new material well to provide a great variety. The band backed up Dylan's mixture of everything from soul, blues, folk, and country with the kind of timing, tune, pitch, and harmony that kept everyone on their feet and feeling the energy. He was able to amp up the audience and get people dancing in their seats throughout the show."[3]

I apologize that my live reports have become so UK-centric, but this was a period of restricted travel for me. Luckily, though, there always seems to be a new Dylan visit to the UK to look forward to, and I was soon to see him again, in June.

For reasons the next chapter will examine in depth, this book has been steadily veering off its main topic to include more and more of what was happening around the tour rather than the shows themselves. For now it is worth noting that the 'Dylan industry' had gone into, and has remained in, overdrive in the new century. Dylan was everywhere: on TV, in adverts, in movies; he had new releases, re-releases, art exhibitions; he wrote books, items such as harmonicas and watches were sold in his name, a veritable deluge of activities concurrent with the NET itself has been pouring over us. Consequently, some straying from the main topic has been inevitable.

To extend that further, I want to detail a live Dylan event during the NET that was a very special occasion for me, although it was not a show in the normal sense of the word, it was not a gig. It occurred, however, just before a singular concert, the last one I want to talk about in detail for some years, because a dramatic change was soon to take place in my relationship with the NET.

I cannot recall now when I first visited St Andrews, known throughout the world as 'the home of golf'. As my family comes from Fife originally, it was a natural place for us to visit for 'days out'. In those days, long before Prince William attended the famous university (third in age and prestige in the UK behind the Oxbridge pair, whose collegiate system it shares), it was one of my father's favourite places. For the history, the ancient ruined cathedral signifying over 1200 years as a major religious centre in Scotland, the natural beauty and the university itself where my sister had elected to go. Although her brief stay as a student was, admirably enough, memorable more for partying and political demonstrations than anything else.

---

3 Rich Bergeron, *The Gilford Citizen*: "*Times may be a-changin,' but fans still love Dylan*" June 5, 2004.

You can therefore imagine my excitement when the University of St Andrews declared that they were going to award Bob Dylan the honorary degree of Doctor of Music. Announcing the honour, the University's Principal and Vice-Chancellor, Dr Brian Lang, said: "Bob Dylan is an iconic figure for the 20th Century, particularly for those of us whose formative years were the 1960s and 70s. His songs, and in particular his lyrics, are still part of our consciousness. We are very pleased to take this opportunity of honouring such a major artist."

I set about organising tickets, pausing only to dash off an e-mail to Stephen Scobie about his idol being awarded the honour by his *alma mater*. This was no easy matter, but rather than go into detail here about the period of uncertainty, and our manic attempts to secure both press and public access tickets, I'll jump to where it all turned out well at the end. This was due to the superb efforts of the staff at St Andrews, two of whom, Gayle and Joyce from the Press and Registry Offices, we will always be indebted to. 'We' being myself, the scurrilous Joe McShane and intrepid photographer Duncan Hume, whose place was assured when a press pass for me was added to the public access tickets I had already obtained.

Getting to St Andrews meant changing my plans for non-Bob reasons, so while Duncan and Joe were at the Newcastle show I was visiting my parents, way out on the edge of the opposite coast of Scotland to St Andrews. The next morning I set off on the first train to ensure that I would be in St Andrews in time even if there were delays in my journey. As this consisted of two trains and one bus, the likelihood of this was high. My own concern over my travelling time was little compared to Joe's. Despite my having built in time to compensate for everything but the most catastrophic of journeys, Joe had been panicking the night before to such an extent that he convinced my friends Catriona and John Kennedy (yes, they were following up on their 2003 debut NET show with more already) that the only way I, and therefore he, would safely make it to the event was for them to pick me up and take me to get the tickets. To do this they would have to intercept me mid-journey and transport me all the way to the venue. For some reason, despite there being no chance of their attending themselves, the Kennedys generously agreed to this.

Therefore at lunchtime on June 23rd, 2004 you could find Joe, Duncan and myself in St Andrews, taking turns to go to the Younger Hall and marvel both at its splendour and the dream-like possibility, it seemed no more than that in truth, that we would soon be seeing a be-robed Bob Dylan there. 'Soon', that is, if a few hours with a clock ticking in seemingly interminable slow motion could be so described.

Picking up my press pass had given me an early warning of the predictably depressing media coverage of this momentous event. Those arriving at the press collection point were not exactly *au fait* with Dylan and pumped me for some information. After telling the chap from Sky TV about "Highlands" (he had never heard of the song) and Robert Burns, I went on to volunteer the name of the album it was from. "No need," he said, not because he already knew the title of the album but because, as he said with frank self-deprecation, "Sky News, mate, I only need one piece of information." With that, he put his hat on and left.

One way of passing the time would be to queue. This being Scotland and out-door Dylan weather, we were drenched within moments. It was a formal dress occasion and umbrellas were strictly for Mary Poppins imitators at this point.

Consequently, we went to a pub and sat where he could keep an eye on the front door of the hall. Convincing Duncan that this was the wisest course of action had not been easy. A few minutes after we sat down, Duncan suddenly announced: "There are people going in." Cue a sharp exit from the pub and a run across the road to be met by the closed doors of Younger Hall. Duncan's impatience and over-active imagination had got the better of us. There was a mini-queue of all of seven people, including us and three cameramen in 'wetsuits'.

We were the only ones not equipped for the elements in the queue; our formal attire proved no match for the weather and within moment we were soaked as our warm table in the snug little bar lay, mockingly, just across the road. Time crawled as we became more and more sodden. An attempt to gain access via a side door, yes, Duncan's bright idea again, led to a rebuff and an accidental meeting with Jim Callahan. This was not exactly what we had planned at that moment in time. Brilliant fellow though Jim Callahan is, to hear him intone "no hollering, no pictures, no this, no that" as we trooped back to stand in the rain again was just no fun at all. Jim seemed to me to grin to himself as he left us to join Dylan for lunch. I like to think he was secretly quite pleased to see some fans there, keeping his eyes on us would at least give him something to do in the long period before Dylan would accept his award.

Meanwhile we were standing in a howling gale with horizontal sheets of rain attacking us and had nothing to do. Or at least not until Duncan asked for the public access ticket that Joe was holding for him. Joe, in a transparent 'let's just fill up the time' ploy, mentioned some inventive reason for not giving Duncan the ticket at that moment. I had been half listening to this mild tease when suddenly I was an attentive, if stunned, witness to a dramatic scene as Duncan lost the plot completely. He seemed to *devolve* into a ferocious creature fighting for a life-preserving meal in some primeval jungle. He was yelling in pure fury: "Just give me the ****ing ticket!"

Oh well, all our desperation for the event to happen and us to witness it was laid bare for all around us to see. No longer were we incognito to anyone in the queue, or possibly the whole of the ancient Kingdom of Fife come to that. The time for 'small talk' had abruptly ended. Dylan was not to appear until 15:40pm. We got in before 2 o'clock and rushed for a seat. The event did not start until half past two and then there would be a long, long list of graduands being announced and clapped off the stage before we saw Dylan.

It is with no little amount of shame that I admit that we were quite proud of seeing no other Bobcats in the audience. The arrival of Mike Sutton along with another fan soon punctured that smug feeling. Still, there was no denying the privilege of being in attendance at such a unique event. All we needed to do now was wait patiently for Bob.

For what seemed like an eternity *'the only person on the scene missing was ...'* Yet, suddenly, *'Big Jim was standing there'* and .... and then, amazingly enough, there was Bob Dylan, after all, really there in all his Immaculateness, topped off by his trademark shock of curls, looking very fine indeed in his robes. Neil Corcoran, sitting on the bottom row outside right of the stage, looked suitably full of himself. Sitting to Corcoran's left, Dylan studiously ignored Neilthroughout. Dylan kept looking straight ahead, other than when Professor Tickle returned after receiving her Honorary Degree of Doctor of Science. Then, Dylan exchanged some words with her as he welcomed her back to her seat.

Dylan was the last of three Honorary Degree recipients, Professor Tickle having been preceded by Professor Emeritus Putnam's award of Honorary Degree of Doctor of Letters. Their two laureations inevitably were detailed and lengthy. Too much so for Dylan it seemed, as he was forced to sit in the full glare of unrelenting scrutiny. Either covering up nerves or displaying boredom, he yawned and spent some considerable time digging something or other out of his teeth with his tongue. The ever-helpful ceremonial booklet was used to cover one or two more yawns, but not all of them.

Following the schedule, the St Salvador's Chapel Choir performed "Benedicamus Domino" and "My Love's An Arbutus". Then, in a polite if musically misguided gesture, an appalling version of "Blowin' In The Wind". There was no reaction from Dylan. This was something he was later berated for, though I tend to think that this was courtesy on his part rather than anything else.

Then came Neil Corcoran's big moment, he gave a generally fine speech of veneration, with lovely statements, such as the following, being especially apt for the occasion:

"Bob Dylan's life as writer and singer has the aspect of vocation, of calling, and his is an art of the most venturesome risk and the most patient endurance. He's spent a lifetime applying himself to such long-sanctioned forms of art as folk, blues, country, and rock music. And, partly by transfusing them with various kinds of poetic art, he's reinvented them so radically that he's moved everything on to a place it had never expected to go and left the deepest imprint on human consciousness."

Dylan's kneeling to accept his commemoration and the resultant award all seemed dream-like. It was a highlight of our lives to applaud him with pride as he accepted the Honorary Doctorate. Then Deputy Principal David Corner brought proceedings to an end with the obligatory reference to coming after Bob Dylan on the bill.

At about this time it became apparent that the people on the stage were going to be led out up the aisle, past where we were sitting. Surely not, surely not Dylan *too*? Oh my God, yes...! Incredibly he walked right past us, close enough to touch. He took a neat little stumble (yes, only Bob can stumble neatly) that meant his head bobbed up right toward us as he passed. Then, with a swish of his cloak, he was gone.

That was my experience of Bob Dylan getting an honorary doctorate at St Andrews University. This was presented to him because: "It seems appropriate that his second such degree should come from Scotland's oldest university, since Scottish border ballads and folksongs have been the inspiration for some of his melodies, and his great song 'Highlands' is an elaborate riff, or descant, on Robert Burns." I would not have missed it for the world.

Unfortunately, the Press responded in a predictable manner, misreporting what happened and inventing slanders on Dylan's behaviour. The most extreme of these was a false claim that he fell asleep, coming from a tabloid without a reporter actually at the event. They also joined with other papers in complaining of Dylan turning up 'late' and 'not saying anything'. As Dylan's behaviour was exactly the same as that of the other two honorary recipients, one would surmise this is the way these things are supposed to happen. A supposition easily checked with the Press Office who confirmed to me that: 'at no point are honorary graduates expected to speak during the ceremony'. Onlookers and reporters would, or at least should, have noticed that neither of the other two honorary degree recipients spoke either.

The other two whinges were that Dylan yawned and left soon after the event. Both of these are undeniably true, the obvious reason for the latter being that he was due to play a concert in Glasgow that night. It is a pity the mainstream media felt the need to report this event in completely the opposite way to the grateful university Press Office: "We were delighted that Mr. Dylan accepted an honorary degree from the University. Staff, students and members of the public were very happy to see him in St Andrews despite a busy touring schedule."

There was no newspaper mention either that Dylan was here a 'fish out of water'; his magisterial presence at the SECC later that night and incandescent one at the Barrowland the night after that revealed him in his true element, that of the stage. Most of the objections were to Dylan's yawning, none of which referred to his hectic schedule, the flight from America and resultant jet-lag, the fact that he was going to expend more energy in the next two nights than most people a third his age could manage or that he would normally be resting at this point in his schedule.

It would have been more fitting coverage if they had addressed these points or noted, as Neil Corcoran did in his laureation that: "It goes without saying that his acceptance of our invitation deeply honours us, and I really can't say what a great privilege and pleasure his presence here is today."

The show at the SECC that night was unsurprisingly unspectacular. Joe had arranged for us to be in the centre of the second row so we had about as good a view as you could have in such an arena. but Dylan must have been thoroughly exhausted by this point. The show must go on, though, and it did, with Dylan appearing dignified and back in his element. An extremely typical show for the summer of 2004 was duly served up, but for most of the tour-following fans our eyes were firmly on the following night, which held the potential, perhaps even promise, of being something different and special.

24th June 2004 The Barrowland Ballroom. Glasgow

1. Drifter's Escape
2. I'll Be Your Baby, Tonight
3. Tweedle Dee & Tweedle Dum
4. Just Like A Woman
5. It's Alright, Ma (I'm Only Bleeding) (Acoustic)
6. Girl From The North Country (Acoustic)
7. Most Likely You'll Go Your Way (And I'll Go Mine)
8. Ballad Of A Thin Man
9. Floater (Too Much To Ask)
10. Highway 61 Revisited
11. It Ain't Me, Babe (Acoustic)
12. Honest With Me
13. I Believe In You
14. Summer Days

*

15. Don't Think Twice, It's All Right (Acoustic)
16. Like A Rolling Stone
17. All Along The Watchtower

The set-list had the same encores as the night before at Glasgow's Scottish Exhibition Centre. Of the fourteen songs in the main set, only four were repeated. Songs in the fifth, twelfth and fourteenth positions remained unchanged. Tweedle Dee & Tweedle Dum was also played both nights, though it moved from eighth song the previous night to third in the concert we are concentrating on. So, ten different songs in the main set from June 23rd to June 24th, but these differences were just the tip of the iceberg.

Dylan was rested, rather than suffering from jet-lag and an exhausting day. Perhaps even more significantly the venue and the crowd it attracted were radically different to the night before. Instead of the SECC's soulless, large metallic aircraft-hangar vibe we had a packed, standing crowd in a sweaty, intimate, vibrant setting. A word on this venue is necessary to set the scene.

If you consider every venue I have seen him play in, the Barrowland Ballroom in Glasgow may not be quite the most surprising place I have seen Dylan. Nonetheless, solely from a personal perspective it is by far the most astonishing. Were you to travel back in time and meet me in a school on the outskirts of Glasgow at the beginning of 1974 and tell me I would see him play at this of all venues, I would have found your prediction far more surprising than your ability to time travel.

Glasgow had yet to transform itself back then and was notorious as the most down-at-heel, violent and unkempt of Britain's major cities. Not all of which reputations it has yet escaped from, admittedly. Given that the Barrowland Ballroom is situated in one of the, to put it politely, less salubrious parts of the city it does not take much working out what kind of place it and the dodgy market which shares its name was. Perhaps unsurprisingly, it boasted a colourful and notorious past. Dizzy Gillespie was one of an enormous roster of eclectic performers to have appeared there. On the darker side of things, Scotland's most infamous serial killer, known as 'Bible John', preyed on his victims at the dance venue.

Back in my first flush of Dylan mania those 30 years previously, the idea of ever seeing him at all seemed a remote possibility. If I did dare imagine such a thing happening, it would be at some huge open-air concert like Blackbushe or the Isle of Wight festival. By 2004, however, both Bob Dylan and the Barrowland Ballroom had reinvented themselves.

No longer was Dylan someone who had not toured for eight years and seemed almost an untouchable recluse, especially to us Europeans. Instead he was sixteen years into the NET, which had featured these kinds of surprises around the world as Bob seemed on a quest to play every type and size of location possible.

As for the Barrowland Ballroom, it had gone through two major changes since opening in 1934. The first was forced upon it by a fire in 1958 which led to a complete rebuilding and it reopened in 1960. The second was the decline of the dance-hall culture and the rise of Rock. Over the decades after I left Glasgow the Barrowland Ballroom had reinvented itself as an intimate concert venue so renowned that it could still attract top acts despite having a capacity of under 2,000. Major benefits it could boast were outstanding acoustics, designed for orchestras in the days before electronic amplification, and its sprung wooden dance floor. Due to all of the above and the wildly enthusiastic crowds that tend to gather there, the Barrowland Ballroom has topped many a chart of 'favourite venues' from both fans and performers alike.

Jennifer Cunningham, writing a history of the venue in what was then called *The Glasgow Herald*, reported that:

"Tom Joyes, manager sums up its secret in two words: atmosphere and character. 'Glasgow audiences,' he says, 'always provide a great atmosphere.' That hardly gives anything away, but, according to Joyes, who has managed the complex of markets and hall for 15 years, there are top bands who prefer three nights at Barrowland to one night at the SECC. His explanation is that his hall is more laid-back. The stand-up hall is better than seating for rock concerts, with fans having access to the bar within the hall throughout the concert. Even with a capacity crowd of 1900, he claims that from the back of the hall you can see the whites of the performers' eyes."[4]

As you can see, there is a double claim building for Dylan's appearance that night being a unique occasion, the claim comprising of both the venue and the local crowd. This idea that both are special and can create the atmosphere to inspire exceptional, even legendary, events becomes self-perpetuating. Audiences attend the shows expecting something extraordinary; the night Bob Dylan came to visit raised the expectation bar exponentially. He may not have been the biggest-selling act ever to appear but he was, unquestionably, the biggest 'name' to grace the fabled stage.

---

4 Jennifer Cunningham, The Herald (Scotland) "Living" Section, "Entertaining Generations" http://www.glasgow-barrowland.com/ballroom.htm

Now, I grew up with gigs in the early 1970s by the likes of the Stones, the Who, Bowie, and so forth in Glasgow being riotous events. These shows were always followed by all the performers saying that they had never known fans or audience reaction like it. It is quite possible they were saying the same thing elsewhere, or even saying it everywhere else. A 15-year-old in those pre-Internet and affordable international phone call days would not know. Nor had I any idea how the concerts I saw compared with the concerts elsewhere, local and national prejudices are always drummed into one by the respective media. It is the same all over the world; every country thinks its army has the 'best damn soldiers in the world'. Similarly, probably every city thinks it contains 'the best damn music venue in the world'.

However, it has been said so often about Glasgow that there seems to be truth attached to it. It is not only musicians who have consistently claimed this, comedians talk about Glasgow stages being the ultimate test: if they take to you, it makes you feel like a God. Conversely, I should quickly acknowledge, they say it is the worst audience to displease. You do not just 'die' in front of such a crowd, you fervently wish for death! The football crowds in the city, too, have long been renowned for being the loudest and most demonstrative on the island.

To return to music, those early 1970s concerts I talked about had been held at a venue now long gone. It was originally called Greens, then The Apollo, which it still was when I queued for three nights for my Earls Court tickets in 1978, and the audiences there were famous for being raucous and boisterous. The much smaller Barrowland Ballroom had taken this reputation on and welded it to its own unique ambience and history.

It hosted quite a show. I was going to write that from the minute Bob sang the opening song, "Drifter's Escape", you knew this was going to be a special night; but if truth be told the incredible atmosphere, the feeling that this was an event of some magnitude was palpable long before Dylan even appeared.

As he took to the stage and performed that first song he was given an ovation worthy of a conquering hero. If anything an even louder roar greeted "I'll Be Your Baby Tonight". In response, Dylan bellowed the song out as loudly as he could. When he got to the 'mockingbird' verse, Dylan lent purposefully over the keyboards peering at the audience, somewhat unfocusedly but still with intent, and somehow combined the poignancy of the song with an aggressive 'I will match your fervour' rendition, before closing with a quieter repeat of the same lines.

The band certainly seemed to revel in the setting, pulling out all the stops throughout the show as the place bounced from beginning to end. "Just Like A Woman" saw the beginning of the main event of the night: the crowd trying to sing along with Bob. Dylan for once was revelling in this, although still trying to maintain control. Yet when the crowd roared out the title line, Dylan had no choice but to let them go, such was the volume they engendered. It seemed like a moveable wall of sound was bouncing all around you, from the stage and the singing crowd, careering off the ceiling and reverberating in one direction before being blasted back from another.

To regain control of the song Dylan followed a few beats behind, originally to try to throw the audience, but by the end of the song just to maintain some kind of parity in the performing stakes. You could see him quite clearly chuckling on one of the choruses before grinning broadly as he allowed the audience to participate at the point they demanded. Given the noise generated from off-stage Dylan's vocals had to be extremely strong all night, even when he changed the pace by playing more contemplative songs, something he strategically did after "Just Like A Woman" ended to huge roars of appreciation.

Although I make it sound, and indeed it often approximated, a football match rather than a concert, there was relative calm when Dylan wanted it. This was evident whether in the slower, quieter numbers or even amidst celebratory singalongs such as "Just Like a Woman", as evidenced by the long instrumental break before it concluded. Perhaps the most conclusive proof of this, though, is that later in the set the contemplative, personal pledge of "I Believe In You" was quite possibly the highlight of the night, and there was a poignant tenderness evident in the moving "Boots Of Spanish Leather" and "Don't Think Twice, It's All Right."

Dylan continued to enjoy a unique rapport with the audience, and as he machine-gunned the lyrics of "It's Alright, Ma" at them it was hard to tell who was enjoying it more, the people on the stage or the people off it. "Girl From The North Country" was instantly recognised and greeted with yet another loud cheer; which may seem unremarkable unless you had heard how Dylan somehow managed to simultaneously spit and gargle the opening words into a series of indecipherable noises. The melody was all but submerged by a strange staccato delivery, though some of the original poignancy resurfaced with a lovely reading of the penultimate verse.

And so the show progressed, building inexorably to the encores which you knew would somehow, although this seemed impossible to contemplate, be even more over the top than what you were experiencing at the time. I should make special mention of "Ballad of a Thin Man" before turning to that incandescent closure to the show. Given where he had been the day before and how scandalously he had been treated in the press that morning, the lines "been with the professors" and "pencil in your hand" could not help but take on added significance to most of the audience. It may be reading too much into things to say that Dylan performed the song with these incidents in his mind, but it was impossible at the time not to feel that way.

The sweat had been dripping off Dylan almost from the very beginning, and by the time we got to the joyous, energy-sapping encores his Stetson hat must have been heavy to wear, so soaked was the wide brim. "Don't Think Twice, It's All Right" seemed to bring the house down but we were all still standing at the end of it and everyone drew breath before the explosive last two songs.

One of the worst things people can say when writing books like this is: "You really had to be there". Yet, for, "Like A Rolling Stone" that night, "you really had to be there". Dylan's voice was a blurred burr and yet powerful and compelling as it competed with a deafening crowd throughout this epic song. Clearly loving the audience reaction and interaction, Dylan was smiling and pointing as he belted out "no direction home"; the band was busting a gut to keep up with, and make as much noise as Dylan and the audience. They clearly sensed the occasion was one where you should just go completely over the top. Dylan was singing lines before and after he knew the crowd would be; it was like being present at an audio wrestling match. This was the kind of tussle that Dylan had had a lifetime of experience of not only dealing with but triumphing in; but on this night he had to admit defeat. This he did graciously, laughingly and with obvious pleasure as the delirious crowd eventually drowned everything but themselves out as they bellowed out the famous chorus.

Visibly moved, Dylan came back to the microphone to say: "*Listen to me: you are the best singing audience we have ever had. We've played that song 1000 times and nobody could sing with it....*" The crowd, naturally, lapped up the compliment and roared even louder, encouraging Dylan to play another encore song. Although all regulars knew he was going to end with "All Along The Watchtower", he seemed to play a little joke on those at the front, affecting surprise that they wanted another song before slamming into an apocalyptic rendition that was so intense you felt it would bring the cliché 'tear the place down' into a physical reality. At the finishing end, with everyone in the building drained, Dylan stood at the centre of the stage like a commander on a field he had conquered, and then some. He gave a dignified bow and left to tumultuous cheers, the pounding feet on the wooden floor sending ricocheting noise slamming back down from the ceiling. Although we knew he had really gone, we remained stomping and cheering for quite some time.

Earlier in this book I have praised Dylan for not mouthing platitudes to audiences or allowing them to sing along, so my enjoyment that night in Glasgow may reek of hypocrisy. I would counter this by saying that it was special simply because he so rarely does these things; were he to say them every night the words would be meaningless. I acknowledge though that the fact it happened in my home city may influence my opinion, even while admitting that such thinking is silly, sentimental nonsense. I should also mention that back on March 1st in St. Louis Dylan also spoke to the audience and the crowd there also forcefully sang along to an incendiary "Like A Rolling Stone".

The reaction of others was most instructive: 'civilians', as Ian Woodward and David Bristow refer to more casual Dylan listeners, absolutely loved the show. A friend who knew of my Dylan interest forwarded discussion pages from an Internet football forum all about the show. It transpired that many of the supporters had gone to the show and were keen to share their experiences, perhaps especially as it was close season in the club football calendar, and many pages were filled with comments on Dylan's appearance at the Barrowland, with hardly a mention of the much larger capacity SECC show the previous night.

There was wall-to-wall praise for a wonderful night out. Dylan, along with the oft-mentioned Neil Young, was continually praised for being an "oldie who still delivered". It was clear from the context that Dylan and Young stood alone in this regard. These were clearly people who followed younger bands and went to see famous old names only when they came to places like The Barrowland Ballroom. These are opinions I rarely hear, surrounded as I am by those who think thirty shows in a year a 'lean spell'. It was eye-opening, too, that most mentioned Dylan speaking to the audience and the sing-alongs. A very different reaction from that of the massed ranks of Dylan foot soldiers. It seems clear that what would be anathema for regular concert goers if repeated nightly, is ideal for the one-off attendees.

It is interesting to note that the concert-goers Dylan supposedly most likes to play for, given his comments in the 'Rome interview' quoted in the 2001 chapter, so rarely get what they most want. This typically Dylanesque paradox caught out the reviewer in *The Herald*:

"The success of the gig, for me, lies in the fact that Dylan played the kind of venue that all bands and performers should play – atmospheric, small and intimate enough to allow a genuine level of communication between band and audience. Dylan doesn't want to play vast barns filled with beard-stroking train-spotters noting down how many times on this tour he's played Ballad Of A Thin Man."[5]

On the surface this fits with what Dylan has often said, and chimes with the reviewer's experience of this one night. However it is palpably nonsense to claim that Dylan "doesn't want to play vast barns". If he did not, he would not have booked himself into them every time in his career he has been able to fill such venues. This same review, albeit erroneously, claims this to be Dylan's most intimate gig in 15 years, which would seem to be a bit of a ridiculously long time to wait to play the kind of place he supposedly prefers. No, it is clear what he prefers from simply comparing the amount of times every year he chooses to "play vast barns" rather than venues "atmospheric, small and intimate enough to allow a genuine level of communication". Which is not to say he does not sometimes revel in moving from his normal arena setting to the more snug.

As for the fans, well that lazy cliché ignores the fact that the fans who go to show after show are usually the ones who are the most boisterous and holler encouragement to Dylan, between the songs, with boundless enthusiasm. Over and above that, there is the other fact that the audience at the Barrowland Ballroom was not just locals seeing Dylan for the only, or one of only a few times. I was surrounded by the same people I was surrounded by the night before and saw many, many other regulars throughout the evening and heard their tales afterwards. Instead of the reviewer's contrast between what he perceived as two separate groups of fans, what he had witnessed was a thorough mixture of the two reacting in identical fashion.

---

5 The Herald (Scotland). *Bob Dylan, Glasgow Barrowland 24th June 2004: Bob Be Praised*; Jun 28 '04. This review can be found on the internet at: http://www99.epinions.com/content_3989872772/ However this does not contain the reviewer's name and the article cannot be located in the paper's archives.

As for the press comments on the show itself, they loved it. *The Herald*'s reviewer, quoted above, was otherwise outstanding in capturing his excitement at the night's events and while admitting that:

"Sometime in the 90s his voice finally waved a white flag and collapsed from 30 years worth of touring, wine and weed. Many performers might have thrown in the towel at that point, their primary instrument broken, but not so Dylan."

He still declared that "Bob Dylan's Barrowland show is the greatest concert I've attended" and gave detailed evidence as to why he felt that way.

"This was not just for the performance but the performance *in situ*: "The audience is here so close to Dylan, so near to the flesh of the myth ... As he strolls out to rapturous applause, we see that Bob Dylan is actually a man, a human being of surprisingly short stature, with a deeply lined, wise face, narrowed eyes and a fetching gold cowboy hat. He stands stage right, plays electric keyboards and harmonica, and radiates genius."

The same paper's *Sunday Review* had a blaring headline of "Bob Almighty!" while another review famously declared that "It's like having Picasso paint your living room". A comment that reminded me of seeing him at Hammersmith, close up for the first time, in 1990.

It is good to read such enthusiasm and while it was a fun night out, it has to be pointed out, with all due respect to *The Herald* reviewer, the Barrowland show was one of the best in recent years but not remotely in contention to be "one of his greatest concerts ever". The very phrase does a grave injustice to hundreds of other shows, not to say entire decades. Which brings me to the bit of this book I have been dreading. In the early days of the novel, British writers would address their readers directly, often to point out a plot development or to indicate action 'off-stage' that affected the peregrinations of the main character. Well, dear reader, your author fell off a cliff at this point, and did not enjoy his attendance at any Dylan show until late in 2011.

As Dylan continued through the year (a summer tour co-headlining with Willie Nelson, followed by a US fall college tour - with the last of the year proving, as had become customary, the strongest) and on, ceaselessly criss-crossing the globe throughout the rest of the decade, I plummeted downwards in a spiral of decline that saw me become increasingly estranged from the NET. To make matters worse, the next two Dylan albums, *Modern Times*, notwithstanding that the chorus of "Nettie Moore" breaks my heart, and *Together Through Life* were dreadfully disappointing. I seemed to have tripped at the top of a mountain and was falling in a downward spiral; I fought for handholds, footholds, tufts of grass to hold onto amidst the rocks that were battering me as I fell. I tried to climb back up but something was inexorably pulling me down, until I finally fell into a deep, dark place.

This is where the next chapter opens, as we fast forward to 2009 in my NET story, before returning to look at where Dylan's story went and why I feel compelled to jump five years.

CHAPTER NINETEEN

2005 – 2009:
In which your author becomes lost

Giant Despair—the Dungeon—the Slough of Despond—the Key of Promise

This might be a good time to reread some of the shows where my excitement was at its peak, or to read appendix one, if you have not already done so. I suggest this because I am now going to deal with the period where I fell out of love with the NET, and relationship break-ups are always hard and messy affairs. Accordingly, a reminder of the joy that preceded the following would not go amiss. I am going to jump to a night in 2009 when I walked out of a show after about half an hour and then retrace the steps of how I got there, in an attempt to explain how the guy who burbled incoherently in the presence of Bob in 1993 came to this sorry pass, sixteen years later.

The Roundhouse 2009

The first thing that should be admitted upfront is that I should not have gone, I knew in advance that I would not enjoy it. I was suffering a crisis not only in my 'Dylan life' but also in what I now called 'real life'. That is not a distinction I would have made in previous years, nor would anything have got in the way of a Dylan tour, but things had changed. So, going to the show was my 'fault'.

I am though, as you may have gathered, a bit of a Dylan addict, and addictions are tough to break. I had gone from having no intention of attending a show to getting tickets for two. Firstly the Roundhouse, a small, intimate venue Dylan was scheduled to play straight after a gig at the huge, impersonal Docklands Arena. Secondly, at the much-loved venue the Edinburgh Playhouse, adjacent to where my sister was now living. This latter event ignited my old self and with much cunning, time, effort and expense I organized front row centre seats – centred around what I still think of as 'Larry's old seat' – for self, family and friends. Brother-in-law Alex and the perennial Joe scrambled at my first 'alarm call' and were at the head of the queue when the tickets went on sale. In the end, though, I stayed at home and let the plane leave Stansted with an empty seat.

Before that happened there was the Roundhouse gig in London, on April 26th. The usual rumours for Dylan playing at such a small venue had circulated: he was going to play his most recent album in its entirety, he was going to play an 'Unplugged' style all-acoustic show; *xxxx* (insert any number of fantasy names here) was going to join him onstage/for the encores/for the whole show. None of these happened. This did not disappoint me; on the contrary I have steadfastly declared throughout this book that I dislike the very idea of such things as a Dylan show had always been more than special enough for me. To catch one in a small venue was enough additional magic on its own without the need for any other 'trimmings', especially as those are often extremely distracting. Dylan did what I had always wanted him to do, he played as standard a show in the small venue as he had the night previously in the Docklands Arena.

The difference now, however, was that I had no liking for the standard show. It should be noted that everyone I knew who went to both shows far preferred the one at the Docklands. Dylan's mood, commitment and vocals were felt to be far stronger at the cavernous arena than at the tiny venue. One long-term Dylan fan who began attending shows in the 1960s and had followed faithfully ever since found the Docklands show to be most enjoyable; yet he left the front of the Roundhouse for the bar after the first song, declaring that he knew what was coming and did not want the memory of the night before to be sullied.

I did not hear about this until after the show, which I approached in a state of trepidation, having long grown to dislike the vocal mannerisms, the overall, seemingly unchanging sound night after night, year after year and the odd little keyboards Dylan spent most of the night hiding behind, vamping aimlessly.

To repeat, attending the show was my own responsibility, undertaken in full knowledge of what to expect. Even if I could have written out the set-list of my dreams, I would still not have been overly keen unless all the factors that put me off the shows were eradicated. However, weakness prevailed and go I did. Here is how it felt, reconstructed from e-mails sent that very night.

My build-up to the show itself was entertaining; this was one of those occasions that attracted Dylan fans from around the globe. Accordingly, I once again met up with many touring friends that have appeared in these pages from throughout the years. Bill Pagel, whose NET website has become something akin to an 'official adjunct' to the yearly touring, was across from America and had, as ever, interesting news to share. Even some fans who felt like I did about the previous five years' touring, but who had taken the more obvious step of therefore no longer attending shows, turned up just to socialize. It was like a tour veterans' convention.

The best bit of the gig for me came before it really began. For about 10 minutes before the show started, Dylan was in full view from my vantage point - near the front, to one side . He was standing side-stage, relaxing and stretching his arms out and looking Bob-cool. Though it would have to be said that his body language did not exactly exude comfort, far less happiness.[1]

When he hit the stage it was a thrill to see him so close, but it soon became apparent that he was not in the best of humours. It cannot have helped that it was bakingly hot, something doubtless exacerbated by Dylan being overdressed in yellow cravat and a heavy black jacket of many buckles. His voice started out even rougher than I had feared, and grew worse as he struggled on through a depressing run of songs.

In a way, the half hour or so that I lasted was longer than might have been predicted in the circumstances. I was encouraged to remain that long by people in front of me continually leaving. This meant that after each song I was nearer

1 From the time I was there and from all reports of his onstage demeanour thereafter, this did not change. Dylan had a treat awaiting him, though. After the show, as he was making his way out Dylan was delighted to see Roger Daltrey of the Who; beaming with pleasure Dylan gave him a big hug. Daltrey has been noted attending Dylan concerts in these pages before and Dylan has been known to return the compliment, witnessing for example the Who's show in Vancouver in October 2006.

to the stage, until I got so very close that it seemed too rude to leave after, say, "Tangled Up In Blue". Although I am duty bound to confess that I did want to.

Dylan had opened with a ramshackle 'Leopard-Skin Pill-Box Hat' but that did not phase me. This book has detailed that, over the years, one has come to expect 'rough and ready' opening salvos. So I expected that, but I certainly did not expect it to be the highlight of those songs I witnessed. It may well have been, however, as Dylan then played a sequence of songs that led me deeper into despair, one step after another. I felt like being taken down a flight of stairs to a destination I instinctively felt must be avoided at all costs.

"Don't Think Twice" was followed by a "Tangled Up In Blue" that I felt at the time was an assault on decency. I thought of leaving, but four people in between me and the stage all left during this song and with close to a perfect position I decided to stay, comforting myself that things onstage could not get any worse. I was wrong. "Million Miles" became the excuse for a ten-minute sludge of 'blues-based' (as it always seems to be described, much to the detriment of the Blues) rocky blancmange that pushed me almost beyond endurance.

"Tryin' to Get to Heaven" retained about one per cent of its melody and consequently, horribly mangled though it was, almost shone like a shimmering jewel in this setting and was enough to keep me in attendance, just. Then the unholy racket of 'Tweedle Dee' found me Tweedling my way out and I was homeward bound, not caring if I were to later hear that Dylan had, indeed, played the whole of his new album.

I was not alone in my mood or my actions. To exit the Roundhouse I had to push though a very crowded concourse, packed with people milling about, crashing out, going to the bar or trying to push their way out altogether, like myself.

Mick Gold was later to write to me: "It was memorable, that weekend of the Roundhouse. All the newspapers overflowed with accounts of the cosmic esteem Dylan was held in. Yet I found myself in an Indian restaurant in Camden Town with some men who'd seen Bob more than 200 times in concert, and they found it a challenge to articulate how much disgust they felt over his current live performances. Journalists miss out on the mood on the street once more."

It seems only fair to quote a favourable review to counterbalance my view. The next day I could read Richard Williams in *The Guardian* writing as though he had been at a different concert than I had. I devoutly wish I had been to the same one as him:

"The patience of the faithful, however, was rewarded with the elegance of a low-slung 'Million Miles', the hard-won grace of 'Tryin' to Get to Heaven', the exhausted wisdom of 'Sugar Babe', the tender croon of 'Po' Boy', the road-house shuffle of 'I Don't Believe You' and perhaps the most compelling version of 'Like a Rolling Stone' since Earls Court 1978."[2]

'Elegance and 'grace' were the last words that would have sprung to my mind as I raced away from the theatre. I did not relax until I was at a coffee stand in Kings Cross station; churning emotions began to settle and my body welcomed the cool air after the fetid conditions in the Roundhouse.

What follows is the story of what went wrong between myself and the NET from approximately the middle of 2004 until 2009. A long fall that had seemed to bring my NET story to an end at that moment when I hurried out of the Roundhouse. Like the NET itself, however, my journey is far from over. Back then, though, it felt like it was; what exactly had gone wrong?

The Interregnum: 2005-2009

Before considering my 2009 situation with a cooler head than the man fleeing the Roundhouse with the extreme reactions typical of a jilted lover, I should mention that I did keep attending shows, every year from 2004 leading up to 2009.

Realising, however, that I was no longer enjoying the shows, I did curtail my attendances. Or at least I attempted to, though even this became an unexpected struggle. I found that I could not just stop; I was, after all, still running *Judas!* at the beginning of these years, so was heavily involved with all things Bob. Also, Dylan, bless him, kept visiting Europe. In 2005 he not only toured the UK but ended the year's touring with a five-night residency at Brixton, where he mixed up the set-lists and sprang many a surprise. Primarily, live debuts of both "Million Dollar Bash" and "Waiting For You" on 21st November being joined by the first run-out of the apt "London Calling" to celebrate Mick Jones's

2 Williams, Richard "Bob Dylan at the Roundhouse". *The Guardian*. 28th April 2009

presence in the audience. Other covers in that week included "Rumble", played as a tribute to the recently deceased Link Wray, and a one-off cover of "Blue Monday", immortalised by Fats Domino who had been reported as lost (but was, thankfully, later rescued) when the Katrina tragedy had unfolded in New Orleans three months prior to these shows.

I knew by then that I had fallen out of love with the NET so I decided on 'one show a year' from then onwards. With remarkable, and uncharacteristic, self-control, I managed to achieve this in 2006. In 2007, though, I was again caught up in going to multiple shows. I say 'caught up', but 'dragged in' would be more accurate; this book's photographer, Duncan Hume, offered free accommodation at one show, then *Judas!* publisher Keith Wootton offered door-to-door transport and a ticket for Wembley. Yes, I was back at that arena again despite all I have written. We had a dreadful journey to the show, seventy miles or so taking about four hours, and although we were relieved to make it just before the start our relief quickly turned to bitter disappointment. It further convinced me that I should really take a break, or at least have stuck to my plan of only one a year. After all, I might not like the shows but you have got to go and see Dylan at least once if he's in the country you are living in, surely.

Definitely 'one show per year in person maximum' I vowed, again. After all, with the ever-improving quality of hand-held smartphone devices, videos were now routinely being taken of shows that exceeded most efforts from the intrepid, dedicated filmers of the NET's earlier years, when capturing such events for posterity was fraught with difficulties. There really was no need to break my vow; I would go once a year to see Himself in person, and thereby not overstrain my relationship with a touring event towards which I no longer felt affinity.

The recommitment to this idea lasted all the way to 2009, when I was unable to resist arranging Roundhouse and Edinburgh Playhouse tickets. But in addition to the knowledge that I was ignoring my own counsel in going at all, familiar old demons that had nothing to do with Dylan were stalking me. Pressure was building from all sides and I just really did not want to be there anymore. This simple truth, something I had known but hitherto refused to fully admit even to myself, had finally sunk in and so I left the hall and, for all I knew at that moment, live music behind.

You may recall that after the Fleadh in 1993 I tried to convince a manager from my company of the time, who had walked out on her one and only Dylan show, that the NET was a two-way street: "The audience has to put in a bit of work to contribute to the occasion...." and she had replied that this was more than she was prepared to do, and saw no sign from the stage that there was anything worth striving for, nor any effort coming from there to contribute towards an enjoyable event.

I think I would have killed myself had I known back then that one day I would feel exactly as she had that day, and would leave a show just as totally disillusioned. Indeed, it was far worse in my case as I had the added misery of being haunted by the inescapable feeling of being a traitor.

I apologise to those who have favourite shows and memories from these years and want to read about them here. On the other hand, I know from experience that you are better off this way. I have received feedback on my reviews of these shows from the 'offended faithful' and they informed me that, to put it mildly, they 'did not enjoy' the experience.

So, I still attended to shows and listened to many other one-off performances as devotees bombarded me with what they saw as sure-fire songs to bring me back into the fold. None did, however, and I do not want to give a five-year litany of complaints and negativity. It would serve no purpose. On the other hand, for this to be the full story of my NET I do have to give an overview and insight into why it stopped working for me. As many thousands still enjoy the experience, we can also finally investigate what causes such violently opposed reactions to Dylan shows from among the fan fraternity. In writing this chapter I finally came to understand what had happened with the reports I received from New Orleans back in 2003.

I realize that those who love this period will find yourself violently disagreeing with my comments; I do try to include repeated caveats that, while many agree with me, others feel differently. I can only answer the question of 'how did it feel' during this period for me, and attempt to pinpoint why I fell out of love with the NET. Much of the ground has already been covered. The many concerns I have raised in the preceding chapters came to dominate the shows for me, progressing from merely distracting me from my enjoyment to obliterating it altogether.

Authenticity: *'that note of something big manifested'*

To get to the bottom of why this happened, we need to step back and take a wider view of why live shows mean so much, what it is that the audience 'gets' from the performance on stage. Before concentrating on the Dylan shows of these years, I will broaden the canvas and look at quotes from or about other performers in the fields of rock, folk and singer-songwriting with regard to the feeling of authenticity in live performance. It would not be unreasonable to claim that Dylan has no peers, but in a spirit of generosity I think most would allow that the names of Bruce Springsteen, Leonard Cohen and Joni Mitchell are among the most worthy of being so considered.

I want to highlight the importance of performances conveying a feeling of authenticity, however crafted or contrived the performances may be in reality. This brings me to the core of what I respond to when listening to Dylan and why I stopped responding during this period. It is a complex matter and I need to take it step by step, beginning from a broad perspective before narrowing it down to the Dylan shows of this period; not because I wish devotees to agree with my 'naysaying', but because I want them to be clear as to my reasons for becoming estranged, and indeed for the return of my enjoyment of the shows in later years.

Here is a very relevant quote from a book on Bruce Springsteen. It involves two staged physical actions that were meant to convey a message to the audience. NET followers will immediately connect this with the aforementioned 'Formation', Dylan's enigmatic staged physical actions when he and the band stood impassive in the face of closing applause. This lasted throughout the period in question and was, as it happens, for me one of the most authentic expressions from the stage during it. However, particular relevance aside, the general points and the conclusion are central to my concerns in this chapter:

"... the tour's most provocative moment came from a less expected source. During the final encore of most shows during that foray, Springsteen, alone on guitar, would start up 'If I Should Fall Behind', a relatively obscure but compelling cut from *Lucky Town* ... After the first verse, Springsteen would step away from the microphone and, one by one, other members of the band would sing verses. At the end, they all sang together. It was a bit stagey and contrived, but moving nonetheless: It was, after all, a song about sticking together ... After guitarist Steve Van Zandt sang his verse, fellow six-stringer Lofgren would step up. Every night, as he stepped toward the microphone, Lofgren would rest his arm on Van Zandt's shoulder, as if to comfort him. Little could be more show-bizzy, full of more contrived emotion, but even for those who knew it was coming, it was one of the most affecting moments in a three-hour performance that was all about community, consolation, and camaraderie. It was fake, everyone knew it was fake, yet it felt real, night after night.

"That's a difficult achievement. Even the E Street Band can't attain it every time they try. Most nights on the Rising tour, the second and final encore would start with 'My City of Ruins'. Springsteen would start the song solo on piano and after the rest of the band joined in, he would step away from the stool and return the piano to rightful owner Roy Bittan. While the band vamped, Springsteen would walk to his centerstage spot, not planting himself there until after he stopped for a moment with each player, standing beside him or her. The last stop was by Clemons's side, and they would sway a bit together, backs to the crowd, and then Springsteen would return to singing the song. I have no idea what Springsteen said to the band members as he worked his way across the stage. He may have complimented them, he may have told them how pleased he was to be playing with them, or he may have said nothing of emotional import. But let's assume he did speak to them about things that matter. It didn't come off that way. It felt like an act. But, as I just asked us to assume, it might not have been an act, but instead something quite real that developed organically. Still, in the end, it didn't matter whether it was real or spontaneous because it didn't feel real or spontaneous. The choreography in 'If I Should Fall Behind' looked fake but felt real; the choreography in 'My City of Ruins' may well have been as real as anything in life but looked fake."[3]

There is much here that has relevance to this book, trying to make something "fake" feel "real, night after night" and it being so difficult that not attaining it "every time they try" is only to be expected. I should note that I would prefer the word 'staged' to 'fake'. This is something we will return to. Even more pertinent is the conclusion: "In the end, it didn't matter whether it was real or spontaneous because it didn't feel real or spontaneous." This will be a key point in my discussion of the NET in these years, and the resultant 'split' amongst Dylan fans in their responses to it.

---

3 Jimmy Guterman *Runaway American Dream* ©The Vineyard group Inc. 2005

To clear up one point first, response to a performance is not necessarily to do with the clarity of the lyrics as heard. This was often decidedly lacking in this period but then that was not exactly anything new. And, after all, songs sung in a language one does not know a word of can be incredibly moving and strike one as a totally authentic expression of emotion. As Icelandic folk-singer Ólöf Arnalds put it in *Mojo* (October 2010): "I believe that whether or not people understand the words, a singer can get a message through simply by being present in the meaning of the lyrics."

For this listener, Dylan felt fully present before certain vocal mannerisms conspired to occlude this presence. This perceived 'lack of artistic/personal presence' leads us deeper than ever into the land of subjectivity, and although what I felt was shared by many (let's refer to these as 'naysayers'), it was not true for others who were still happily on board the good ship NET (the 'devotees'). For those for whom Dylan still felt 'present', these were top-notch shows and they reacted to the naysayers' disaffection with virulent scorn.

A scenario of mutual incomprehension quickly developed. Few things create such rabid reactions as apostates, and the situation was further exacerbated because for those who 'lost their faith' the process was a gradual one. Naysayers rarely agree on the exact point the NET turned sour for them; there may have been a general feeling of estrangement, but as everyone's experience of each year or leg is so varied, as there are so many shows some attended and some did not, our 'last show I really enjoyed' was unlikely, almost to the point of impossibility, to be an identical one. One could and did enjoy, as I have written about above, portions, albeit ever-diminishing, of shows even in 'down' periods; it is not as though we are talking about a situation where a switch was suddenly turned off. The division among fans was therefore continually highlighted as 'devotees' turned apostate in dribs and drabs, suddenly finding themselves estranged, reviled and unable to communicate their point of view to the remaining true believers, who interpreted their actions and words as heresy.

Two long-term lovers of Dylan live shows, both of whom have appeared in my story already, demonstrate this ongoing division clearly in the following excerpts from an e-mail exchange I was party to in 2005:

Nick Hawthorne (NH): "I basically think that Dylan can no longer sing, or even transmit much of any emotion into his vocal at all."

Duncan Hume (DH): *"You've obviously NOT heard or* listened *to many of the recent shows then."*

(NH): "Not true. What you hear and what I hear are clearly different to each of us. ... The sound of Dylan's voice has been with me and will be with me until I pack in and die. What I hear from Dylan now, and have heard for a while, is a voice so ugly and removed from that great voice that I can't stand to hear it. And not just by comparison. I can cope with change, with something different. It is not all nostalgia with me. Taken on its own, in isolation, this current voice is horrific to me."

(DH): *"You have really not heard many of the recent shows have you?"*

(NH): "I have heard them and I am telling you what I have heard. You disagree. We just disagree. "

(NH): "Every song has been arranged to sound like the other songs. The rockers all sound alike and create a mash of sound with Dylan yelling above it."

(DH): *"Nonsense. Utter nonsense. Have you heard 'Til I Fell In Love With You? How is that that the same as Stuck Inside of Mobile? How is Highway 61 like Honest With Me?"*

(NH): "The slower songs bring awful vocals from Dylan and tedious playing from the band ... [I repeat] the rockers all sound alike and create a mash of sound with Dylan yelling above it."

(DH): *"NEC Hattie Carroll, Visions of Johanna, awful vocals? Afraid not Nick. Quite the opposite in fact. "*

(NH): "The shows on this tour have had the same format, sound and group of songs that we saw in summer 2004, and autumn 2003 for that matter. Not much has changed."

(DH): *"Goodness, Bob Dylan is still Bob Dylan and the nerve; he still sings the same songs and for the most part sounds the same and not like someone else. What do you want, Caruso? Bob on banjo? What do you expect? That's the problem probably. You expect something more of Bob Dylan, but Nick, I don't think you know what it is. "*

(NH): "That is not the problem at all, Duncan. Your loyalty to Bob is admirable and I know you are genuine in what you say. So am I. His show has been the same for years. That is not Bob just being Bob. I don't want him to be anyone else. I just would like him to do something that interests and excites me. Is that selfish? Nope. It struck me that the people at the SECC this year saw the same show that they saw the year before and the year before that etc. And it isn't a very good show. I expect nothing from Bob."

And so they went on, never resolving their differences, always circling back to examples where one heard one thing and the other did not. Which is not to say that Nick disliked everything and Duncan liked everything, far from it, but in general one felt the presence of the 'authentic Dylan live experience' most of the time and the other simply could not apprehend how.

This divide kept widening until we got to the stage where in the pages of the same issue of *Isis* magazine in 2009 Toby Richards Carpenter referred to a recent show as one of "the best ever" and Henry Porter declared it one of "the worst ever". For those young enough to have only followed Dylan in the new millennium the whole thing was totally baffling. This is the only Dylan they know. If they do not like it, they only go to one show and if they do like it, they go to more. The angst, anguish and bitter fall-outs of longer-term Dylan fans must seem extreme and inexplicable to them. Yet, it is a well known truism that people react sourly when they lose the love for something that was so dear to them. Samuel Taylor Coleridge, writing all those years ago, noted, astutely in his *Letters* (Volume 1, page 588): "'Life were so flat a thing without Enthusiasm – that if for a moment it leave me, I have a sort of stomach-sensation attach to all my Thoughts, like those which succeed to the pleasurable operation of a dose of Opium.'

This "stomach-sensation" is also totally understandable when you remember that at stake was something of the utmost importance. Leonard Cohen deepens and expands upon Ólöf Arnalds's earlier observation:

"I guess that's some kind of basic view I hold about the thing, that it doesn't really matter what the singer is speaking of, it doesn't really matter what the song is. There's something I listen for in a singer's voice and that's some kind of truth. It may even be truth of deception, it may even be the truth of the scam, the truth of the hustle in the singer's own presentation, but something is coming across that is true, and if that isn't there the song dies. And the singer deserves to die too, and will, in time, die. So the thing that I listen for is that note of something big manifested that is beyond the singer's control."[4]

It is becoming clear that everyone I am quoting is using words in a heightened manner that differs from their everyday meaning. 'Fake' and 'scam' and 'hustle' are all referring to performance art and indicating that the truth it reveals is a kind of 'über sincerity': the artifice of performing art touching some universal truth.

There are obvious correspondences with actors here, both in the film star sense equating with the pop star and, more revealingly, the actor on live stage performing a character night after night in almost (but never quite, human nature being what it is) the same manner. Correspondences certainly, but it is not analogous. The singer on stage is mainly singing his songs, his creations, the actor is acting out someone else's. Even in covers of others' songs Dylan usually, as I trust I have amply demonstrated, inhabits those vehicles with his own unique personality, via what Barthes termed "the grain of his voice".

It is the person on stage who is singing to you, in the audience, directly. This is, after all, why you go. The actor is playing at someone else, the character talking to you, indirectly transmitting someone else's words via the mask of another.

Dylan, as you would expect, comprehends this better than anyone, and he makes a very pertinent observation in a 2009 interview 'with' Bill Flanagan. I put the word 'with' in quotation marks as well-placed sources are adamant that Dylan set and answered his own questions in this interview. I have no way of fully confirming this, but it certainly reads that way. Similarly to most of his interviews since that question misquoting "Visions of Johanna" in Rome 2001, this comes across as though Dylan has either posed the questions or at the very least has vetted and arranged them to allow him say exactly what he wants to, when and how he prefers. Artifice, again, and again leading to a greater honesty: if Dylan pronounces on a subject in these interviews, one can be certain it is something he really wanted to get off his chest rather than just an off-hand response to a question he has no interest in. Here we find him carefully distancing himself from live performance as acting and stressing the personal sincerity of the singer in contrast to the character acting of thespians:

---

4 Tim Footman: Leonard Cohen *Hallelujah – A New Biography* Chrome Dreams, 2009

Bill Flanagan: The character in the song ("Dream Of You") reminds me a lot of the guy who is in the song "Across The Borderline".

Bob Dylan: *I know what you're saying, but it's not a character like in a book or a movie. He's not a bus driver. He doesn't drive a forklift. He's not a serial killer. It's me who's singing that, plain and simple. We shouldn't confuse singers and performers with actors. Actors will say, "My character this, and my character that." Like beating a dead horse. Who cares about the character? Just get up and act. You don't have to explain it to me.*

Bill Flanagan: Well can't a singer act out a song?

Bob Dylan: *Yeah sure, a lot of them do. But the more you act the further you get away from the truth. And a lot of those singers lose who they are after a while. You sing, "I'm a lineman for the county," enough times and you start to scamper up poles.*[5]

One of the things that was always so admirable about Dylan's singing was the feeling of authenticity. You simply had to 'think he thinks he's right'; Dylan was never one to 'lose who he was' but he could sure make you believe he really had started to "scamper up poles". It was ever thus; the great Sam Cooke, on hearing Dylan's early 'protest' songs, declared that the future of singing was not in how beautiful one sounded but how sincere. Captivated by Dylan singing "Blowin' In the Wind", but understandably a little miffed that it was white voices singing out against racism, Cooke used "The Times They Are A-Changin'" as a starting point for his own tremendous outburst "A Change is Gonna Come". A song that Dylan, appropriately enough, covered at the Apollo Theater Foundation 70th Anniversary Benefit Celebration on March 28, 2004.

Dylan gigs were the antithesis of Diana Ross fashion shows, not some event choreographed over note-for-note replication of the songs as on disc (literally or mimetically). Of course, it was not really authentic in a literal, on-the-surface sense; yes we knew that it was a *show*, but it never felt that way. Although there was artifice, the artistic sincerity seemed overwhelming.

One thinks of Suze Rotolo describing the young Dylan getting ready for his shows and trying to deliberately dress as though he had just been blown in from

5 'Bill Flanagan interviews Bob Dylan' 2009

the dust bowls with no time to dress properly. When he hit the stage everyone believed in the pretence, it was convincing, just as, only a few years later, he was totally convincing as the coolest, dandiest rock star on the planet. This was to continue through his incarnations as a country singer, a fire and brimstone preacher and so forth.

You knew, in the years before the NET, even when it felt totally special that he was playing the same show somewhere else the night after and it had been the identical set-list the night before, too, and that everything had been well rehearsed. Nonetheless the magic of feeling direct communication from the singer on-stage, of the song alive in this particular version in these time-stopping moments was palpable and real.

To pick a shining exemplar from my own concert-attending history, each of the performances of "Tangled Up In Blue" that I witnessed at Earls Court in 1978 seemed the most transcendent moments of artist connecting with fan to deliver his personal vision I had ever experienced. I mean by this that I had that same sensation of a 'peak' on each of the nights I attended. Sometime later I would hear a version from a Paris show the following month that communicated even more intensely and directly, even via tape, than those I had been in attendance for in the UK. Intellectually, though, even before hearing that, I knew not every night at Earls Court could be my 'best ever'; that would have made no logical sense even though that is most certainly the way I experienced them.

Dylan's style of transmitting his visions changed with the NET. There was an inevitable loss of consistency of performance, but this was felt to be a fair trade for increased spontaneity and, consequently, a different form of authenticity. We were dispensing with much of the artifice to get closer, we felt, to the truth, unvarnished though that be. This is a large part of what this book has been about. However, in this period I lost that feeling entirely, this 'trade-off' no longer worked for me. I felt that Dublin and Leicester 1966, for example, for all their identical set-lists had far more variety of performance than any two shows from forty years later, were you to select two gigs where over half the set-list had been altered from night to night.

Previously, Dylan had always had the ability to make me believe in him totally, to feel he was 'present in the meaning of the lyrics', which he always sang with intelligence, care and empathy. If you refer back to the 1988 chapter and see how 'authentic' Dylan's singing from a downtrodden female perspective appeared to be in "Wagoner's Lad" (from the Radio City Music Hall show near the close of that chapter), you will comprehend exactly what Leonard Cohen means and why the "truth of the deception" leads to a Greater Truth. As Joni Mitchell remarked, in her March 1997 Grammy Interview, on 'sincerity' in songs: "Well, I do hear it in Bob, absolutely, Bob can connect up to his stuff really sincerely. In that way he's a great singer. And then he puts his jive in where it belongs. Bob's a great singer."

The Dylan I heard in the years 2005-2009 did not come close to communicating with me in this manner; he no longer was "putting in his jive where it belongs". Like Leonard Cohen, "(t)here's something I listen for in a singer's voice and that's some kind of truth." For the first time in my life I had stopped hearing it when I went to see Dylan or listened to the recordings of the shows. The questions for me now were, why had I stopped hearing what I had heard for some thirty years, and why did others still hear it?

I used to think that all my problems with the shows stemmed from the decline in Dylan's vocal range; however, as I was to enjoy shows as well as albums in future years, it was clearly something in how he was compensating for this decline that left me feeling estranged at the time.

Even mentioning Dylan's reduced vocal abilities raises hackles amongst many fans but it is something we can all agree is a fact, surely, before making variable value judgements on the effect this has had on his shows for most of the 21st century. Naturally there are also varied opinions as to when, or even if, this became a big enough problem to interfere with his ability to perform well or satisfactorily. After all, an argument could be made that the last time a Dylan performance showcased his full vocal range in all its near operatic glory was way back in 1981. This would then cast the entire NET as an exercise in performing within a comparatively restricted vocal range. There are degrees, however, many of them, between 'less than full range' and 'almost no range whatsoever'.

In addition, I acknowledge that I am, of necessity, generalizing, and that some argue that the shows in the period under scrutiny neither lack authenticity nor unduly suffer from Dylan's restricted voice. Which leads me to stress, once again, this chapter deals with my difficulties with the tour at this time, I know while many had the same struggle to find anything to enjoy that I did, many others did not. This is the way of things in such a subjective field. What is objectively traceable are the strategies, the vocal tricks, that Dylan employed and which unquestionably led to a drastically altered NET experience, whether one found that experience joyous or not.

I do not wish to enumerate and examine these merely to criticize in a negative sense, although for me as they were introduced over the years they had a seriously deleterious impact on how I valued the shows. It seems an unavoidable conclusion that Dylan employed these devices in an effort to partially compensate for his inability to express the emotions he wished to evoke in the way he once could, so seemingly effortlessly, when his voice was stronger and his range greater.

To recap these infelicitous techniques, the much discussed 'upsinging' trend was the starting point and was followed by: an odd mix of garbling and growling (sometimes referred to as the 'Wolfman' voice)'; the habit of repeating last or other crucial lines or half-lines; a weird, high-pitched 'singing' to indicate extreme emotion; and the inclusion of staccato, tick-tock passages that seem beyond rational or emotional comprehension.

For many of us the feeling we are witnessing a Dylan show where "something is coming across that is true" is impossible with any of the above too much in evidence, far less a combination, or heaven help us, all of them. It may be possible that a show, if unhindered by some of the other factors we will look at later (Dylan hiding at the edge of the stage behind a plinkety-plonkety keyboard springs to mind as an example), could still be engaging if you felt enough of what Leonard Cohen refers to as the artist's "presence".

'Upsinging' has been covered in detail already and you will by now have surely come to your own conclusions. I will never complain about Dylan trying something new, especially if it is because his vocal cords can no longer cope with the demands of the songs as originally envisaged. The problem here was that this seemed to become, for a period, the default ending of any and every line. This gave the impression that the singer neither cared for nor differentiated one song from another. As there also seemed to be at most three set musical default styles for early folk, all-out crowd-pleasing rockers and the dominating sound – a kind of chugging, soft-blues shuffle mélange – song blended into song and show merged with show in a way that was the polar opposite of how the NET started.

'The wolfman', a growling-garbling sound that seemed to emit from deep inside a choked chest, inevitably brings the immortal Howlin' Wolf to mind. One would have assumed that Dylan playing his late live shows like an old bluesman would sound transcendent. Indeed, at the time of *World Gone Wrong* that is exactly what many people, this author included, were crying out for. You would expect him to be carrying himself in this century, as he says on the back of *Freewheelin'*, like the older performers his youthful self so admired:

"I can sing it sometimes, but I ain't that good yet. I don't carry myself yet the way that Big Joe Williams, Woody Guthrie, Leadbelly and Lightnin' Hopkins have carried themselves. I hope to be able to someday, but they're older people."

Yet it did not sound in the latter half of the new century's opening decade as though he had taken this path at all. I had previously declared, when the NET was younger and I was so impressed with Dylan's ability to compensate for an already diminished vocal power and subtlety, that I would happily go to a show where he merely recited the words, so dazzling and elastic was his control of phrasing. We are often warned to be careful what we wish for, and in the second half of the twenty-first century's opening decade I found myself squirming with embarrassment when listening to Dylan recite words and lines that once pierced my soul.

The reality was not at all what I had anticipated with such relish. Instead of the envisaged subtle and dramatic phrasing communicating through his boundlessly effective internal assonance and half-hidden rhyming schemes, we were faced with a recitation that involved throat clearing to cover up forgotten words and lines, a long growl to indicate that 'there used to be something I wanted to say here but now this noise will suffice'. It seemed to indicate that he either did not remember or did not care what the words had been or had once expressed. The occasional use of this to cover up memory loss or because he felt the urge to 'reinvent' the song onstage but had no new words to hand, would be more than forgivable. Unfortunately, as with the upsinging, it soon developed into a kind of indiscriminate shorthand of a technique just to get through another song on another night. There is no point in recitation when the audience cannot hear what is supposedly being recited; when trickery replaces any attempt at communication, you lose faith no matter how you hard you try to cling on to it.

This brings us to the heart of the split in the Dylan audience at that time: some apprehended that the seemingly authentic had been replaced by the obviously fake, while others still felt the magic. In the previously quoted words of Ólöf Arnalds, they still felt Dylan's *presence* where we mourned his *absence*: "Whether or not people understand the words, a singer can get a message through simply by being present in the meaning of the lyrics."

The two 'vocal tricks' already discussed were, as mentioned, followed by others as the years progressed. Dylan developed an extremely annoying habit of repeating lines to indicate their importance or that a song had ended; a cheap device which he had had no need to stoop to in the past. When Dylan first introduced the trick of repeating the last line in a vain attempt to achieve dramatic effect, it was hammy in the extreme; but also it was almost endearing to hear him be so gauche, and it highlighted how he never used such tawdry trickery before. However, when it continued and spread to chorus and other important lines that he had once sung with such exquisite, time-defying phrasing, it became clear that Dylan actually meant you to accept it as signifying passion. A deep uneasiness over this technique grew in me and this soon turned to queasiness as he repeated the repetitive effect song after song, year after year.

By the time we got to 2009, things had lurched alarmingly further away from the heady days when his performing art communicated that '*über* sincerity' that Leonard Cohen and Joni Mitchell talked about. Songs were now punctured by odd staccato passages and/or an even stranger 'tick-tock' replacement of the previous melody line.

As the point of the NET always seemed to be for Dylan to experiment with his songs, to find new ways of expressing them or to find new things in them, I do not complain simply because I find no enjoyment in how he chooses to experiment at a certain time. I can only report that I was one of a huge swathe of those who had taken everything the first fifteen years of the NET had given us, things we had liked as well as things we had not, who found themselves left with nothing to appreciate in the shows because we no longer felt the artist was expressing anything real to us. These experiments, if that is what they were, became ossified into sets that seemed more or less interchangeable over a period of years far less months; the very opposite of the radical and daring on-stage experimentation that had formerly made the NET such a roller-coaster of an ever-changing experience.

The seemingly endless years of Dylan tinkling keyboards at the side of the stage is an exemplar of this. I am not fixated on Dylan having to play guitar, nor averse to him playing any other instrument on stage. On the contrary, earlier in this book I was crying out for Dylan to play piano. I do care, however, about how he plays whatever instrument he is employing. Dylan has often thrilled me when at the piano both in the studio and live. The extraordinary performances of "Ballad Of A Thin Man" from 1966 are surely amongst the most exciting things he has ever done. I originally thought the move to keyboards an interesting, innovative and potentially inspiring one in the context of the Never Ending Tour. Dylan had not been adding much to the sound via his guitar playing, whether through physical inability or conscious choice, for a number of years. I just do not care for what he did on the keyboards at any of the shows I attended or listened to from the period in question. I am delighted others did and envious of them come to that, I would much rather be writing that I loved what he did than that I did not. I was not alone in my disgruntlement, the instrument in question was known to some fans as the IOT, short for 'Instrument Of Torture'.

On a side note, but a fairly important one regarding the live experience, I do prefer to see him when I attend a concert. I concede that if he wants to play a show with his back to large portions of the audience that is his choice and right. At the same time, I surely cannot be alone in preferring to see the person I had travelled far and paid to witness. I can hear him whenever I want to, after all. When people talk about attending gigs they discuss who they are going 'to see'.

The general press reaction to Dylan in 2009, I should point out, bore no relation to my views. Indeed, nearly every article I read perfectly described the Dylan of 1989, while most of the press reviews of 1989 shows could stand very well for how I felt about the shows twenty years later.

So we return, as we always do, to the interchange between performer and audience member. When you feel this as real, you forgive everything else. You ignore the childish keyboard playing, you put aside his back being all that many in the audience ever see, you overlook that money is being charged for people to get front row access ahead of those who have queued overnight, and all the other depressing and money-grabbing things that happen both around the tour and outside of it. Regarding that last point, there have been too many depressing developments in the aggressive merchandising of all manner of things connected to Bob to go into here, but one example was so shocking in its naked greed and exploitation that it can stand for all the relentless pushing of the 'Dylan brand'.

In 2008 *The Bootleg Series Vol. 8 – Tell Tale Signs: Rare and Unreleased 1989-2006* was released. The standard 2cd version retailed at $18.99, while the deluxe version with one extra CD was a staggering $129.99. This price was all the more extortionate considering that it was for a Dylan item consisting almost entirely of digital music (there was also the 'bonus' of what Michal Gray called "an almost insultingly redundant booklet of photos of singles covers"[6]), given Dylan's recent remarks that such things are worthless and it was right they were available for free because that accurately reflected the actual value of digital music.

You may say that this has nothing to do with the NET, but it affected the ambience around the shows. It was not exactly a stretch to see them as events taking place in temples of greed where everything was overpriced and 'customers' were encouraged to legally bribe their way into queue-jumping.

Others shared my perceptions and suffered the same agonies. We were struggling through a very modern *Slough of Despond*, and the uncertainty that a consistently unconvincing live Dylan brought to our lives was bewildering and disorientating. Here is rock critic Peter Doggett suffering a similar experience at this time, and how it spread to encompass all things related to Dylan:

"Years ago, my friend Mark Paytress wrote a biography of Marc Bolan, and in his initial draft, he made what seemed to me reprehensible claims about Bolan's superiority over Dylan. Nonsense, I replied, scribbling across his manuscript. The gist of my argument was that whereas Bolan represented artifice – a conscious shifting of personality and style in a desperate bid for commercial acceptance, from the mock-Donovan of 1965 to the glittery teen idol of 1971 – Dylan's business was authenticity, rooted in the soul and in the unambiguous honesty of America's folk traditions, black and white. I bullied him into softening his tone in the final draft. But *Modern Times*, *Together Through Life* and *Chronicles* made me think that I owe Paytress an apology. I still don't rate Bolan as any kind of artist (though he was a magnificent opportunist, and a halfway decent pop star

6 Michael Gray *Bob Dylan Encyclopedia blog* «Tell Tale Signs Pt. 3, Money Doesn›t Talk...». Bob Dylan Encyclopedia blog. August 14th 2008.

for about 12 months). But I don't think that Dylan is a proud beacon of authenticity any more, either. Maybe he never was ...

"The next time I heard him, I didn't think so, and I don't to this day. But remember that the first Dylan we heard – the archetype of the man we've stalked ever since – introduced himself as an orphan, a teenage rambler, a recidivist hobo with rambling', gamblin' spirit in his blood. That wasn't true, but we wanted to believe it, the same way as we wanted him to be Woody Guthrie and Robert Johnson, Allen Ginsberg and Chuck Berry, Elvis Presley and Jack London, Scott Fitzgerald and Little Richard, only with a voice without restraint and the eye that could pierce the soul. It's that Dylan I hear, still, in my head and on my stereo. But I need to be aware that it's an invention, a marvellous cultural creation, which touches me in a way Marc Bolan never could but comes from the same school of magic known as Art. As distinct from Life ...

"The problem with certainty is that once it starts to ebb away, it's difficult to stem the tide. If you believe that the auteur of *Modern Times* is faking it, the sense of doubt seeps backwards through Dylan's career..."[7]

I know that dread feeling so well; in the case of live performances the same effect is even stronger and much more pervasive. You find a feeling of disillusionment rippling back through the last three decades, casting deficiencies hitherto tolerated into an unforgivingly stark light. I am conscious that this has much to do with our projecting onto Dylan and reacting too extremely in all situations; even so, acceptance and balance seemed impossible to achieve. I was adrift on a sea of negativity, trying to salvage what I could of previous certainties. I can barely express to you how depressing this was. If only someone had been able to time-travel back from November 2011 and tell me that I had really enjoyed a show or played me a tape from Spring 2013.

Back in 2009, other help was at hand, however, for both Mr Doggett and me. It came from a most unexpected source. Earlier in the year I had heard, with proverbial jaw-dropping incredulity, that Dylan had recorded a *bona fide* traditional Christmas album. I was sworn to unbreakable secrecy on the matter and impatiently awaited for the news to leak so I could discuss this astonishing development. Then the 'preview snippets' were released and sounded so appallingly

---

7 "Sweet and Sour Turkey" Peter Doggett *ISIS* Issue 147, November 2009

crass and disingenuous that I plummeted to my lowest stage of despair. I was at rock-bottom, from here the only way was up. The last thing I would have anticipated, though, was that it would be the very album these horrendous previews came from that would lift my Dylan life back to a state of grace.

As I listened to the Christmas album for the first time, I found myself, much to my surprise, rather enjoying it. Where the snippets had sounded horrendous, the effect of the thing itself was rather endearing, and that was on the first listen. As early as the second or third playing of the album in its entirety, I already found that songs and phrases were vying for my attention. In succeeding plays I realized that fully flowering pleasure of a new Dylan album unfolding layer by layer, peeling back to reveal itself in the combination effect of track after track. Far from sounding artificial it could not have came across as more sincere. Dylan is totally loyal to his material; he invests everything he can muster into it with clear-sighted honesty and can be heard enjoying the well-earned fruits of his labours.

Peter Doggett was similarly lifted from despair and doubt: "It's the work of a man who, for once in his life, is prepared to let down his defences and be real – in the confident assumption that his motives will be scrutinised and interpreted with such sand-stirring energy that his path across the desert will be obscured, just the way he always likes it to be."[8]

It was my own Christmas miracle, I felt that Dylan was back in my life with that presence, that ability to convince, transcend and transport. It brought to mind a Christmas episode of the TV series *M*A*S*H*. A rather extravagant comparison, I acknowledge, but it sums up how the album made me feel. In that programme, the character Charles Winchester had lost his way, he was bereft of hope marooned in Korea, totally cut off from his previous life. As a result, Father Mulcahy engineered it so that Charles's parents sent something from his past, something that would anchor Charles and bring him back to himself. When he unwrapped this surprise Xmas gift, his old toboggan cap, Charles declared himself 'saved', as though a light had been handed down to him in the darkness.

8 *Ibid.*

I felt something similar that Christmas. For most of my adult life I had staunchly defended Dylan against the naysayers. Then, for seven years or so, while everything he did was acclaimed as genius I could only see sloppiness and pretension. I was seen to have changed sides, I was lost and it seemed I had suffered an irrevocable breakdown in my relationship with Dylan and his music. This daft, yet precious, Christmas album led me back from estrangement. I had thought that 'I'd been down to the bottom with a bad man', but now 'I was back where I belonged'.

CHAPTER TWENTY

2010 – 2011:
In which your author is mysteriously saved

River of Life—Giant Despair killed—the Delectable Mountains—the Enchanted Ground

It will be clear from my comments when he was previously in the band that I was delighted when Charlie Sexton rejoined it in the autumn of 2009. This was the first step in a rejuvenation and transformation of my NET experience.

Despite various signs of encouragement from audio and video sources, I was not to see Dylan in 2010. I was resistant to his only UK appearance as that was a festival in a field and my days for those types of events were by now firmly in the past. While I agree that 'you can repeat the past, of course you can', I was not quite ready to go that far. This was in no small measure due to the coverage you get in these days of internet superhighways. In the pre-'everything is recorded and information overload' days I would have gone to see him somewhere. This was the first year I had not since 1988, but I was still listening.

Dylan was as busy as ever in 2010 and in 2011, the year he turned 70. Before beginning 2010's touring with his first visit to Japan since 2002, he performed "The Times They Are A-Changin'" at 'Performance at the White House: A Celebration of Music From the Civil Rights Movement' on February 11th.

President Barack Obama introduced Dylan by using the 'never ending tour' term Dylan so dislikes: 'The man who was good enough to take time off from his never-ending tour, Mr Bob Dylan'.

As 2010 and 2011 unfolded I followed developments with very contradictory feelings. Often 'The Voice' and the band sounded better, then, just when my optimism was rising, a truly horrific version of one classic or another would send me scuttling back towards depression. This was to occur throughout 2010, but David Bristow, who was still attending many shows, told me that audio alone was no longer a guide to what was happening; the show was now as much a visual performance as an auditory one. I dismissed his claims out of hand, the idea that the greatest vocal artist I have ever heard needed to be seen to be appreciated seemed too ridiculous to contemplate.

April 2011 saw Dylan's first ever shows in Taiwan, Vietnam and mainland China, followed by shows in Australia and New Zealand. The Chinese dates produced the kind of media storm that we have become all too wearily familiar with. Journalists with no knowledge of their subject and too lazy to even make a few mouse clicks, spreading lies and distortions about things that never happened and a 'Bob Dylan' who, if he ever existed at all, was a passing character role in a brief 1960s cameo appearance.

Maureen Dowd used the *New York Times* as a platform to condemn Dylan for bowing to pressure and allowing his set-list to be censored by the Chinese authorities. The lack of "Blowin' in the Wind" and "The Times They Are A-Changin'" seemed to particularly invoke her ire. It would have taken her less than a minute to ascertain that in the previous year's touring the former had been played at approximately ten percent of the shows and the latter not at all. Dowd clearly thought this was 1963 not 2011, and an alternate 1963 at that as back then, in the real world she seems unacquainted with, Dylan's anthems were viewed by mainstream American opinion as un-American and pro-Communist. More risibly yet, the absence of "Hurricane" was also condemned, yes, a song only ever performed in 1975-6. It was no laughing matter though as paper after paper regurgitated this nonsense. Dylan bowing to censorship in China became a hot debating topic as though it had actually happened. Then the same kind of rubbish was spewed forth again when he reached Vietnam.

Dylan was rattled enough to take the unprecedented and very un-cool, un-Dylan like step of issuing a rebuttal from his own 'propaganda organ', www.

bobdylan.com. It was striking to find Dylan still, after all these years, trying to throw off his 1960's mantle or, to be more accurate, one of his 1960's mantles:

TO MY FANS AND FOLLOWERS

Allow me to clarify a couple of things about this so-called China controversy which has been going on for over a year. First of all, we were never denied permission to play in China. This was all drummed up by a Chinese promoter who was trying to get me to come there after playing Japan and Korea. My guess is that the guy printed up tickets and made promises to certain groups without any agreements being made. We had no intention of playing China at that time, and when it didn't happen most likely the promoter had to save face by issuing statements that the Chinese Ministry had refused permission for me to play there to get himself off the hook. If anybody had bothered to check with the Chinese authorities, it would have been clear that the Chinese authorities were unaware of the whole thing.

We did go there this year under a different promoter. According to Mojo *magazine the concerts were attended mostly by ex-pats and there were a lot of empty seats. Not true. If anybody wants to check with any of the concert-goers they will see that it was mostly Chinese young people that came. Very few ex-pats if any. The ex-pats were mostly in Hong Kong not Beijing. Out of 13,000 seats we sold about 12,000 of them, and the rest of the tickets were given away to orphanages. The Chinese press did tout me as a sixties icon, however, and posted my picture all over the place with Joan Baez, Che Guevara, Jack Kerouac and Allen Ginsberg. The concert attendees probably wouldn't have known about any of those people. Regardless, they responded enthusiastically to the songs on my last 4 or 5 records. Ask anyone who was there. They were young and my feeling was that they wouldn't have known my early songs anyway.*

As far as censorship goes, the Chinese government had asked for the names of the songs that I would be playing. There's no logical answer to that, so we sent them the set lists from the previous 3 months. If there were any songs, verses or lines censored, nobody ever told me about it and we played all the songs that we intended to play.

Everybody knows by now that there's a gazillion books on me either out or coming out in the near future. So I'm encouraging anybody who's ever met me, heard me or even seen me, to get in on the action and scribble their own book. You never know, somebody might have a great book in them.

OK Bob, whatever you say.

I went to two shows in 2011, Glasgow in October and London in November. This took me back full circle to the cities I first saw NET shows in, back in 1989. I had deliberately refrained from following too closely and especially from listening to shows just prior to going, so that whatever happened would affect me as if I were a normal punter. Although I suspect that normal punters would still think of me as extremely obsessive; especially as it had become even easier to keep up to date, via the Internet, with anything you are interested in. The myriad of Dylan sites had been joined by the *Bob Dylan Examiner*, dedicated to providing an online Dylan daily news digest and which consequently provides continual commentary, often with audio and video links, on all that is happening on the NET. Inevitably, I did know everything that was going on, but by my standards I was extremely detached and for once I could go along to a show without any great expectations or knowledge of exactly what I would see.

Naturally I was hoping for it to be better than I had last seen, indeed I had every reason to expect it to be, having heard a number of encouraging performances in the interim. On the other hand I also had reasons to worry, given the previous chapter of this book and some of the other live songs that I had heard. As it turned out, I got a little bit of everything; the main thing to report, though, is that I thoroughly enjoyed the evening.

October 8th 2011 Braehead Arena Glasgow

1. Leopard-Skin Pill-Box Hat
2. It's All Over Now, Baby Blue
3. Things Have Changed
4. Tangled Up In Blue
5. Honest With Me
6. The Lonesome Death Of Hattie Carroll
7. Summer Days
8. A Hard Rain's A-Gonna Fall

9. Highway 61 Revisited
10. Tryin' To Get To Heaven
11. Thunder On The Mountain
12. Ballad Of A Thin Man

*

13. Like A Rolling Stone
14. All Along The Watchtower

The very first thing that struck me when Dylan took to the stage was how much healthier he looked; all his boxing training and cycling exertions were really paying off. Bob was slim, wiry and fighting fit and, perhaps not coincidentally, he also appeared happier within himself and with what he was doing. He carried himself with the swaggering authority of old.

It seemed to me that there were a lot of people on stage these days, but as far as I could tell the entire night was visually and aurally centred on Bob, or Bob interplaying with Sexton. This may have been because I could not take my eyes off Dylan, but the others seemed distant both physically and in the mix. Dylan moved around the stage all night, the 'retreats' behind the keyboards now had a part to play in an overall context of ever-changing focal points and goodness gracious great balls of fire, he was animated when there too. A tremendous amount was going on to keep the audience's interest high, and all the while Dylan kept eye contact with them as he orchestrated the on-stage drama like an energetic circus master.

This increase in visual entertainment did not detract from the musical performance. On the contrary, that too had improved in important respects since last I had seen Dylan and the band. Yes, there were some of the silly arrangements, but his voice was stronger and deeper than I had heard in many a year, with hardly a hint of upsinging, although it was still extremely limited in range for most of the night. I have noted before during this century that there are sudden increases in singing power, as though he had found some sort of steroids for vocal cords. I have no idea if such things exist, I am just saying that this is what these sudden boosts make you think of, that is how dramatic they can be. It is probably natural that in years of approximately one hundred shows there will be periods of comparative diminution and improvement in vocal power, but the difference was startling to my ears. Now he could belt out an intimidating "Ballad of a Thin Man", for one example, and he could heighten the contrast between different songs or parts of songs far more than he could in some earlier years.

Before this sounds like a total conversion to all things then current on the NET, I should point out that he still messed about on those silly keyboards and would shift a song a key too high for no reason, but at least he had stopped always doing that and,. Dylan now distracted from this by being centre stage for much of the time, giving an extraordinary display of visual gestures, body contortions and facial engagement. Basically, Dylan was clearly having a ball whether he was centre stage or at the keyboards, as was especially evident in a raucous, over the top "Thunder On the Mountain". However, I get ahead of myself.

As at the Roundhouse, Bob and the band opened with "Leopard-Skin Pill-Box Hat". This time, however, I felt a different attitude coming from the stage. The start of this evening's event was really strong, renewed energy, commitment and engagement poured from the stage from the first minute of ""Leopard-Skin", through "Baby Blue" and into an extraordinary "Things Have Changed". A video of Dylan's movements would be essential to see what I mean by calling his performance of it 'extraordinary'. It was an interpretative piece that relied on a combination of singing and acting. "Tangled Up In Blue" had a strange, melody-destroying rhythm. This peculiar arrangement is not without point; it allows what is left of his voice to spit out the lines, broken as they are into spit-able chunks.

This technique, I will concede, does not always work, and indeed sounds absolutely appalling on certain songs, but at that moment in the audience in Glasgow, what I was experiencing was exhilarating when compared to the shows I had seen in 2006 to 2009. I was not spending the evening wishing I were somewhere else.

"Honest With Me" was forceful, perhaps too forceful; whether the sound was simply too loud or something, somewhere was not set-up as it should have been, I could hardly hear a word Dylan was singing. My evening took another turn for the worse when Dylan started to get into his 'find-a-doodle-on-the-organ-and-then-adapt-the-melody-of-the-song-to-it' mode. This was especially the case on "The Lonesome Death of Hattie Carroll" and "A Hard Rain's A-Gonna Fall". I actually was less offended by "Hattie Carroll", because I thought the silly melody he found was quite pretty, albeint totally inappropriate. The nadir for me was "Hard Rain", where the three-note fairground-organ-cum-nursery-jingle just sounded inane. After each of these songs Dylan blew away the uncomfortable feelings they had left me with by delivering pounding rock-outs on "Summer Days" and "Highway 61 Revisited".

One of the highlights of the night was "Tryin' To Get To Heaven", which Dylan really sang, Lord be praised. It was unblemished by anything bar a couple of phony line endings and surely we can all forgive a couple. After this tender rendition, Dylan switched moods dramatically and tore into a "Thunder On the Mountain" which was so bad that it was ludicrous, and yet most enjoyable visually. Dylan was having such fun shouting out words, randomly perhaps in one verse but as it was just a barking growl played so loudly through the sound system that there was double distortion, it was hard to tell. Bob was grinning and half-imitating his odd mixture of Jerry Lee Lewis and Jerry Lewis with such abandon that you felt it would be churlish not to just enjoy it with him.

"Ballad of a Thin Man" was done with great panache, electronic echoes giving extra bite to words like "lepers and crooks". Bob"s voice positively caressed the line "you're very well read, it's well known". It was, I later realized, very mixed in regards to vocal delivery, but the phony-sounding trick endings to many lines passed me by when I was at the show, engrossed as I was in his crazy movements while my ears were being pounded by the huge speakers and exposed to the, admittedly somewhat hammy, 'echo effect' for the first time.

The encores were upon me all too quickly, again this was back to the way I used to feel at Dylan shows. In brief, I had not had as much fun at a Dylan show in a long time, maybe since Barrowlands 2004 (though I am very willing to accept that this may be because I attended the 'wrong' UK shows in 2005) and I certainly had not seen Dylan getting into a show as much since then. He was clearly enjoying himself and more than happy to let everyone know it. While the crowd at Braehead were much less enthusiastic than the audience at that raucous night from seven years ago, Dylan was no less enthusiastic, or raucous.

Although I have stressed that Dylan's voice was stronger in these last months of 2011's touring than I had heard it for a long time, it was, obviously, still not The Voice. Much as I would love to say that sufficient range and tone has been restored to allow Dylan to sing his songs with nuance, to inhabit them in at least in a semblance of the way he once so effortlessly did, I cannot do so. I detest all the reviews that include observations like 'his voice, never a thing of beauty, has now deteriorated to (insert animal-related 'humorous' description)' and I detest them for the first part far more than for the second. The second, if unkind, may have a smidgeon of truth in it. The first constitutes barbarism of the worst kind, being an exact reversal of the aesthetic truth so often and amply displayed in a whole range of singing styles and mediums.

His voice was a thing of rare and spectacular beauty and I miss it terribly, it was the single most attractive thing about Dylan shows for me and it has gone. The range and subtlety are still severely restricted; it is hardly to be expected, after all, that his vocal cords will regenerate as he goes through his seventies. And yet this time I still enjoyed the show and that cannot be solely down to an injection of comparatively more vocal power and dynamism and Dylan being dominant in the mix. Although it was partly due to those factors there was a whole new, and very different, aspect to the way Dylan was performing.

The following observations cover both my Glasgow and London experience(s) and, indeed, stand as a general commentary on how the NET had, once again, morphed into a new entity. Or, as Dylan would have it, how I compare this new tour to the one that preceded it. The odd thing is that what I am going to tell you is exactly what I had been told, repeatedly, for about a year prior to this by my good friend David Bristow. 'Odd' in that I never listened to him, or rather I gave no credence to his words and now I have to hope that you are more generous than I was in buying into the view that a major factor in the experience nowadays is visual and that, to use an old cliché, 'you really have to be there'.

I never used to believe that, in fact I have opposed the whole idea throughout this book. Just to remind you, as I have said before, were I to pick my favourite 100 Dylan shows I would have attended none of them; the same is true of my favourite fifty shows in the last 25 years. Being there was obviously the best thing of all, but it was never essential to my enjoyment and appreciation; now, it is. This constitutes a major shift in the parameters of Dylan concert enjoyment and it can lead to understandable cynicism in one listening only to the audio, but more on that below.

I did not listen to David and you will probably be resistant to taking my word for it, but I urge you to go along and see a show for yourself. Yes, after all I have said against the phrase 'you really had to be there', I am now saying that 'you really have to be there'. "Things Have Changed" from Glasgow on October

8th is a shining exemplar of why this is so. The audio alone conveys only a fraction of what was performed that night, which was an interpretative drama created by Dylan's on-stage enactment of his feelings while singing the piece. A remarkable display that began with him crouching, arms wide, before the song even started. The drama continued with leg movements and body-squeezing crouches as Dylan enacted the meaning of the words and music, pouring his very being into communicating the song for his audience.

As I later listened to "Ballad of a Thin Man" from the same show, I had to get past some ridiculous 'upsinging-lite' line endings in verse one. At the show, however, when I was standing *watching* him I never even noticed them. "Thunder On The Mountain" would be yet another prime example. On a recording it sounds terrible, but at the time it was a riot of exuberant fun, releasing the poignant tension created by the preceding, heartfelt, "Tryin' To Get To Heaven". These specific examples are representative of the nature of Dylan"s whole dramatic performance and carefully-structured shows.

A multitude of seemingly small gestures illuminate the songs, it is enthralling to see Dylan put the songs over visually with his strange movements, as idiosyncratic as his trademark, thrilling phrasing always was and sometimes still can be.

Clearly it is impossible for me to show you exactly what I mean, hence my exhortation for you to go along to a show as soon as you can, but perhaps I can give you an idea by concentrating on one, single example of gesture and song combining to create variable effects. This occurs in "Tangled Up In Blue", Dylan moves his arm toward himself and then outwards again as he sings *"from me to you"*. Depending on where the song is taking him (or he is taking it) on any given night, his arm, on its outward swing, can gesticulate to the air, perhaps signifying his muse, a lover from the past (or present); or to the audience, that shadowy entity he is attracted to and repulsed by and which seems to confuse him just as much as muses and lovers.

That is a description of merely one arm, at one moment, of one song - bending and shaping the meaning even as the words reach us. Imagine entire shows with Dylan's whole body and face contributing at different and apt times and you can start to build up in your mind how much of a drama the whole experience is. Photos of the tours, and some truly amazing photos have been taken, show Dylan in a myriad of poses, his hands and face particularly alive with expressive power and, as can perhaps better be seen on videos, at times his entire body is contorted or dancing, staggering, jigging and jiving to help convey whatever it is that he wants to convey at that particular moment of live performance.

The whole event has changed, it is now predicated on the interaction of the visual with the songs; it must be being assumed that nearly all the audience know nearly all the songs intimately or it wouldn't work nearly as well as it does, but work it most certainly does.

I can envisage the cynical reply 'So now you want us to believe the shows are great because even though his voice is shot his movements make it all worthwhile?' Ridiculous as it may sound at first, that is indeed what I mean and I believed it even more after seeing a stronger show in London in November, that brought the year's touring to a close.

Naturally this transformation in the NET was heavily debated in the Dylan fan world. Rainer Vesely, a regular contributor to Michal Gray's blog, underlined these very points in an excellent post entitled "How Dylan Concert Expectations Have Changed". Rainer was describing how since Dylan "crawled out from his hiding place behind the keyboard, where he ducked away from 2005-2009 – he is staging a 90-100 minute drama, in which he puts much, much more emphasis on his physical presence than ever before. He really acts(!) and recites, gestures, mimics, uses – very consciously!! – his weird way of walking, knee-bending, staring, half-closing or wide-opening his eyes etc."

Mr Vesely was propounding the same view that David Bristow had previously been putting forward to me, and unsurprisingly Rainer's points were met with reactions similar to mine to David: incredulity that one was being asked to accept that the greatest live vocal performer now had to be *seen* to be appreciated. So, we now have three distinct camps; the naysayers, the devotees and the naysayers who were devotees again as long as they were in the building and close enough to see Dylan's bodily movements and facial expressions, or were equipped with binoculars.

A good video can give a general impression of what I am describing. However, it would still only be an approximation and it would need to be multi-angled and professionally filmed to give anything like a proper representation of the performance. Something like the Globe Theatre's films of its Shakespeare productions, for example. However, even this is still 2-D and therefore 'flat' in more ways than one. Even as the fledging 3-D technology develops it will still miss the ambience and is restrictive in that your eyes can only follow what the cameras capture. You, as viewer, do not have the choice to change the angle of view, whether to stare at the ceiling, observe at the exact moment you want to how the band are reacting to Dylan's movements and so forth. Even the magnificent Globe DVDs of *Henry IV parts I and II*, for example, are a much weaker dramatic experience than you got when you were at the theatre.

Before looking at the final show of the year at the whatever-it-was-now-called Hammersmith Odeon, I should report that the feedback from the shows following those in Glasgow became more and more favourable, peaking with a much-raved about performance in Nottingham which seemed to combine the best of all vocal and visual aspects. Now that I had been convinced that the only way to appreciate a show was to be there, I mostly refrained from listening to anything until after I saw a show again myself. I had adapted my approach to NET-following, as what was happening now was not the equivalent of the shows I used to adore. It was a different experience, a different tour. Dylan's point about 'Never Ending Tour' being a wrong description of a succession of different tours has never been so clearly proven. What one was now witnessing was not the same tour that this book began describing, and while it may not be my favourite of the many incarnations it has produced more enjoyable shows and provided me with much more pleasure than most of the immediately preceding 500 or so gigs. The reports I had read were proven correct; by the time Dylan got to the last show of the year he had taken things forward to a whole other level.

Despite not being in such a good position, I still enjoyed it more as the songs (apart from the three *Modern Times* representatives, none of which came close to working) were stronger and Dylan's voice comparatively stronger. I thought the standout songs were "Ballad Of A Thin Man", "Things Have Changed", "Man In The Long Black Coat" (though I still miss the "people just float" line), "Desolation Row", "Forgetful Heart" and the closing benediction of "Forever Young".

This strong spine to the set avoided the likes of his 2011 treatments of "A Hard Rain's A-Gonna Fall" and "The Lonesome Death of Hattie Carroll", which were not so much deconstructed as disembowelled. Basically, what I am saying is simply that there were more songs better sung at the Hammersmith show I saw compared to the Glasgow show I saw. A Dylan show is never 'simple', however, and the devilish delight is in the detail.

November 21st 2011 HMV Hammersmith Apollo London

1. Leopard-Skin Pill-Box Hat
2. It's All Over Now, Baby Blue
3. Things Have Changed
4. Spirit On The Water
5. Honest With Me
6. Forgetful Heart
7. The Levee's Gonna Break
8. Man In The Long Black Coat
9. Highway 61 Revisited
10. Desolation Row
11. Thunder On The Mountain
12. Ballad Of A Thin Man
13. All Along The Watchtower
14. Like A Rolling Stone
15. Forever Young

This event, the last night of the 26th consecutive year of touring, brought with it another 'gathering of the tribes' and it was marvellous to meet or bump into so many familiar faces before, during and after the show. So many people who have featured at the scene of so many key points in this book were in evidence, including Andy and Michelle, who had ushered Pia and I into a good viewing slot back in 1994 at Roseland. Were I to list everyone I met that day it would make a list to rival that of the acknowledgements at the end of this book, and feature many of the same names.

I was further back in London than I had been in Glasgow, but I could imagine the look on Dylan's face, project what I had seen there during the repeated songs. I was in general admission, standing near the back to get the elevation my diminutive stature requires. I had perhaps underestimated how constant the stream of people entering and leaving and re-entering the floor for drinks, food, smoke, toilet and whatever else they required would be. Yet, although I was bumped and barged from beginning to end, I did know all along that this was the price you pay for moving in such venues to the elevated level of the floor where the cinema stall seats used to be. It is part of the live experience and a trade-off you have to juggle with; old campaigners like me know the score, after all. My rather smug reasoning was apparently justified as, seconds before the show began, I was revelling in an outstanding view of the entire stage.

Then, just as Dylan came on, a guy about six foot six inches tall stepped right in front of me and stood there with his back all but touching my nose and blocking out everything except said back. So, I had to shuffle along a bit and find another reasonable vantage point; this recurred throughout the show, though Duncan Hume was kind enough at one point between songs to motion me into a superior vantage point that he had either created or noticed. Although I was too far away to be completely happy, I did have a good overall view of the stage and the crowd stretching from the front of the stage back to my location.

A striking difference from when I had last been in such a position was the overwhelming presence of held-aloft mobile phones recording or photographing throughout the entire event. I had seen smatterings of this before and numerous, simultaneous use during the final song but it was now like a never-ending sea. Perhaps most people present felt they were not really there, in the same building as Bob Dylan, unless they recorded the experience. All in all it was rather surreal and I pushed it from my mind and trained my eyes to discount this distraction.

In a throwback to the variable NET shows of earlier incarnations, the opening three songs, despite being the same numbers as I had witnessed a month previously, were already very different. Mark Knopfler joined Dylan on stage and his fluid guitar lines changed the way the band sounded and the songs were put across. Visually things were different too, as Mr Knopfler played unusually close to Dylan; a brave move on his part, most musicians tend to prefer being at a safe distance.

The show entered its mid section, alternating slow and fast versions of songs from the new century. Vocally and musically this was the evening's only unsatisfying period for me, though with one shining exception to that description. "Spirit On The Water" was as close to mundane as anything in such a setting with Dylan on harp can be. "Honest With Me" was loud and hoarse; at these times, not seeing him up-close was most detrimental. "Honest With Me" had sounded the same in Glasgow, but watching his facial expressions had made it enjoyable there.

Although I am writing in praise of the new visual elements of the show it is an undeniable fact that a dependence on this is clearly a problem, unless the entire audience are equipped with and comfortable using binoculars. From my distance and without binoculars, there was only Dylan's 2011 voice and his body movements to go on and these were not enough, on this night, to transform these songs into something engaging. His voice was about to be unleashed, however, in a startling demonstration of his power still to captivate and transport an audience.

"Forgetful Heart" was the sixth song of the night and a contender for the show's stand-out performance. This live torch-ballad had been a highlight of shows since it first appeared. When I was writing earlier about encouraging performances I had heard throughout 2010 this was always one of them, show after show it provided a dramatic counterpoint to the overall loud rock base of the gigs. This is a bit surprising, coming as it does from *Together Through Life,* an album almost entirely co-written with Robert Hunter (who also co-wrote that old NET warhorse, "Silvio") and, perhaps not unexpectedly, a leading contender for the weakest album of Dylan's career.

This album was, however, risibly lauded upon its release, garnering far more praise than, say, *Highway 61 Revisited*, *Blonde on Blonde* and *Blood On The Tracks* had when they first came out. The dregs acclaimed as a masterpiece while the masterpieces are received with only tepid enthusiasm: it is all part of the crazy world of Bob Dylan and of how much of the music press, far less the mainstream press, have been totally incapable of judging him in anything bar hindsight. On the other hand, I should also note that there are nowadays a fair number of knowledgeable and insightful critics in newspapers, magazines and blogs who have lived with Dylan's music for decades and are very well attuned to the pitfalls of rushing to accept an instant and 'popular' interpretation of whatever he is doing; their voices are easily lost in the torrent of mindless fawning that greets even total throwaways like *Together Through Life*, however.

In any case, "Forgetful Heart" was one of the better efforts from the disc and ended on a Dylan-song-history-redolent, extremely moving and meaningful couplet that played off "Knocking on Heaven's Door" and "Tryin' To Get to Heaven":

"The door has closed for evermore,
If indeed there ever was a door"

Live, it was a jewel illuminating the mid-section of the show; a dark ruby sending shards of nuance, subtlety and emotional insight through all that enveloped it. The band were there on stage, I could hear Donnie's fiddle, Stu's acoustic guitar and the ever-loyal Tony on his standup bass, but my eyes were trained solely on Dylan, at the still point of the stage and night as he sang and played harmonica with breathtaking poise and control and heart-rending emotion. As T.S. Eliot put it, in *Burnt Norton:* "At the still point, there the dance is."

"The Levee's Gonna Break" saw Dylan retreat back to his keyboard and, like the other *Modern Times* songs, sounded much the same as it always does. Realizing this, I spent most of it remembering how moving Dylan had just been and how affecting his harp playing had been the song before, and tried not to concentrate on the rather lame and ham-fisted performance he was currently serving up. If nothing else it produced some breathing space before I was again completely captivated, this time by "Man In The Long Black Coat", which again found Bob centre stage with harp but in a very different persona to the one who had delivered "Forgetful Heart".

Now he was energized and the song fairly bounced along. As with "Tangled Up In Blue" in Glasgow, Dylan spat some of the lines out with clipped and chiselled intonation that set them out from the general growling delivery. The song was recast, it remained 'mysterious and dark', but now with an unsettling urgency.

Dylan's biting enunciation of "He had a face like a mask" had a profound effect on me. My mind raced with thoughts of Dylan himself in masks, his joking declaration at the All Hallows Eve 1964 show "I have my Bob Dylan mask on, I'm *masque*-r- ading", his Richard Nixon mask in 1975 on the Rolling Thunder Tour, his whiteface on the same tour for the *Renaldo and Clara* film and all the metaphorical masks he had worn by now for some five decades. Another phrase was snarled from the stage and snapped me out of my reverie, and I was once again immersed in one of the highlights of the evening.

It could fairly be argued that the following "Highway 61 Revisited" sounded, as I complained of regarding "The Levee's Going To Break", 'much the same as it always does', yet I enjoyed it. It is such an incomparably better song and Dylan's combination of actions and delivery was so superior that I was once more an engaged member of the audience. Then the succeeding song, "Desolation Row", had me once more enraptured.

A waltz-time version of the epic found Dylan totally engaged. I was transported and with him every step of the way until a guy returning from the bar tripped, stumbled and somehow managed not to fall as he passed me. He clearly thought I had made it difficult for him to squeeze between me and the person on my right shoulder. I had done nothing, I didn't even know he was there but he stood stock still right in front of me staring at me for some time with a look in his eye that said: 'If I wasn't holding a drink in each hand I would punch you right now.'

I had to try and ignore this and keep my eyes and ears trained on Bob; as is the way with interruptions, one is convinced what one missed was the highlight of the night. Either way it was a captivating rendition and I said to Duncan Hume during the break before "Thunder On The Mountain" that I was already looking forward to the next time I could see a show.

"Thunder" initiated a period of all-out, apocalyptic noise-level rock, "Ballad Of A Thin Man" and "All Along The Watchtower" followed in one blistering version after another, the last again showcasing Dylan's ability to break melody and lyrics into new shapes even in the midst of a pile-driving arrangement. It was akin to being machine-gunned by flying, famous aphorisms. Dylan stalked the stage in the most majestic of manners; he was revelling in his total control over the song, the band, the audience – the whole damn shooting match. "Phew! Rock 'n' Roll." We emerged panting, sweating and drained from one classic to be faced with that classic of all classics, the greatest rock song of all time, "Like A Rolling Stone".

Again, yes, I know I am repeating myself, the visuals were essential. As my mind ranged through those thoughts it was simultaneously drinking in a *tour-de-force* Dylan on-stage drama that involved incredible arrogance, affecting weakness and nervousness within an overall context of resolute, clear-eyed sureness and total command of the stage and the audience. His body and although I could not see it his face too, I knew, as well as his voice were communicating a multitude of the myriad emotions that song connotes.

A comparatively stately and compassionate version sent my thoughts ranging throughout its sadness-tinged delivery. I knew the show, and the year's touring, was ending (or, at least, I thought I did) and that my own journey had come to safe harbour. I did not want it to end, I was back to wanting another show tomorrow, or at the very least next week. Yet I knew it was ending for 2011 and it was with bittersweet feelings that I both followed the song being played and pondered on how Dylan had, throughout the night, been encapsulating the whole tradition he speaks so eloquently of belonging to. Dylan the minstrel, the super-smart cowboy, the riverboat gambler, the troubadour, the bluesman, the crooner, the man in the mask, the rocker, the man who changed everything, the man who defies everyone and everything that tries to label him (as I vainly strive to do here) – the man with the never-ending tour.

And so, that was it. Yet, wait, the thunderous applause does not greet the night's end. Something is happening and this time even Mr Jones could see what it was.

Mark Knopfler appeared again, strapping on his guitar and adjusting the microphone in the middle of the stage. The crowd is buoyed by the thought of the imminent duet. However good they thought it might, be it was to surpass their expectations; doubly so for an old 'duet cynic' like myself.

"Forever Young" began with Dylan singing the opening verse, Knopfler sang the second and after some hesitancy they were bold enough to try sharing the third. As Mark sang the lines

"May your heart always be joyful, may your song always be sung,
and may you stay forever young"

he underlined the central importance of gestures in the modern Dylan show by turning to and extending his arm towards Dylan as he sang "may your song always be sung". The whole auditorium erupted and if there were any dry eyes in the house, well, they were nowhere in the range of my swimming vision.

It probably reads as though this was just a corny gesture that should not have worked, but it seemed so natural and the crowd response was so spontaneous that it was irresistible. It was a very moving moment and a perfect note for me to end on.

I applauded until my hands smarted and my voice was hoarse and left what I will forever call 'the Hammersmith Odeon' with a chill wind at my back. It did not feel cold, however; rather it was strangely comforting, carrying, as it did, a ghostly voice calling, repeatedly:

"Thanks for coming, Bobby! Thanks for coming............."

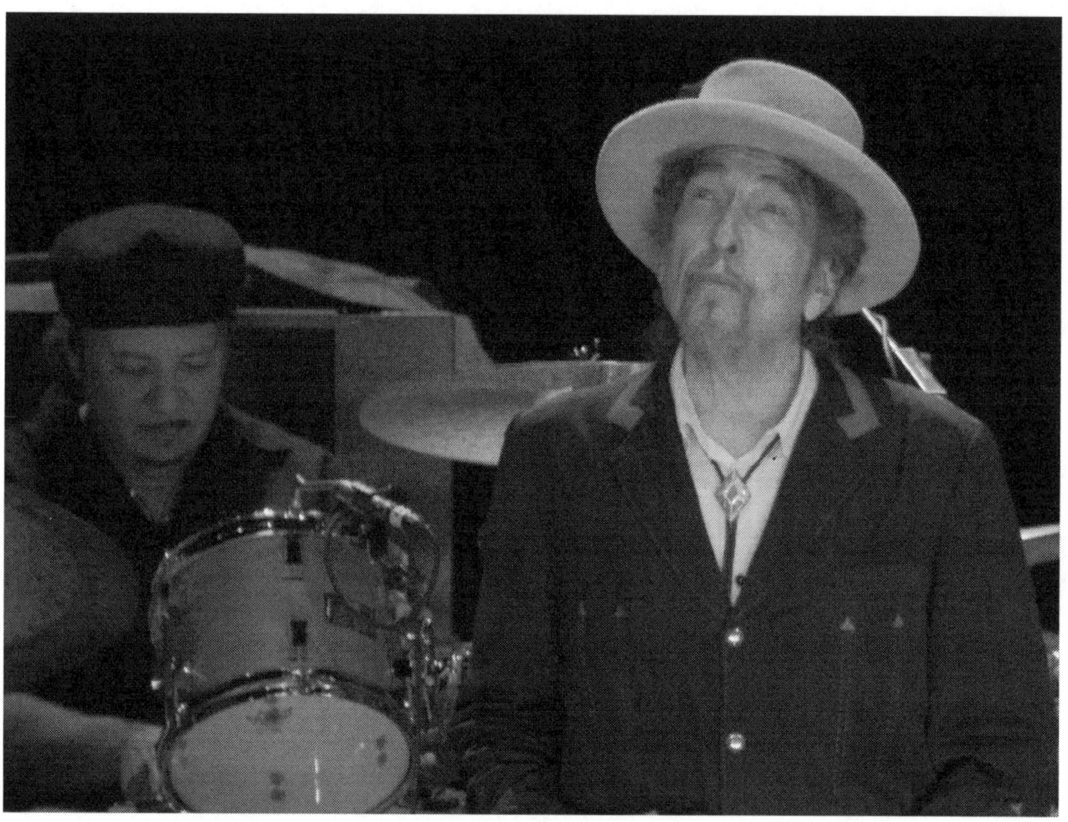

MERRIWEATHER POST PAVILION, COLUMBIA, MD. AUG 16, 2011

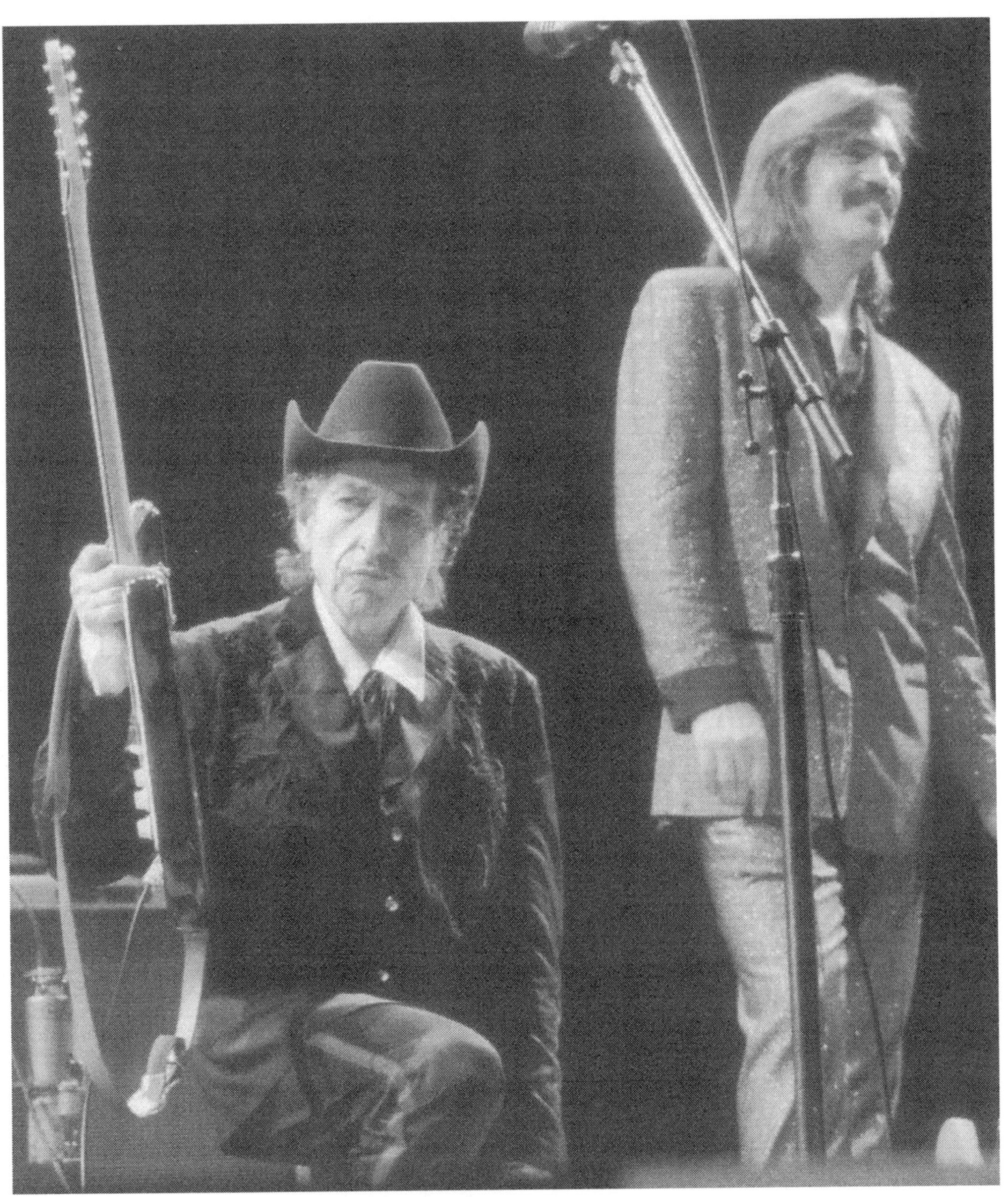

PARIS, APRIL 30TH 2002

APPENDIX ONE

21st July 1993: "Hey, that's great..."

I am due to return to an important meeting after a short lunch break. I get a message that Alex, my brother-in-law, wants me to call him immediately. I gather it is something very urgent indeed. I have to go into the meeting as I'm already late. I reckon that it can only be one of two things: an illness in the family or something Dylan-related. If the former he surely would have said so. I have to assume it is the latter, and sit in a ferment of worry and nerves; I presume, for the eternity of the 100 minutes that follow, that Dylan is on television or that some big news has broken.

The minute the meeting ends, I rush out to phone Alex. I am more than stunned to hear that Dylan has been in Camden and that Alex has stood next to him. Although he had had no opportunity to speak to Dylan, he was at least rewarded by seeing Dylan walk backwards into a café as part of a video shoot. One of Alex's colleagues even spoke to Bob and obtained an autograph with a lovely little personal message for Alex.

Overwhelmed, pleased, a bit jealous – all those feelings at once, with the nagging question: could he still be there?

Alex is still talking: of a song possibly called "Blood In My Eyes", of Dylan singing with a busker, of the autograph he has. This is all too much. He goes. I call Larry. General disbelief and astonishment later, Larry says he cannot possibly get there but will phone Mike Sutton[1] in Camden to see if anything is still happening. He tells me to call back in 20 minutes. Five minutes later I call him back. He hasn't got through to Mike. I ask him, very precisely, to tell me that there is no possibility that Dylan is still there and that I've to be sensible and go home. He follows my instructions to the letter; I hang up, step into the street and hail the first taxi I see.

Within three minutes we hit a traffic jam. I gnaw at my fingernails, knuckles, wrists and arms, still the taxi crawls along. I have the bright idea of calling Compendium Books,[2] who sell my fanzine, ***Homer**, the slut*. I tell the driver that I'll be back but must run and make a phone call; I have no worries that I'll catch him up. I think that I'd better appear cool and collected – after all, Dylan probably left ages ago.

After a few rings, I'm greeted by the familiar voice of Compendium's buyer, Mike. I interrupt him hurriedly "Hello, I supply you with ***Homer**, the slut*, a Dylan magazine, do you need any more copies?" "Funny you should ring just now, he's sitting straight across the road at the window of a restaurant...." click, *GRRRR*!

Within seconds I am back in the cab, impressing upon the driver that, traffic jam notwithstanding, I have to be in Camden High Street *NOW*. I expect he couldn't make out many of my words, but he got the idea. Sooner than I'd thought possible, we were in Camden High Street.

I get the taxi to stop straight across from Compendium Books. Sure enough there is a restaurant there, called Fluke's Cradle.[3] I walk in. For Mike to have seen him from the bookstore, Dylan would have had to have been in the room where I now stand. The room was empty of Dylan, bereft of Bob.

---

1 Mike Sutton has been going to Dylan shows around the world for over 30 years. Known for his dedication in queuing for hours before the door opens so he can be as near Dylan as possible, he usually spends Saturdays in Camden High Street near Compendium Bookshop. On this particular Saturday he went to a local supermarket instead and missed everything. I always point out how amusingly ironic this was. He has not laughed yet, no matter how wittily I put it.

2 Sadly Compendium Books closed in the year 2000.

3 Fluke's Cradle featured heavily in the "Blood In My Eyes" video. It had paintings on the walls for sale, and Bob is sitting beneath one such on the cover of *World Gone Wrong*. Alas, Fluke's Cradle is no more. Shortly after my Dylan experience it was sold, redecorated and renamed.

I trudge across to Compendium to ask when he left, what they saw etc. They kindly grab me at the door and say: "He's still there, he's in the back now, having a meal." "Can I have a ***Homer**, the slut?*" "Yes, but don't take the top one, it's dog-eared. Take two and bring one back signed." "On your bike!"

I take two and go back across to Fluke's Cradle. My plan is simple; I'll go into the restaurant and sit as close to Dylan as possible, and ask for his autograph if there is a convenient opportunity as he leaves. I pass through the bar, thinking that above all I must be inconspicuous. I go into the restaurant and... *Oh my God He's really there!* OK, I went in knowing he would be there but seeing him really there, like really him, really sitting there ... too much! I've read that in moments of shock the body is supposed to have a kind of automatic defence system. I've obviously been programmed wrongly as when I went into shock my body went on the attack. Knees buckling, head spinning and heart attempting to smash through the ribs.

Dylan is wearing a top hat, sitting in profile, that nose, those curls; visions of Blackbushe and all that '78 meant to me seeing him live for the first time, visions of so many years before and after that. I stand stock still. I somehow remember that I am supposed to be inconspicuous. Dylan's table was down a few stairs to the left. I go to sit at the nearest table to him on my level of the restaurant (a whole other level) and try to be cool. I pick up a menu, though I know I'll never swallow anything I order. The menu slips through my sweaty paws. I decide I'm too conspicuous so I move to the next nearest table, which just happens to have a better view of our man. I realize I am, in fact, totally conspicuous as Dylan and his entourage are the only people in the restaurant apart from me. Maybe I am not supposed to be there, I think, and this thought prompts others that remind me I had always said I would never disturb him in this way and that I was acting very stupidly. I leave the dining area and go back to the front bar.

I am still feeling pretty happy though, seeing Him so close is a big thrill. I order a drink. I sit down. I stand up. I sit down again. I move table. I decide on an alternate strategy. I could go downstairs again and ask someone if they could get Dylan to sign a *Homer*. This I do, whispering my request and stressing that I only want it if it will not unduly trouble Dylan. "Go and ask him yourself." I glance up at Dylan, a mere four seats away.

"No, I don't want to disturb him and anyway it isn't physically possible." "OK, maybe." "I'll be sitting in the bar if you manage to get it signed. Thanks a lot."

I sneak back out and wait. A few minutes – or eternity – pass. My *Homer* is returned, this person doesn't feel it is right for him to present it to Dylan. "Fair enough," I think. I'm happy enough and have remembered all the stories about him being pestered by fans. I'll just sit and watch him leave.

A few more minutes pass and someone comes over to me and says: "Go now! Now's a good time." I stand up, hesitate, look doubtful. "You'll never have a better chance in your life, go now." I go. Back in the restaurant only Dylan's table is now occupied. The furthest away table; Dylan, naturally, the most difficult person to get near to. To get to him I will have to push past someone I do not recognise and then Dave Stewart.

If I had thought that my heart was pounding before – and, hey, it had been – it was doing something else altogether this time. There were four young-looking people at the table; three on the far side, one nearest me, then next to him Dave Stewart and next to him, Himself. Looking absolutely gorgeous.

You know what they say about 'an aura around him'? Well, I had always thought that was nonsense; or, rather, a projection of our feelings. I was wrong. The aura is almost tangible. My legs are threatening to give way, as is my rib cage. I try to detach my tongue from the roof of my mouth and my jaw from the floor.

At this moment there is a babble of conversation in the room. Dave Stewart is facing Dylan – who is staring straight ahead in profile (and what a profile) – asking a series of questions quite vehemently. I cannot make the questions out due to the conversation amongst the others. Dylan is not responding at all. I push past the first person between me and Bob.

A silence falls around the table, with the exception of Dave Stewart's drumming questions. I cannot make out the words because my heart is beating so hard that my ears are drumming louder. I try my pen for the last time, but I had tried it once too many times and it had run out; luckily I had brought eight with me, so I fished out my seventh last. I'm now standing right beside Dave Stewart's chair. Dylan is within arm's reach.

The movement in getting *Homer* and the working pen out alerts Dave Stewart to the fact that there is someone behind him and that everything has gone quiet. He stops talking and looks around and up at me. His look is marvellous: it says "Oh no, not another one of these Dylan nutters". (In a kindly way, however, and later I admire his ready acceptance of himself as a mere pop star beside someone who is a real Star.) He moves his chair slightly, I help him move it a little more.

I am now standing right beside Bob Dylan. There is total silence. Dylan just keeps staring ahead, not reacting to the sudden silence or anything. This lasts for seven zillion aeons, or about two seconds in real time.

Well this is it, after 18 years of interest, some have called it obsessive, in the Man, I am at the point many of us have dreamed of over and over. What am I going to say?

I have no idea. Staying alive is only barely within my grasp at this moment. Thinking stopped some time ago. I tear my tongue from the roof of my mouth. "Excuse me, Mr. Dylan," I squeak. HE MOVES – and *how* – the head swivels round in an instant. Dylan is staring me in the face (or, at least, the rivers of sweat where my face should be) and says – 'says' is the wrong word but, since the real description does not exist, it will have to do – pointedly and interrogatively: "*Yeeaah*?"

I am dead. It is not a pleasant feeling. I want my mummy and daddy. I want the ground to swallow me up and never let me out again.

Suddenly I am reborn and mysteriously function. I hold out a copy of *Homer* issue 9. I force the Sahara Desert above my chin to respond; the sand becomes a torrent of burbling water. Something along the following lines pours out:

"Could you please sign this? Of course, it doesn't matter if you don't and I'm very sorry for disturbing you, I realize it is a stupid thing to do, and it has been great being this close to you and I'll leave now."

I do not know how much of this Dylan made out; maybe "please" and "sign" or possibly he just guessed what the pen and magazine were for. "*Yeah, sure ...*" He took the magazine in his left hand and the pen in his right I was pleased to see. However, the pen was upside-down! A tale flashed through my mind of someone asking for his autograph who didn't have a pen and his devastating response ... maybe if he tries to sign it now he'll get annoyed. Oh No ....

Fate, however, intervened. Or perhaps it was the whole point of the suggestion that I "go in now" (if so I owe that gentleman so much I could never, ever repay him). Dylan laid the magazine down and jabbed a beautiful finger at the embroidery on the jacket sleeve pictured on the front cover: *"That's it, that's the jacket I'm talking about."* They'd been discussing that very jacket???! Someone says from the far side of the table "Well, that's it then, it's Hammersmith." I answered, in a very small voice, without taking my eyes off Dylan's right hand which was signing the front cover of *Homer* at that very moment: "Actually it is Belfast. But, hey, if you guys want it to be Hammersmith, then Hammersmith it is." I take the signed copy from Himself and slither backwards out of the room. I am aware of acute physical pain. Yet the thought resounds that IT HAS HAPPENED.

I sit in the bar again. Stunned. Staring at *Homer*. More stunningly stunned. Slowly my brain tries to re-establish a modicum of control. "Sit where he'll have to pass you on the way out," it urges. I do. I get crafty, I get a table where they will have to pass in single file as they approach the door. I take away the second seat and wedge myself into a perfect viewing position as they leave the restaurant. I place the signed *Homer* by my right hand and lay the other one on the table in such a manner that anyone looking as they passed would have to see it.

Another few zillion years (about two minutes) later they start to leave. Stewart and some of the others (three, I think) are talking quite animatedly and, gesticulating over to me, one says something along the lines of: "Oh yes they still do, look at that lad over there."

They all laugh, in a friendly fashion. I keep my eyes glued straight ahead waiting for Bob Dylan. I can scarcely believe that this is what I am doing. Everything seems surreal. I am dragged back to something approximating reality when, attracted by the laughter, the next person out – a young American – stops at my table (thereby blocking the passageway, so I have another hero) and, pointing to the unsigned *Home*r, asks "Do you subscribe to all of these?" "Yes, and, actually, I run this one." "Really, how?" "Well I type it up on computer and I've a photocopier at home ..."

As those last three words came out, every sensory input in my being went into overdrive again. Dylan had majestically walked up the stairs and was now heading straight for my table. Do not believe he is 5' 7", this man is at least 9 feet not including the top hat. He rests one hand on the table and lifts *Homer* from the young man's hands. The youngster backs off a little, Dylan moves in. I self-liquidise.

Dylan starts reading the inside cover page. He says something about the information line number and laughs and then flicks a few pages, sometimes pausing to read. There is a smile, a grunt, an "uh-huh". Some of my senses are still working, I realise that behind me everyone has left except Dylan and the youngster who first stopped at my table. He is shifting his feet as though to leave, Dylan is still reading but I feel he is about to go.

"Please take it Bob.[4] And thanks for a great year ..." "*Yeah*" he replies, in a 'I've heard it a million times before' voice. He is still standing, reading. "*Did you write this?*" I have no idea what page he is on. Remember I am sitting down, wedged in, he is right ahead and above me. I can see the front and back page and *him*. Having written virtually none of Issue Nine, I answer anyway. "No, I edit it ... it's not a very good issue anyway Bob ..."[5]

He raises an eyebrow and flicks a few more pages, keeps on reading.

Suddenly Dylan realises it is time to go, very regretfully he says: "*This is eh, uh, really interesting but you know I just don't have time ...*" "Please take it, Bob, take it with you ..." He leans towards me with a look that says: "There's a puddle on this chair and it is trying to speak to me, but I don't know what it is burbling." Thankfully, the young man translates: "He's trying to tell you it is yours to take, Bob." (How can he say that so easily, I wonder.) Bob, still pretty close, in a very surprised and grateful voice: "*Really? I can take this one?*"

Utter panic, his face is now too close for its own safety. I gasp/scream/whisper "Nothing would give me greater pleasure in life ..." He – Bob FUCKING Dylan – puts the hand with *Homer* (his left) toward my right shoulder and his right hand squeezes my left shoulder as he leans forward and says gratefully "*Hey, that's great ...*" I am now beyond death, beyond rebirth, beyond Nirvana. I am also almost completely incapable of movement. However, Dylan is still nearby so I manage to get up and follow him to the car waiting outside.

---

4 At least I think I called him "Bob" from here on in but I cannot be sure.

5 Why did I say that? How should I know? Maybe I thought he had read a nasty comment. More likely that it was just another blurted-out answer. You may think I was handling this very badly – and you'd be correct – but wait till you try it. I contend that the wittiest, most informed mind ever would gibber in the Presence. So what chance did I have? Anyway, at least I hadn't fainted or vomited, both of which were distinct possibilities ...

I notice Dylan is still being generous with his time, a denim-clad man is shaking his hand and they are exchanging greetings. I notice too that Dave Stewart is in the back of the car videoing everything. But mostly I notice Dylan, how friendly he's being, how people are drawn to him and, finally, something which even he may never understand, how even the ordinary things he does do not lessen the aura, the mystique.

He is doing normal things, but he is set apart. I never believed such a thing possible; but he just doesn't walk and talk like anybody else. He is Bob Dylan. He walks around the back of the car and goes in the far side back seat. (They let him walk near the cars? – dear Christ, I wouldn't.) He is waving to people on the street, unfortunately this brings too many of them across the road. They press against the car, staring in at him. He opens the *Homer* and buries his face in it as the car speeds away.

I have a feeling that I will never be able to describe; the way the fear, pain, hesitation, wonderment changes to an unbelievable rush of adrenalin. I want to tell everybody in the world what happened. I realised that I could start at Compendium and Alex's office and thank them at the same time. I ran across the road to Compendium. In my delirium I had forgotten such things as traffic. It was coming straight for me. Screeching brakes, burning rubber. Chaotic hubbub. My hero from the entourage shouting "Hey, watch the cars!!!" I spin round in the middle of the road and yell back: "What the hell does it matter now?!"

APPENDIX TWO

Why Not?

Is there something strange about touring? About playing live shows? If there is, tell me what it is.[1]

BOB DYLAN, 2012

Gregory Peck has already been quoted as saying of Dylan: "He is surprises and disguises; he is a searcher with his songs. In him we hear the echo of old American voices: Whitman and Mark Twain, blues singers, fiddlers and balladeers. Bob Dylan's voice reaches just as high and will linger just as long."

These well-chosen lines encapsulate the twin Romantic views of Dylan on the NET. He is seen as a physical and artistic embodiment of one of the main strands of the American literary tradition, still out 'on the road', restlessly searching for some higher truth. Alternatively, or simultaneously, NET Dylan is the troubadour, in the great oral tradition of Woody Guthrie, Hank Williams, old bluesmen and the cast of Greil Marcus's *Invisible Republic*.[2]

---

1 Mikal Gilmore, *Rolling Stone* interview, September 27, 2012

2 Greil Marcus – *Invisible Republic* Henry Holt & Co., New York, 1997

It is an enticing image, bolstered by the fact that Dylan keeps on travelling and touring and by Dylan's repeated comments on how much he enjoys playing on stage, as well as his avowed insights into what the covers he is playing mean to him:

"I love that whole pantheon. To me there's no difference between Muddy Waters and Bill Monroe ... Those old songs are my lexicon and my prayer book... All my beliefs come out of those old songs, literally, anything from 'Let Me Rest on That Peaceful Mountain' to 'Keep On The Sunny Side.' You can find all my philosophy in those old songs. I believe in a God of time and space, but if people ask me about that, my impulse is to point them back toward those songs. I believe in Hank Williams singing 'I Saw The Light.' I've seen the light, too."[3]

Occasionally, Dylan seems attracted to a Romantic view of touring; in one of his many responses to the question "Why do you keep touring?", he declared how appealing it was to see the sunrise over a new road every morning.

Combining the two Romantic views of Dylan on tour, the entire NET experience can be seen as a vehicle akin to Mark Twain's Mississippi raft on which Huck Finn and Jim drifted downstream, uncompromised by the 'civilising' effects of settled society on the land either side. Or you can see the NET convoy as Herman Melville's *Pequod*, with Dylan at the helm, separated from home and family; though the White Whale Dylan is determined to chase and slay is his own myth.

Many years before the NET, Dylan had alluded to both Twain and Melville at different times. Interestingly, this was at a time when he returned to touring after a lengthy absence. Certainly he sees the NET as a way of dispensing with his own myth: "*It was important for me to come to the bottom of this legend thing, which has no reality at all,*" he said in 1992. "*What's important isn't the legend but the art, the work.*" Yet one cannot help but recall the amount of times Dylan himself has kept that myth going in the NET through crazy publicity stunts and stadium appearances with other 'icons'.

Nonetheless, the view of Bob as Ahab or Ethan on a never ending Quest, year after year without respite, does not really add up. For most of the NET, Dylan

3 Jon Pareles 1997 N.Y. Times News Service

has spent more time off the road than on it. Dylan has a more restrained schedule than the travelling bluesmen he is often compared to, as he himself has stressed. *"I do about 125 shows a year,"* he has commented. *"It may sound a lot to people who aren't working that much, but it isn't. B.B. King is working 350 nights a year."* Dylan may have been overestimating B.B. King's pre-'retiral'[4] gigs per year here, but his overall contrast is valid. King usually plays at least twice as many shows a year as Dylan does.

Bob's adherence to touring does not necessarily make him a Romantic/Kerouac figure. It is too simplistic an explanation, not that explanations, as we shall see, are actually necessary in the first place.

After his motorcycle accident in 1966 Dylan stopped touring to be with his family. In 1974 he toured again after the lay-off. The Rolling Thunder Revue tours of 1975 and 1976 were specifically an attempt to root his psyche in the Romantic Artist/Genius/Travelling Minstrel figure in the American Dream. This period of his life ended up in divorce and born-again Christianity. So, Dylan knows such traditions inside out in both a personal and artistic sense. He had already lived through them and progressed to the next stages of his life a long time ago. Obviously, the NET as a stirring, mythic quest would be a wonderfully uplifting note on which to end my book, but it would also be a cop-out as it offers only a partial truth. It is only one of the many categories critics try to force the whole concept into.

At the other extreme we have the cynical view. The cynics portray Dylan as a different kind of fictional character, a far less attractive Huck Finn, who rather than being admirably unsullied by civilisation simply doesn't want to grow up. Instead of a Romantic hero we have a grown man playing at Peter Pan, using the NET to avoid responsibility and as a substitute for lasting relationships.

In fact, closer examination shows Dylan's life is actually far more balanced than either this theory or the driven Romantic artist in torment idea suggest. Away from the NET for half the year, Dylan can spend his time in any way he wants. He is not avoiding his children, who are all grown up, nor as far as we know his ex-wives. For much of the NET, what little information we have on his private

4 B.B. King (born in 1925) undertook a farewell tour in 2006. He was canny enough to quote Sean Connery's James Bond movie title *"Never Say Never Again"* and King has played some shows since then, including a European tour in 2009.

life (and the less we have the better, I very much believe; it is called 'private' life for a reason) indicates that he spends much of the Thanksgiving to January holiday periods with as many of them as possible. Dylan has a private life; he has family, children, ex-wives. Dylan 'grew up' and accepted his responsibilities a long, long time ago. One could easily make a case from the little we know of his private life that he takes his role as a father more seriously than anything else.

Another charge levelled at Dylan's NET is that he does it because he has nothing else; he is 'trapped' on the road because he hasn't a clue what to do if he stops. Occasionally Dylan himself will give this theory a boost as, unsurprisingly, given that he views the NET as his 'trade', his 'job', he sometimes tires of it. At worst he feels his 'job', as perhaps we all do from time to time, to be nothing more than the mundane routine. Some even take the rather inelegant lines in the otherwise beautifully assured "Highlands", from *Time Out Of Mind,* autobiographically:

"Woke up this morning and I looked at the same old page,
Same ol' rat race, life in the same ol' cage."

Dylan himself may occasionally, wistfully dream of an alternate life – "*I would prefer to start my life anew over and over again. Learn a new trade, marry another girl, live in another place.*"[5] – yet these are just natural human sentiments. Most of us daydream about alternate lives where the fantasy grass looks so much greener. To make out of them a case for Dylan being chained to a life he hates is to ignore a whole swathe of countering points.

Undoubtedly the NET pays Dylan well, allegedly commanding some $50,000 per show and playing over a hundred of them a year plus festivals. Yet Dylan does not need the money, he could stop whenever he wanted. Apart from all his other income, Dylan could, and in some cases does, make money by the occasional special show, such as the three-song mega-grossing Pope bash, or by releasing old or new songs, by putting out a book, doing a movie cameo and so forth. There are a multitude of ways Dylan could make money were that his only aim, in other words. Selling a few copyrights to advertisers would be another, strikingly lucrative, example. Or, as he has recently discovered, via art exhibitions and selling paintings and prints.

5 *Der Spiegel* 16-10-1997.

So, if the NET were *only* a grind, why would he keep doing it? The point is that it is much more than just a paying job. Yes Dylan views it as his 'trade' but, as he has pointed out many times, it's a trade he still loves carrying out:

"There's a certain part of you that becomes addicted to a live audience. I wouldn't keep doing it if I was tired of it."[6]

These are views he has reiterated for decades now. In 2012, he answered the question, "So, live performance is a purpose you find fulfilling?" by saying:

If you're not fulfilled in other ways, performing can never make you happy. Performing is something you have to learn how to do. You do it, you get better at it and you keep going. And if you don't get better at it, you have to give it up.[7]

He went on to add that touring, his 'calling', was *"not any different to anyone else's. Some people are called to be a good sailor. Some have a calling to be a good tiller of land."*

The final 'charge' against the NET by those who seem determined to find a sinister explanation for it was that Dylan was only performing so much because he could no longer write songs or make albums. This kept cropping up in the first half of the NET, as it was true that Dylan wrote little in the first dozen years of the NET compared to the prolific output of the first twelve years of his career. It is worth remembering that *Oh Mercy, under the red sky* and *Time Out Of Mind*, along with the second Traveling Wilburys album and two albums of covers, did come out, however.

Dylan partly 'inspired' these comments by mentioning in interviews of this period that writing has become more difficult for him, that the flow of songs had been reduced to a comparative trickle. Dylan has often contrasted the falseness of trying to create in the studio with the natural feeling of conceiving new art on stage.

"Yeah. The recording process is very difficult for me. I lose my inspiration in the studio real easy, and it's very difficult for me to think that I'm going to eclipse

---

6 *Ibid.*, Note iii

7 *Ibid.*, Note i

anything I've ever done before. I get bored easily, and my mission, which starts out wide, becomes very dim after a few failed takes and this and that."[8]

Yet, surely this seems more like an artist knowing exactly what he wants than someone being 'forced' into touring because he cannot do anything else. In 2012 Dylan still felt the need to remind those who question his motives for touring exactly where his priorities lie. Mikal Gilmore asked: "Miles Davis had this idea that music was best heard in the moments in which it was performed – that that's where music is truly alive. Is your view similar?" Dylan responded with:

Yeah, it's exactly the same as Miles' is. We used to talk about that. Songs don't come alive in a recording studio. You try your best, but there's always something missing. What's missing is a live audience. Sinatra used to make records like that - used to bring people into the studio as an audience. It helped him get into the songs better.[9]

This 'theory' has by now been completely blown out of the water by the *"Love And Theft"*, *Modern Times, Together Through Life, Christmas In The Heart* and *Tempest album* releases. To which can be added the *Masked and Anonymous* movie, the *Chronicles* book and all Dylan's painting exhibitions. These latter activities aren't song-writing, but they are further evidence that Dylan is not forced into touring because he 'cannot do anything else'.

It may not be that all the theories above hold absolutely no validity whatsoever; though the very best that could be said for them is that they are very partial views, propounded by people who are pretending that they know Dylan's mind. Even if Dylan was not writing new songs, there would be no need to jump to the conclusion that therefore he would have to tour. He could do anything he wanted; luckily for us he wants to perform.

I am not claiming that I can read his mind any more than any other commentator can, but some straightforward points can be made and Dylan's own comments taken into account. Granted a certain amount of care is required here as it would be highly unreasonable to expect that Dylan's motivations for, and

---

8 *Guitar World* interview, published in March 1999 edition

9 *Ibid.*, Note i

feelings towards, the NET are going to have remained the same every day since 1988. Some fluctuation is surely inevitable; in addition there is nothing to stop contradictory reasons being at work simultaneously. In Dylan's art and career, contradictory states often hold the greatest truths.

When introducing Dylan at the 1991 Grammy Awards, Jack Nicholson said that he had searched the dictionary for the 'fairest word' to describe Dylan. He decided on 'paradox' because it meant: "A statement seemingly self-contradictory but in reality possibly expressing a truth." More prosaically, Dylan sees himself as "inconsistent":

"*That's just the nature of my personality,*" he says. "*I can be jubilant one moment and pensive the next, and a cloud could go by and make that happen. I'm inconsistent, even to myself.*"[10]

Notwithstanding paradox and inconsistency, it is easy to propose a more balanced view than the extreme Romantic and Cynic positions discussed above. A view based on those of Dylan's own comments that have remained consistent throughout the NET and on the facts we can be sure of, rather than on speculation about Dylan's personal life and current mindset.

From the first year of the Never Ending Tour onwards, Dylan has equated his touring with day-to-day work rather than the Romantic, beat-style existence. Speaking near the beginning of the NET:

"*There's just something instinctive that tells me that a man must support his family, no matter what. As it is, I'm doing what I do because I've been given to do it, but most of the people who work 'nine-to-five' have got to support families, and there is a tremendous disregard for that. You don't see much of that being heralded with heroic words and fancy awards. But that's what makes the world either rise or fall, that commitment to family.*"[11]

It is a theme he has returned to; he sees himself as doing his job, his trade, his craft. It is, simply, what he does. This was the same interview in which he succinctly answered all these questions about touring by saying "*We want to play because we want to play.*" What seems complicated comes down to those

10 *Ibid.*, Note 3

11 Interviewed by Kathryn Baker for *Associated Press*,1988

simple, oft-repeated but just as oft-ignored truths. He has even told us how this happens:

"A lot of people don't like the road, but it's as natural to me as breathing. I do it because I'm driven to do it, and I either hate it or love it. I'm mortified to be on the stage, but then again, it's the only place where I'm happy. It's the only place you can be who you want to be. You can't be who you want to be in daily life. I don't care who you are, you're going to be disappointed in daily life. But the cure-all for all that is to get on the stage, and that's why performers do it. But in saying that, I don't want to put on the mask of celebrity. I'd rather just do my work and see it as a trade."[12]

We are fast approaching the time when the NET alone will have covered half of his entire career, indeed if you include the Petty tours, Dylan has toured every year now for the majority of his lengthy vocation. Yet he still has to answer the same questions on why he tours. He has been uncharacteristically consistent in his replies. In 2012, he explains it, yet again:

"Touring is about anything you want it to be about. Is there something strange about touring? About playing live shows? If there is, tell me what it is. Willie [Nelson]'s been playing them for years, and nobody ever asks him why he still tours. Look, you travel to different places and you encounter things that you might not encounter every day if you stayed home. And you get to play music for the people – all of the people, every nationality and in every country. Ask any performer or entertainer that does this, they'll all tell you the same thing. That they like doing it and that it means a lot to people. It's just like any other line of work, only different."[13]

In a nutshell, as he wrote in *Blood On the Tracks*' "Buckets Of Rain":

"All ya can do is do what you must
You do what you must do and ya do it well."

To bring this somewhat spurious 'debate' to a conclusion; as I wrote at the end of *Razor's Edge*, it is better to turn the question around and ask (as Dylan does above, I wish I had had that quote twelve years ago): why shouldn't Dylan be

12 *Ibid.*, Note iii

13 *Ibid.*, Note i

touring? What is so surprising about him practising his particular trade? Can you imagine the job advert? It would go something like this:

Situation vacant

Description: Tour the world, working evenings only! You decide how to spend the rest of your time. Only work about 1 evening in 3, the rest of the day and night is yours to do whatever you please. Pick and choose when and where you want to work. Accommodation = luxury bus or the very best hotels or wherever takes your fancy. Your choice whether to dine out at a different top-class restaurant every night or not.

Duties: Your only obligation is to work at your trade, your calling, what you most enjoy doing .

Bonus package: Have lots of parties, garner worldwide acclaim, have young women desperate to meet you every time you turn up for work. There will always people on hand to carry out your every wish.

Remuneration and holidays: "Name your salary", fantastic pay and as many holidays as you want.

Yet still people wonder why he does it, or even scorn him for so doing. Not that these people are prone to proposing an alternative even a tenth as attractive. It is as though they are desperate for Dylan to disappear for some reason; bizarrely, this includes people who think of themselves as Bob Dylan fans. After all these years and all he has done and said and sung to dissuade them, people still think they know him, still think he owes them something (when it is the opposite that is the case), still think they own him. It makes no sense to keep asking "Why?" Dylan has answered this the same way all through the NET; in any case the answer seems, self-evidently, "Whyever not?"

Thank goodness Dylan had the sense to 'apply for the vacancy'. Out of that decision has come the munificent bounty that is the NET; we get the greatest artist of his time going out year after year, recreating his magic in front of our very eyes and ears. Far from the ceaseless reworking of his old songs being a sign of loss of artistic creativity, it is the very centre and expression of his art. The refusal to take the easy option and just sing the songs the same way time after time is borne out of his inherent understanding that the core of his art is the never ending challenge of the new performance.

AFTERWORD:

The Road Goes Ever On

The Road goes ever on and on
Down from the door where it began.
Now far ahead the Road has gone,
And I must follow, if I can
Pursuing it with eager feet.

J.R.R. TOLKIEN, *THE LORD OF THE RINGS*[1]

The road goes ever on and on, indeed. As I have been typing the NET has rolled on, completing 25 years by the close of 2012 and heading for its silver anniversary on June 7th 2013. Although there was only one show in the UK in 2012, again at the Hop Farm Festival, this provided the startling introduction of a grand piano to the stage. This was not done just as a one-off and the piano has, obviously, dramatically changed the sound and the stage set-up.

There was also another wild interview, with Dylan harping back to the themes and sometimes mistaken claims of his 2001 Rome interview; views that have been regurgitated so often over the last dozen years that they are now generally accepted as 'the truth'. Dylan was in extreme mode, describing the critical fans

1 This is a later version of the song that first appeared in *The Hobbit*, 2012's big Xmas cinematic release.

of 1966 as "evil motherfuckers" that he hoped would rot in hell and ranting on about how he had been transfigured. Much more importantly than all that posturing (or at least let's hope it was no more than that), the interview was in support of an excellent album, *Tempest*, easily his best since 2001's *"Love And Theft"* and reliant for its success and powerful effect on his delivery and use of The Voice. Regretfully, songs from this terrific album were not much in evidence in the later 2012 shows.

The shows had kept on coming in 2012, and the Knopfler tie-up in the last leg of 2011 was replicated in the US a year later, and books on Bob kept coming too. I spotted one with a subtitle that suggested it would be highly relevant to my main topics in these pages: *It Ain't Me Babe: Bob Dylan and the Performance of Authenticity* by Andrea Cusso[2]. The suggestion was fully confirmed in the extremely interesting, closing portion of the book, which contains, for one thing, an insightful comparison of the Supper Club shows and *MTV Unplugged.* That Mr. Cusso's themes are akin to mine in this book in general, and the last few chapters in particular, is strikingly clear as he draws to his conclusion:

"The authentic Dylan, thus, reveals himself through performance, and at this point whether a performance is good or bad matters less than the very effort to be 'authentic'. I have seen an authentic Dylan barking through the lines of 'Tomorrow Is a Long Time' in 2008 (my favorite love song torn to pieces on a November night in New York) and so intoxicated in 1992 that he was hardly able to remember the words to 'All along the Watchtower'. And yet the feeling that what I was seeing was an authentic artist struggling to give an authentic performance never went away.

"... Performances, indeed, reveal the emotional side of authenticity, and the link between the artist and the audience is more often than not an affective one, effervescent and contingent because it can find its way only in performance. This is probably the reason why fans return to Dylan even when they know the melodic rope-walking, the adventurous phrasing, the exciting setlists are long gone, unlikely to re-appear now that Dylan is aging. Yet there are still moments when Dylan does it again, and they can be witnessed only if one is there, on

---

2 *It Ain't Me Babe: Bob Dylan and the Performance of Authenticity,* Andrea Cusso, Paradigm Publishers, 2012.

a particular night and at a particular moment. A few days ago (November 14, 2011), I heard my third 'Desolation Row' in five days. 'They're selling postcards of the hanging.' Something special was beginning to take shape."

Cusso is a sociologist and his book is indicative of a trend that is seeing more and more academic studies focussing on the work of Bob Dylan, no longer just in the 'lit crit' departments but also in other fields such as 'media and culture studies'. Dylan's career is a Postmodernist theorising dreamland and cross-cultural and cross-academic studies are bound to continue to proliferate alongside academic analysis of his words, music and voice.

While welcoming all of these, it is my deeply held hope that there will be more fan books and NET histories too, to provide different perspectives to mine. We all carry our own NET with us and it would be beneficial for future generations to read accounts written while the NET was still going; there will, after all, doubtless be many a book written in the future that looks back and reflects on these many, extraordinary years. I envisage that one day a philosopher with the necessary background will draw up an objective aesthetic of live performance of popular music (pop, rock, blues, folk etc.) in general, which will prompt another to produce a similar framework for discussing Dylan's live work and maybe even for the NET in particular. Each year, leg and night could then be considered in that overarching context. Well, that is all speculation for the future. For now, the road goes ever on and on, so let us pursue it with eager feet...

...even unto 2013. You will have gathered that this book really ends at Hammersmith in November 2011; however the time it takes to get a book out means that events have been unfolding even as the proofs come back and changes are made and more delays are incurred. So, I am taking this opportunity to add a few more paragraphs to this postscript to mention that 2013's touring has begun, and once again it is all change on the good ship NET.

First of all, the band has changed again. Charlie Sexton has oft been justifiably praised in this book but, for whatever reasons, had become an increasingly troubled looking and peripheral figure as time passed in his second NET stint. He was replaced for the tour that began in April 2013 by the outstanding Duke Robillard, quite an attraction in his own right as well as having the experience of the *Time Out of Mind* sessions behind him.

The whole dynamics and sound of the band has altered. Sensibly sticking to unchanging set-lists to bed in the new guitarist, Dylan is concentrating on his singing and allowing Robillard to play compelling leads and develop an interplay between all members onstage. From what I have heard thus far, it all promises to be quite something to behold when it is fully formed. The grand piano was already established as a standard feature of the shows and has added magnificently to the new ensemble of sounds.

When he is in the mood to communicate fully with his audience, Dylan's focus on the songs themselves is exemplary. The set-lists staying the same is only ever a problem when it is a sign of *ennui*. In the first weeks of this tour, the twenty-sixth consecutive NET year, twenty-eighth in terms of unbroken touring, leading up to the 'silver anniversary' of the very first NET show on June 7th, we are blessed with a Dylan fully engaged. The names of the songs may not be changing every night but the nature of the experience does as emphasis and nuances shift.

Dylan's increased focus has been shone on certain numbers in particular: "Pay in Blood" boasts a reworked arrangement, fully highlighting the drama of the song while the masterly "Blind Willie McTell" finds Dylan probing its profundities with an alluring, shifting mix of musical and vocal emotions stretching from the jaunty to the brooding.

The star turn of each night that I have heard, however, has been spell-binding readings of "What Good Am I?" Dylan gives this his all, both vocally and on exquisite piano, so much so that the "naked truth" no longer seems to be "taboo". As with all songs from *Oh Mercy*, I find the balance tips from seeming to be a dramatisation of Biblical times with personal Dylan overtones to a Dylan speaking about himself with Christian-Everyman overtones depending on whether one is listening to the album (the former) or live performances (the latter). Here, the dramatisation takes on the nature of a Shakespearean soliloquy with Dylan using every ounce of his remaining vocal power to portray the song in all its compelling depth.

On a more trivial note, but nonetheless important to the NET experience, the visual experience has also been transformed. Dylan even appears hatless, quite a surprise, as the photos through the years in this book will testify. There is a strange assortment of mirrors on the stage facing out at the audience, placed in curious patterns. Someone suggested that it must be Feng Shui, which certainly makes more sense than the other theories that are circulating. The opening has altered too: there is no more Aaron Copland, and with the Miers' introduction also having been retired after nearly a decade's service we are back to Dylan striding on stage and getting straight down to business. As the NET heads towards its 25th anniversary, thrilling audiences is still the "business" in question.

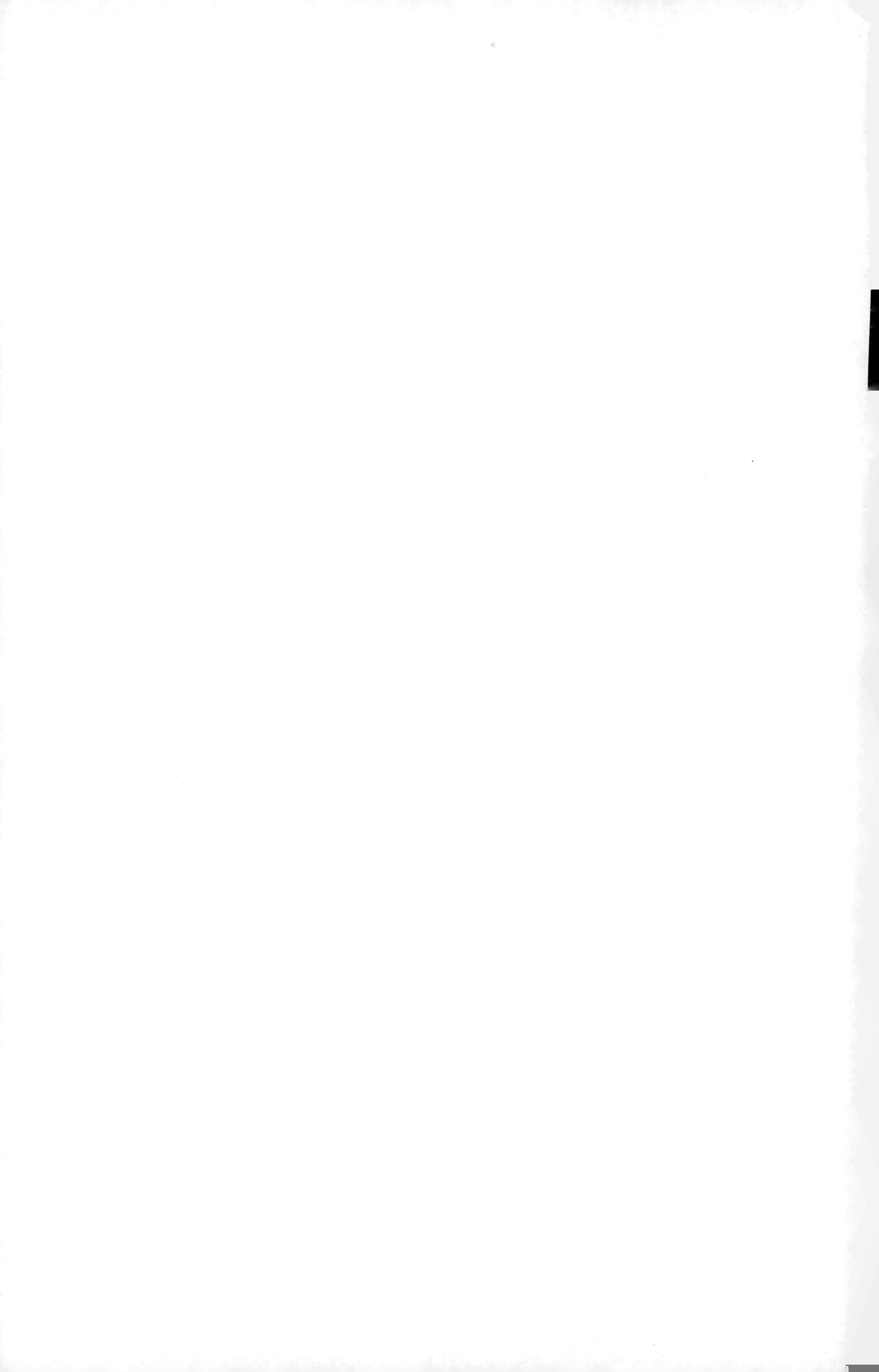

Thanks and Acknowledgements

From 1988 to 2013 there are so very many people to thank that this list could become another example of something so long as to appear 'never-ending'. With apologies to whomsoever I may have missed, the following roll-call is for specific help with the book and/or on the road. Sadly, there are quite a few names here who are no longer with us, but their help and friendship shall never be forgotten:

Garret Baker, Derek Barker, Clive Barrett, James Bishop, Olof Björner, Sean Body, Jim Brady, David Bristow, Mark Carter, Jon Casper, Ben Clayton, Dangerous Daniel, John Denley, Peter Doggett, Glen and Madge Dundas, Larry Eden (Lambchop), Michelle Engert, Stephan & Chris Fehlau, Robert & Elaine Forryan, Alan Fraser, Michael Gray, John Green, Jim Heppell, Clinton Heylin, Sara Hill, Nigel Hinton, Duncan Hume, Jailhouse John, Jim Johnson, Raymond Landry, Rod Macbeath, Joe McShane, Paul Maxin, James and Olive Muir, Josh Nelson, Pia Parviainen, John Perry, Christopher Rollason, Stephen Scobie, Nigel Simms, Lucas Stensland, John Stokes, Manny & Philly Vardavas (you know why), Peter Vincent , Roy Whiteaker, Paul Williams, Ian Woodward, Keith Wootton, Andy Wright.

Plus, of course, numerous Dylan fan groups, sites, magazines, forums, blogs and so forth. A number of the concert reviews herein have appeared, in some form or another, in **Homer**, *the slut*, *Isis,* and *Judas!*

Special thanks to Peter Vincent for copy-editing and proof-reading and to Duncan Hume for access to his vast and impressive Dylan photograph collection.

All photographs by Duncan Hume. Front cover photograph is from Paris, April 30th 2002. Back cover photograph is from Brussels, 6th April 2007.

Cover by Scott Greenway (Feedbacker Design).

29351401R00233

Made in the USA
Lexington, KY
23 January 2014